DATE DUE

Lincoln's Journalist

John Hay

Lincoln's Journalist

JOHN HAY'S ANONYMOUS
WRITINGS FOR THE PRESS,
1860–1864

Edited by

MICHAEL BURLINGAME

SOUTHERN ILLINOIS UNIVERSITY PRESS

Carbondale and Edwardsville

01   00   99   98   4   3   2   1

Frontispiece: Photograph of John Hay, 1861, by Albert Bierstadt,
signed by Hay, courtesy of Brown University Library.

Library of Congress Cataloging-in-Publication Data
Hay, John, 1838–1905.
Lincoln's journalist : John Hay's anonymous writings for the press,
1860–1864 / edited by Michael Burlingame.
p.   cm.
Includes bibliographical references and index.
1. Lincoln, Abraham, 1809–1865. 2. United States—
History—Civil War, 1861–1865—Sources.
I. Burlingame, Michael, 1941– .
II. Title.
E457.H39 1998
973.7'092—dc21   98–6013
ISBN 0-8093-2205-6 (alk. paper)   CIP

The paper used in this publication meets the minimum
requirements of American National Standard for
Information Sciences—Permanence of Paper for Printed Library
Materials, ANSI Z39.48-1984. ∞

For David Herbert Donald,
mentor extraordinaire

CONTENTS

ACKNOWLEDGMENTS

ONE DAY IN 1992 WHILE I WAS WORKING AT THE JOHN HAY LIBRARY AT Brown University, Jennifer Lee, curator of the Lincoln Collection, suggested that I might like to examine a scrapbook in which Hay had pasted some of his own writings. Without her prompting, I would doubtless have ignored that valuable source and its counterparts in the Hay Papers at the Library of Congress, and this volume would never have come to be. To Ms. Lee, now head of the manuscripts department at the New York Public Library, I extend heartfelt thanks. Among the other librarians at Brown who have been especially helpful and cordial over the years are Samuel Streit, Jean Rainwater, Pat Sirois, Mary Jo Kline, and Andrew Moul.

I also owe a debt of gratitude to Robert Hoffman of Rochester, New York, who kindly let me examine and quote from one of Hay's scrapbooks that he owns. His friend Joseph Buberger was most helpful in expediting the copying of the scrapbook.

John Y. Simon, the dean of documentary editors in American history, has supported me unstintingly as I labored over the manuscript of this and other Lincoln-related volumes. His friendship, encouragement, and guidance are deeply appreciated.

While spending endless weeks at the Library of Congress on this and related projects, I was the beneficiary of the generous hospitality of my sister and brother-in-law, Sue and Edwin Coover, which extended far above and beyond the call of family duty.

Thomas F. Schwartz, the Illinois state historian, and Wayne C. Temple, the chief deputy director of the Illinois State Archives, kindly agreed to read the manuscript and give me the benefit of their extensive knowledge of Lincoln and his times. Connecticut College's R. Francis Johnson Faculty Development Fund helped defray some of the expenses incurred in researching and editing this volume. Regina B. Foster and Anita L. Allen have cheerfully and efficiently helped type the manuscript.

As the dedication indicates, I owe a great deal to David Herbert Donald, under whom I studied at Princeton and Johns Hopkins Universities.

Lois McDonald deserves more credit than I can express for making it possible for me to edit this volume.

INTRODUCTION

THIS VOLUME COMPLEMENTS JOHN HAY'S CIVIL WAR DIARY, AN invaluable document despite its many gaps.[1] To help caulk some of those gaps, Hay's anonymous and pseudonymous journalism written between 1860 and 1864 is collected here. These dispatches and editorials shed both direct and indirect light on Abraham Lincoln. Not only does Hay quote the president and describe his activities but he also offers opinions that may reflect Lincoln's views. Referring to writings by both of Lincoln's personal secretaries, one scholar observed: "Hay and [John G.] Nicolay seem generally to have adopted Lincoln's opinions as their own; and it may be surmised that the observations in their Letters, Diary, and Notes, were not far out of line with what Lincoln thought at the time, even when they do not quote him directly."[2] The historian and journalist Walter B. Stevens maintained that Hay's 1860 and 1861 Springfield dispatches to the *Missouri Democrat* in St. Louis were "sent direct from Lincoln's office" and were "inspired by Lincoln." Stevens added that, according to a tradition among Missouri journalists, "Lincoln wrote some of the political correspondence which Hay sent to St. Louis."[3]

Hay began his journalistic career in 1860, when James B. Angell, one of his professors at Brown University in the mid-1850s, asked him to describe Lincoln for the *Providence Journal*. Writing under the pseudonym "Ecarte" (a kind of card game), Hay sent a detailed sketch full of revealing anecdotes that Angell excised in his eagerness to have the Republican candidate seem properly statesmanlike. Later Angell regretted wielding a ruthless blue pencil on Hay's four "Ecarte" letters for the Providence paper.[4] Using the same nom de plume, Hay also contributed several items to the *Illinois Daily State Journal* in Springfield and the *Missouri Democrat*. On April 26, 1861, the editor of the *Illinois Daily State Journal* thanked him for his dispatch dated April 16. Those dispatches by "Ecarte," many of which Hay pasted into his personal scrapbooks of his own writings, are included in this volume.

Among the scrapbooks in the Hay Papers at the Library of Congress is one (volume 54) devoted to writings by and about Hay dating from the Civil

War. The first forty-six pages contain dispatches from the *Missouri Republican* with the following dates: October 11, 14, 17, 21, November 2, 4, 7, 13, 18, 24, December 3, 5, 12, 13, 17, 19, 26, 28, 1861; January 6, 20, 22, 27, February 6, 11, 14, 21, 25, 28, March 9, April 6, 21, 23, 27, May 11, 19, June 18, 19, 26, July 13, 27, August 20, 31, September 22, 25, October 20, and December 21, 1862. Forty-four of these dispatches are datelined Washington, one is datelined Norfolk, Virginia (June 18, 1862), and one is datelined White House Point, Virginia (June 19, 1862).

The contents of the rest of this scrapbook are as follows:

Page 47: blank.

Page 48: "Ecarte's" May 21, 1860, dispatch from Springfield, which is definitely by Hay.

Pages 49–55: blank.

Pages 56–60: five editorials from the *Washington National Republican,* three dated in Hay's handwriting.

Pages 61–63: blank.

Page 64: a Washington dispatch of August 12, 1861, to the *New York World.*

Pages 65–66: a St. Louis dispatch to the *New York World,* dated September 20, 1861.

Pages 67–69: blank.

Page 70: an unidentified clipping of a letter from Hay's friend Gen. Quincy A. Gillmore, asking to be relieved from command under Gen. Benjamin F. Butler; a clipping from the *Washington National Republican* of May 26, 1864, challenging the *New York Tribune*'s account of a Cabinet meeting; and an unidentified editorial.

Page 71: a description of a private theatrical like the ones Hay attended in Washington; a clipping relating Lincoln's remarks about the tightrope walker Blondin; and clippings of Lincoln's letters to L. B. Wyman (December 11, 1861) and to F. B. Loomis (May 12, 1864).

Page 72: a brief editorial from the *Washington Chronicle* entitled "Hon. Schuyler Colfax," which, Hay told Colfax, came from his pen; an editorial from the *Washington National Republican,* "Meade vs. Lee," dated in Hay's hand; an 1860 clipping from the *Illinois Daily State Journal* of a humorous letter by "Lily White," bristling with Hay-like puns and banter; and an unidentified clipping about a steamboat trip that Hay took with other dignitaries.

Pages 73–74: blank.

Pages 75–90: Springfield dispatches by "Ecarte" for the *Missouri Democrat,* June–November 1860.

Page 91: a small handbill listing the 1860 Illinois Democratic nominees for national and state office.

Pages 92–106: Springfield dispatches to the *Missouri Democrat* (one signed "Ecarte") dated November 1860 and January 1861.

Pages 107–9: an editorial from the January 22, 1861, issue of the *Illinois Daily State Journal*. Page 109 also contains a clipping of a letter by Hay to Cornell Jewett (July 18, 1864) and Jewett's reply (July 30, 1864).

Page 110: clippings of Hay's letters to Charles Gibson (July 25, 1864) and to John A. Dix (December 1, 1863).

Page 111: an article about Hay's visit to Florida in 1864.

Page 112: Lincoln's response to a serenade; Lincoln's celebrated letter of November 21, 1864, to Lydia Bixby (almost certainly composed by Hay),[5] and Lincoln's letter of the same date to John Phillips.

Page 113: an item dated March 30, 1865, about Hay's appointment as secretary of the U.S. legation in Paris and one about Nicolay's appointment as consul in the same city.

Page 114: a humorous article about Hay's literary reputation and his health.

Pages 115–16: an editorial from the May 2, 1865, issue of the *Washington National Republican*.

Page 117: an article about Hay from the *New South* (May 30, 1863).

Pages 118–19: an article by Whitelaw Reid, dated August 10, [1863], which mentions Hay's literary endeavors.

Between pages 119 and 120 is a loose clipping about Hay's doings in South Carolina in the spring of 1863.

Page 120: blank.

Pages 121–25: several articles about Hay's lecture on "The Progress of Democracy in Europe."

Page 126: a clipping from a St. Louis newspaper.

The remaining pages are blank, save one to which is attached a printed list of the passengers, including Hay, who accompanied Lincoln on his journey from Springfield to Washington in February 1861.

While Hay's authorship of the "Ecarte" letters in the *Providence Journal* and the *Missouri Democrat* seems indisputable, it is not as certain that he penned the above items for the *New York World* and the *Missouri Republican,* though the evidence is highly suggestive. One item in the *World* definitely can be attributed to Hay, who on September 28, 1861, recorded in his diary: "I wrote articles in the [New York] World and [Springfield] Journal for Frémont." The *World*'s dispatch about Frémont dated St. Louis, September 20, 1861, is pasted into volume 54 in the Hay Papers at the Library of Congress. Hay was in St. Louis on that date. In the same scrapbook are Washington dispatches to the *World* dated August 5 and 12, 1861, composed in Hay's distinctive style, marked by long sentences, baroque syntax, verbal pyrotechnics, cocksure tone (combining acid contempt and extravagant praise), offbeat adverbs, and scornful adjectives. It is a literary voice hard to mistake. In another scrapbook, now owned by Robert Hoffman of Rochester, New York, Hay pasted dispatches from the *World,* dated February 11, 12, and 18, 1861, written aboard the train carrying Lincoln (and Hay) from Springfield to Washington. These items, also in Hay's distinctively baroque style, are almost certainly by Hay. It seems plausible that the other *World* dispatches, in that same style by "our special correspondent" aboard the train, were also Hay's handiwork.

"Our special correspondent" continued to write for the *World* from Washington after Lincoln arrived in the capital. These dispatches complemented the work of "our own correspondent," whose articles appeared in the *World* almost daily throughout January 1861. On March 4 and 5, the *World* ran Washington dispatches by both "our own correspondent" and "our special correspondent." In the spring of 1861, these two journalists continued reporting from Washington. It seems likely that the baroque dispatches in March 1861 by "our special correspondent" are Hay's; the bland style of "our own correspondent" at that time is quite unlike Hay's. From March 8 until April 15, the *World* ran no story by either correspondent.

Internal evidence suggests that Hay continued writing for the *World* after March. On May 7, 1861, he described in his diary an episode involving his beloved friend, Elmer E. Ellsworth:

> The youthful Colonel formed his men in a hollow square, and made a great speech at them. . . . He spoke to them as men, made them proud in their good name, spoke bitterly & witheringly of the disgrace of the recreant, contrasted with cutting emphasis which his men delighted in, the enlistment of the dandy regiment for thirty days, with *theirs* for the war— spoke solemnly & impressively of the disgrace of expulsion—roused them to wild enthusiasm by announcing that he had heard of one officer who treated his men with less consideration than himself and that, if on inquiry the rumor proved true, he would strip him & send him home in

irons. The men yelled with delight clapped their hands & shouted "Bully for you." He closed with wonderful tact and dramatic spirit, by saying "Now laddies, if any one of you wants to go home, he had better sneak around the back alleys, crawl over fences, and get out of sight before we see him," which got them again.

The Washington dispatch of May 7 in the *New York World* (see chapter 2) described the scene with many of the same words: "So far as the officers are concerned, I believe they are doing, with one exception, their duties like soldiers and like men. I am informed that one of them believes he can treat you like dogs, as if in manhood you were not his equals. I shall find him out, and if it be so, I will put him, too, in irons, and send him back. [Tremendous applause, and a voice 'bully for you.'] We have come here to fight traitors, and we are ready for the war!"

Other internal evidence suggests that Hay composed the dispatches to the *World* pasted in his scrapbook, volume 54 of the Hay Papers in the Library of Congress. In one dispatch, written on the train carrying Lincoln to Washington in 1861, the anonymous author declares: "But a sudden incursion of giants like that which Cincinnati has known to-day is an event fraught with as much dread, at least to correspondents of five feet eight, as the stampeding of rhinoceri across a colony of anthills would be to the occupants." Hay's height was about five feet, eight inches, according to his cousin.[6] Another dispatch in the *World,* dated February 26, 1861, describes the correspondence addressed to Lincoln, which only Hay and Nicolay (aside from the president) were privileged to see. In November 1861, Hay described in his diary how he, Lincoln, and Seward visited the home of General McClellan. That same month, the Washington correspondent for the *Missouri Republican* noted that the president, the secretary of state, and a private secretary to the president called on McClellan. In June 1862, the correspondent for the *Missouri Republican* said that his ancestors had lived in Virginia. Hay's paternal great-grandfather migrated from Pennsylvania to Virginia, and his grandfather migrated from Virginia to Kentucky.

"Our own correspondent" did not write to the *World* from Washington between August 13 and 22, when Hay accompanied Mary Lincoln on her trip to Long Branch, N.J. Just at that time, "our own correspondent" filed stories from that resort, a town that did not enchant him. "The drizzle seems wetter there than other wheres, the sky grayer and colder, nor is there refuge except in suicide or intoxication," the *World*'s correspondent complained.[7] In a letter to James A. Hamilton on August 19, Hay referred to "suicide or intoxication" as he bemoaned the dullness of Long Branch:

> I did not receive the kind note you sent me, until Friday night at Long Branch. As it was horribly dull there, I concluded, instantly upon reading your kind invitation, to return to New York and go to you Saturday afternoon. But then I found there was no telegraphic station at Irvington or Dobbs' Ferry and that I could not apprize you of my coming. I went down town and lunched with Mr. Roosevelt at Exchange Place. Coming back I was thunderstruck to find you had been at my hotel and were gone. There were only three recourses left me. Suicide, intoxication, or profanity.[8]

Neither "our own" nor "our special" correspondent wrote from Washington after August 26. In this volume the dispatches by "our special correspondent" on the train bearing Lincoln from Springfield to Washington and "our own correspondent" written in Hay's distinctive style from Washington, Long Branch, and St. Louis, are included.

It is not clear how Hay came to write for the *World*. Perhaps Simon Cameron facilitated the arrangement. At that time, according to S. L. M. Barlow, the *World* had "the reputation of being controlled wholly by Mr. Cameron," Lincoln's secretary of war.[9] In 1864 Cameron helped Nicolay and Hay in their abortive attempt to gain control of the *Baltimore Sun*.[10]

Hay did not abandon journalism in September 1861. From the following month until the end of 1862, he seems to have written frequently for the *Missouri Republican* of St. Louis. In a scrapbook (volume 54 of the Hay Papers in the Library of Congress) are pasted many Washington dispatches clipped from that newspaper; although their authorship is not identified, their style is Hay's. It is hard to imagine why he would have pasted them in a scrapbook of his own writings if they were by another author. Many journalists keep scrapbooks of their own articles. In Hay's Papers at the Library of Congress are scrapbooks containing editorials from the *New York Tribune* dated 1870–75, when Hay was the chief editorial writer for that newspaper. Volume 58, dated 1871–72, contains 146 pages of triple-columned, closely packed clippings, mostly editorials, with a smattering of art criticism, some poetry, and occasional accounts of Hay's lectures. The first two clippings, describing the 1871 Chicago fire, are signed "J. H." Volume 59, dated 1873–74, contains 125 similar pages.

Not all the scrapbooks in the Hay Papers at the Library of Congress are filled with writings by Hay himself. Volumes 55 and 56 contain articles about Lincoln, Hay, and the Civil War that are clearly not by Hay. But volume 56 also contains dispatches from Madrid in 1869 and 1870, when Hay was stationed there as a diplomat, as well as *New York Tribune* editorials from the early 1870s. In two of those editorials appears the word *beguile,* a favorite of Hay's.[11] In 1872 an editorial declared: "Only the life-long habit of saying what he does not mean, could *beguile* an elderly man into standing up before a large number of his neighbors and telling them what he and they knew to be silly and false."[12] Two years later another editorial contained this sentence: "This is a plan by which even municipal dignitaries from the interior are sometimes *beguiled.*"[13]

Since Hay kept scrapbooks of his journalism during the 1870s, it seems plausible that he did so in the previous decade. A few of the 1861–62 dispatches in volumes 54 and 55 contain information to which only someone in Hay's position could have been privy. For example, on October 21, 1861, Lincoln's close friend Edward D. Baker was killed in battle. A Washington dispatch of that date to the *Missouri Republican* contains the following passage: "A king might have been proud of the simple and hearty eulogies uttered last night in McClellan's room, where the President, and Seward, and Cameron, and M'Clellan, and another [doubtless Hay], in deep but not unmanly grief, received the heavy news of the fate of their friend. . . . And McClellan pronounced his bluff and soldierly epitaph: 'I would rather have lost a battle than Baker; yet no loss is so great but it can be repaired, and though many a good fellow with shoulder straps go under the sod before this row is over, the cause must triumph.'" The next day, Hay recorded in his diary: "This has been a heavy day. Last night Col. Baker was killed at Leesburg at the head of his Brigade. McClellan & the President talked sadly over it. McClellan said, 'There is many a good fellow that wears the shoulder-straps going under the sod before this thing is over.'"

In that dispatch, Baker's oratory is praised lavishly: "He was utterly at home on the hustings. His ready, sparkling ebullient wit, his glancing and playful satire, mirthful and merciless, his keen sharp syllogisms and his brilliant sophisms, whose fallacies though undiscoverable were perplexing, and the fierce splendors of his eloquence, made him one of the most popular stump orators that ever lived." In Hay's obituary of Baker, published in December 1861 in *Harper's Magazine*, virtually identical language appears:

"He was utterly at home on the hustings. Those who are acquainted only with his grave senatorial efforts can form no adequate idea of the ready, sparkling ebullient wit—the glancing and playful satire, mirthful while merciless—the keen syllogisms—and the sharp sophisms, whose fallacies though undiscoverable, were perplexing—and the sudden splendors of eloquence that formed the wonderful charm of his backwoods harangues."[14] Thus it seems quite likely that Hay wrote this dispatch.

Another conversation between McClellan and Lincoln appears in the Washington correspondence of October 26, 1861: "The other day, McClellan said to the president, 'I think we will succeed entirely if our friends will be patient, and not hurry us.'

"'I promise you,' said the President, 'you shall have your own way.'"

On October 10, Hay recorded in his diary the following words of McClellan: "I intend to be careful, and do as well as possible. Don't let them hurry me, is all I ask." Lincoln replied: "You shall have your own way in the matter I assure you."

On November 4, a Washington correspondent told readers of the *Missouri Republican:* "Plain people began to think princes a bore. Fortunately for the class, at this time came our young soldiers of the house of Orleans, to redeem from contempt the princely character. Roused by a noble and glorious impulse of abstract honor and principle, they came to fight in the Western world the battle of freedom and constitutional law. De Joinville came with them—three honest, earnest and gallant men." In November 1861, Hay recorded in his diary that "we went up and talked a little while to the Orleans princes. De Joinville is deaf and says little."

In his dispatch of November 11, the *Missouri Republican*'s Washington correspondent commented on Benjamin F. Butler: "He will give an admirable account of himself, for though in his character you may discover elements of vanity and arrogance which somewhat mar its symmetry, yet his worst enemies cannot call him unsoldierly, or deny him the possession of those rare native powers which place men at the head of armies in trying times." Three days earlier Hay had copied into his diary a letter from Butler that he called "a wild and absurd miracle of cheek."

On September 26, 1862, Hay wrote in his diary: "Last night September 25 the President and I were riding to Soldiers Home; he said he had heard of an officer who had said they did not mean to gain any decisive victory but to keep things running on so that the army might manage things to suit themselves. He said he should have the matter examined and if any such language had been used, his head should go off." In a dispatch to the *Missouri Republican* dated October 1, 1862, the Washington correspondent reported:

> Major John J. Key . . . said, in answer to the question propounded to him by another officer, "Why were not the rebels bagged by McClellan after the battle of Antietam?—"That is not the game. The object is for the two armies to keep the field as long as possible, neither gaining any decisive advantage, until both are tired out, and a compromise may be made by which we can save slavery."
>
> This shameful utterance was reported to the President. He sent a message to Major Key, through Mr. Hay, his secretary, requesting that he would, within twenty-four hours, disprove the charges of having made the above remark.

Other internal evidence suggests that Hay composed the *Missouri Republican* dispatches contained in his scrapbooks. In one dated October 11, 1861, the Washington correspondent wrote:

> Yesterday . . . Gen. McClellan and his staff were galloping through the chilly mist, over the steaming and soggy roads, looking along the lines, rectifying mistakes and filling up omissions, and, in short, finishing well what had been well begun. The discipline of the troops is very cheering. They march well and behave themselves when they halt. A few days more will be spent in taking up the loose edges of the work already done, cautiously feeling the way to other points of advantage, and the general limbering of the muscles that precedes and prepares for violent exercise. Circumstances point strongly to the probability, that at an early day next week, a strong reconnaissance will be made, whose result will, of course, be most momentous.

The previous day, Hay had written in his diary: "We came to McClellan's quarters. . . . McClellan came in hurriedly and began to talk with the President. They discussed the events of today and yesterday. McClellan was much pleased at the conduct of his men—no rowdyism or plundering today. He was merely today finishing yesterdays work. . . . As we left, McClellan said, 'I think we shall have our arrangements made for a strong reconnaissance about Monday to feel the strength of the enemy.'"

Similar parallels may be found between Hay's diary and the Washington dispatch of October 14, 1861, which states that:

From sources whose trustworthiness cannot be for an instant impugned, our Government has information that only the kindest and heartiest expressions of good will and sympathy are heard in the best circle of the best class of England. Recent conversations, in the unrestrained freedom of friendly intimacy with men so high in fame, and position, and power as Earl Russell, Mr. Layard, the Under-Secretary of State, Mr. Cobden, Earl Grey, Colonial Secretary, His Royal Highness Albert, Prince Consort, and the gracious lady, Victoria herself, evince only the most cordial sympathy with the Federal Government, and show conclusively that the bearings of this great controversy between civilization and barbarism, between law and anarchy, is as fully understood and appreciated in the Court of St. James as in the Cabinet at Washington.

On October 12, Hay recorded in his diary: "Seward spoke also of [John Lothrop] Motley's despatch which seems to contain a most cheering account of the real sentiment of honest sympathy existing in the best class of English Society towards us. Motleys letter embraced free and cordial conversations with Earl Russell, Earl Grey, Cobden, Mr. Layard Prince Albert and the Queen."

On January 22, 1862, the special Washington correspondent of the *Missouri Republican* vividly described Andrew Johnson's reaction to news of a Confederate defeat:

The happiest man in town all day yesterday was Andrew Johnson, United States Senator from Tennessee. Early on Monday the welcome news of the victory at Somerset elated him. Exultation checkered with doubt filled up the afternoon. He went to bed thinking that a great thing had happened if the news were true. At midnight, a dispatch from the President, announcing the official confirmation of the news roused him from his bed at the St. Charles, and he indulged in a *marche de triomphe* over the certainty of success. He considers the victory most cheering in character, most important in results.

On January 20 Hay dashed off a note to Johnson and evidently delivered it to him personally: "The President directs me to send you copy of dispatch just received from Baltimore: 'We have dispatch from Cincinnati announcing that Schoeff killed Zollicofer and routed his army at Somerset on Saturday. Twelve hours fight. Heavy loss both.'"[15] Thus it seems likely that this Washington dispatch for the *Missouri Republican* was written by Hay.

On September 25, 1862, the *Missouri Republican*'s Washington correspondent described Lincoln's brief reply to a serenade: "He said only half a dozen words, but his voice was full of an earnest solemnity, and there was something of unusual dignity in his manner." The day before, Hay had written in his diary, "He did say half a dozen words, & said them with great grace and dignity." In that same dispatch appears an account of a celebration at Salmon P. Chase's home; Hay described that celebration in his diary.

Unfortunately, Hay kept his diary only sporadically in 1861 and 1862, so that document cannot be used to check the authorship of other dispatches in the *Missouri Republican* and the *New York World*. But if the items dated May 7, October 11, 14, 22, and 26, and November 4 and 11, 1861, and January 22, September 25, and October 1, 1862, are by Hay—as his diary suggests—then it seems plausible that he wrote others. Occasionally another correspondent wrote to the *Missouri Republican* from Washington but in a style quite unlike Hay's. I have included in this volume not only the items pasted into Hay's scrapbooks but also other dispatches apparently by the same author.

When Hay quit writing for the *Missouri Republican* in late 1862, he did not lay down his journalistic pen; he composed editorials for the *Washington Chronicle*. In December 1862, John Wien Forney, editor of the *Chronicle,* told Hay, "I have taken some liberties with your MSS. which will not, I hope, be objected to." He added "I am very anxious for your assistance, and earnestly ask you for it."[16] Eight months later Hay told John G. Nicolay, "I am getting apathetic & write blackguardly articles for the *Chronicle* from which West extracts the dirt & fun & publishes the dreary remains."[17] Whitelaw Reid reported that Hay "is charged with occasional sparkling editorials in the *Chronicle.*"[18] Hay pasted some *Chronicle* editorials into his scrapbook of his own writings, but since he thus preserved few of them, they are hard to identify. I have included only those which he referred to in his diary or which are preserved in the scrapbook, volume 54 of the Hay Papers in the Library of Congress.

Inferring from this journalism Lincoln's own views is difficult, although it can be safely assumed that he would seldom have uttered such scornful judgments as did Hay in his Civil War dispatches. In the preface to an 1890 version of a book originally published two decades earlier, Hay apologized for his opinionated style, begging readers to "pass over with an indulgent smile the rapid judgments, the hot prejudices, the pitiless condemnations, the lyric eulogies, born of an honest enthusiasm and unchecked by the reserve which comes of age and experience."[19] The same caveat could be applied to the documents presented here.

Hay scribbled for the press partly to supplement his income and partly to satisfy his compulsive need to write. As a diplomat in Paris in 1865 and later in Spain, he continued writing for American newspapers, including the *New York Tribune.* In the fall of 1866, he told his uncle that "the magazines & newspapers begin to pay me decent prices."[20] In the decade after the Civil War, Hay pursued his journalistic career on the *Illinois Daily State Journal,* the *Chicago Republican,* and the *New York Tribune.*[21]

Hay may also have written for the press at the behest of Lincoln, who valued friendly publicity. During the quarter century before his presidency, Lincoln had written anonymous and pseudonymous pieces for the *Illinois Daily State Journal.*[22] In 1857 Lincoln drafted an agreement stipulating that he and six others would contribute to a five-hundred-dollar fund "to be used in giving circulation, in Southern and Middle Illinois, to the newspaper published at St. Louis, Missouri, and called 'The Missouri Democrat.'"[23] At first, Nicolay was the Springfield correspondent for that paper, but its editors grew disappointed in him, complaining that he lacked the "mental force" and "the requisite enterprise and activity." In seeking a replacement for Nicolay, they appealed to Ozias M. Hatch to recommend "an intelligent, active young man, one who is, or may immediately become, familiar with the policy of our party in Illinois, [and] who can write a sprightly and comprehensive letter." By mid-1860, they had determined that Hay was just such "an intelligent, active young man."[24] (Hay may have written for the *Missouri Republican* of St. Louis at the suggestion of Lincoln, who was understandably concerned about building support for his administration in heavily Democratic central and southern Illinois.) In 1859 Lincoln secretly purchased the *Springfield Illinois Staats-Zeitung,* which was to support the Republican cause.[25] In 1861 he appointed many Republican journalists to important offices. The following year Lincoln evidently urged John W. Forney to establish the *Daily Morning Chronicle* in Washington to support the administration.[26] Lincoln told Noah Brooks that, if he were to become the chief presidential secretary in 1865, he could continue writing his regular dispatches for the *Sacramento Daily Union.*[27]

Useful as the documents presented here may be for students of Lincoln and the Civil War, it is unfortunate that Hay did not devote to his diary the time and energy he lavished on composing them. If he had, history would be even more beholden to him than it is.

Born in 1838 in Salem, Indiana, Hay grew up in Warsaw, Illinois, on the banks of the Mississippi River. A precocious boy, Hay quickly outgrew the town's schools and was sent to live with his uncle, Milton Hay, in Pittsfield, where the schools were more challenging. There he befriended John G. Nicolay, who would later serve with him as Lincoln's secretary. After graduating from Brown University in 1858, Hay returned to Illinois, where he once again stayed with his uncle, who had moved to Springfield.

Upon winning the Republican Party's nomination in May 1860, Lincoln required help with his correspondence. He knew Nicolay, who had been assisting the Illinois secretary of state, Ozias M. Hatch, for three years. Lincoln enjoyed spending time in Hatch's office, which was "practically the Republican campaign headquarters for both city and State," and there he became well acquainted with Nicolay, whom he decided to employ as a secretary.[28] When Milton Hay suggested that his nephew assist Nicolay, Lincoln agreed. Following his triumph at the polls in November, Lincoln hoped to keep both Nicolay and Hay in his employ, but Congress appropriated funds for only one personal secretary. Milton Hay, who observed that his nephew "had much enjoyed working with Mr. Lincoln," offered to cover John's expenses in Washington for six months. Lincoln wanted the young man on his staff, but rejected the generous offer, insisting on paying Hay with his own money. That proved unnecessary when Hay received an appointment as a clerk in the Interior Department and was assigned to work in the Executive Mansion. In 1864 he became a major in the army.[29]

In the White House, Hay worked closely with Lincoln, who "loved him as a son."[30] Galusha Grow, Speaker of the House from 1861 to 1863, said that "Lincoln was very much attached" to Hay "and often spoke to me in high terms of his ability and trustworthiness." Grow knew of "no person in whom the great President reposed more confidence and to whom he confided secrets of State as well as his own personal affairs with such great freedom."[31] Hay and Nicolay were (as they later wrote) "daily and nightly witnesses of the incidents, the anxieties, the fears, and the hopes, which pervaded the Executive Mansion and the National Capital." Lincoln, they said, "gave them his unlimited confidence."[32]

The relationship between Hay and Lincoln was like that which had developed between Alexander Hamilton and George Washington. As the journalist John Russell Young recalled, Hay "knew the social graces and amenities, and did much to make the atmosphere of the war[-]environed White House grateful, tempering unreasonable aspirations, giving to disappointed ambitions the soft answer which turneth away wrath, showing, as Hamilton did in similar offices, the tact and common sense which were to serve him as they served Hamilton in wider spheres of public duty." Young, who frequently visited the Executive Mansion during the Civil War, portrayed Hay as "exceedingly handsome—a slight, graceful, boyish figure—'girl in boy's clothes,' as I heard in a sniff from some angry politician." Young thought that Hay was "brilliant" and "chivalrous," quite "independent, with opinions on most questions," which he was not shy about expressing. Endowed with "a poetic nature," Hay could be "reserved" and aloof, "with just a shade of pride that did not make acquaintanceship spontaneous." Young described him as "a comely young man with [a] peach-blossom face." This "young, almost beardless, and almost boyish countenance did not seem to match with official responsibilities and the tumult of action in time of pressure, but he did what he had to do, was always graceful, composed, polite, and equal to the complexities of any situation which might arise." Hay's "old-fashioned speech" was "smooth, low-toned, quick in comprehension, sententious, reserved." People were "not quite sure whether it was the reserve of diffidence or aristocracy," Young recalled. Hay was "high-bred, courteous," and "not one with whom the breezy overflowing politician would be apt to take liberties." Young detected "a touch of sadness in his temperament" and thought Hay "had the personal attractiveness as well as the youth of Byron" and "was what Byron might have been if grounded on good principles and with the wholesome discipline of home."[33] (Commenting on this portrait in 1891, Hay told Young: "I read what you say of me, with the tender interest with which we hear a dead friend praised. The boy you describe in such charming language was once very dear to me—and although I cannot rate him so highly as you do, I am pleased and flattered more than I can tell you to know he made any such impression on a mind like yours.")[34]

Others made similar observations about the assistant presidential secretary. Clark E. Carr depicted Hay in 1856 as a "bright, rosy-faced, boyish-looking young man." Carr had never met "a young man or boy who charmed me as he did when he looked at me with his mischievous hazel eyes from under a wealth of dark brown hair. He was, for those days, elegantly dressed,—better than any of us; so neatly, indeed, that he would . . . have been set down as a 'dude' at sight."[35] Logan Hay thought his cousin "a different type from the rest of the Hay family. He had a magnetic personality—more culture."[36] A journalist who knew him during the Civil War called Hay "a young, good-looking fellow, well, almost foppishly dressed, with by no means a low down opinion of himself, either physically or mentally, with plenty of self-confidence for anybody's use, a brain active and intellectual, with a full budget of small talk for the ladies or anybody else, and both eyes keeping a steady lookout for the interests of 'number one.'"[37] When F. A. Mitchel congratulated him on his appointment as assistant presidential secretary early in 1861, Hay replied: "Yes. I'm Keeper of the President's Conscience."[38] His college roommate, William Leete Stone, described Hay as "of a singularly modest and retiring disposition," yet with "so winning a manner that no one could be in his presence, even for a few moments, without falling under the spell which his conversation and companionship invariably cast upon all who came within his influence."[39]

Among those most susceptible to Hay's charm were members of the opposite sex. At Brown, William Leete Stone recalled, Hay "was always a great favorite with the ladies."[40] In Springfield, Anna Ridgely thought him "a very pleasant young fellow & very intelligent," a "bright, handsome fellow of medium height and slight build, with good features, especially the eyes, which were dark, lustrous brown; red cheeks and clear dark complexion; small, well-shaped hands which he had a habit of locking together interlacing the fingers, and carrying at arm's length, which the girls thought particularly fetching." His clothing also appealed to young ladies, Miss Ridgely observed: "He wore a long, loose overcoat, flying open, his hands thrust into the pockets, which was also thought very graceful and attractive as he swung himself along the street, for he had a rocking walk in those days."[41] A young woman wrote from Washington during the Civil War that the "nicest looking man I have seen since I have been here is Mr. Hay, the President's Secretary. I do not know him personally but he came into the Senate the other day to deliver a message from the President. He is very nice looking with the loveliest voice."[42] Hay's eyes also appealed to young ladies. "Hay's marked feature was his eyes," Helen Nicolay recollected; they were "always kindly" and "sometimes depressed."[43] His college sweetheart recalled with pleasure his "wonderful hazel eyes." She said, "You could look into them a mile, & he looked a mile into yours." She also found him "very attractive as a talker," with his "abrupt, swift phrases."[44] (This high opinion was not universally shared. In 1864 a Springfield young woman "was disgusted with him" because "he talked in a most affected manner.")[45]

The journalist T. C. Evans, who saw Hay in Washington often during the Civil War, said that he "was born to moderation and calmness in mien as in action, and they walked with him on either hand throughout his length of days, tokens of the equity of a balanced character, working with Nature as one who had discovered that her central note is calm and that she is commanded only by those who obey her." He appeared "to possess in a high degree a silent power of work, doing a great deal and saying little about it," while "his spirit was ever of unruffled serenity, his manner of invariable sweetness and charm, and . . . his talk was apt, varied, refined, and of a markedly literary quality."[46]

A fellow diner at the Metropolitan Club during the Lincoln administration recalled that Hay was "smooth-faced, ruddy-cheeked, vivacious, witty, polished, urbane and withal as full of intellectual activity as an egg of meat." A "hard practical worker" who spent "twelve or fourteen hours a day of hard work at the White House," Hay nevertheless "constantly pursued his *belles lettres* studies and went much into society." He was a "trusted and intimate friend of Lincoln's," who "probably lived nearer to that good man's heart during the years of the civil war, than any other man." Throughout the war "he was always the same witty, genial, agreeable, effervescent and fascinating fellow." Hay obviously "had decided genius and unusual literary culture."[47]

In 1866 William O. Stoddard, who had assisted Hay and Nicolay during the Civil War, said that Hay was "quite young, and looks younger than he is; of a fresh and almost boyish complexion; quite a favorite among the ladies, and with a gift for epigram and repartee." He was able to tell a joke well, Stoddard testified. One calm Sunday, Hay entered Stoddard's office, "all one bubble," and recounted a funny story, first to Stoddard, then to Nicolay. Overhearing the merriment, Lincoln came to Stoddard's room and said,

"Now, John, just tell that thing again." As Stoddard recalled, "His feet had made no sound in coming from his room, or our own racket had drowned any footfall, but here was the President, and he sank into Andrew Jackson's chair, facing the table, with Nicolay seated by him and Hay still standing by the mantel. The story was as fresh and was even better told that third time up to its first explosive place. Down came the President's foot from across his knee with a heavy stamp on the floor, and out through the hall went the uproarious peal of laughter."[48]

Hay's friend Charles H. Philbrick, who worked at the White House in 1864 and 1865, told an Illinoisan, "Hay does the ornamental . . . and the main labor is divided between three others of us who manage to get along tolerably well with it."[49] In 1863 Thomas Wentworth Higginson called Hay "a nice young fellow, who unfortunately looks about seventeen and is oppressed with the necessity of behaving like seventy."[50] Captain Henry King thought Hay physically "most resembles Edgar A. Poe" and considered him "a thorough gentlemen, and one of the best fellows in the world."[51] Thurlow Weed termed Hay "a bright, gifted young man, with agreeable manners and refined tastes."[52]

Hay had his detractors, too. Henry M. Smith, who covered Lincoln's 1861 journey to Washington for the *Chicago Tribune,* called him "a nice beardless boy" and lamented that "Mr. Lincoln has no private secretary that fills the bill and the loss is a national one."[53] Another journalist thought him epicene: "He was esteemed of the better sex as a proper ladies' man, and might with due change of garb have passed creditably as a lady's maid."[54] Some found Hay's "vanity" "inordinate almost to the point of being disgusting."[55] The historian David Rankin Barbee was even more severe: "Hay was such a damned intellectual snob, . . . so superior to everybody, including Jehovah, that you want to puke as you read him."[56] In fact, Hay disprized modesty, which he deemed "the most fatal and most unsympathetic of vices."[57] He hoped his newborn nephew would "shun Modesty! It is the bane of genius, the chain-and-ball of enterprise."[58]

Whenever possible, persons mentioned by Hay are identified in notes when their names first appear. I have identified the sources for annotations derived from manuscript collections, newspapers, and specialized monographs and biographies but not those derived from easily available published sources.

Obvious typographical errors have been silently corrected. Otherwise, the spelling of the original has been retained. All editorial insertions appear in italic type inside brackets. Words that are difficult to decipher in the original are enclosed in brackets with a question mark: [*word?*]. Words that are completely illegible are replaced by open brackets: [   ].

Lincoln's Journalist

1

1860

As the events of the last week have rendered Springfield, in one respect at least, the central city of the north, I have thought that some mention of the occurrences that have recently disturbed its monotonous quietude, might not be devoid of interest to the readers of the Journal. Having had greatness thus suddenly thrust upon her, she deports herself in the eye of the nation as bravely as if she had achieved greatness or been born great. With the undisturbed self-possession that seems the exclusive heritage of *la jeunesse Americaine*, she has quietly taken her position as the political "object of interest," and bears her honors as coolly as if rockets and cannon were no novelty in the backwoods, and as if it were the most natural thing in the world that rail maulers should walk composedly into the company of princes.

When the lightning came down from Chicago, on Friday [*May 18*], to tell us that the nation had honored the honest man whom we have so long delighted to honor, the deep and earnest enthusiasm of the hearty western populace burst forth in the wildest manifestations of joy. The Cerro Gordo cannon—*El Cyclope*—was dragged from its dignified repose in the State House, to rouse on alien prairies the echoes that once sounded over the chaparral of the south—Lincoln banners, decked in every style of rude splendor, fluttered in the high west wind, and the very church bells signalled the triumph of stainless honor and pure conservatism by clangor that was unecclesiastically merry. At night the town gathered in the rotunda of the capitol, and listened to the speeches of several gentlemen who were kind enough to furnish a thread to hang shouts and cheers on; then proceeded with banners and music to the residence of the illustrious nominee. Soon the tall, gaunt form of the future anchor of the republic appeared in his

1

doorway, and in a few good-humored and dignified words he thanked them for their kind manifestations of regard. For a while the clear air trembled with their noisy joy, and then the hard-handed multitude rushed to grasp the hand that years ago was as hard as any there, and that is as honest now as the one which wrote "Aristides" on the envious Democrat's shell in the time that sophomores love to call the "grand old days."

On Saturday morning an immense concourse of the people met at the Great Western railroad depot to receive the committee appointed by the late convention to make to Mr. Lincoln the formal announcement of his nomination. As the train came rushing in, the delegation was welcomed with round after round of rousing, electrifying western cheers. A procession was speedily formed to escort the committee to their hotel. Conspicuous in the line of march was a squad of enthusiastic Republicans, with venerable fence rails, borne *a la militaire,* which Lincoln might have rived in his stalwart youth, in the days when a pen would have been an awkward toy in his hand, and the coon-skin cap shaded his black locks so comfortably as to leave no want for the civic crown.

From the hotel the crowd adjourned to the State House, and listened with eager interest to a series of brief and effective speeches, by Hassaurek, a keen and logical German from Ohio, whose sharp hits and clear deductions elicited frequent applause; two noble representatives of Yankee Republicanism, Amos Tuck of New Hampshire, and the genial Gov. Boutwell of Massachusetts, who lives kindly in the commencement dinner memories of Brunonians [*graduates of Brown University*]; Carter of Ohio, and Kelly of Pennsylvania; and that wonderful German of the northwest, whose knowledge of our institutions is no less perfect than his mastery of our language, Carl Schurz, whose name has become a watchword of freedom on two continents.

A noteworthy feature in these speeches was the spirit of absolute confidence and certainty of complete triumph that animated them. No more of the martyr-spirit of four years ago; no more of the forlorn-hope appeals; no more of that feeling of contention against overwhelming odds, or of that blind dependence on the offices of Providence, which animated the champions of freedom in that glorious defeat. But every heart seemed filled with the dauntless energy which comes from a premonition of success, and fired with the infectious enthusiasm which kindles through the vast extent of a great and growing and victorious organization.

While the people were enjoying themselves in the State House, and feeling that it was good for them to be there, the committee, accompanied by the State officers and a few prominent citizens, went to the house of Mr. Lincoln to announce his nomination. The announcement was formally made by Mr. Ashmun, the president of the late convention, and Mr. Lincoln very briefly responded. His letter of acceptance will be published in a few days.

Until nearly midnight the rejoicings continued. The principal streets were ablaze with illuminations. Bonfires flamed and roared in public places, and bursting rockets paled the splendor of the calm May star-light.

The Republicans of the Prairie State feel large-hearted and jubilant. That victory which they would cheerfully and earnestly have labored to secure under the leadership of the great New Yorker, they are sure of now. Mr. Seward would have received every Republican vote in the northwest, for the man is unworthy to be called a Republican who does not love and revere him. But Abraham Lincoln will receive thousands of votes that never were Republican before. The skies are bright.[1]

Springfield correspondence, 9 August 1860

Of course you will not expect any coherency of language, or any sobriety of style, after a day like yesterday. All Springfield is speaking in hoarse whispers. All the voice that was in us went up yesterday in shouting. The deluge of enthusiasm that has swept over us has left no soul unsubmerged by the swelling waters. Lincoln men are too jolly to give any particular reason for the faith that is in them; and Douglas men, if such a race exists, are in a state of hypnotism. We may be able to exhume a few fossils from the wreck next week, so as to have something to hit, but at present they seem as extinct as the Dodo. We cannot characterize this demonstration by words. Superlatives grow tame and insipid in view of the facts. We can only say, with Walt Whitman:

I will not say it was this, I will not allege it was that—
I will swear it was glorious.

It was certainly the greatest political demonstration that our State has ever seen. Veteran stumpers, who have mingled in every fight since Jackson's time, fail of comparisons to describe it. Editors and reporters who have haunted for years the mass meetings of the nation, say they have seen nothing to be compared to it. Grey-haired Whigs, who shouted and drank hard cider on the Tippecanoe battle field, at the monster meeting of twenty years ago, and have lived ever since in the confident belief that no other meeting ever would be held like it, shake their heads since yesterday, and mourn over a broken idol, an ideal eclipsed.

Although every preparation had been made for an immense crowd, and all the appointments of the affair were on the most liberal and extensive scale, the vast influx of the enthusiastic yeomanry of the State so far exceeded the most sanguine expectations of the managers, that it was only by the most strenuous exertions that the immense procession could be arranged in order, and the programme of the day carried out. Although there was a telegraphic apparatus set up in the cupola of the State House, to telegraph to the twenty-five marshals on the ground the positions of arriving delegations, so as to obviate the necessity of any superfluous labor, the arrangement of the stupendous concourse occupied the severest exertions of the entire force of the Marshals, from early morning to high noon. When the crowd had been passing out of the city in one continuous stream for hours to the fair grounds, until the large enclosure was filled almost to its utmost capacity by the throng, there still seemed to be no perceptible diminution of the vast crowds that swayed to and fro on the streets and sidewalks. The fact is, we cannot tell the truth about a crowd like this, without seeming to romance. But all Illinois was here, and will testify to the day's glory to after times. You might have carved the greatest Douglas crowd that ever staggered and swore through a summer's day, out of this meeting, and then have had enough left to whip a young earthquake and outroar a Comanche hurricane.

And then the quality of the crowd was something to boast of. You know how (and the Lord knows why) our Democratic friends are accustomed, like the Pharisee, to "thank God they are not as other men are, even as this (Re)publican."

We could, in the soberest sadness, return the compliment yesterday. There was none of that affectation of rowdy plebeianism which outcrops in all Douglas crowds, as if dirt and Democracy were somehow inseparable. No pandering to the vile ground swell of ruffian passions; no barefooted rangers; no hangings in effigy; no brutal defiances, were anywhere to be seen in the vast procession. And in the human ocean that surged along the pave, you might look in vain for those floating islands of yelling diabolism that spiced the Douglas turnout of July. The enthusiasm, though hearty and genuine, and often going up in rousing, electrifying Western cheers, was very decorously restrained and generally distributed, not bursting out in sporadic spasms around doggery doors, and whisky-haunted corners. As old Joe Gillespie observed, the crowd combined the distinguished characteristics of the old Whig and the old Democratic parties—intense decency and tremendous cohesion.

It is useless to attempt a full description of a demonstration such as this has been. If you are a man of lively imagination, take a dose of Hasheesh, and turn your mind to some such brilliant subjects as the Feast of Lanterns, the Vale of Cashmere, Bengal lights, and Choate's oratory, and you will drift into a kaleidoscope of fantastic design and gorgeous colors, which may realize to your perceptions the show that yesterday's parade gave us. There was great taste and ingenuity in some cases displayed. A power-loom, for instance, was worked by steam as the procession moved on, and wove several yards of Kentucky jeans, which was passed on and cut by a tailor, and made up with a sewing machine into a pair of pantaloons, to encase the limbs of the future President, who merits as well as King Edward, the English Justinian, did, the title of Long-shanks. Then there were log cabins and monster flatboats, and big Indians, and allegorical representations of all the trades, and beautiful young women clothed in innocence and tarleton, personating the Union-loving States, and every conceivable variety of mottoes, inscriptions, and devices on banners, globes, and transparencies, that swayed and floated and revolved along a seemingly interminable line of eight miles of procession, where ingenuity and taste seemed to have exhausted themselves in making the details of this colossal parade worthy of the occasion, worthy of the cause, and worthy of the man whom they delighted to honor.

The speeches were in keeping. Trumbull spoke with that clear energy and irresistible logic which have gained our State such honor in the Senate. Doolittle, of Wisconsin, with that earnest eloquence which is building him the foundation of a substantial fame; and Browning, his Websterian dignity vitalized with Western fire; and Palmer, the idol of the central counties; and heroic John Wilson, who would not bow the knee to Baal, under Bell-Everett colors; and Case, and Cowan, and Oglesby, whose very names will "start a spirit."

It was worth many years of ordinary life to see the wild rush and impetuous enthusiasm of the crowd when Mr. Lincoln appeared upon the grounds, to see for a moment, and be seen by the eager thousands who had come so many miles with that one purpose and hope; and to hear, when he had been forced on to the stand by their loving violence, the friendly, yet dignified words by which he stilled their clamorous plaudits, always keeping, as he has hitherto kept, his position of

Fine reserve and noble reticence.

Is it not a contrast to the vulgar antics of the little man [*Stephen A. Douglas*], who is now stumping the East, with his one thread-bare speech, and his superannuated "gar-reat pur-rinciple"?

Well, night came at last, and the enthusiasm rekindled under the stars. The torch-light parade of the Wide-Awakes (among whom, all honor to a heroic few who are the salt that shall save Hannibal, Mo.!) was the most magnificent thing that could have been devised to close worthily a demonstration like this. Viewed from an elevated position, it wound its sinuous track over a length of two miles, seeming, in its blazing lights and glittering uniforms, like a beautiful serpent of fire. As the companies successively reached the corner of Fifth and Adams streets, they ignited vast quantities of Roman candles, and as the drilled battalions moved steadily on, canopied and crowded with a hissing and bursting blaze of fiery splendor, that cast a lurid glare on the upturned faces of the excited thousands, the enthusiasm of the people broke out in wild cheerings, that came back in redoubled echoes from the four sides of the square.

And this morning, "decently and in order," the vast crowd melted away. With banners flying, and music sounding, and with the thunder of salutes, the several delegations returned to their homes, with memories enriched by experiences of a day, such as it is seldom granted for men to witness. It is this style of thing that causes the patriot to gain heart and hope for the future of the Republic. The Commonwealth is safe, as long as the huge heart of the people beats right for freedom, for justice and for National honor.[2]

SPRINGFIELD CORRESPONDENCE, 23 AUGUST 1860

Lying as you do "in the hollow Lotus land" of perfect security and a healthy public sentiment, it may be pleasant for you to hear occasionally a voice from the midst of the smoke of the prairie-fires that are kindled in the western skies. I would advise all zealous Republicans, eager for a new sensation, to leave for a while the east, lapped in the languor of easy and certain victory, and sail like Hiawatha "into the fiery sunset." They will find a fight waging such as they never saw before. It is true that in the north of this State—the land of Canaan as its denizens call it—Puritan morals and Yankee thrift have made their results apparent in large and certain Republican majorities. In our splendid fight of 1856 the north came thundering down to Springfield with 35,000 majority. But Egypt [*southern Illinois*], exulting in ignorance, and like Forrest, "thanking the gods she was barbarian," sent up a solid vote out of the darkness that "seized the pile" of Canaan and gave our electoral vote to the Pecksniff of Wheatland [*James Buchanan*]. She has bitterly repented, and will show it by works.

This year, while as I remarked, the north of Illinois stands ready to honor any draft you may make on her for Republican votes, the south and the centre are straining every nerve to remove the necessity of these immense majorities, and to make the 50,000 the north has promised them, a merely ornamental trophy of victory. All through the darkest nooks of the southern counties the watchfires of liberty are lighting. Republicans are multiplying at every coigne of vantage. Wide-Awake clubs are flashing the sheen of their caps and shoulders in the heart of Cimmerian glooms. Our young and chivalrous candidate for Governor, Richard Yates, has carried the war into Africa, and is stealing away as many hearts by his frank blue eyes and sunshiny smile, as by the truth and eloquence of his fervid orations. Swett and Oglesby are doing wonders down there also, in removing prejudices and bringing over the wavering vote that has long been inclining the right way, and that is coming over in platoons when success becomes certain. The sight of gentlemen, speaking in a gentlemanlike way, is a new revelation in politics to the Egyptians, and is charming from its very novelty. Then the local oracles are breaking silence and beginning to respond, filled with Apollo. There is a minister of the gospel who has buckled on his armor and gone forth to meet the foe, and is astonishingly successful. Mr. Ferree, this Egyptian Garibaldi, has been egged and mobbed two or three times, but flourishes under the regimen wonderfully. He knows that these foul proceedings are enlisting the feelings of the people on his side, and often declares that to him "*un oeuf* is as good as a feast." The Republican phalanx in the south is compact and resolute, and though unable of course to redeem at once the southern districts, they will divide the vote very respectably.

But it is in the central counties that you would see the Laocoön struggle. The Douglas adherents, although convinced that Lincoln must carry the State, still fight with the energy of desperation for the possession of the county offices. After working, cheating, and perjuring themselves for years for the advancement of the little man who lately distinguished himself by a disquisition on mollusks at Rocky Point, and seeing at last that this labor has been all in vain, they have rallied for this last time, hungry and heart-sick, to keep possession, if possible, of the sheriffalties and clerkships, and the privileges the appurtenances thereunto appertaining. This is the explanation of their great parades, their temporary structures, their free whisky, and malt enthusiasm.

Meanwhile the Republicans are exultant but not apathetic. Conscious of being in harmony with the moral sense of the world; confident of a State triumph and a national victory; uncorrupted as yet by office, and rejoicing in a monopoly of decency and clean linen, they build their wigwams, turn out their torchlights, applaud their speakers, gaze with mild contempt at Douglas blow-outs, and go quietly and get up demonstrations five times as large. Have you heard in the far east the thunder of our earthquake on the 8th of August? To adopt the style of Sir Bohort's lament over Launcelot du Lac, it was the vastest crowd that ever filled a prairie; and the happiest crowd that ever hurrahed for a winning candidate; and the soberest crowd that ever drank three hundred barrels of ice water; and the most respectable crowd that ever brought its wife and children to a political festival; and the quietest crowd, when it listened, that ever sat under the harangues of a Senator; and the loudest crowd, when it spoke, that ever out-roared a Comanche hurricane.

It was a day to be remembered for the benefit of grand-children. It was a day that gave encouragement to many who were doubting for the future of pure Democracy. It was the only day that ever surpassed that monster gathering that swept from four States, like an avalanche, upon the battle-field of Tippecanoe, in the cider-delirium of twenty years ago.

I am afraid to tell the truth about the respective merits of our State candidates, it sounds so much like western blowing. Let me give you an instance. Against the calm and venerable Dubois, whose grand old head has silvered in the service of the State from the infancy of this century till now, the Douglas men have nominated for Auditor a little Dutch druggist's clerk, whose one, sole, and only qualification is that he speaks his own language flippantly, though with a villainous Suabian accent. An Irish cooper of Chicago, fresh from the sod, who has somehow recently blundered into a fortune, was pitched on for Treasurer, to make the race against the present sagacious and far-sighted incumbent, Hon. William Butler. *Ex pede Herculem.* I will not bore you with carrying out the contrast farther.

Every day, as I attend conventions, loaf at mass meetings, talk with the people and read the newspapers of this State, I am more and more convinced of the truth and felicity of the classification made by the gentleman who wrote to his friend in the east: "Every man is a Republican out here, who fears God and can write a legible hand without rolling out his tongue."[3]

Springfield correspondence, September 1860

It is one of the truest evidences of the innate nobility of Abraham Lincoln, that he impresses all with whom he is brought in contact, lofty or lowly, with the irresistible magnetism of a large and catholic nature. Politicians cannot but admire his clear, practical sagacity and unerring judgment; patriots and philanthropists can recognize in his public speeches the utterances of a mind that is able to rise above the mists of party passion, and look with undazzled eyes upon the radiance of eternal truths; and the honest back-woodsmen of the Sangamo Bottom, with whom his early life was passed, still love to tell, with scarcely less of affection than respect, their memories of the man.

And among those who are never weary of singing the praises of Our Abe, old Tom Edwards is best known to the citizens of Springfield. To the lo-quacity of a Yankee notion dealer, Tom adds the frankness and the easy *abord* of the west, and these are adorned and height[*en*]ed by a certain sympathetic quality of mind, that saves him from vulgarity or common-placeness, and that, under other circumstances, would have made him a fanatic or a poet. I came across him the other evening, as he was making for home, in his odd, toddling, western gait. The shadows were lengthening, and he was getting homesick for the woods. He says he can't sleep in towns—they smother him. Anxious as he was to go, the name of Lincoln brought him up with a round turn, and he instantly began a stream of reminiscences. Old Tom may certainly be believed in matters *quorum magna pars fuit* [*of which he was a large part*].

In reply to my question, he began:

> Well, young man, I reckon I *kin* tell you the first time I ever seen Abe Lincoln. It was at the big wrastling match at Clary's grove. It was gettin to be pretty well on in the spring of the year; winter work was over, and summer work wasn't ready, and the boys used to meet of the fine after-noons in the round clearing of the maple grove. That was afore the time when these river fellers fust began to bring their greasy euchre-decks,

9

and their monte-tables, and their all-fired Mexican puzzles, to snake more money out'n a honest man's wallet in a day than he could put thar in a month. We wasn't up to so many thieves' tricks as they larnt us sence, but we could do a thing or two that I'm afeared we never shall see our grand-children a doing. We had hard knuckles and hot blood; we could give tough knocks and take em, without ither whining or bearing malice. Ef bad blood was bred at a raising or a shooting-match, it was middlin sure to be spilt afore sundown, and that, you know, is better than to have it a-cankering around a man's heart.

Well, this day as I was a telling you about, we was all gathered to-gether at Clary's Grove. All our particular crowd was thar. And you couldn't have found a better set of men,—regular out-and-out sons of natur—anywhere than was loafing under the sugar trees that day. There wasn't our equals any place, from where the Indians was catching muska-longe on the big lakes, to where the Parley-Vous was eating bull frogs and cheating the redskins on the Missouri shore. Many a crowd from the other settlements we had bantered and licked as easy as a pointer could flax out a ground hog. This always winning had kind o' spilt us—made us feel cagey and sassy, like. We always felt like knocking off somebody's hat, or tramping on somebody's moccasins.

Well, the day I was talking at, we had been running, and jumping, and wrestling a little, and was laying around kind o' loose under the maples, when Dent Offert came out amongst us and commenced blowing about a clerk of his'n, that he said could throw any man in the crowd. The boys haw-hawed at this a little, but thought it was some of Dent's "wind," for Dent could lie like a peddler when it was wanted, and something when it wasn't. But Jack Armstrong, the pride of our settlement, him that we used to call Salem's Glory, tough as whit-leather, and wiry as a wild-cat, the man that had never been throwed, and we believed never could be throwed, commenced talking back at Dent, saying that his bones was aching with nothing but strength, that he had been laying lazy long enough, and would like a good freshener of a wrestle fust-rate. After he and Offert had jawed a little, they ended by anteing up five dollars a piece on the wrestle, which you know was a heap bigger bet than fifty is now.

"Now bring on your long-legged Hoosier," says Jack, "and I'll flax him in three jerks of a gar's tail, and then eat him ef youre not satisfied."

Dent moved off with a queer kind of grin on him that always meant business, and walked towards his little store where we got our notions, and hollered, "Abe! come out here a minute." And that was the fust sight I ever got at Abraham Lincoln.

10

I have not space to recount all the adventures of the day which Old Tom rehearsed in his characteristic manner, telling how Lincoln won the friendship of the whole company. But his conclusion of that narrative forms a fitting introduction to another which he gave.

That's the way long Abe Lincoln walked into all our hearts. And when he got a friend he never lost him. He took his place kind o' natural as king of our crowd, and we made him captain of our regiment in the Mexican war [*the Black Hawk War of 1832*], and we sent him to the legislature, and at last he got so big that our settlement cramped him, and he went up to Springfield, and did the same thing there.

Jack Armstrong and Abe Lincoln was always firm friends from that day, and Abe's friendship didn't die even when Jack was cold in his grave. He had a chance to show it once.

It was some twenty years arter "Offert's clerk" first come to New Salem, there was a camp meeting in Clary's Grove. One night there was a drinking spree in a tent on the camp ground, and a parcel of young fellers got into a fight. Old Peter Cartwright, who was a preaching, heard of the row, and off with his coat and come a-running down to the tent to take a hand. But when he and the crowd got there, the fuss was over. A young man was laying dead on the grass, and Jack Armstrong's oldest boy standing, looking kind o' scared and sobered, by the body. He had always been a wild sort of youngster, though not malicious, and they immediately caught him and held him to trial for the murder. It looked pretty hard for the boy. Old Peter Cartwright (and he had the keenest nose for blood of any preacher you ever [*did*] see) was in for hanging him. The boy and his mother, the widder Armstrong, were getting mighty down-hearted.

All at once I begun to think of Abraham Lincoln. He had got to be a big man in the State by this time, and once in a while the winds would blow the reports of his doings way down into old Menard [*County*]. I spoke to some of the Armstrong kin, and walked up to Springfield. There I seen Abe; I seen the same old feller; a great sight changed in looks and talk, but the same old heart beat in him. I set down and told him all about the boy's fix and the widder's trouble, and asked what could be done. He set there a minute, pushing his gold specks up into his hair, looking kind o' serious at the floor. I imagined that, like the balance of the lawyers, he was thinking about his fee. So I told him that would be all right; that all the boy's rich kin would sign as "we, the signers, promise to pay" as much as he asked. He looked up, smiling quietly, a way he has got, more with his eyes than his mouth, and says: "You Ed'ards! you ought to know me better than to think I'd take a fee from any of Jack Armstrong's blood." Then he laid his hand on my shoulder in his old fashion, and says: "Why, bless your soul, I've danced that boy on my knee a hundred times in the long winter nights by his father's fire, down in old Howard. I wouldn't be worthy to take your hand, Tom, if I turned on him now. Go back and tell old Hannah to keep up a good heart, and we will see what can be done." Now, I am such a tender-hearted old fool, and the wind that day had made my eyes so weak, that I could not say nothing nor do nothing, but got out of the office. He got me down so bad with his old-fashioned way, that I couldn't trust my voice with a Thank ye. I went down and told the widder that Abe was coming, and the poor old soul fell on her knees and commenced praising the Lord and blessing Abe Lincoln.

The old man's voice was beginning to grow treacherous as he told the story. He suddenly rose as if to recommence his journey. I, wishing to hear the end of the matter, said, "Well, Tom, how did it come out? Did he clear him?" He turned upon me a little petulantly and answered:

That's a funny question. Certainly he cleared him—slick as a whistle. The jury never left the box. Some of 'em was crying like four-year-olds. The judge was chawing up his pen to keep his face straight. But old Hannah was cool as a cowcumber. She knowed it was all right when I told her Abe was a coming, and she had her cry then. She walked home happy with her boy. The light of the sunset was blazin through the west windows of the court house as he finished his speech, and he looked, somehow, different from the rest of us. I've heerd some little squirts around town say he isn't pretty. Blast their little souls, I wish they could have seen him then.

After a little pause he continued:

When I was a youngster, and fust begun to read a little and talk with travellers, I had an idee that somewhere in the great outside world, there was living a great man that knowed it all. He was my idee of a man. I looked at all our crack politicians, and it wasn't any of them. As I growed older, I never saw my man. I used sometimes to think it would have been Lincoln if he had been born somewhere else. I've voted many and many a time for Douglas, but I never thought it was him. Ned Baker had some mighty fine streaks in him, and they say he's a going to the Senate from Oregon. But I never thought *he* was my great man. And I heard Daniel Webster once. There was something sort of awful about his eyes that made common men feel small. So he was not my man, for all would have to love him. But that night as I went home, after hearing Lincoln's speech, I gave up my idee of a great man; for, as I told you, I never thought Lincoln was the man, and if Lincoln wasn't him, he did not live anywhere in the world.

It was getting near sun-down, and Old Tom took up his stick and moved off towards the woods.[4]

Springfield correspondence, 11 October 1860

Ever since the glad tidings of great joy came flashing over the wires from Pennsylvania and Indiana (I name these two States as returned prodigals, for Ohio is the elder son who is ever with us), the citizens of the home of Lincoln have been too happy to take any particular interest in mundane affairs. They recognized the propriety of having some manifestation of rejoicing, to show the world they were not ungrateful for the blessings of Providence, but in-tended to wait till the majorities were done growing, and they knew how much to shout. This was all very well in theory, but the enthusiasm of the rising generation could not remain bottled up so long. So to-night "there was a sound of German band by night, and the Sucker capital had gathered her torches and her Wide-Awakes, and bright" the camphene blaze fell on their japanned mantles, which may certainly be called, since Tuesday, "Capes of Good Hope." The quiet October air was frightened with rockets and other pyrotechnics, and nervous ladies were periodically startled by the culiarly vi-cious tone of the small but plucky Wide-Awake cannon.

A very large procession rapidly formed at the Republican Headquarters and marched through the illuminated streets to the inspiring music of the band, which seemed to have caught a novel charm from the general joy, up to the residence of Mr. Lincoln. Having arrived there, they roused the Eighth street echoes with fifteen tremendous cheers, equally distributed between Lincoln, Trumbull, and the three victory crowned States.[5]

Springfield correspondence, 7 November 1860

"Republicans of Sangamon, the eyes of the nation are upon you!" These words greeted us yesterday morning in the columns of our paper, stared at us from the placards blotching every dead wall, and seemed to set themselves to the music that our brass bands showered upon us all day. We acted as if the suggestion were heeded, albeit the eyes of the nation were probably more divergently employed on that busy day. We began our work in the morning, we continued it at noon, and hung threateningly around the polls till the judges prudently closed them at six o'clock. But the sun went down behind the hills of Menard, leaving twilight to gather over Sangamon redeemed.

You must permit western men to brag a little. Besides, the coming man is among us, and the light of his presence glorifies our mean estate. So let me say what Sangamon has done. In the face of a Democratic majority, estimated this spring at six hundred, we have elected our entire county ticket, gained two members of the Legislature and our State Senator, and effectually broken the back of Democratic rule in the centre.

The work for a few weeks past has been intense. But the bugles sang truce on election day. I have rarely seen a more quiet and peaceful collision of the sovereigns than on yesterday. The explanation is easy. Douglas men were despondent and frightened, and Republicans were hopeful enough to be magnanimous.

It was a sight full of pleasant suggestions to a mind not too partisan to be patriotic, to see Lincoln vote here yesterday. When he first appeared, walking with Mr. Hatch from the State House to the polls, the dense crowd immediately began to shout with the wild abandon that characterizes the impulsive heart of the west. The crowded throng respectfully opened a passage for him from the street to the polls, and continued to cheer with the energy of insanity as he quietly deposited his ballot and retired. There was something infinitely delightful to the people in the spectacle of a man, great in character and in circumstance, ignoring the dignity of his position and quietly acknowledging the supremacy of the law and the inherent nobleness of the institutions to which we all owe all that we are. The quick sympathy with which the people saw and appreciated this, evinces the refining power of a free education and the high moral capabilities of the American mob.

At night, a large crowd, impelled by the irresistible sociableness which a joyous sympathy produces, gathered in the State House to talk things over, and shout at the news as it came. Nearly all the good fellows in the State were there; the glee club was there; across the street, the ladies had prepared the finest collation that the Watsons could supply on a day's notice; and at the end of the hall was Lincoln's own room, for the time being the ear of the nation and the hub of the solar system. Was it not good to be there? The crowd thought so. They commenced rejoicing over precinct majorities, but finally lost all sense of restricted glories or provincial contests in the magnificent roll of Republican thunder that came echoing out from New York and Pennsylvania. There was a forty horse-power shout that went up, tearing the concave and gladdening the hearts of the Rhode Islanders sprinkled though the hall, when the secretary read the report from the Providence Plantations, of the vote that has covered the dear little State with glory a mile deep, from Burrillville to Block Island. I could only think of the words of Walt Whitman, and in my heart I said them: "Bully for you, old State!"

All this day a crowd has been gathering. The office of the Secretary of State has been thronged by strangers and by friends. I noticed the ponderous frame of Judge [*David*] Davis making a liberal avenue through the press, and near him the deep-brained [*John M.*] Palmer of Macoupin. And always affable and always dignified, ever ready with a word for his friends and a thought for his country, with a cordial hand, and with honest eyes behind his gold-mounted spectacles, Lyman Trumbull was there. It is an honor to western people that they can honor this man. He is a far-thoughted statesman, with no demagogic arts and no bombastic glitter. It speaks well for advancing civilization, that devotion to such a man could nerve the masses of a border State to fight like the one we have come out of victorious. The fight for the Legislature has been Trumbull's. And the glory of a signal victory is his. In the face of an infamous apportionment, we have secured a neat and ornamental majority in both branches of our Legislature. So let us shout with the Belleville Germans, "Es lebe Lyman Trumbull!" [*Long live Lyman Trumbull!*]

To-night, a tumultuously happy crew came down from the north. After holding a sort of love-feast at the Chenery House, they came up to the square, and the obliging secretary gave them the Representatives Hall to be merry in. They sent imploring appeals for Lincoln, and the kind-hearted [*president*] elect could not refuse their request. He came in with a retinue of choice spirits, and was received with a strange outburst of enthusiasm which never for an instant grew disrespectful. There was none of that insolent familiarity of which Douglas was the victim in this place a few weeks ago, when grimy blackguards would slap him on the back and roar, "How goes it, my buck!" Lincoln, who was always a gentleman, is now surrounded with something of that "divinity that doth hedge a king." He staid for a little while, and retired.

Relieved of the presence of Republican royalty, the crowd had speeches and songs. They grew uproarious over some telegraphic dispatches that Mr. Nicolay read to them. One was from Judd: "The four northern districts of Illinois send greeting to Springfield, with 41,000 majority." For such mercies may we be truly thankful.

It seems absurd to write about the good time here, when the whole continent is aglow with the same good feeling. But the peculiar warmth that lives on the rejoicing here seems to me worthy of especial notice. It is not so much the return of purity and the triumph of freedom that the people here hail, as it is the recognition by the world of the great soul that they have honored and loved for many years. I will never say again, "A prophet is not without honor, save in his own country."[6]

2

1861

SPRINGFIELD CORRESPONDENCE, 7 JANUARY 1861

M R. LINCOLN HAS GIVEN UP HIS ROOM AT THE STATE HOUSE, AND his public receptions are at an end. His private Secretary, Mr. Nicolay, has an office in Johnson's Building, where he receives all who wish to see Mr. Lincoln upon important business.

The President's whiskers continue to flourish vigorously. Some assume to say that he is putting on 'airs, and the following is a frantic distich that I rescued to-day on its way to the stove:

> Election news Abe's hirsute fancy warrant—
> Apparent hair becomes heir apparent.[1]

SPRINGFIELD CORRESPONDENCE, 9 JANUARY 1861

At an early hour the hall of the House was densely packed by an eager auditory. Nearly every public man in the State was present. Norman B. Judd, the Judges of the Supreme Court, Hoffman, Koerner, and others as distinguished, were inside of the bar. The galleries were black with humanity. . . . The Senate came in at the moment appointed, led by the urbane and dignified President.

Hardly were they seated when there was a slight sensation observable by the door, and the crowd parted to make room for Abraham Lincoln. He cordially saluted the Supreme Judges and quietly took his seat near them. He glanced up at the crowded galleries. Perhaps he thought of the times when his friends had filled them, twice before, and gone away heavy hearted. He did not think of it long, certainly, for he soon dived into his capacious coat pocket, and bringing up a handful of letters began to look over them. He reads letters constantly—at home—in the street—among his friends. I believe he is strongly tempted in church.

The balloting began, and ended. It was a foregone conclusion. Applause tried to follow the announcement of Mr. Cullom that Lyman Trumbull was our Senator for six more years, but was instantly checked by the Speaker. . . . Mr. Lincoln rose from his chair, and was straightway overwhelmed. He began to shake hands. Mr. Judd stood near, holding that inevitable unlighted cigar between his lips, surveying the mature climax of a work that has been greatly his. All Lincoln's old time friends were gathered around him.[2]

SPRINGFIELD CORRESPONDENCE, 10 JANUARY 1861

The President elect views the present posture of affairs with great equanimity, though with all proper earnestness. Those who see him every day, those who know him best, have most cause to congratulate the country upon falling into hands at the same time so generous and so firm. He has Jacksonian energy, with more than Jacksonian breadth and liberality of statesmanship. Whatever betide, the hour will have its man.[3]

SPRINGFIELD CORRESPONDENCE, 12 JANUARY 1861

An elegant and significant tribute was to-day received by Mr. Lincoln, which shows the deep hold he possesses on the popular heart. It is an exquisitely executed cane, the staff made of South American wood, and the carved head of solid gold, a perfectly polished specimen of the Nevada quartz being set in the massive metal. It is of great cost and unimpeachable taste. It is the gift of a California mechanic, who did not even care to have his name connected with the princely present. It was brought from the Pacific shore to this town by Mr. Churchman, a friend of Lincoln's earlier days.[4]

SPRINGFIELD CORRESPONDENCE, 14 JANUARY 1861

Mr. Cowan, the new Senator from Pennsylvania, and Mr. Sanderson, from the same Commonwealth, have been here since Saturday night [*January 12*] very earnest and importunate for the nomination of Mr. Cameron. It is thought, by those most entitled to speak, that Mr. Cameron will be appointed. The claim of so powerful a State, when concentrated upon one man, cannot be disregarded.[5]

SPRINGFIELD CORRESPONDENCE, 15 JANUARY 1861

Rumors are busily circulating in regard to a supposed compromise, originated by the veteran Joseph Gillespie, and supported by all the central politicians, to which some unauthorized correspondents have already pledged Mr. Lincoln in advance. The report is wholly without foundation. Mr. Lincoln will be very slow to pledge himself to any policy which shall open the door to indefinite filibustering, and a man of the deep sagacity and sterling integrity of Joseph Gillespie would be the last to recommend it. The present troubles are the subject of earnest consultations among the Republican leaders collected here, but as yet no conclusion has been reached as to measures remedial.

Hon. N. B. Judd is still here.[6]

SPRINGFIELD CORRESPONDENCE, 19 JANUARY 1861

The dispatch in regard to the recent patriotic stand taken by Senator Crittenden in the United States Senate reached here at noon, and was received with deep gratification. The opinion is surely and slowly gaining ground that a peaceful solution of the present difficulties will be reached. Any one who appreciates the calm and elevated attitude in which Mr. Lincoln stands, in regard to the present complications, can never despair of the Republic when he controls its destinies. I have reason to believe that he coincides with Gov. Seward in favoring a convention of the people to suggest amendments to the Constitution. Conscious of nothing in his acts or sentiments which should justly excite alarm, he will insist upon his quiet inauguration, without further assurances on his part; but when once at the head of the nation, those who are laboring for peace with singleness of heart, will never find their plans balked by any factious opposition from him. He holds the principles of truth and justice as dear as ever; he holds as dear the peace of the country. . . .

The anti-Cameron and pro-Judd delegation went back to Chicago to-day. The politicians come and go, and always find that the President lives in Springfield, and that no clique or party has a bill of sale of him.[7]

Springfield correspondence, 22 January 1861

Mr. Lincoln received this morning a delegation from the Legislature of the State of Indiana, empowered to invite him to pass through their capital city on his way to Washington. He has previously received such an invitation from the Legislature of Ohio. He will probably accept both. He holds that an invitation coming from the Legislature of a State in their official capacity carries with it too great an authority to be disregarded.

Although Mr. Lincoln has not yet definitely decided upon the time of his departure, or the exact route of his progress, it is thought that the capital cities of Ohio, Indiana, New York, Pennsylvania and Maryland, will be honored by his presence.

There has been a cloud of delegations hovering around this town, offering all possible inducements to a Presidential visit. . . .

The estimation in which the incoming administration is held by neighboring powers, is clearly shown by the deep respect and consideration, which marks the intercourse of Matias Romero, the Mexican Minister, with Mr. Lincoln.[8]

Springfield correspondence, 23 January 1861

A strong article appeared in the *Journal* yesterday morning, denying that secession was a legal right, and that the enforcement of the laws was coercion. Its unusual closeness and compactness of logic excited the suspicions of the *Register,* which reviews it weakly and inconsequentially this morning, attributing it to Mr. Lincoln. If Mr. Lincoln has written it, the *Register* man would have shown great courage though scanty discretion in attacking it. Mr. Lincoln has other matters to engage him besides "writing for the *Ledger,*" or any other paper, however respectable.[9]

Springfield correspondence, 28 January 1861

The item hunters have recently been ignoring Pennsylvania, and keeping a vigilant eye upon the proceedings of the Hoosier pilgrims, who still stray out in large and respectable delegations to this political Mecca, to kiss the sacred Kaaba, and intimate to Abraham, that Caleb, called Smith, would make a most capital Postmaster General; and Uncle Sam's mail, equally interested in such matters, groans under the weight of letters innumerable, all to the tenor and effect that if you want a good, energetic, progressive, trustworthy, honest, Young America Postmaster General, Schuyler Colfax is your man. Indiana seems to prefer Caleb, while the general public calls for Schuyler. Mr. Judd's friends hope to win the day by a dexterous flank movement, which will leave the distinguished Hoosiers out in the cold. It is lucky that we have such men. The Post Office Department will certainly not suffer, whatever befalls.

Mr. Lincoln will not only make no further announcement of his intentions in regard to the selection and disposition of his ministry, but will not even *decide* as to his appointments until he arrives at Washington, and has the benefit and advantages of the fuller information which is accessible there, in regard to the subject.

There is another point, whose publication may set at rest the anxiety of the holy army of self-appointed Union savers, and relieve Mr. Lincoln from an immense amount of daily terebration. Mr. Lincoln will not be scared or coaxed into any expression of what everybody knows are his opinions until the will of the people and the established institutions of the Government are vindicated by his inauguration. Then if anybody doubts his integrity, his liberality, his large-hearted forbearance and his conservatism, their doubts will be removed. Until then let them possess their souls in patience.

It is now definitely settled that Mr. Lincoln will leave Springfield on the 11th day of the coming February. He will be accompanied by his family, Major Hunter and Colonel Sumner, of the United States army, and a few distinguished Illinoisans. His route will be through Indianapolis, Columbus, Pittsburgh, Cleveland, Albany, New York, Philadelphia, Harrisburg and Baltimore. The programme is liable to further modification, but will not differ essentially from that.

From the Legislatures of Ohio, Indiana, Pennsylvania, and from the citizens of the respective capitals of those States, Mr. Lincoln has received the most cordial invitations to honor them with a passing visit. Such invitations cannot decorously be disregarded. The progress of the President elect cannot but be fortunate in its influence upon the tone of public feeling in the Union. The devotion which men in general feel for their government is a rather vague and shadowy emotion. This will be intensified, and will receive form and coloring, by personal interviews of the people themselves with their constitutional head.

Mrs. Lincoln, and her eldest son, Robert T. Lincoln, the Prince of Rails, have returned from the East, and are now at home. . . .

An opportunity for removing misapprehensions is presented by an article in the *Journal* this morning. The papers who have been holding Mr. Lincoln responsible for the uncompromising editorials of the *Journal* had better print the leader of to-day, which, while it is for the principles of the Republican party, tells what those principles are, and deprecates the misrepresentation to which they have been subjected.[10]

SPRINGFIELD CORRESPONDENCE, 29 JANUARY 1861

Mr. Rodgers, a prominent conservative politician of Nashville, Tennessee, has been here for a few days, bearing with him letters from the leading conservatives of that State, endeavoring to arrange some terms of compromise by which they could make some successful resistance to the tide of secession in Tennessee. His interviews with the President were strictly private, but those who have enjoyed his confidence inform me that he will return to his home with the assurance that Mr. Lincoln is earnestly devoted to the preservation of the Union with all its constitutional guaranties, and that everything consistent with honor and with principle will be done by him to keep them intact. He appreciates also the dignified reticence which Mr. Lincoln preserves, as concessions at this time would be a confession that the minority may at any election rebel against the constitutionally expressed decision of the majority.[11]

SPRINGFIELD CORRESPONDENCE, 30 JANUARY 1861

Hon. Edward Bates arrived here last evening, and had a protracted interview with Mr. Lincoln, who left the city this morning on a visit to an aged relative in Coles county. He will return in two or three days.[12]

SPRINGFIELD CORRESPONDENCE, 31 JANUARY 1861

Mr. Lincoln arrived at his home this morning, much refreshed by his late excursion into the woods. He is one of those men who, having carried into middle age the stamina of a vigorous youth, always feel a new pulse of energy upon returning for a while, to the haunts of early exercise. He is never better than after a fatiguing journey or a continuous series of laborious speeches. He gained fifteen pounds in weight during that energetic campaign of 1858. He bears renewed vigor back from this little excursion into the country. An earth-giant, like autumnus, he always gains strength by contact with his mother earth.

Mr. Judd, and a phalanx of his Chicago friends, are here. The indications at present in political circles seem to be that Illinois must waive, for the present, her claim to a seat in the Cabinet. The conflicting interests of distant sections will probably result in the sacrifice of a man, than whom none is more worthy.

Mr. Nunez, of California, called upon Mr. Lincoln to-day. It is difficult for us who are civilized to fully appreciate the magnitude of the triumph and the merit of the achievement of the Pacific Republicans. Mr. Nunez, who is a remarkably clear headed, practical gentleman, ridicules the idea of a Pacific Republic. He regards it as a mere chimera of disappointed politicians, which if successful would be disastrous in the extreme to all hopes of material progress on the western shore.[13]

Indianapolis correspondence, 11 February 1861

The first day of the presidential tour is over; the crowds, which from 5 P.M. till nearly midnight have besieged the Bates house, the quarters of the President elect, are beginning to disperse, and something as near silence as a correspondent has any right to expect has fallen upon the city, which, for the past twenty-four hours, has been in a state of uproar and enthusiasm which nothing but an occurrence of unusual importance could have induced.

Nothing in the magnificent pageantry which attended the recent progress through the West of the Prince of Wales could have surpassed the display and the enthusiasm with which, all along the route from Springfield hither, the people of the West greeted the President elect. It has been a continuous carnival; rounds of cheers, salvos of artillery, flags, banners, handkerchiefs, enthusiastic gatherings—in short, all the accessories of a grand popular ovation, have been essayed along the line, and made the most of. It would seem that the entire population, without distinction of age, sex, political or religious belief, had turned out with the design of controverting finally that mouldy maxim, that a prophet hath no honor in his own country.

Sunday, Mr. Lincoln's last day in Springfield, was spent in the society of a few intimate and favored friends. The President is said to have exhibited much sadness at his approaching departure, and to have been quite forsaken by his usual hilarious good spirits. He does not attempt to conceal from himself or his friends his sense of the gravity of the mission which calls him in this troubled time from his household friends and gods, nor that the future is one whereof the horoscope may not be cast. The great German orator, Carl Schurz, arrived in Springfield on Saturday night for the purpose of bidding Mr. Lincoln farewell, and was received with the utmost distinction. He was invited to accompany the presidential party to Washington, but was compelled to decline, owing to business engagements. The gentlemen invited comprise members of all the political parties, with the exception of the secessionists. Govs. Gales [*Yates*] and Moore [*Morton*], the Hon. Messrs. Hatch, Bateman, Grimshaw, Morrison, Underwood, Cols. Sumner and Burgess, Major Hunter and others, compose the party which will be joined at some point on the route by Mrs. Lincoln and her two younger sons. There is a report that Mrs. Lincoln was induced to abandon her design of following her husband a week later by a telegram from Gen. Scott, who represented that her absence from the train might be regarded as proceeding from an apprehension of danger to the President. So many vapory rumors of contemplated assault upon Mr. Lincoln have been current in Washington for months, that the general may have come at last to regard such a contingency as at least possible.

The scene at the depot before starting was impressive and touching in the last degree. Upward of a thousand people were assembled, and Mr. Lincoln, taking his place in one of the rooms at the station, bade farewell to his friends and neighbors, to the number of several hundreds, with an affectionate grasp of the hand. As the time approached for the departure of the train, he mounted the platform, and, in a brief and touching speech, which left hardly a dry eye in the assemblage, bade them farewell, invoking the assistance of Divine Providence in the difficult mission upon which he was embarking, and with visible emotion requested their prayers to the power which alone could bring day out of the night which had fallen upon us. As he entered the car, after a final adieu to Mrs. Lincoln and a few near friends, three cheers were given, every hat in the assemblage was lifted, and the crowd stood silent as the train moved slowly from the depot.

At the half dozen stations between Springfield and Decatur, there was no stoppage. There were assemblages, however, at each place, and the flying train was greeted with cheers and the waving of flags and handkerchiefs. At Decatur the train bowled into the depot, where apparently several thousand people, gathered from the surrounding country, had assembled, and the air rung with cheer on cheer. Mr. Lincoln left the car, moving rapidly through the crowd, shaking hands vigorously, and incurring embraces and blessings to an extent that must have given him a slight premonition of what was in store for him. No one could witness this frank, hearty display of enthusiasm and affection on the one side, and cordial, generous fraternity on the other, without recognizing in the tall, stalwart Illinoisan the genuine Son of the West, as perfectly *en rapport* with its people now, with his purple honors and his imperial cares upon him, as when he was the simple advocate, the kindly neighbor, the beloved and respected citizen. Having spent his life in the very heart of the mighty West, having mingled with its people for a lifetime, the sympathy between the constituent and the elect is as perfect as that between near kindred. The stay here was brief, the train again moved on, cheered out of sight, whirled through the quaint little towns of Sangamon, Cerro Gordo, Iresdale, Sadorus, at each of which clusters of several hundred people were assembled, all enthusiastic, vociferous, and fluttering with handkerchiefs and flags. At Tolono, where the second stop was made, what with the cheers, the cannon, and the general intensity of welcome, the President was fairly bullied into a little speech, which, although merely a graceful recognition of his welcome, was received by the crowd with as wild an intensity of delight as if it had been a condensed embodiment of the substance of his inaugural.

Something of the gloom of parting with neighbors and friends, bidding farewell to the community in the midst of which he has lived for a quarter of a century, seemed to rest upon the President during the greater part of the day. He was abstracted, sad, thoughtful, and spent much of his time in the private car appropriated to his use. The train arrived at Indianapolis at 5 P.M. The depot was populous with vehement Indianans: thirty-four guns in rapid succession were fired, after which, accompanied by Gov. Morton, and attended by a procession comprising both houses of the legislature, the municipality, the firemen, civic and other dignitaries, he proceeded in the direction of the Bates house, standing uncovered in the barouche, and bowing to the cheering multitudes which lined the streets. After a few moments of rest, he was escorted to the balcony and introduced by Governor Morton, and made a speech, the report of which the telegraph will have given you in advance of the receipt of this letter. At its conclusion the applause was deafening, and there were loud exclamations from the crowd, of "That's the talk," "We've got a President now," &c.

The Bates house does not appear to have been built or equipped with special reference to such raids as have been made upon it this afternoon. The halls, passages, and rooms have been congested with turbulent congregations of men, all of whom had too many elbows, too much curiosity, and a perfectly gushing desire to shake hands with somebody—the President, if possible; if not, with somebody who had shaken hands with him. The supper table was overcrowded and the columbiad of the occasion, the great elect himself, was forced to wait at least twenty minutes before his supper was brought him. The servitors were willing, apparently, but confused; several wandered vaguely about with plates in either hand, engaged in a severe struggle with a complication of orders. Biscuits were handed to hungry persons who had solicited ham, and who thereupon became maniacal; cold pickles were invariably proffered to the meek suppliant for tea. A gentleman connected with the local press received the contents of a sugar bowl down his back, and has not since been heard from. The supper was altogether a comedy of errors, and seemed to amuse the President quite as highly as the gentlemen, whose perception of the fun of the thing was sharpened by getting nothing whatever to eat. After the repast, a levee was held in one of the large rooms of the hotel. From what I saw of the President's coolness under the terrific infliction of several thousand hand-shakings, I should say that he unites to the courage of Andrew Jackson the insensibility to physical suffering which is usually assigned to bronze statues. I have made some amateur studies of the art of hand-shaking at the West, and I think I may say that the rack, the thumb screw, King James's boot, the cap of silence, with all the other dark and recondite paraphernalia of torture, become instruments of cheerful and enlivening pastime, beside the ferocious grip and the demoniac wrench of the muscular citizen of the West. When it is not one citizen merely but a frantic succession of citizens, each more muscular and more wildly appreciative than the other, the result may, perhaps, be faintly conceived.

Since the termination of the levee the crowd in all the thoroughfares of the house, in the bar and adjoining rooms, has been generally occupied in discussing the President's speech. The resolute silence, which he has maintained since his election, broken at last—the politicians here are, in an informal manner, fathoming the significance of his words. The speech meets with universal approval. It has been doubtless carefully considered (indeed, it is understood that its substance was decided upon before leaving Springfield), and although he assured his hearers that his remarks were rather suggestions for their consideration than statements of his policy, none can fail to discern in them the index which points the executive way. The manner of the speech was quite as admirable as its matter. Mr. Lincoln has a clear, sonorous voice, and although his style is rather colloquial than declamatory or oratorical, it is singularly effective and admirable. Moreover, there is something inspiring in the individual presence of the man. His manners are simple almost to naiveté; he has always a friendly, sometimes a jocose word for those who approach him; but beneath all this, the resolute, determined character to the man is apparent. The fury of enthusiasm into which has lashed the usually (if report be true) tranquil Indianapolitans is quite touching, when witnessed from a distance, but alarming to come in contact with. Men embrace each other wildly without provocation; shorthand reporters, with the great speech in phonetic characters, resembling flys' legs, are surrounded and smothered. The bar-room throbs with patriotic sentiments and calls for drinks. "Lincoln and Union forever" is intoned with subdued emphasis in every direction. Indianapolis is not one of the great western towns, but a stranger, visiting it to-day for the first time, would have suspected its population numbering several millions. The train containing the presidential party leaves to-morrow at 11 A.M.[14]

CINCINNATI CORRESPONDENCE, 12 FEBRUARY 1861

Within a few months, the Queen City of the West has known two convulsive sensations; the metropolis of Pig has twice been stirred to its very marrow, its last resources of enthusiasm and hospitality called out, its aggregate lungs dragooned into that exercise of freeman, the copious huzza. The visit here of the Prince of Wales was the cause of the first of these emotional pangs; that of the new President the present. It is now a trifle after midnight, and, judging from the proceedings since the great arrival, one would imagine that every inhabitant of Cincinnati, with the exception of some fellows who are making a row in the adjoining room, had gone to bed in a state of delirious devotion to republican principles, as embodied in the tall person of "Old Abe." The reception here, just finished, has been a thorough and magnificent success. Not less than one hundred and fifty thousand people crowded the depot and thronged the streets through which the presidential cortege passed. The city has waved with flags (upon which the number of stars was undiminished), with handkerchiefs, brandished by fair hands; has resounded with the thunder of guns and the roll of music, and the tramp of feet and peal of countless hurrahs. It has taken on its robes of festival, and greeted the republican chief with even a statelier grace than that with which, a few months since, she welcomed the young prince, who dropped in upon her *en passant*, tasted her toasted pig (luxurious but penitential viand), looked at her villas, talked to her bores, danced with her pretty women, and whirled away. The ovation in honor of Lincoln quite eclipses that in honor of Albert Edward, and I am assured by enthusiastic "oldest citizens" here that the splendors of all precedent festivals and days of display which Cincinnati has witnessed are eclipsed to-day.

But to be consecutive. The President breakfasted this morning with Gov. Dennison. Several members of his suite were also invited; and the occasion, though necessarily brief, was brilliant, convivial and elegant. Mr. Lincoln charmed all whom he met with his graceful *bonhomie*, his quaint western wit and his adroit repartee. He has shaken off the despondency which was noticed during the first day's journey, and now, as his friends say, looks and talks like himself. Good humor, wit and geniality are so prominently associated with him in the minds of those who know him familiarly, that to see him in a melancholy frame of mind, is much as seeing Reeve or Liston in high tragedy would have been. The party returned to the hotel at 9 o'clock. A crowd, the nucleus of which had gathered at daylight, blocked up the streets in the vicinity of the Bates house to an extent which was quite embarrassing, and which called for the exercise of a good deal of energy to penetrate. There was such vociferous and prolonged cheering that the President, on behalf of his ears, proceeded to the balcony and made a little speech a minute long, whereat the noise was redoubled. The call this time was for Bob [*Lincoln*], of whom rumors had percolated the assemblage, rendering it wild. Bob, with a fine display of pluck, came forward, and with a still firmer display of pluck declined to make a speech. He waved his hat, however, bowed, and retired, his debut being pronounced a success. Bob seems to inherit the paternal energy, is visible everywhere simultaneously, and wears the plume of his new title, "the prince of rails," with jaunty self possession and grace.

The brief interval which elapsed between the speech and the departure was rendered riotous by the proceedings of two gentlemen, early friends of the President, who threw themselves upon Abraham's bosom, and sought to macadamize him with hydraulic embraces. They then feloniously abstracted a lock of his hair, gravely divided the trophy between them, and disappeared.

The party, attended by apparently the entire population of Indianapolis and the surrounding territory, started for the depot at half past 10. The crowd there was excessive, and its enthusiasm at fever heat. Shortly after the arrival at the depot, the special train bearing Mrs. Lincoln appeared, and she was conducted to the car reserved for her in the President's train. At 11 o'clock the start took place, shortly after which a committee from Cincinnati and adjoining towns in Kentucky were introduced to the President, who received them with the utmost affability. All the towns along the route were gayly decorated with flags and streamers; in some places guns were fired, and the train seemed to ride upon the crest of one continued wave of cheers. Only four stoppages were made at the principal places where crowds were gathered, to whom Mr. Lincoln addressed a few words of thanks and recognition. The train arrived at Cincinnati at 3 P.M. The gathering along the track was so dense that the train was forced to stop for a time. The depot was so fully packed that the municipal and military authorities were forced to intervene before the train could enter. Mr. Lincoln was received by the mayor, conducted to a carriage drawn by six horses, and, escorted by militia and a deputation of citizens, started for the Burnet house.

The streets along the line were populous as the cities of the Orient. Every window was thronged, every balcony glittered with bright colors and fluttered with handkerchiefs; the sidewalks were packed; even the ledges and cornices of the houses swarmed with intrepid lookers-on. The steps of the Burnet house rise in a succession of terraces, and those swarming with men and women, as the cavalcade appeared in sight, presented a most impressive spectacle. The display of flags from the roof was almost laughably profuse. The stars and stripes flouted the sky from every corner, and in the interspaces, in a manner which would have fanned the most fiery secessionist cold, had there been one there to see. The post office in the immediate vicinity was radiant with half a score of silken constellations; there were flags everywhere where there were not patriots; and patriots everywhere there were not flags; and in the midst of all, to the excellent not yet wholly discredited tunes of "Hail Columbia" and "Yankee Doodle," done upon brass, the President descends, and enters the house. Tremendous cheering—a phrase which is apt to become slightly repetitive in chronicles like this—is an actual essential here. A speech from the balcony followed. It was apparently unpremeditated, and had the happiest effect. He quoted from a speech he had made at a time when he could not have dreamed of the crescent honors which were in store for him, and the patriotic, kindly and conciliatory tone of Abraham Lincoln, citizen, came gracefully and nobly from the lips of the citizen-made President. When, as a simple citizen of the West, he told his audience, composed partly of Kentuckians, a year ago, that "we mean to remember that you are as good as we, that there is no difference between us other than the difference of circumstances, we mean to recognize always that you have as good hearts in your bosoms as other people, or as we claim to have, and treat you accordingly,["] it probably did not occur to him that he was so soon to repeat the same sentiments to the same audience as President of the states which he is to reunite.

There is a plethora of politicians here. Some from the neighboring state of Kentucky, a few from New-York, and a legion from the West and Northwest. Some of them are much given to embracing the President, as if he required a little of that sort of affectionate fortification. He puts up with it gravely, although I think he wishes they wouldn't. After the speech he retired till after supper, which was served in private apartments to the President, his lady and sons, and a few guests. A repetition of the Indiana levee on a more extended scale, took place in the great dining-room from seven till ten, at which hour, although the crowd still hungered and thirsted for an opportunity of shaking his hand, he succumbed, leaving the disappointed to shake their own hands, or find some friend upon which to vent that painful ceremonial.

Mrs. Lincoln, in another apartment, held a levee, whereat the beauty and fashion of Cincinnati did graceful homage to the prospective queen of our republican court.

A large number of Kentuckians are here. Those whom I have seen are conspicuous for their reticence and their length. I am of the opinion that Kentuckians, as a general rule, should not leave home in one piece. In communities where the average of stature is from seven to eight feet they might not be regarded as objects of terror. But a sudden incursion of giants like that which Cincinnati has known to-day is an event fraught with as much dread, at least to correspondents of five feet eight, as the stampeding of rhinoceri across a colony of anthills would be to the occupants. Most of the gentlemen from across the river speak hopefully of the future, and express their appreciation of Mr. Lincoln; but a few dark of aspect gather in overhanging groups and gesticulate. The mayor of Covington, a Kentucky town into which, from the roof of the Burnet house, an arrow might almost be shot, is one of the disaffected. He declines to wait upon and pay his respects to the President elect, a circumstance of no further consequence than that it saves the presidential hand a violent grip and his arm a tremendous wrench.

The arrangements here throughout were admirable. Cincinnati has honored herself in her manner of honoring the President.

The weather has been delightful. The party leaves for Cleveland to-morrow morning.[15]

BUFFALO CORRESPONDENCE, 16 FEBRUARY 1861

The train bearing the President and suite left Cleveland this morning at 9 o'-clock. Quite a large crowd was assembled at the depot and along the line of the track for some distance. The train consisted of one baggage and three passenger cars, one of the latter beautifully carpeted, curtained, and upholstered for the occupancy of the President's party.

At Euclid, a station near Cleveland, a man was injured by the premature discharge of a cannon. A telegraphic report of this death, received at the next station, was subsequently contradicted. At Wickliffe, Willoughby, Painesville, and other small stations, clusters of people, gathered from the adjacent county, were assembled, ranged along platforms, swarming upon adjoining roofs, clinging upon posts and fences, and exhibiting the heartiest enthusiasm. At Westfield an interesting incident occurred. Shortly after his nomination Mr. Lincoln had received from that place a letter from a little girl, who urged him, as a means of improving his personal appearance, to wear whiskers. Mr. Lincoln at the time replied, stating that although he was obliged by the suggestion, he feared his habits of life were too fixed to admit of even so slight a change as that which letting his beard grow involved. To-day, on reaching the place, he related the incident, and said that if that young lady was in the crowd he should be glad to see her. There was a momentary commotion, in the midst of which an old man, struggling through the crowd, approached, leading his daughter, a girl of apparently twelve or thirteen years of age, whom he introduced to Mr. Lincoln as his Westfield correspondent. Mr. Lincoln stooped down and kissed the child, and talked with her for some minutes. Her advice has not been thrown away upon the rugged chieftain. A beard of several months' growth covers (perhaps adorns) the lower part of his face. The young girl's peachy cheek must have been tickled with a stiff whisker, for the growth of which she was herself responsible. At Ashtabula, the home of Senator Giddings, something more than the brief and formal speech with which he usually responds to the public manifestations of welcome, was expected from the President. The republican constituency of this district is noted as being more intensely republican than the most republican of republicans in other localities. No speech was made, however. The train stopped; the crowd stared at the man of the hour for an instant, then burst into an irrepressible huzza, to the echo of which we rolled away, leaving every inhabitant of Ashtabula upon the platform, with his or her mouth open in a state of din-bewildered enthusiasm.

At Girard, a station near Erie, a profound sensation was created by the sudden appearance of Mr. Horace Greeley. He wore that mysteriously durable garment, the white coat, and carried in his hand a yellow bag, labelled with his name and address, in characters which might be read across Lake Erie. He had, it was said, mistaken the special for the general train, and was a good deal embarrassed on finding himself so suddenly cheek by jowl with the chief of the great and triumphant party which he had so large a hand in establishing, and of which he is one of the most powerful and least judicious supporters. He at first made an incursion into the reporters' car, where he was captured, and marched off in triumph, by Mr. Secretary Nicolay, to the President's car. Here he was introduced for the first time to Mrs. Lincoln. At the next stopping place Greeley suddenly disappeared. His arrival and departure were altogether so unexpected, so mysterious, so comical, that they supplied an amusing topic of conversation during the rest of the journey.

At Erie a dinner had been prepared in the station, and the inhabitants had gathered upon the platform for the purpose of making a noise, and destroying the quietude of that repast. The station swarmed with people, chiefly very old men and very young boys, and as the train drew up cannon were fired, Hail Columbia experimented upon by a brass band, and the roof of an adjoining shed broken through. No injuries were occasioned, but some unreasonable persons who had been precipitated to the bottom of the structure, made a vow and wanted to get out. No attention was paid to them, however. It is possible that they may have been released during the day. The dining room was crowded. There were elderly women, with umbrellas and spectacles, mounted upon chairs; aged gentlemen, with crutches and benedictions; local politicians, with fluffy white cravats and tremendous appetites; colored persons of both sexes, one or two infants at the breast, together with all the other varieties which make up western life. The dinner was excellent and profuse. At its conclusion Mr. Lincoln was conducted to the balcony and spoke a few words to the assembly, after which the suite formed in line and again entered the cars.

At Dunkirk, at the conclusion of a brief speech, Mr. Lincoln, placing his hand upon a flag staff from which the stars and stripes waved, said, "I stand by the flag of the Union, and all I ask of you is that you stand by me as long as I stand by it." It is impossible to describe the applause and the acclamation with which this Jacksonian peroration was greeted. The arches of the depot echoed and re-echoed with the ring of countless cheers. Men swung their hats wildly, women waved their handkerchiefs, and, as the train moved on, the crowd, animated by a common impulse, followed, as if they intended to keep it company to the next station. Inside the cars the enthusiasm created by the conclusion of the speech was scarcely less than the outside assemblage had exhibited. The company evinced a general disposition to intone hurrahs and sing patriotic songs out of tune.[16]

BUFFALO CORRESPONDENCE, 18 FEBRUARY 1861

The train arrived at Buffalo at 5 o'clock P.M. The crowd at the depot was something unprecedented in the history of popular gatherings in this part of the country. It is estimated that at least seventy-five thousand persons must have participated in the turbulent ceremonials which greeted the arrival of the President elect. The military arrangements, organized with reference to previous gatherings of the sort, were found to be utterly inadequate. As the train rumbled into the great depot—a structure capable of containing at least ten thousand people, the single company on duty, together with a few struggling policeman, were swept away like weeds before an angry current. The crush was terrific. Thousands and thousands of men without, urging, pushing, and struggling, endeavored to force an entrance to the depot, which was already packed to its utmost capacity. The President himself narrowly escaped unpleasant personal contact with the crowd. An intrepid body-guard, composed partly of soldiers and partly of members of his suite, succeeded, however, in protecting him from maceration, but only at the expense of incurring themselves a pressure to which the hug of Barnum's grizzly bear would have been a tender and fraternal embrace. Major Hunter was crushed violently against the wall, receiving serious injuries. It was at first thought that his shoulder was dislocated. An old gentleman from Lancaster had three ribs broken, and was otherwise badly bruised. When recovered from the press the blood was running from his mouth and nose, and it is believed that he has sustained serious internal injuries. There are one or two minor accidents, the details of which it was impossible to obtain.

The President was received by his predecessor, Mr. Fillmore, who uttered the briefest possible words of welcome to the distinguished guest, after which they entered carriages and proceeded in the direction of the American Hotel. The streets were densely thronged, the cheers unremitting, the stars and stripes waved everywhere, from roofs, from windows, from balconies, festoons of drapery, banners with inscriptions of welcome, in fact all the traditionary accessories of popular demonstration were copiously distributed throughout the entire route.

On arriving at the hotel, in front of which the throng was so dense that the cortege found it extremely difficult to approach, the President was received by Mayor Bemis in a speech, to which he responded. Immediately upon his entrance the doors of the house were shut in the faces of the crowd. It was only in this manner that the hotel was protected from an incursion, which would have entirely subverted the order of the establishment.

Mr. and Mrs. Lincoln immediately retired to their private apartments, where they remained till after supper.

A deputation, consisting of officers of Governor Morgan's staff, arrived to-day from Albany, and were received by Mr. Lincoln this evening before the levee. The reception of the public did not differ in any essential particular from those at other cities: the crowd came up one staircase, crossed the corridor bowing to Mr. Lincoln, and descended by another staircase to the street. Occasionally one of the sovereigns would address the President in an informal manner, eliciting always a prompt, sometimes a felicitous, repartee. Several little girls, who were introduced, Mr. Lincoln lifted in his arms and kissed, sending them and their parents away entirely enchanted by his unaffected cordiality. Mrs. Lincoln's levee, in an adjoining room, was well attended.

A committee, representing the German citizens of Buffalo, waited upon the President during the evening, an attention which he recognized pleasantly in a little speech.[17]

Albany correspondence, 18 February 1861

When the train bearing the President stopped at the imaginary line which constitutes the western boundary of the state, a few excited persons with much toil and travail hoisted a shred of bunting, upon which were inscribed the words, "Welcome to the Empire State." There were a few heavy persons upon the platform; a few small boys, who persisted in getting under the car; a few elderly women, and a blooming bouquet of girls; there were horses hitched at fences; farm wagons of a rude sort ranged about the roads; there were small flags, making up for their lack of size by an intensity of flutter; there were all and singular the objects which one expects to see at a rural railway station, but there was little in the clusters of men, women and children in the snowy, desolate reach of wintry fields, intersected by zigzag fences and winding roads, to indicate it as the porch of the Empire State. Nothing holding a promise of that magnificent central range of cities through which the plumed and bannered train was to whirl the grim chieftain; nothing of that wondrous tidal wave of life drawn up from leagues and leagues of territory, upon the crests of which, welcomed with acclamations and sped with blessings, he was to ride. It was like entering St. Peter's through a trap door, or Aladdin's palace through the ventilator. But the reception upon which the President entered, as the train spun across the line, has been one which the century is not likely again to see, one of which the suggestions are pregnant with events, of which the history will strike deep into the coming time, coloring it the world will see how. The greatest, richest and most powerful of the states has slapped the President upon the shoulder emphatically, told him to "go it," and be sure of at least one "backer." The state will keep its word. The question is, will "old Abe" go it?

If the reader could see him, as the writer hereof sees him, sitting upon yonder seat, deep-eyed, bending forward, his face channeled with deep wrinkles, which hold a shadowy significance of the man within—large-browed, thoughtful, an aspect generally expressive of rugged strength in repose, and of resolute decision in action—the reader would probably arrive at the conclusion that he was the man, of all others, to see first that he was right, and then to go ahead. If he be not such a man, why, then physiognomy is a delusion and a snare, and Lavater may go hang.

The telegraph has anticipated this letter, of course. It ceases to be news before I have moistened the syrupy gum arabic rim which seals its envelope. Why then may I not be inconsecutive, throw details where Macbeth, with a lordly contempt for the apothecaries, desired physic to be thrown, and recreate merely those cloudy impressions which a winter ride across the state leaves upon the mind. I have seen the snow flakes melt upon a million up-turned faces to-day; dissolve in lucent globules as if those eager herds of men had just come drenched from the vale of tears—have seen the long white mystery of the snow stretch away into the gray horizon, till of crowd and cannon, plume and banner, of city, town and hamlet, of spire and forest and mountain, little remains except a visionary procession moving amid the feathery desolation of a world of snow. It will not therefore, perhaps, be expected of me that I should here repeat what Mayor Smith said, nor need I enter upon elaborate conjectures as to the sentiments which fired the bosom of Alderman Jones. I need not record the inscriptions upon divers banners, need not allude to the numerous platforms fruitlessly erected along the route; need not refer to that pusillanimous example of the American eagle which, catching an accidental sight of the President elect, turned away in terror and hid its head in the bosom of a sympathetic policeman. Are these and other incidents of the sort not written in the chronicles of that natural enemy of the scribe, whose letters go by mail—the telegraphic reporter? They are. Accursed be his memory forever and a day.

What peculiar exigence of time tables may have led Mr. Superintendent Wood to indicate 5 A.M. as the hour upon which to start from Buffalo, I do not know. I only know that Mr. Wood did indicate that hour, and that that relentlessly executive person, like time, tide and rent day, waits for no man. We were, consequently, compelled to rise at 4 A.M. At that hour the waking human heart yearneth to behold its enemy; at that hour, suddenly aroused, men habitually milder than the sherbet of the oriental wax vitriolic of temper, and demand explanations. Need I intimate that of the weird cluster of men, cloaked and muffled, who gathered gloomily in the dim corridors of the American, not one but thirsted for the blood of Wood, as the hart thirsteth for the running brooks? I need not. The anathemas which were intoned from the double shotted columbiad of objurgation fired off by the stout gentleman who had an opinion to the piping maledictory treble of the thin man who had lost his spectacles. Let them lie in the lap of that silence whereto they have wandered and fallen asleep. I do not intend to become their historian.

There is something weird in that mysterious light which comes before the dawn. Somebody says that for one hour in the twenty-four the world is overspread with an atmosphere of old. I do not feel inclined to disbelieve it, for now as I look upon the file of soldiers ranged before the door, stiff, silent, spectral and motionless, they seem to me transfigured and to have taken on something of that shadowy presence which the phantom legions seen in the night season by Zhabile, the monk, moving slowly down the Alps wore. The houses, too, look wan and distant, and the snow under foot glimmers with the faint phosphorescent light, which is neither of the moon nor of the stars. When we reach the depot and look beneath the arch, there is such a grim cavernous darkness within that it seems as if we were entering a magnified example of the house apportioned for all the living. There are a few winking lamps, a few pallid officials rushing hither and thither, a hissing demon of an engine glimmering with pendent, motionless flags; there is a momentary silence succeeded by a zouave charge upon the baggage man, who retreats in good order, executing a flank movement and disappears. Finally the start is effected.

By and by the dawn rises. It is really melancholy to contemplate the hour at which agricultural people rise. Men in farm yards, distributing hay to herds of cattle, men chopping wood in door yards, men driving teams along the country roads, men standing at the porches of rural hostelries, endeavoring to express in their attitudes their conviction that early rising is a good thing, and to be cultivated, as if the unanimous reluctance of the human race to getting up before daylight were a thing to be whistled down the wind. Out upon those mouldy proverbs which teach the beauty and utility of turning out upon hours wherein only owls and milkmen should be stirring.

The vital history of that day's ride is to be written in three words: "Crowds, cannon, and cheers." Such crowds—surging through long arches, cursing the military and blessing Old Abe; swinging hats, banners, handkerchiefs, and every possible variety of festival bunting, and standing with open mouths as the train, relentlessly punctual, moved away. The history of one is the history of all; depots in waves, as if the multitudinous seas had been let loose, and its billows transformed into patriots, clinging along roofs and balconies and pillars, fringing long embankments, swarming upon adjacent trains of motionless cars, shouting, bellowing, shrieking, howling, all were boisterous; all bubbling with patriotism. The enthusiasm for the President was spontaneous and universal; and when we reached Albany, everybody present congratulated himself that he had been a witness of one of the most memorable of triumphal processions which this or any other country has ever witnessed.

There is something dispiriting in the consciousness that we are in for it for the day. A day, superficially considered, is a mere dot upon that great map of time, sown with multitudinous constellations of similar dots; only a globule in the great ocean of the ages. But there are days which sink into the soul and take on certain airs of being infinitely longer than other days—days which look the human race in the eye and controvert the ancient maxim, *tempus fugit*—the day before that on which you are to be hung; those in which you wait for expected remittances; those which drag their weariness along when men are shipwrecked upon desolate islands, dying of thirst. Why may I not add those upon which one starts, before daylight, for a day's ride in the cars.

But if any thing could enliven it, if any thing could blunt the numerous moral augurs with which the hours probe us, it would be this wild arrival of crowds past which we are whirled. The echo of acclamation scarcely dying behind us, before that far onward breaks upon our ears. But any steration whatsoever wearies at length. Crowds are singularly alike. They are always seen from an elevated point of view, dotted with a bright, almost tropical arabesque of color, and they always bellow. They invariably call for speeches, and then make such a row that the speaker's voice is inaudible. They are curiously wavy and undulating, like tides which rise and fall and currents which drift across each other. What a world of human experience—of joy and woe, of remorse, anguish, triumph, and what not, belonging to man the animal, and man the spiritual, is represented in this herd of men and women, stretching down the bannered street as far as our eyes can penetrate amid the snow!

One naturally thinks something of this heavy irrelevant sort, as he looks upon the tiers of upturned faces, pallid with the cold; but at the next station there is another crowd, with another history. It bellows like the former, and waves its flags; its official persons flutter with sashes of a similar sort, and make similar little speeches of welcome; its boys intone similar howls—it is, in fact, so thorough a counterpart of the preceding one, that any meditation upon the subject whatever becomes tedious, or if the correspondent falls asleep, it is no fault of his, but of Mr. Wood, who outraged all the finer feelings of his nature by making him get up at that penitential hour of 4 A.M. The assumption of having fallen asleep affords a fair excuse for closing this letter, which I proceed to do.[18]

Philadelphia correspondence, 21 February 1861

The journey through New Jersey to-day was unexpectedly brilliant. The crowd which greeted Mr. Lincoln at the depot, at Jersey City, was one of the largest, as it was certainly the most picturesque, which he has yet seen gathered to welcome him. The "light, aerial gallery" which fringes the interior of the structure was crowded with women and children, [who] waved with handkerchiefs, and fluttered with ribbons and frills of lace, and intoned treble huzzahs as the tall chief strode up the depot and mounted the platform car provided for him. Excellent order was preserved. The policemen, with maces longer than the stave of Dogberry, punched unoffending old gentlemen, of a peaceable turn of mind, off the platform, administered severe discipline to the ribs of correspondents and reporters, and put a plume upon the climax of their efficiency by struggling to restrain the majority of the members of the suite from entering the car. The start was duly effected at length, and from that point to Trenton, where a legislative reception and a lunch awaited his future excellency, there was nothing memorable, beyond that which is expressed in this stereotyped formula—cheers, cannon, crowds, etc. At Trenton it was apparent that unusual arrangements had been made. The number of mounted marshals, with white satin badges upon their hats, riding vaguely about in the mud, made it evident that the capital of New Jersey, in her reception of the man of the hour, was resolved to be "equaled by few, excelled by none." The official display was embarrassingly elaborate, but it rather increased than mitigated the prevalent disorder. Several members of the suite, after fruitless endeavors to get a seat in one of the carriages—primitive conveyances open at the front, and externally very red with the soil of the territory—plunged wildly into a neighboring restaurant where they dined frugally on a small sardine. The more fortunate following in the presidential wake, through streets thronged with people apparently from remote rural districts, through parallel ranges of windows, clustered at which were fair smiling faces—reached the state house, and after a little delay obtained admission to the senate chamber. This was already thronged, but by some system of compression imperfectly known to me, room was made for the half hundred or more whom the special train had brought. There was rather more tumult than would generally be considered consistent with the owl-like gravity of a legislative assembly, and a large number of persons, unhappily in the background, made the chamber resound with cries of "Down in front"—"Hats off." The appearance of Mr. Lincoln was the signal for tumultuous applause, lasting several minutes.

The speech having before this been given to your readers in full, I have nothing to do with its matter, but its manner is worthy of special mention. His voice was as soft and sympathetic as a girl's. Although not lifted above the tone of average conversation, it was distinctly audible throughout the entire hall. When, after avowing his devotion to peace and conciliation, he said, "but yet I fear we shall have to put the foot down firmly," he spoke with great deliberation and with a subdued intensity of tone, lifted his foot lightly, and pressed it with a quick, but not violent, gesture upon the floor. He evidently meant it. The hall rang long and loud with acclamations. It was some minutes before Mr. Lincoln was able to proceed. When silence fell again, he asked them to stand by him so long as he did right. There was a peculiar naiveté in his manner and voice, which produced a strange effect upon the audience. It was hushed for a moment to a silence which was like that of the dead. I have never seen an assemblage more thoroughly captivated and entranced by a speaker than were his listeners yesterday by the grim and stalwart Illinoisan.

The dinner, or rather lunch, was profuse, and admirably served, but the delay experienced before the dining hall was thrown open seemed to have been unnecessary, as it certainly was tedious and irritating. The crowds were unmanageable; the police moved moodily about, expostulating and uncertain what to do; the wrong persons were admitted through private doors, and the right ones debarred therefrom; everybody called for the landlord, who was not to be seen; and in this way from half to three quarters of an hour were spent. The President was conducted in state through the kitchen, where a number of men in paper caps, and smelling of burnt pie, saluted him gravely and made gestures with ladles. It would hardly have occasioned surprise if one of them had pulled some congratulatory remarks from his apron pocket, and proceeded to read them, by way of testifying his respect for the President, and his confidence in the incoming administration.

The lunch was admirable, but imperfectly arranged; those who had forks could find but little to put those utensils into; those surrounded by all the luxurious varieties of cold cut had no forks. However, by dint of perseverance, about three hundred people managed to eat or drink something, at somebody else's expense; after which, the suite departed.

From Trenton to Philadelphia nothing of special note occurred. The arrangements at the Philadelphia depot were ample, but an unaccountable delay occurred in the starting of the carriages. The route laid down by the committee was in distance about four miles, and throughout the whole way the streets, windows, and balconies were crowded. The reception at the hotel and the ceremonies of the evening I shall give in a future letter.

Great preparations are being made for the impressive ceremonial, by the President elect, of hoisting the American flag above Independence hall, to-morrow morning. An immense crowd is anticipated, notwithstanding the earliness of the hour at which the event takes place. The day will be observed in this city as a public holiday.[19]

Harrisburg correspondence, 22 February 1861

All along the route from Philadelphia, and especially at Lancaster, receptions seemed more the result of curiosity than enthusiasm. Even at Harrisburg, not one man in a hundred cheered.

The crowds everywhere were uniformly rough, unruly, and ill bred. Mr. Lincoln was so unwell he could hardly be persuaded to show himself.

Harrisburg is swarming with soldiery, some of whom came from Philadelphia, and there are hardly enough persons out of uniform to balance the display. The corps of Zouaves elicited special attention. Colonel Ellsworth was in his glory to-day.

The Jones house, where the party stopped, was fairly mobbed. The arrangements there were unprecedentedly bad; some of the suite and party were unaccommodated with rooms; several in one bed, and others had no rooms at all. The crowd, and the fatiguing ceremonies of the day, and the annoyances and vexation at the badly conducted hotel, proved too much for the patience of the party, who vented their disgust loudly. The committeemen did nothing, and were in every one's way. Completely exhausted, Mr. Lincoln retired at 8 o'clock, and Mrs. Lincoln, on account of the crowd, disorder, confusion, want of accommodation, and her own fatigue, declined to hold any reception.

A drunken, fighting, noisy crowd infested the city all the evening, cheering, calling for "Old Abe," and giving him all sorts of unmelodious serenades. No terms are too severe to characterize the conduct of the crowd about the hotel and the arrangements there.

The route to Baltimore to-morrow was not determined till this evening, as it was debated whether or not Mr. Lincoln should ride from depot to depot or go by a route which avoided a change of cars.

The party call Baltimore an infested district, and doubted what to do. Finally it was arranged to leave here at 9 o'clock, arriving at Baltimore and Washington at different hours than were before arranged. They go by direct route from here, and ride through Baltimore, dining, by invitation of Mr. Coleman, at the Eutaw house.

The Baltimore committee are reported to commissariat Wood as not truly representing the people of the city. It has therefore been determined that the committee shall not be received by Mr. Lincoln, nor allowed on board the train. This is decided, and may create some disturbance.

The Presidential party tomorrow will consist of thirty-five persons, the original number, the Pennsylvania committee having arranged with Mr. Wood not to accompany the train.[20]

WASHINGTON CORRESPONDENCE, 25 FEBRUARY 1861

When, with the daylight of last Saturday, arrived the Great Western, in this city, unbored with attendants, bothered by no committees of reception, hungry, weary, pallid, with a borrowed hat, and somebody else's overcoat; and when, a few moments thereafter, the news was first whispered, then spoken, and finally bellowed from one end of the town to the other, the people here resident, without distinction of age, sex, or condition, organized themselves into a committee on rumors and surmises. That committee has been in session ever since. The number of conjectures which have been hazarded would, if they were dollars, pay the national debt. The stupid opinions which have been expressed, the illogical explanations of the matter which have been offered, the amount, in brief, of vapor which has been conversationally emitted, may fairly be spoken of as the unknown quantity.

The effect here was certainly miraculous. Sagacious persons, in a general way up to all dedges, when informed of the great arrival, pulled down their lower eyelids and requested bystanders to inform them whether they saw anything green there. Correspondents were dragged from reluctant beds and sent flying upon missions of discovery. Men gathered at street corners and in bar-rooms, talked earnestly with vehement gesticulations; the street took on a holiday aspect, and women and children, as the forenoon rose, blushed a gentle mauve color, under the influence of the universal excitement. Amid it all, the President elect, having caught a wink of sleep and taken a little breakfast, proceeded to pay his respects to the President, whereafter he went about his business, leaving the town agog.

Now the rumors hitherto nebulous began to take definite form. Plots, it was said, had been discovered. The vendetta had been proclaimed against Old Abe. Oaths, deeper than wells, had been taken that he should never pass the Monumental city [*Baltimore*] alive. Certain detectives, of unparalleled shrewdness, had recently been resident at Baltimore, and in the divers characters of the music teacher, the southern planter, the gentleman of liberal means and elegant leisure, the barber, and so on, had accumulated such a mass of discoveries, had discovered such an uncommon number of mares-nests; had, in fact, opened up so cheerful a vista of conspiracy, fringed with bowie knives and pistols, that the President elect, esteeming discretion, if not the better, at least a respectable part of valor, concluded to give the disaffected town the slip, pay his fare through it like an ordinary traveler, and leave the conspirators howling.

As curiosities of the occasion, I can do no better than to give in detail a record of the more sanguinary and bloodthirsty of these rumors, appending thereto a simple, unadorned statement of the facts in the case. It is a pity to eviscerate the interesting and very readable dispatches from Harrisburg of your contemporaries. It is a melancholy circumstance which forces me to dispel the picturesque illusion of the President in a Scotch plaid cap—the midnight arrival of that extra-ordinary party, who, after enjoining secrecy and receiving assurance thereof, fortified by words of honor, oaths, etc., hardly wrung from reluctant correspondents, proceeded to lock everybody in separate rooms, ought certainly to stand untouched. The episode is too dramatic to be squelched. As to those rumors:

One Mr. Detective Pinkerton, of Chicago—a gentleman of Vidocquean repute in the way of thief-taking—a very Napoleon in the respect of laying his hand upon the right man—a person who has populated the penal institutions of the West with elaborate scoundrels, whose villainy eluded all save the Pinkertonean investigations—was several weeks since sent to Baltimore for the purpose of working up the case, *i.e.*, discovering whether any peril menaced Mr. Lincoln in his passage through that city. Rumor attributes to Pinkerton the discovery of secret organizations, the members of which, sworn upon their daggers, had taken oath to assassinate the President. An Italian barber wanders vaguely through this shadowy surmise; a leader of the Baltimore carbonari, probably, who wears a slouch hat and gives an easy shave for six cents. This tonsorial person was recently summoned before a secret committee of investigation at Washington; he resigned his membership upon receiving the summons, proceeded to Washington, swore black and blue, returned to Baltimore, and resumed his membership of the conspiratory cabal.

It is highly probable that Pinkerton made, according to current rumor, other discoveries of a similar refreshing sort, but the barber's slouch hat in some manner extinguishes him at this point, and a squad of New-York detectives loom mysteriously through the general fog. They are said to have discovered that an organized plan to throw the train off an embankment, somewhere between the state line and Baltimore, had been laid. Two of the railway flagmen had been suborned, a hundred armed men were to lie in wait in the vicinity for the gentle purpose of bayoneting any possible survivors among the occupants of the train. They discover (still according to Madame Rumor) that the police arrangements at Baltimore are being unaccountably slackened, that not more than twenty men are to be detailed at the depot, and that the chief has intimated his inability to guarantee the President's safe conduct through the town.

There are reports concerning certain sharpshooting desperadoes, animated with the heroic design of picking off the President from attic easements; recondite varieties of explosives are hinted at; torpedoes are to be thrown beneath the carriage; so many desperate and murderous things are to be done, that if the President elect had all the lives of a cat he would lose them all, one after another, before reaching the Eutaw house.

It will be observed that thus far I have dealt only with the rumors vaguely adrift upon the surface of conversation, hereabout. I give them as rumors merely—as accessory incidents of the most serio-comic event of the time. It is now generally believed that Mr. Lincoln's sudden change of the plan of his journey was founded upon no apprehensions of violence or insult to himself. It is possible that statements to the effect that unpleasant, perhaps dangerous, demonstrations toward him were contemplated may have been laid before him, but that these influenced his action is disbelieved. He had received no invitation from either the municipality or the citizens of Baltimore to visit that city; it was represented to him that the ceremonials of welcome, contemplated by the thousand or fifteen hundred republicans, would needlessly inflame the public mind, not so much against him as against those who received him. This view of the matter was strongly urged by his advisers. Meantime arrived a special messenger, the son of Senator Seward, bearing, it is said, a letter from Hon. Erastus Corning, dispatches from Gen. Scott, and a message from the future Secretary of State, urging his immediate presence in Washington, and the inutility of tempting the possibilities of an outbreak at Baltimore. Mr. Lincoln, thereupon, submitting entirely to the direction of his friends, left Harrisburg at once, and reached Washington as has been before recounted.

There will, of course, be future disclosures concerning the matter. Even up to this time it is impossible to form an opinion which may not be controverted by the revelations of tomorrow. I do not think, however, that the existence of an organized plot against the President's life will be established.

The President today visited both houses of Congress. The southern members, with one or two exceptions, declined introductions to him.[21]

WASHINGTON CORRESPONDENCE, 26 FEBRUARY 1861

If the President was in any respect an object of sympathy while on his travels, he is certainly doubly so now. He has exchanged the minor tribulations of hand-shaking and speech-making for the graver woes which attach to the martyr toasted between two fires. The conservatives have chiefly had the presidential ear since the unexpected arrival last Saturday morning. Last night a deputation of the straight-outs had an interview with him, their rumored object being to defeat the appointment of Gen. Cameron to the cabinet. A protest, signed by a number of senators, to a similar effect was yesterday sent him, and every effort possible in his disfavor is being made.

The belief is current, however, that his appointment is a fixed fact. There will, of course, be a good deal of squirming among the not-an-inch men, but there can be no doubt that the conciliatory disposition manifested by the President, in calling to his council the conservative rather than the belligerent men of his party, will give satisfaction to the country at large. Bell, of Tennessee, had an interview with Lincoln this morning. The substance of their conversation has not transpired, but enough is known to occasion the deepest gratification to the conservatives here of all political classes.

A strong effort has been made by republican senators here to force Seward from the place assigned him in the cabinet. It is rumored that a protest, numerously signed, greeted "Old Abe" almost immediately upon his arrival, and that he did the business for that interesting document by putting it in the fire. Mr. Lincoln resents the assumption which such a protest implies that he will be unduly under the influence of any individual among his advisers.

Among the recent arrivals are those of Horace Greeley, and Giddings, of Ohio. In fact, nearly all the prominent straight-outs are here. It is expected that if their protestations and solicitations are overborne by Seward's influence in the construction of the cabinet, an immediate rupture of the party will ensue—the *Tribune* (among newspapers) leading the opposition. The truth is, the personal animosities, jealousies and heart-burnings engendered by the recent contest are fanned to a white heat. With the not-an-inch men it is rule or ruin; with the conservatives a deprecatory attitude of defense. The former have the advantage in point of numbers, the latter in the respect of being headed by Seward, the man of all others most entirely in the confidence of the new President.

Mr. Lincoln's quarters at the National are violently besieged, but generally with unsatisfactory results. The rabble of office seekers are not admitted. He receives deputations, touches up his inaugural, consults with prominent men, and talks very little. He has disclosed a talent for listening since his arrival, from which many infer that when he does speak officially he will mean what he says, and abide by it. Little has transpired in respect to the tone of the inaugural, although it is stated that the changes in that document since reaching Washington have been but slight.

The preparations for the ceremonial of the inauguration are in progress. The steps leading to the eastern entrance of the capitol are being boarded over, forming a platform, in the midst of which a canopy is to be arranged, beneath which the President will stand while delivering his inaugural. The preparations for the ball, which is intended to be one of the accessory splendors of the occasion, are also going on. A temporary building, capable of accommodating six thousand people, is in course of erection in the immediate vicinity of the post office. It is worthy of remark that the flying artillery and a detachment of U. S. troops are quartered near the place. There is a report that some of the most distinguished ladies in Washington society will decline to attend the ball, and that in consequence something of the prestige of the entertainment will be impaired.

The number of western politicians here is beginning to tell with fearful effect upon the market for alcoholic beverages. The rush for offices is perhaps greater than was ever before known. Applicants outnumber places in a proportion which is really laughable. The President very justly declines even to consider claims for other offices than those of his cabinet, until after the inauguration and the establishment of his government.

Mrs. Lincoln receives nightly at her parlors at Willard's. She has won all hearts by her frank, unaffected cordiality of manner, and the unconventional simplicity with which she greets those who call to pay the respect due the wife of the President. Young Bob has been extensively lionized, and a good deal of regret is expressed by the ladies at his approaching departure for Harvard. The private secretaries of the President, Nicolay and Hay, are toiling early and late with a mass of correspondence, of the extent of which I can convey no adequate idea. Some of the communications are pious, some blasphemous, many long, a few threatening, and all contain applications for some little office. Judging from the number of these missives, it would seem that the number of people in the United States who find it impossible to earn an honest living must be appalling.

The defection of General Twiggs, and his surrender of nearly two millions of state property to the rebels, occasions but little surprise. He has been for some time known to be disaffected toward the government under which he holds his commission, and to sympathize strongly with the traitors.

Gen. Cass left this city for Detroit to-night. The car occupied by the Prince of Wales had been provided for his accommodation.

Rumors of the discovery of a league, at Richmond, consisting of thirty members, among whom lots were to be cast for the selection of the assassin of the President elect, are current. At this late hour it is impossible to trace them to any reliable source.[22]

WASHINGTON CORRESPONDENCE, 1 MARCH 1861

The golden days have fallen upon the capital. The air hath in it all of June except the breath of roses and that drifting incense which the censers of the honeysuckle hold. I think this premature balminess and warmth of atmosphere superinduces a general languor and lassitude. People of extreme opinions whom I meet look, in a moist, disheveled way, open to conviction. Men of profound aggressive energies wander vaguely along the avenue, shirt collars limp and pendent, moist globules upon their brows and maps of Asia, in yellow dust, upon their coat-tails, with such a nerveless incertitude of purpose that one might think them about to stop a policeman for the purpose of inquiring whether they were really awake, and this was March, and that, yonder, the capitol, and so on. Seriously, there is a grim reality in the clutch of this velvet-handed demon, the spring fever. I think it has even tempered the acerbity of legislative debate. I passed an hour in the gallery to-day, and really the tranquillity and peace of that asylum of bald-headed sinners I can liken to nothing save, perhaps, the council chamber (if there be one) of those mild-eyed dwellers in the happy isles, sought long and fruitlessly beyond the baths of all the western stars by the mariner Ulysses. Some question of coffee, I think, was being discussed—something anent the duties thereon—and a mild vow was made by a thin gentleman, with a bald head and blue spectacles. I am conversant with coffee, but know little of duties; consequently the discourse presently waxed tedious. When the gentleman with blue spectacles reached "fifthly," I reached for my hat, and, shaking the dust of the gallery from my sandals, ascended the dome, or rather the pillared tiers whereon that stupendous convexity, crested with Crawford's masterpiece, is to be reared.

It is a good place—this light, aerial gallery, iron-railed—from which panoramically to view this sprawling, chaotic town. Seen from this point, the city unrolls its dusty magnificences of distance; the stupendous harmonies of its design reveal themselves in broad avenues, which converge upon the capitol as all the roads of the Roman empire converged upon that golden milestone by the Pincian gate; moreover, distance lends enchantment here as elsewhere. The town is a congeries of hovels, inharmoniously sown with temples, as the Napoleonic tapestries were sown with golden bees, but something in the dust, the remoteness, the sunlight, touches them into respectability, if it does not glorify them. For the chief thoroughfare of a capital it would be difficult to conceive of a meaner street in architectural adornments than Pennsylvania avenue, but from this point it takes on the stately airs of a grand Appian Way among thoroughfares. Very straight, very broad, and, seen from a distance, it makes a false pretense of being splendid, which it is not, but only escapes squalor by a hair's breadth. Why did they attempt to build a city where no city was ever intended to be reared? It will never be a capital, except only in name; never a metropolis like Rome, or London, or Paris. The "eternal blazon" is against it. Yet it will sometime, of course, be clustered about with historic memories. Caesar will be slain in the capitol, and Brutus harangue the roughs from the terrace. Who knows but captives from Patagonia, or some terra incognita elsewhere—some undiscovered tropic isle jeweling the tawny forehead of the orient ocean—may be somehow brought hither to rear a new Coliseum. Our civilization must retrograde first, it is true, but history sobs with the records of its retrogressions. It has been swinging backward and forward like a pendulum since ever the flaming sword was fixed at the first garden gate whereof we have knowledge.

It is very cool and invigorating, this wandering around the circular gallery. One falls insensibly to wondering how the men with paint-pots and hammers cling to such slight projections at such dizzy altitudes. I recollect hearing a story of a correspondent who reported the proceedings of some crowded occasion, clinging the while with his teeth to the bell-rope, writing with one hand and reversing the sheets with the other. But the feats of some of these artisans are even more astounding. They sit astride the slender iron bars which gird the framework of the dome, flourish their brushes or their hammers, chant patriotic staves, make their little jokes, and (who knows?) dream of days wherein they shall be chieftains, like the mighty and much badgered Abe. Up from the Nazareth of rails a prophet has come; why may not one come up from the paint-pot and forge?

I am not sure that these excellent and intrepid artisans, with whom now and again I stop to exchange such observations as my aerial outlook suggests, cherish any hidden ambitions of the sort. Probably they do not. If one be bitten with the desire of legislative or other fame, Washington is a good place to disillusionise him. You see here, it may be, a reverend senator blind with a bad article of whisky; an eloquent representative, purpureal of nose and moist with the perspiration of yesterday. You shall see crowding the bars, shuffling along the aisles, populating the corridors of the blear caravanserai of hotels, at once represented every stage of official eminence and every grade of inebriety. There are generals, and colonels, and majors, and captains, governors, senators, honorables; all chew tobacco; all spit; a good many swear, and not a few make a merit of being able to keep two cocktails in the air at once. The hotel halls are littered with a mixture of dirt, scraps of paper, cigar stumps and discarded envelopes, and the whole is embroidered with an irregular arabesque of expectoration. Exceedingly small and very dirty boys take a good deal of trouble and make an unnecessary amount of noise in the endeavor to induce you to purchase the *Star* and *States* for five cents. Heavy persons, whom you have never seen before, with moist hands, eyes luminous with intoxicating beverages, break through the crowd and wildly shake your hand. They convict you of having met them before somewhere. You say you have been there, whereupon you are instantly saddled with an acquaintance who grasps your hand fifty times a day, and whom you heartily wish at the—antipodes.

As to news, there is very little, and even of that little the Ariel of the telegraph informs you almost before we know it here. The President elect exhibits symptoms of having been recently subjected to a good deal of hydraulic pressure. Probably his cares sit as lightly upon his shoulders as they would upon those of any conscientious man, alive to the gravity of the duties which the inauguration on Monday next will usher in. But the burden is heavier than that which Atlas bears. The President elect encounters not only the difficulties of rule at this most momentous crisis in our history, but the added complication of a most formidable schism in his party. He has been, during the week, pulled hither and thither, alternately by the conservatives and the ultraists, till I am much mistaken if, in his inner heart, he does not wish himself back in the quiet village of Springfield again.[23]

WASHINGTON CORRESPONDENCE, 2 MARCH 1861

The sun, thank God, has risen upon the last day of the administration of James Buchanan. He sits in the White House, with the chalice of power upturned, making wry faces at the unspeakable bitterness of its dregs. A weak, pottering old man, with much of the industry but none of the power of Philip the Second of Spain, who sat, velvet-capped, rugose, swarthy, impenetrable—a mystery to the world, to himself, to history—in the Escurial, docketing minutes and scribbling inane commentaries upon the margins of dispatches. He has left—the weak, bad old man, from whose hand the wand of rule is falling—a dark footprint upon our history, one which a century will hardly obliterate. There will be prayers tomorrow in the churches; in thousands of pulpits the Divine guidance will be invoked for the President of the United States and all others in authority—how much of thanksgiving, I wonder, will mingle with this formula of invocation, that the scepter passes with another sunrise into other and worthier hands? How much of blessing and how much execration shall go with the ex-President to that tranquil country home which, four years ago, was the shrine whereto unwashed political pilgrims journeyed? The Lancastrians, it is said, sought to purchase this quiet country seat, that it might be no more inhabited by the man at mention of whose name, hereafter, the muse of history will avert her eyes and weep. Yet, no asylum for his waning years could be so retributively appropriate as that wherein, day by day, he shall meet the rebuking eyes of those who once honored him, were proud of his fame, and followed his rising fortunes with a fidelity deserving of a better requital. Pray for him, good souls; and the tenderest prayer that could be uttered would be, that *resuryum* might not be written above him when he is dead.

The new man, whom all the joy bells are to ring in with golden chimings on Monday, sits all day in his parlor at Willard's, receiving moist delegations of bores. That he is not before this torn in pieces, like Actaeon, is due to the vigor of his constitution, and the imperturbability of his temperament. The feuds in his party rage with a wilder fury than did those between the rival roses—the Guadeloupe and Ghibbelines, the Montagues or the Capulets. Whether Chase or Cameron shall hold the keys of the strong boxes, is the question. The rival parties have been kept in breathless suspense, awaiting its solution for days and days. Up to this hour it is unsettled. Probably to-day will witness the finale of the contest.

Meantime comes bad news from the South. Virginia and Maryland are confidently expected to secede to-day. John Tyler, the greatest political blunder of this or any other age, denounces the peace conference, reviles its conciliatory final action, and, with all his feeble strength, slams the door in the face of compromise. If the apprehensions concerning the action of Virginia be realized, it will, of course, gravely complicate existing difficulties, and throw a new obstacle in the way of the new President. The current feeling here is expressed in the phrase which one may hear at the capitol, in the street, at the hotels, from all sorts of people: "If Virginia goes out, good-bye to the Union." The sanguine and the hopeful, in view of even so lamentable a contingency as the defection of the Mother of Presidents, are not disposed to intone so lugubrious a farewell. "If Virginia goes out," say they, "[*there will be*] a firmer attitude on the part of the North." And, in truth, they are about right. Conciliation has already been stretched to the extremest tension without avail.

The overpowering strength of the republican element here renders the peaceful inauguration of Mr. Lincoln a certainty, even if under other circumstances there were just grounds of apprehension. The display, according to the published programme, will be in the highest degree impressive. The military, the civic authorities, the diplomatic corps, together with associations, and the citizens generally, will unite in forming the presidential escort. The avenue will be gaily decorated, and the capitol draped with flags and banners. Every thing of pageantry which can lend impressiveness to the august ceremonial will be made accessory. As to the ball little is known, save that the building in which it is to be held approaches completion, and that the tickets of admission are about a hand in length. It is quite doubtful whether the festival will be a success.[24]

WASHINGTON CORRESPONDENCE, 4 MARCH 1861

The openness, candor, and magnanimity in which President Lincoln's inaugural is conceived, exhibit him as a man of probity, from whose love of justice and fair play the country has everything to hope. He stands ready to concede to every section its full constitutional rights, without quibbling over phrases or seeking to take advantage of doubtful constructions. The inaugural is as conciliatory as it could possibly be in consistency with the obligation imposed by the official oath to preserve, protect, and defend the Constitution. The keynote of the whole address will be found in this passage, which is so wise and excellent that we cannot forbear to repeat it:

> So far as possible, *the people everywhere shall have that sense of perfect security which is most favorable to calm thought and reflection.* The course here indicated will be followed, unless current events and experience shall show a modification or change to be proper; and in every case and exigency *my best discretion will be exercised, according to the circumstances actually existing, and with a view and a hope of a peaceful solution of the national troubles, and the restoration of fraternal sympathies and affections.*

President Lincoln does not regard the Union as dissolved, and he looks not to coercion, but "to calm thought and reflection," to bring the disaffected states to again recognize their constitutional obligations. Instead of acts of hostility against those states, calculated to arouse their passions, it will be the aim of his administration to give them a "sense of perfect security." Even if current events should make it wise to change his present purpose, everything will be done "with a view and a hope of a peaceful solution of the national troubles, and the restoration of fraternal sympathies and affections." We are thus particular in calling attention to these pacific declarations, because, from the heartiness with which they are uttered, they are calculated to have a reassuring effect on the public mind, especially as the whole address is in harmony with their spirit.

If, contrary to the wishes of the President, there should be a collision between any of the states and the federal government, it will be only because those states wantonly provoke it. The government will not assail them. If resident citizens cannot be found to accept the federal offices in any of those states, there will be no attempt to force obnoxious strangers among the people for that object. Though the government may have the *right* to fill these offices from abroad, President Lincoln thinks it wise to waive the enforcement of this right, since it could only lead to irritation. If those states should suffer from domestic violence or foreign invasion, and ask aid of the general government, his administration will be as prompt to afford it to them as to any other part of the Union. So long as they do not refuse the mail facilities they now enjoy, the postal service will be continued to them. But while no right will be withheld from those states and no act of aggression committed against them, and while everything like a high handed assertion of authority will be carefully avoided, the President cannot release himself from his obligation to enforce the laws. "In doing this," he says, "there need be no bloodshed nor violence, and there shall be none unless it is forced upon the national authority. The power confided to me will be used to hold, occupy and possess the property and places belonging to the government, and collect the duties and imposts; but, beyond what may be necessary for these objects, there will be no invasion, no using of force against or among the people anywhere."

This language respecting the public property is not quite free from ambiguity, and, taken by itself, it would not make it quite clear whether it is the intention of the President to *retake* the forts in possession of the seceding states. It is, no doubt, purposely left ambiguous, in order that the administration may be free to act as future exigencies may render proper. It must be interpreted in accordance with the kind and fraternal spirit which animates the whole address, and with the President's avowed wish to avoid irritation, and to produce a temper in the public mind favorable to calm reflection.

In regard to the rights of the South, President Lincoln maintains that the slave states have a valid claim to their fugitive slaves, and that it is the duty of the government to enforce that provision of the Constitution in its plain and obvious meaning. He also maintains that the southern states have the fullest right to manage their domestic institutions according to their own pleasure, without interference. But he pretty clearly intimates that the political question relating to slavery in the territories cannot be irrevocably decided by the Supreme Court. In regard to remedies for the existing state of public feeling he seems to favor a national convention for amending the Constitution, and recognizes the authority of the people so to alter that instrument as either to grant new guarantees to the slave states, or to fix terms for the separation of the states.

On the whole, President Lincoln is very firm in his determination to execute the laws, but very desirous, at the same time, to cause no needless irritation, and to restore friendly sentiments. A carping and captious spirit may distort the inaugural, and so find matter to condemn; but no candid citizen can fail to approve it, and augur well of the new administration.[25]

WASHINGTON CORRESPONDENCE, 6 MARCH 1861

The "irrepressible conflict" of office seekers has fairly set in, and the members of Congress are waylaid, dogged, importuned, buttonholed, coaxed and threatened persistently, systematically, and without mercy, by day and by night. There seems to be no way to abate the nuisance, and they must bear the infliction with the best grace they can assume. It is astonishing how many gentlemen are now in Washington, from all parts of the country, who have served the nation or served states, elected Lincoln, or elected congressmen, or performed some signal political service, for which they claim, modestly of course, to be rewarded by the party. It is singular, too, while their merits loom up in their own estimation into magnificent proportions the offices which they claim dwindle into relative insignificance. The members of the cabinet have the charming prospect of being in a state of regular siege for months to come. Secretary Smith entered upon the duties of the Interior to-day. In five minutes the ante-room was filled with a motley crowd of applicants, each anxious to gain immediate audience and have his little matter attended to; but they were, most of them, doomed to disappointment, and could not even effect an entrance.

The appointment, which is understood to be determined, of Mr. Crittenden as judge of the Supreme Court, gives the most unqualified satisfaction to all union men, and is regarded as indicating the national and conservative policy of the new administration. The secessionists are greatly enraged, from the apprehension that an act of so much magnanimity and wisdom will further conciliate the border states. It is impossible to please these gentlemen. They are horrified at any thing on the part of Mr. Lincoln which looks towards firmness in the support of the government, and they are equally discontented at any evidence of his pursuing a conciliatory course. It is all done for effect, they say. Of course it is, and, what is better, will be very likely to produce it. A few more such appointments would do more to check the secession movement than anything else whatever. They would be a practical commentary upon the inaugural which all men could read and understand, and would convince southern men who have been honestly apprehensive of a sectional administration, that the professions of that document were to be honestly reduced to practice. The more the inaugural is studied, the more general and profound is the satisfaction it gives. It is understood to convey Mr. Lincoln's own sentiments, and to have emanated from a sound mind and an honest heart.

Those who are most opposed to it can find no salient points of criticism in it. Its remarkable unity of thought and tone compel its acceptance or rejection as a whole, and drive objectors into the loosest of generalities in its condemnation. The real objection, which lies at the bottom of all complaints against it, is simply that it announces the intention to carry on the government. If it was necessary to say this—and how can it be doubted?—then certainly it could not be said less offensively or with greater calmness and freedom from passion. If any fears existed that the President would be in any respect an instrument in other hands they are, I apprehend, pretty well dispersed. He does his own thinking and acting, and, while he will take counsel from his constitutional advisers, he will never shrink from the responsibility of decision upon all measures of government.

The demand of the commissioners from the southern confederacy for the giving up [*of*] the forts will be at once made. Of course there can be but one answer to this demand, and when it is given the attack on Fort Sumter will immediately follow. This course will be adopted both as a matter of pride and consistency, and it is now viewed as the only policy by which the border states can be drawn into the revolution; and this, even, cannot be done without inaugurating a counter revolution in some if not in all of them. The union men in them have gone too far to recede; they have taken too bold a stand now to succumb. Their determined resistance to secession will either prevent it in these states, or it will paralyze it, and the cotton states can hope for no effective co-operation from them in their revolutionary course. When the Union standard is raised in the South there will be more flock to it than secession leaders are at all aware of. Men now yield to the current who would not if they could have assurance of support in resisting it.[26]

WASHINGTON CORRESPONDENCE, 16 APRIL 1861

A long course of peace and prosperity has not quite cankered the heart out of our people. The rust of money-getting has gathered thickly enough over the heart and conscience of the trading North; but the friction of actual battle removes it with instantaneous ease. Through all the long, cowardly, compromising years that have crept away in inaction and dishonor since this century was young, marked only by a succession of enactments that stand on the statute books like the grave-stones of national honor, the Northern mind has seemed to sink deeper every day into the listless apathy which subdues all impulses of freedom and moral independence to the dominion of avarice and cowardice. The activity of peaceful trade salved the wounds of insulted honor, Southern cotton stopped the ears of the North to every sound but the jingling of dollars. People began to wonder if a resurrection ever would come. The lethargy seemed terrible, when the shame of the last four years was powerless to break it. Occasional signs of disturbed slumber were seen. Cass throwing his portfolio in the face of the President—the glad shouts of millions hailing the progress of the sun that, scorning astronomical laws, rose in the west and travelled eastward—the sudden burst of applause that followed "Anderson's fine cut" from Moultrie to Sumter—all heralded a return of the Northern spirit that used to be.

There was a deep sigh of relief when the babbling old helmsman [*President Buchanan*] left the reeling vessel, and a younger and stronger man took his seat, in silence. Every man of the crew breathed easier, for the ship felt the helm.

The crowning insult came at last, and the rebel batteries forced a surrender from Sumter. The morning after, the President wrote his proclamation, and the swift tongue of the lightning [*the telegraph*] spoke the simple, firm, and dignified words that night, over the continent.

The response proves that the nation was not dead, but sleeping. From every State the answer comes, eagerly begging for the privilege of doing more than is asked of them. The Governor of Rhode Island, elected by Democratic votes, clothed with the moral power of his position and the material power of five millions of inherited wealth, whose villages dot the Mosahssuck river for miles, who pays his servants salaries that would buy Florida, telegraphs to the War Department, that a regiment is ready at once, and that he will leave his spinning-wheels and lead them to the field in person. You cannot too highly estimate the significance of this fact. Cameron instantly answered "come."

New England is saved by this storm. We see now that the voice of a Puritan conscience is louder than the hum of a thousand looms.

Pennsylvania is on the war-path. John Covode offers to take $50,000 of the loan to arm the militia. Philadelphia forces the mayor into decency, and Southern swaggerers are slapped and cuffed into silence on the streets.

And Old Manhattan renews the glories of her better days. The magnificent infection of a patriotic rage seizes the people in the throng of the thoroughfares. Treason turns pale before their quiet earnestness. The hoary traitor of the *Herald* is hooted on the streets, and rushes to his office in dismay, to find it invested by a threatening multitude. He shouts to his foreman: "Deil tak ye, mon! why dinna ye rin up the stars and stripes? Stop, Jamie! Ye had best hoist *twa* flags, mon!" then sits down to write an editorial, indorsing in full the Administration, and proving that he has been with it all along.

We are still waiting for the response of the West. We have no doubt of her. The first low notes of the coming thunder are reaching us now.

There is something splendid, yet terrible, about this roused anger of the North. It is stern, quiet, implacable, irresistible. On whomsoever it falls it will grind them to powder.—The necessity of war makes its very cruelty a source of hope and mercy to mankind. Let it be bloody and short, in pity to the maniac South. They are weak, ignorant, bankrupt in money and credit. Their army is a vast mob, insubordinate and hungry. Their state, based on a thin crust of custom and law that covers a sea of hidden fire. What is before them but defeat, poverty, dissensions, insurrections and ruin. They have sown the wind. They will reap the whirlwind.

The North will not have mercy, for mercy would be cruelty now. The Government must die or crush its assailants. Freedom and Slavery stand in the field, like the hosts of good and evil in the Apocalypse, for a final fight on Armageddon's plain. There is no question as to the issue. Leaving out of view the Rights of the matter, we have the Might. The rebels must yield or they and their institution must be swept into the Gulf. The longer the fight lasts the worse for them. Let them look to it, that the crash of jarring claims in their worn-out States does not break, once and forever, the shackles of the slave.[27]

WASHINGTON CORRESPONDENCE, 7 MAY 1861

To-day May has really dawned upon Washington. The cold, rainy, sluggish and inclement weather of its primal days, that would have made hypochondriacs of any but real live patriotic soldiers has, thanks to the neglects of Pluvian Jove, at last terminated in sunshine. The avenues are waving with richly foliaged trees, and the air is bracing, cool and genial. I have just returned from the camp of the Seventh Regiment after a journey of about two miles through a mucky, muddy stratum that could scarcely be equaled in all Jersey, and molded and thoroughly baked, would make good brick-bats for a Baltimore mob. Carriages and omnibuses in great numbers are constantly troubling this mud, either for the gratification of those citizens who are impelled thence by a curiosity to look in upon a genuine military camp and "survey the tented field," or to bear to and from the ground those sons of the Seventh who, on a two hour furlough are permitted to visit the city. Ten from each company are permitted by the command to be absent at once, and the gray jackets have during the day quite a representation upon the Avenue Pennsylvania.

Arriving at the entrance of the grounds which lead to the camp, a mile and a half west of Willard's, the gates were flung open, and two sentinels with an array of brass buttons and bristling steel, demanded of me a "pass." This matter arranged, a walk of about two minutes up a road bordered with luxuriant grass and shaded by trees in full foliage, brought me *vis à vis* to two other sentinels whose business and equipments were similar to those just passed. Turning then to the left I passed through a gate. On the right stood the tents of the guard, with two brazen-throated howitzers pointing toward the road. A few rods further on is the "tented field" with its carpeting of green clover and dingy red mud. The Seventh literally "live in clover." A beautiful little city of tents it is; well divided off and laid out with avenues and streets. The tents, I should think, must cover more than an acre of ground. Some of them are trimmed and ornamented tastefully with the national colors, and are very cosily furnished with tables swung on cords from the roof, and camp chairs and carpets, wardrobes, &c., &c. I was there at the very important hour of dinner, and saw many young men who have waltzed in the gay parlors of the New-York *elite*, while the bright light of gorgeous chandeliers rained down upon loveliness and beauty bedecked with pearls and diamonds, were, on this occasion, engaged in the far less poetical occupation of cooking steak before a little fire afront the tent door, and watching the savory juices as they fell spattering and crackling among the flames. Others, six in a tent, while partaking of their romantic repast, with the fresh air of heaven pouring in upon their table, were telling jovial stories, like as many jack-tars in a forecastle. Everybody seemed happy and healthy and hungry; and when the muddy feature of the picture is disposed of, and the warm, genial summer air and summer sunshine makes all beautiful around and comfortable within, those who live with roaches in dark rooms in high hotels may well envy the pleasant camp-life of these gallant soldiers, with nothing but white canvas and blue sky above them, and the cheek of mother earth close beneath them.

The tents bear many evidences of patriotism, of wit, and of luxury. The red, white, and blue wave at nearly every door. Comical and grotesque figures and descriptions are drawn or pasted here and there upon the canvas, and on many of the tables I observed a lavish display of those little dainties which invest life with pleasure and elegance. In one corner of each tent lay the mattresses which, spread upon the floor, are pressed for a sleep more refreshing and visions more delightful than many a couch of eider, veiled by Tyrian tapestry, has ever yielded.

Passing through an avenue, I came near stumbling over a striped pole, and looking on a tent at the right, saw King Tonsor himself, with soft white napkin and glittering razor and foaming lather, sitting in the regality of *bar-bar*-ism and ready to treat the qualities of one of Wade & Butcher's brightest blades. A little further on a black boy was endeavoring with box and brush to impart some of his own ebony hue to a pile of muddy boots, and singing jovially,

> Black your boots and make 'em shine,
> And charge you only *half a dime!*

His efforts to contribute a polish to the society in his vicinity seemed commendable and well appreciated, and when he grinned, every tooth in his head glistened like a newly-minted piece of silver. My visit to the laundry convinced me at once of its simplicity, but I have not at present time to describe it.

In several tents the soldiers were singing, and in all the universal sentiment seemed to prevail of contentment and happiness. Every one with whom I conversed seemed anxious for war, and a chance for the regiment to prove its valor and effectiveness. The puerile anathemas and threats which have been uttered through the southern press against the Seventh Regiment have had their effect, and if ever the "tug of war" shall come—and I see now many reasons for believing that it soon will—the Confederate States will find, when they meet these sons of New-York, their ribaldry returned to them, with interest, in coins of lead and steel.

I witnessed this afternoon the administering of the oath to the New York Zouaves, under Col. Ellsworth. It was a most imposing spectacle, and in many of its features quite different from the usual scenes attendant upon the ceremony. When the regiment arrived in Washington last Friday evening, many of them obtained leave of absence, and many who could not, *took* leave of absence with sundry significant gyrations of their digits from their noses at the commanders who refused the recreation demanded. The consequence was that Friday night and Saturday they swarmed down upon the city from their quarters in the Capitol and commenced warlike experience by invading several of the liquor stores and low resorts. Ultimately several separate rows resulted, in which a few of the Zouave fireman soldiers behaved themselves shamefully. Saturday evening all the stores were closed at a very early hour, and the citizens actually kept away from the street in terror. The following card from Col. Ellsworth appeared in the *Republican* Saturday morning:

Mr. Editor: Will you do me the favor to state that the regiment of Zouaves were recruited in great haste, and we could not avoid taking some men unknown to the majority of the regiment. A few of these men have been conducting themselves in a discreditable manner, and I will regard it as a favor if, in the future, all persons who have been in any way annoyed by any one claiming to be a member of this regiment, will present himself at 10 o'clock on the morning following the occurrence for the purpose of identifying such person. It is the intention of the regiment, and my own determination, to free ourselves, by the most summary process, of all such characters, the moment we can identify them.

E. E. Ellsworth
Colonel First Zouaves

The demonstration made seemed to be one of pure mischieviouness and a happy-go-easy feeling that made everything legal in time of war, and I am happy to know, from conversation with the regiment yesterday, that the disgraceful conduct of a small portion of the soldiers is regarded with supreme contempt and sorrow by the regiment at large.

At about 4 o'clock this afternoon the whole regiment, fully equipped, formed in a hollow square about the statue of Washington, in the grounds east of the Capitol. At a signal every man was silent and stood erect in the ranks. Col. Ellsworth stepped forward, facing the beautiful stand of colors, and with a firm voice announced that the oath was about to be administered, and then alluded to the members who had disgraced themselves, in the following words:

Boys: I have an unpleasant duty to perform this afternoon; I am obliged to disgrace some who, by their acts, have brought a *seeming* disgrace upon the regiment. They have not stained our fair reputation though as a regiment of soldiers; they are, thank God, but a few; they have disgraced themselves—not us. [Applause] We regret most profoundly their deeds for the sake of our friends in New-York who have been so kind to us; but no ten or dozen men can bring disgrace upon this regiment if they are sought out and punished. They are now in irons, and will be given over to the civil authorities to answer to the law for their infamous conduct. So far as the officers are concerned, I believe they are doing, with one exception, their duties like soldiers and like men. I am informed that one of them believes he can treat you like dogs, as if in manhood you were not his equals. I shall find him out, and if it be so, I will put him, too, in irons, and send him back. [Tremendous applause, and a voice "bully for you."] We have come here to fight traitors, and we are ready for the war! [Cries of "Yes," "yes!" "Go in!" etc., etc.] If you will do your duty, my laddies, bravely, we shall go home exulting in victory, when the war is over. [Cheers] A word about our future. It is my privilege to select our camping ground, and in a few days we shall have a house of our own. [Cheers, and a voice, "Bully!"] These Sharp's rifles which we now carry are to be all exchanged for new and more beautiful and efficient weapons, which I have been permitted to select for you. They will be Minie rifles with saber bayonets, and are among the first of the kind that have been given out by the government. [Loud cheers.]

You are now about to be mustered into the service of the United States, and are the first regiment who will pledge yourselves not for thirty days or sixty days, but *for the war!* [Tremendous applause, and nine loud, long and hearty cheers] Now if any man of you has any desire to back out, and wants to leave this glorious war and go home, now is the time. Let him sneak away like a hound, and crawl over the fence and be off! [Cries of "No!" "no!" "Not one!" and three cheers for Colonel Ellsworth.]

After the applause had subsided, a number of evolutions were performed by the regiment, much to the admiration of thousands of spectators who gazed upon the scene through the iron fence which surrounds the grounds, very few being admitted within, and none except those having "passes." The regiment then formed in close straight double column, reaching entirely across the center of the inclosure, from the north to the south fence. President Lincoln now came upon the grounds, leading his little son, and escorted by Col. Thomas, Adjutant General of the army. Several of the cabinet were present, who stepped forward to greet him. He then proceeded to a review of the entire line of Zouaves, and expressed much satisfaction at their soldierly enthusiasm to Major McDowell and Col. Thomas, who accompanied him. The colors were gracefully waved as he passed, in token of respect.

While the work of calling the regimental roll was progressing, I paid the standard bearers a brief visit. The ten flags carried in the Zouave regiment form the most beautiful stand of colors which has so far been brought into Washington by the volunteer troops. The pride with which they are borne is certainly unequaled in any other regiment. Each in turn was displayed to me, and a most enthusiastic and glowing description given of its donor or donors, and its history. The one given by Mrs. Astor recently is, I should judge, the pet of the ten at present.

"There's no prettier flags than these in [the] world!" said a little hard-visaged fellow, as [he] looked at the one he unfurled; and an honest tear of enthusiastic pride started to [his] eye and told how sincerely he spoke. "The red, white and blue! God bless them!" continued he, a moment after, and he laid his arm affectionately around the flag that trailed down by the side of the staff. "We boys is goin' to fight for these pieces of cloth till we die!" "We're goin' to have one more flag when we come back!" said another with a sagacious wink. "It'll be the flag o' secession, nailed on to the bottom o' this flag staff!" "That's so!" chimed in several of his comrades.

I do not believe there is a member of the regiment who is not absolutely thirsting for a chance to capture a stand of secession colors in battle and bear it home as a trophy.

It was nearly 8 o'clock and the sun had two hours ago disappeared behind the grand old Capitol, which loomed up facing the interesting scene, when the regiment had wheeled again into [a] hollow square, with sides flanked five deep, to take the oath. In the inside, around that beautiful statue of the Goddess of Liberty, stood the colors of the regiment and the drum corps. The stars in the blue sky looked brightly down upon the scene, and the stars upon the national banner waved over it in the pulse-like breathings of the warm summer air. Silence reigned for a moment supreme. Then Col. Thomas stepped forward, and in a loud voice announced the ceremony, followed by Major McDowell, who read the oath. A phenomenon occurred here which added a strange impressiveness to the ceremony, and at first seemed to cause Col. Thomas to pause. Accidentally the position taken by him was such that a clear thrilling echo from the front of the old Capitol rolled back his sentences, word for word, almost as distinctly as they had been uttered. The effect was one of the most impressive I have ever witnessed, and the throng seemed paralyzed with a superstitious awe, as if the God of Nations spoke in every echo-tone.

Three times the announcement and the oath were repeated. Then the regiment raised their right hands solemnly into the night air, and, in one great, thrilling, rolling thunder of more than a thousand voices blended into one, repeated the oath after the officer, and sent their "So help me God!" up into the clear, blue sky for the angels to record. Cheer after cheer, loud and hearty then broke from the ranks, until "order" was commanded. "If there be any," said Col. Thomas, as he then passed before each company in turn, "who have refused or neglected to take this oath, let him step from the ranks." "No!"—"No!"—"Never!"—"Never!"—"Nary one!" &c., &c.,

were the cries of the companies as he passed. Only about twelve were found, and they were greeted with hisses and groans as they stepped forward. They objected to enlisting for the entire war, being very ready and willing for the "three months" term of service, and then, as they said, if necessary, to enlist for three months more. Col. Ellsworth and Major McDowell, after a short conference with them, arranged the matter, and they were regularly sworn in with their comrades.

At the close of the scene, the regiment retired to their quarter. Col. Ellsworth is full of energy, and his popularity among the firemen seems unbounded. In war his men will be among the most courageous of our soldiers. The traitors may well dread them. They will fight like tigers![28]

WASHINGTON CORRESPONDENCE, 15 MAY 1861

A few weeks ago, a sudden raid from the south side of the Potomac could have annoyed Washington terribly; but now we have nothing to do, but amuse ourselves listening to martial music, visiting the camps, and slandering the Zouaves.

The last division has grown the most popular in the city. When the fire brigade first appeared in this city, "magnificent at a distance," as somebody said—some half-a-dozen cultivated life by gaslight very extensively for a day or two. The Colonel, however, soon had them adorned with iron bracelets, and the place that knew them will know them no more.

But, to grow quotational again, "The evil that men do, lives after them;" and the town still persists in believing Ellsworth's "pet lambs" to be the most graceless *mauvais sujects*. Girls who never were kissed before, complain dolefully of rude salutes. Every bummer who experiences collision with a lamp-post, charges his black eye to the shoulder-hitting heroes. There is not a chicken leaves its roost desolate, without damaging in its flight the reputation of the 1st N. Y. Zouaves.

Meanwhile the muscular patriots live and flourish in the delights of camp life, unmindful of the carping world without. They love the Colonel, fear nothing, eat their rations with trimmings beguiled from neighboring cabbage-patches, play in the sun, sleep in the shade, and pass all their time in a state of bewildered conjecture as to "why in thunder they don't get something to whip." Their principal amusement seems to be cursing Ellsworth's body-servant—a very jolly darkey, with an irrepressible grin, and a wonderful alacrity in dodging kicks and potato-peelings.

The poor white trash regard them with unmingled awe. They are en-camped about five miles from the city, near the bank of a beautiful stream. Their word is law to the rustics. Last night a sentinel at the out-posts hailed a skulking passer-by:

"Who goes there?"

"Don't shoot sir! It's me. I've been fishing and am going home."

"Advance, fisherman!" cried the intrepid Zou-zou, "drop two shad and re-tire!"

The order was promptly obeyed, and a smell of preparation soon issued from the tent of the relieved guard.

Zouave stock went up wonderfully the day after the great fire adjoining Willard's Hotel. It was one of the greatest achievements of the Fire Depart-ment. They rolled in a red-shirted avalanche down the Avenue and swarmed like Salamanders over the flames. They tore down a burning building in the middle of a solid block and saved the square.

Their devotion to Ellsworth is something very singular and interesting. It springs from his mingled severity and kindness. He never sleeps till he is sure that every man in the camp is comfortable. He never eats till every man has his rations. But he regards the honor of the regiment as his own, and pun-ishes with relentless vigor any symptom of disorder or insubordination. You will hear of these men in the first great fight.

The Dandy Regiment, the New York Seventh, are encamped at Stone's Farm, north of the city. They are the perfected flower of civilization—pride and boast of Young America. Their officers hold sinecures. Every man is a gentleman and a soldier. They need neither instruction nor control. I think such a camp never was seen before. Scattered around the tents, under the trees—fine, slender, sinewy frames—thoughtful, clear-cut faces—hair shaved to pugilistic brevity—hands bronzed by the weather, but delicate—wonder of the camp—clean. This regiment includes every variety of a cer-tain social grade. Authors, artists, merchants and fops. Men whose names are an "open sesame" to the vaults of Wall street, men whose waltzing is the delight of the Avenue. This is the blood which is to be shed for the final bap-tism of freedom. The expense is enormous, but it will pay. The best blood of England smoked along the Valley of Death, in a fight for a political abstrac-tion. What better way of dying could there be for gentlemen, than in battle for the institutions that made them what they are?

In the red days that are to come on this Eastern shore, you may look for a report from two regiments: from the Seventh, pre-eminent in the honor

that *fears* to be cowardly; and from the muscle and heart of the unconquerable Northern men, the stern, vindictive dash of the Gothic fury that
actuates the well-ordered battalions of Ellsworth's Pet Lambs.[29]

HAY'S OBITUARY OF ELMER E. ELLSWORTH, 3 JUNE 1861

There has not been an evening since Sumter fell, so full of life and hope, so
redolent of the eager whispers of the waiting crowd—as was last Thursday
evening. The town was murmurous with flying rumors—all hopeful and
promising. Gen. Scott was going to show his hand, and the dandies of the
Seventh and the lambs of the Fire Department were to have an opportunity to wear off the dust of a month's idleness. People talked cheerfully of
Alexandria and Arlington, and invented model campaigns for the departing
regiments, with all the spirited ignorance and illogical enterprise with which
civilians essay warlike vatication.

But on Friday morning the tone of feeling and conversation was strangely
changed. With the earliest dawn a ghastly horror of floating surmise clouded
the town. The rumor ran rapidly through the usual gamut of shocked assertion and reckless contradiction, until doubt was hunted out from every
resting-place, and we all knew that "Ellsworth was dead."

When that was ascertained no one cared to ask further questions. The details of the assassination, the projected defenses, the march of the regiments—which at any other time would have furnished the most palatable
food to the jaded news hunters at Willard's—were unnoted and disregarded.
It seemed enough for one day that we had lost the cheering presence of the
brave young colonel. It seemed impertinent to speak of other things.

A sudden gloom fell on the city. A hundred banners slipped sadly to half-
mast. Men walked quietly through the streets, forgetting their business.
Soldiers talked low and earnestly, with clenched hands.

Why was this so? This public grief seemed to scorn precedents. He was
not an old and honored warrior, but a boy of twenty-four, who had never
seen a battle. The praise of the people naturally follows wealth; but Ellsworth
had no fortune but his sword, and his aged parents live in the quiet seclusion of a country village in New York. It was not the murmur that rises when
a giant dies. This young hero was only five feet six from spur to plume. Why
should the people mourn for him?

No man ever possessed in a more eminent degree the power of personal fascination. That faculty, which when exercised upon masses of men, Halleck styles "the Art of Napoleon—of winning, fettering, moving and commanding the souls of thousands till they move as one," he enjoyed, in a measure, of which the world will ever remain ignorant. He exercised an influence almost mesmeric, upon bodies of organized individuals with whom he was brought in contact. I have seen him enter an armory where a score of awkward youths were going sleepily through their manual, and his first order, sharply and crisply given, would open every eye and straighten every spine. No matter how severe the drill, his men never thought of fatigue. His own indomitable spirit sustained them all.

Besides that, his *personale* was very prepossessing. There was something cheery and hopeful about the flash of his white teeth when he smiled, his face was always alert and intelligent, and the honest and sincere good fellow looked serenely out of his handsome eyes. His heavy black curls never looked affected or vain. They set off admirably the firm and statuesque pose of the head. And his dress was always in keeping with the man we knew.

Add to this his youth and his fame, his patriotism which no rebuffs could daunt, his energy, which people began to recognize, the work he had done, and the work he was expected to do, and you have some idea of the reasons that made people deplore a victory that his sacrifice made a thousand times worse than a defeat.

And the people for once are right. You shall not find between the seas a man who can in all things take his place. In the hearts of his friends, and in the ranks of his country's defenders, he has left a void which is not to be filled.

His life presents few salient points of romance or interest. He was at a very early age thrown upon his own resources by the financial reverses of his father, (of whom in his stricken age let a generous Republic be not unmindful,) and his whole career from boyhood to his death is a touching drama of struggle with circumstances, always strenuous and severe, but always self-reliant and stout-hearted. Very dark would have been the passage through some scenes of his life in Chicago, had it not been lit with a healthy good humor that nothing could repress, an energy that misfortune was powerless to daunt, and a stainless honor that freed him from even the temptation to wrong. In spite of mean lodgings and scanty fare the great soul kept a firm foot-hold in the muscular body, and outside of the daily toil and privation, the young student reveled in an ideal realm, not of selfish indulgence or sordid fame, but use and beneficence to his fellow men. This aim and purpose did not exhaust itself in dreams. He worked steadily towards its realization.

The first fruit of his efforts was the perfect training of the Chicago Zouaves. The vast flutter of interest and gale of applause that their challenge trip occasioned, though the great military sensation of the age, was utterly unworthy of the subject, as it failed to distinguish the real spirit of Ellsworth's work. While it dwelt on the agility and unerring precision with which these scarlet machines performed their gymnastic lesson, they left out of view the entire discipline—the identification of spirit of commander and men— the *animus* they derived from their idolized leader, inspired these slight young men, and annihilated their susceptibility to hunger and fatigue. Was it not, also, a great triumph for this water-drinking Colonel to abolish by the force of his own iron will, a practice against which all the anti-alcoholic forces, under a thousand aliases, have warred for years in vain?

I know the trial excursion of the Zouave Cadets was not undertaken from any motives of display, but by the force of contrast, to demonstrate the fact in a way that people could understand, that our ordinary militia is a very unwieldy and useless affair, and cannot be made serviceable except by a vast expenditure and endless annoyance and delay. And although in the last six weeks the people have wonderfully seconded the effort of the Government, a candid review of their operations, from the proclamation until to-day, will convince any one of the necessity of a thorough reconstruction of the militia laws of most of the States, and such a re-organization of the citizen soldiery as will nourish a more decided military spirit, and establish a higher standard of discipline.

To a great extent, that trip was a great success. In its wake sprang up hundreds of new military companies, like phosphorescent sparks in the track of a ship. Several States reconstructed their militia laws, and a general military revival was perceptible throughout the land. It had an effect, also, in disseminating some sensible ideas in regard to uniform. Inside of the flashy absurdities of crimson and gold, for which it was responsible, there was a germ of sound judgment in the easy, careless flow of the Zouave costume, which hardly touches the wearer.

Ellsworth went back to Chicago, for his brief hour the most talked-of man in the country. He quietly organized a skeleton regiment upon a plan of his own, and made his best men the officers of it. He offered this to the Governor of Illinois and to the President, "for any service consistent with honor." This was the first offer of any organized force to sustain the Constitution and the laws. With soldierly instinct he foresaw the inevitable struggle, and predicted the very manner of its beginning.

Leaving Chicago, he came to Springfield in the midst of the most exciting campaign known to political history. It was not possible for Ellsworth to be neutral in anything, or idle while others were working. With the whole energy of his nature he entered into the struggle. He became one of the most popular speakers known to the school-houses and barns of Central Illinois. The magnificent volume of his voice, which I never heard surpassed, the unfailing flow of his hearty humor, and the deep earnestness of conviction that lived in his looks and tones, were the qualities that struck the fancy of the Western crowd. Besides, it was very novel and delightful to see a soldier who could talk.

An administration in harmony with him was elected, and Ellsworth hoped to be able to put into practical operation those plans which had formed the goal of all his former efforts. My space will not permit an analysis of these plans. They looked to an entire reorganization of the militia of the United States. They had the approbation of some of the best military minds on the continent. With the hope of being placed in a position where he could be of service in this way, he accepted Mr. Lincoln's invitation and joined the Presidential traveling party. He soon became indispensable. No one could manage like him the assemblage of turbulent loyalty that crowded and jostled at every station.

At Washington he was placed in a false position. He never wished office for its honor or its profit, but you never can get office-seekers or office-dispensers to believe any such story. His delicate sense of honor felt a stain like a wound, and the amiable gentlemen of the press never can withhold the sly stab when they think a man is failing.

These weeks were the least pleasant of Ellsworth's life. They were brightened only by the society of those he trusted most, and by the unvarying friendship and confidence of the President and his family. But Sumter fell, and the gale of aroused patriotism, sweeping down from the North, scattered away the cobwebs of political chicane, and educed the true men of the time. When war was in the land, there was no dancing attendance for a man who knew that God had made him a soldier. There was only a moment of hesitation—it was whether Chicago or New York should have the glory of his regiment. His friends remembered the malignant jealousy that hampered what he and they would have done for the State of Illinois last winter, and feared a repetition of the scene. New York was Catholic and Metropolitan. He went to New York.

The rest transcends memoir and passes into the sphere of history.

How he conceived the novel idea of a fire brigade—how he formed the most muscular regiment that the annals of warfare have mentioned—how by the mere force of intellect, he controlled the fierce turbulence of these untamable men—how he armed them and brought them to the capital—how he made soldiers of them, turning the stern Gothic spirit of fight into well-ordered channels—how he captured the first rebel town—and how he made that splendid morning memorable to all time by his death—shall all be told when some future historian writes the story of the new crusade of freedom.

His loss at this time cannot be too deeply deplored. He had every requisite for great military success; he had a wonderful memory and command of details—immense industry and capability of enormous mental and bodily labor, great coolness of mind, an original and inventive brain, and more than all, the power of grappling to his heart with hooks of steel the affections of every man with whom he came in contact.

Then there is a smaller circle who mourn him in tears as the truest, tenderest, most loyal-hearted man that ever died.

This is the bead-roll of his virtues. I do not remember but two faults that he had, and they were magnificent ones. He was too generous and too brave.

The one subjected him to the most cruel slanders from sordid men, and the other caused the disaster which has plunged a people into mourning.

All classes seem to regard his death as a personal affliction. The family of the President went down to the navy yard on Friday and gazed long and tearfully on the still face which had so often brought sunshine with it, into the Executive Mansion. Five minutes afterwards Ned Buntline came in, and quietly laid a dewy wreath of laurel over the brave dead heart. A tear came to his hard eyes as he passed out and said to a Zouave standing gloomily by the door; "We'll mourn him to-day, boys, and avenge him to-morrow."

As for the Zouaves, all other emotions are swallowed up in the manly grief that hallows revenge into religion. They have surprised every one by their silence. Bitter as is their rage and despair, they remember that they are

Ellsworth's men, and are too soldierly to be lawless. But they have sworn, with the grim earnestness that never trifles, to have a life for every hair of the dead Colonel's head. But even that will not repay.

The ripples of private grief are never taken into the account of the grand swell of a public sorrow, but it is certain that no man could have died more deeply lamented than the young hero who is moving to-day in solemn grandeur toward the crushed hearts that sadly wait him in the North. Scattered over the land, severed by wide leagues of mountain and prairie, the few who knew him well are mourning in the utter abandon of irremediable anguish, as if all the earth had for them of bright or beautiful or brave, went out with his last breath. Yet they are giving thanks to God that they were permitted to know him, and are vowing to keep ever green in their souls the memory of him who always seemed to his friends not like the people one meets every day, but like a splendid type of the courtesy and valor that dignified the leal-hearted cavaliers of the great days that are gone.

One last word. May he rest forever in peace, under the Northern violets and the Northern snows. May his example sink into the heart of Northern youth, and blossom into deeds of valor and honor. His dauntless and stainless life has renewed the bright possibilities of the antique chivalry, and in his death we may give him unblamed the grand cognizance of which the world has long been unworthy—

"Le chavalier sans peur et sans reproche."[30]

WASHINGTON CORRESPONDENCE, 9 JULY 1861

The combined energies of the Senate and House seem to be devoted to measures having exclusive reference to the war. The numerous bills that have been framed for the action of Congress are rapidly passing through the machinery of committee, and will soon be before the two houses for consideration. Owing to the extensive preparation which has been made by senators and members for the extra session, in the way of drafting bills, resolutions, etc., there is little or no delay either in the Senate and House, or in committee, and many measures which would have been pending a long time in an ordinary session, are rapidly transformed into laws at this one. There are objections made to this hasty legislation in some quarters, but no strong reasons against it can be offered at this critical juncture. Aside from the necessity for immediate legislation, senators and members are desirous of lengthening their season for recreation as much as possible. Should this session be protracted until the 1st of September, but three short months would intervene before the commencement of the regular session, and another and very potent reason, and one which was looked forward to several sessions ago, is, that no mileage or salary is paid members at an extra session. All of these facts tend to make this session a very brief one. In three weeks the halls of Congress will be vacated.

The question of revenue—and it really is the most important one before Congress—is one which is claiming the attention of every senator and member. It cannot be denied that there is opposition to some of the recommendations of the recent report of the Treasury Department. A higher tariff and a popular loan are advocated in the most influential quarters in preference to direct taxation, and it is not improbable that this plan will be adopted by the House Committee on Ways and Means. It is contended that the present tariff can be so modified as to yield a revenue of one hundred millions per annum. But New-York merchants will probably have something to say on this point, and will doubtless be heard. Congress should authorize a large loan immediately. One offer of ten millions has been made to Secretary Chase at a medium rate, if he will advertise now for a loan.

The Senate and House have devoted most of today's session in eulogies on the late Judge [*Stephen A.*] Douglas. In the Senate, it seemed to me that the occasion offered but little of the solemnity of those of other times. The opening remarks were made by Senator Trumbull, who offered the customary resolutions of respect and condolence. He was followed by Senator McDougall, of California, whose brief tribute was totally inaudible in the galleries, and mostly so on the floor. Judge Collamer, of Vermont, succeeded him in the most eloquent and appropriate words which were uttered, and which tended to deeply impress upon the rapidly-forgetting mind many of the sterling traits of the lamented deceased, and the great loss with which the nation had met in his death. The eulogy of Judge D.'s successor, Senator [*Orville Hickman*] Browning, created a favorable impression. It was delivered with good emphasis and discretion, and interwoven with many little incidents of the personal relations of the speaker and his predecessor. In the House no less than ten speeches were delivered, nearly every one of them being in the same eulogistic strain, and of course very wearisome.

It was anticipated that [*John C.*] Breckinridge would make a few remarks in the Senate, inasmuch as his relations with Douglas were known to be of the most cordial nature, but the Kentucky Senator sat firmly in his seat, with his head bowed, carelessly twirling a paper cutter, but intently listening to all that was passing around him. Hon. Robert J. Walker, one of the most devoted friends of Douglas, was the only distinguished spectator present, excepting a few members of the diplomatic corps. The scene was in striking contrast with some of the occasions on which Douglas addressed the Senate.

The telegraphic correspondents were not a little surprised this morning at the following official order of Gen. Scott, prohibiting them from transmitting army movements over the wires:

> Henceforward the telegraph will convey no dispatches concerning the operations of the army not permitted by the Commanding General.
>
> Winfield Scott.
>
> Department of War, July 8, 1861.
> The above order is confirmed.
>
> Simon Cameron, Secretary of War.

For the past two weeks there has been no government inspector in the office here, and no restrictions on dispatches; consequently, the *Tribune* has run the gauntlet of its *canards,* deceiving the public, and annoying the government. Its astounding falsifications in yesterday's issue out-Heroded Herod, and the government put a stop to them. You may rest assured that neither Gen. Scott nor the President consult the *Tribune's* correspondent more than once a week. The telegraph company are making efforts to have the embargo raised, but I doubt if it succeeds.

The Thirty-third New-York Regiment arrived to-day, and went into quarters on the avenue. The handsome manner in which New-York is throwing in regiments here, day after day, is the theme of enthusiastic praise on every hand.[31]

Washington correspondence, 10 July 1861

To-day an interesting meeting of the correspondents of the New-York dailies was held at the capitol for a conference with the government on the publication of important movements of the army. It seems that General Scott and Secretary Cameron have arrived at the conclusion that the details of military movements transmitted to the New-York papers have been of infinite service to the rebel cause, giving them early and reliable information via Louisville of the intentions of the government. In view, therefore, of the impending importance of the movements of troops, it has been necessary to prevent the transmission of telegraphic dispatches detailing army affairs. But the government, ever zealous of the rights of the press and the rights of individuals, has appealed to the patriotism of the correspondents to co-operate with it in affording themselves as ample liberty as is consistent with the protection desired by the government, and has entered into an arrangement whereby the press shall not be furnished with telegraphic information of army movements. At the same time, however, it was protested that the ends which the government is trying to secure would not be subserved, and the correspondents also insisted that when a battle should occur they should have full license to telegraph not only the official dispatches which come to hand, but all other information which could be obtained. This "compromise" will doubtless be granted by the government.

During this interview, the fact was freely stated and commented on, that the rebel spies in this city furnished the enemy as full and earlier information than it was possible for correspondents to obtain. The government has been informed of this, time and again, but has taken no measures to prevent it. These spies leave the city by a land route down the Potomac, to a point ten or twenty miles below where they cross over in small boats and enter the rebel lines.

There can be but little doubt but that every twenty-four hours Beauregard is in possession of every movement of the federal troops of the day before, while this government rarely obtains any information from Manassas. The Potomac is not sufficiently guarded for seven miles above and below Washington to prevent the rebel spies from crossing. It was likewise a notorious fact that until the *St. Nicholas* was seized, spies were daily landed on the Maryland shore at any point on the Potomac, from whence they could cross into Virginia. Until the government remedies all of the evil it cannot expect to keep its movements a secret from the enemy.

The House to-day passed the crisis. Vallandigham, of Ohio, made his speech within the hour rule, with perfect satisfaction to himself and to the House. Not the least objection was made to his taking the floor, and the members and galleries listened to him very patiently and quietly. No demonstrations of either approval or censure were made. The Ohio member is the object of no inconsiderable attraction. He stands boldly forth as the type of a class so insignificant in numbers that it would be lost sight of altogether were it not for just such an element as that illustrated today. Vallandigham is a man of respectable talents, a good lawyer, a finished scholar, and withal a good speaker. His appearance is that of a tall, handsome man, and his address is of a bland and courteous character. He is a ready debater, and seldom makes a speech without attracting the entire attention of the House. Although no one respected his opinions he was listened to by most of those present. The presiding officer, however, busied himself with a newspaper. It is probable that but one or two speeches of this character will be made during the present session. The vigorous manner in which the House pushed on its business to-day may be regarded as indicative of the spirit of the members throughout the session. There is a determination to make it as brief as possible, and I have heard one week from Saturday suggested as the day on which Congress would probably adjourn *sine die.*

It is the impression that the Senate Committee on Foreign Relations will present such evidence as to necessitate the recall of Harvey as minister to Portugal. Aside from the seized telegrams, it is alleged that the government has oral and written evidence of Harvey's complicity with the traitors. His most earnest defenders cannot rid him of the responsibility of so telegraphing the rebels that detection was for a time impossible. If his object was peace, he would have honorably used his own name.

Three thousand troops have arrived here during this week, one thousand of whom have been sent across the Potomac.[32]

WASHINGTON CORRESPONDENCE, 22 JULY 1861

Since the memorable day when the British captured Washington, in the last war, the federal capital has never been the scene of such excitement as now. The solemn midnight march of the grand army across the Potomac roused an intensity of feeling and expectancy. The popular heart was moved to its deepest depths. The marching regiments so long encamped here were cheered on their departure with a lusty enthusiasm and hopefulness unprecedented in war annals. It was believed that the federal forces had started on a march to be crowned with brilliant victories; that the enemy would be routed from their fastnesses among the mountainous ravines and glens, their cannon captured, and intrenchments demolished. Under the bold leadership of our officers, the thunder of our batteries, and the heroic courage of our infantry columns, we were to march victoriously to Richmond. This was to break the bone of the rebellion, to end the war, to restore again our nationality.

News of the battle of Bull Run reached us. The defeat was not a defeat— only a victory of vastly superior numbers over a few segmentary regiments. An engagement of the whole army would tell a different story. This engagement was announced to take place on Sunday.

At an early hour in the morning the thundering roar of the distant artillery was first heard. The excitement here was renewed. It waxed intense and grew intenser. Every sort of conveyance was in requisition to convey persons to the battle field. Senators, congressmen, heads of departments, and civilians of every rank and degree showed eagerness to go to the battle field. Those who remained were impatient to catch each fragmentary item of news from the scene of conflict. Thousand-voiced rumor was busy with its multitudinous recitals of the progress of the battle. Meantime Gen. Scott remained the same unimpassioned man he ever has been. Through all the exciting scenes of the day and evening there was no visible token of the emotions that stirred him. He opened his dispatches, read them, and gave his orders with the same characteristic coolness that has always marked his official acts. About the telegraph office there was a curious throng of anxious inquirers after the news. Where a returning visitor presented himself from the battle ground he was at once surrounded and stormed with a series of questions.

First of importance came the news that Bull Run had been taken and the enemy completely routed. This caused universal demonstrations of delight. The great key of the rebels' position had been captured, and the way to complete victory was sure and of speedy accomplishment. Close upon the heels of this statement came the intelligence of the recapture of Bull Run by the confederate troops, with terrific loss of life on both sides. The wildest rumors prevailed. It was said that all our leading officers had been killed, that entire regiments had been cut to pieces, and that our heaviest artillery was in the hands of the enemy. Stories were recited to gaping multitudes of terrific hand-to-hand fights, of dead bodies strewing the fields, and the reddening of the water of Bull Run creek by the blood of the slain. Our lines were reported as broken up, and officers and men retreating in the wildest confusion. A climax to the whole story was magnifying the rebel troops to the number with which Wellington marched to battle on the field of Waterloo, and starting these in pursuit of our retreating army, the pursuit to continue to this city, which was to be shelled and captured at once.

Gradually authentic news of the disastrous results of the fight began to be received. It was terrible to witness the effect it produced everywhere. Every one foresaw the consequence of the defeat in the future movements of our army. Crowds remained up all night, in their excitement unmindful of sleep, talking over the events of the day. There were all sorts of opinions expressed, some charging the blame upon Gen. Scott, some upon the administration, urging that Mr. Lincoln and the cabinet had pushed him into ordering an advance of our army when its number, compared with that of the enemy, made an advance suicidal; and some berating the *Tribune* as the sole cause of the defeat, in its foolhardy persistence that an advance should be made forthwith on Richmond. The last was the most current opinion, and it was expressed with a vigor of language and style of denunciation possessing all the emphasis capable of utterance in the English tongue. Connected with the news of the victory of the army of Jeff. Davis, it was feared that the secessionists of Alexandria and Baltimore would at once rise in rebellion against the regiments that thus far have awed them into seeming submission, and, overcoming them, rush to the aid of the confederate troops. Is it a wonder that there was excitement here? It was a beautiful moonlight night, but there was none of the calmness of a moonlight Sabbath evening. The streets echoed the clattering hoofs of hurrying cavalry; regiments marched to and fro, their bristling bayonets gleaming in the bright moonbeams. There was the heavy sound of rolling army wagons, dispatched for the wounded soldiers and army baggage. At two o'clock in the morning, your special army correspondent arrived from the battle field, having remained at the scene of action two hours later than any of his associate representatives of the press. He brought the latest tidings. As, covered with dust, he rode his horse—although having been thirty-six hours in the saddle—at a dashing pace in front of the National, he was at once surrounded with eager inquirers. He confirmed the tidings of defeat, and reported that Col. Montgomery, with a division of New Jersey troops, had arrested the flight of the main body of the fugitives, and that there were then about 11,000 men under Col.

Richardson, who were not in the fight, at Centreville where the rest had made a stand with a battery to guard against further advance of the enemy. This put an end to the story that all the army was retreating to their intrenchments across the river.

A continuation of the excitement of yesterday although different in kind, has been that of to-day. There was never such a day here before—it is to be hoped there will never be such another. With the ushering in of daylight there came pouring into the city crowds of soldiers, some with muskets, some without muskets, some with knapsacks, and some without knapsack, or canteen, or belt, or anything but their soiled and dirty uniform, burned faces and eyes, that looked as [if] they had seen no sleep for days, to indicate that they were soldiers. One by one came wagons filled with the dead and wounded. Most horrible were the sights presented to view, and never to be forgotten by those who witnessed them. The bodies of the dead were piled on top of one another; the pallid faces and blood-stained garments telling a fearfully mute but sad story of the horrors of war. And the appearance of the wounded, bereft of arms, of legs, eyes put out, flesh wounds in the face and body, and uniforms crimsoned with blood, proclaimed with equal force the savage horrors of human battling with weapons of war. Crowds gathered about these wagons, and those of the wounded who were able to talk were questioned as to the incidents of the battle. To the hospital the crowd followed, and it was with difficulty the physicians in attendance could keep them back, so earnest were many to learn the fate of relatives and friends. And now came into beneficent use the lint and bandages so generously furnished by the ladies of your city.

All the forenoon fugitive soldiers have come straggling into the city. They were like lost sheep without a shepherd. Notices at length appeared at the different hotels, calling upon the members of the various regiments to assemble at such and such a place, at an appointed hour, the object being to discover how many and who were missing. Meantime the returned soldiers clustered about the hotels, and some in their weariness lay down on doorsteps, or any place they could find where the rain would not touch them—it rained all day from early in the morning—to rest and refresh themselves by sleep. By the middle of the afternoon the meetings took place, the rolls were called and a knowledge thus gained of those missing. It is gratifying to know that many of the statements and suppositions as to the lost and missing of certain regiments prove to have been greatly exaggerated. At night most of the men had reported themselves at their recent headquarters, and gone into camp again. Officers as well as privates are missing. Many of the regimental headquarters show a meager array of numbers to what they exhibited recently, and the sad faces of soldiers are apparent everywhere. All day the telegraph office has been besieged with those sending telegrams to friends of the safety or death of soldiers in whose fate they were interested.

This evening some regiments were ordered to march to Centreville tomorrow. This is interpreted as an intention on the part of the government to hold, if nothing more, the ground thus far occupied by our troops. As to the immediate intentions of the War Department, nothing has definitely transpired. A rumor prevailed this evening that a blockade had been ordered upon the railroad lines leading northward, in order to keep them exclusively for the use of regiments directed to come on to this city, but inquiry at the army headquarters proved the rumor incorrect.[33]

WASHINGTON CORRESPONDENCE, 28 JULY 1861

I have spent a good portion of to-day among the wounded soldiers at the different hospitals in and about the city. Only few of the wounded will die. Many will be disabled from fighting again; but the great majority are on the swift way to recovery, and burning with restlessness to join their regiments and renew the conflict with the enemy.

There are three hospitals where the wounded are being taken care of—one in this city, one in Georgetown, and the third at Alexandria. At the hospital in this city there are seventy-three patients, at Georgetown two hundred and fifty-seven; and at Alexandria one hundred and thirty-one—four hundred and sixty-one all told. At each place there is a competent corps of medical attendants, the rooms in the main well ventilated, and every care shown the men that medical skill and humanity can suggest. The hospital here is the government hospital, a large four-story brick building, of drab color, some one hundred and fifty feet long, including the two wings, with an extension ninety feet deep in the rear of the easterly wing. There are thirty-two wards. What was formerly the Union Hotel, at Georgetown, is now the hospital. It is a three-story brown-stuccoed building, and in a fine airy location. A private dwelling serves as the hospital at Alexandria. It is an old-fashioned residence, and large, as must be seen from the number accommodated in it. Beside those confined at the hospitals, there are a good many being taken care of at private residences—some fifty altogether.

I might write by the hour, did my time and your space permit, thrilling incidents connected with the recent battle, recited to me by the suffering and gallant wounded. Capt. Laing, of the Seventy-ninth [*New York*] Regiment (Highlanders), has six wounds. One ball passed through his neck, just grazing the jugular vein. He heard Col. Cameron's last command, "Come on, gallant Scots!" and was by his side when he was shot. The fatal ball entered near the temple; not a drop of blood came from the wound. He fell with his sword in his right hand, and revolver in his left. Capt. Laing walked six miles after receiving his own wounds, bringing from the field Col. Cameron's sword and revolver, which have since been delivered to Secretary Cameron. Capt. Laing is cheerful. "If I die," he said, "I shall die contented, knowing that I die for my country," and with a smile added, "but I would like first to get another brush at them." John S. Evans, of the Eighteenth N.Y. Volunteer Regiment, occupied the cot next to Capt. Laing. He has shown himself a hero. His left arm had just been amputated close to the elbow. "You done for fighting," a gentleman present remarked. "That is all that troubles me," was the noble reply. In the same ward is Ferguson Wilson, of the Second Vermont Regiment. He escaped with a rifle ball in his left hand. He takes the matter jocosely. "I got my foot in it," he said, "but I shall be on hand at the next tussel, when I expect to see the enemy get their feet, legs, body, and all into it." Clifford A. Fuller, of the Second Rhode Island Regiment, was within ten feet of Col. Slocum when the latter was shot and fell from his horse. A crowd of officers gathered around their leader. "Leave me," said the dying colonel, "and avenge my death." George B. Arnigh, Fire Zouave, was shot in the arm by a Minie ball. He was in a wagon with several others who had been wounded. A crowd of the Black Horse Cavalry dashed upon them and ordered them to halt. He leaped from the wagon, scaled a fence, and made rapid tracks for the woods. A shower of shot came after him, but none took effect. All in the wagon were taken prisoner. Among the wounded who showed greatest courage was Col. Farnham, of the Fire Zouaves. He left a sick bed to go to the battle, and rode in an ambulance to the scene of action. He was in the thickest of the fight. One bullet grazed the side of his head, inflicting a severe scalp wound. The stunning force of the ball knocked him from his horse, but he was soon mounted again, and leading on his "red-legged devils" with heroic bravery. He will be ready in a few days to assume command of his regiment.

The returns of the killed and wounded are yet very imperfect. Several three months regiments went home before their correct returns were made out, while others are yet incomplete. The number killed is now stated at 317; wounded, 532; missing and prisoners, 788.

Major-General McClellan has assumed charge of the men here and entered upon a vigorous prosecution of the duties of his command, including the army on both sides of the Potomac. He promises to be as popular and efficient as at his recent post of duty. New and important changes will be inaugurated forthwith. Foremost, it is understood, he will make a thorough overhauling of the commissariat department. There has long been most palpable and grievous neglect here, creating great dissatisfaction among the men. He will put a stop to the absence of so many officers and soldiers from their encampments, and under his regime the rum-shop keepers here will not reap the golden harvest they have been reaping.

A large majority of the three months regiments have gone home. As I write, the Fifth Massachusetts regiment is on its way with music and flying colors to the railroad depot. They are loudly cheered. Nearly all our departing regiments go home full of military and patriotic spirit, and many will come to us again.

The prevailing belief here now is that the rebel army are maturing plans for an attack on this city. Present movements of the War Department plainly indicate a supposition that such is the case. Every thing now done looks to an inceare [*increase*] of our defenses. More regiments are being thrown across the river; our intrenchments there are being made more impassable, and additional cannons are being placed on the commanding heights. The necessity of these preparations is evident. The enemy are in large force near[*er*] us than they have been at any one time since the commencement of hostilities. Madly enthusiastic over their recent victory, and believing our troops are thoroughly demoralized and disheartened, it is easy to conceive the insane supposition on their part that they have only to advance upon us and the victory is surely theirs.

Let them come says our veteran chieftain: let them come say our soldiers; let them come say our loyal citizens; and there are thousands of loyal beating hearts here; and they would get a reception they do not look for; a reception that would send them howling and hurrying back to their masked batteries and intrenchments at Manassas. Such fool-hardiness would end in the enemy's rout and ruin. It is to be hoped they will attempt it; the fear is that they will not.[34]

WASHINGTON CORRESPONDENCE, 30 JULY 1861

The city is continually stirred with exciting rumors. Now the gleaming cohorts of Beauregard are marching straight upon our intrenchments across the river; and again we hear of the rapid advance of his serried columns toward Edward's Ferry, a point forty miles up the Potomac—the attack thence to be made upon the federal capital. Mingling with these conflicting rumors are stories of the uprising of secessionists in Baltimore, and terrific routing and killing of the federal troops there; that Banks's command has been scattered like spray before the wind; that Fortress Monroe has been taken; that we are beaten on every side; that there is no hope for us; that the President, cabinet and Congress are putting themselves into a succumbing attitude, and are going to acknowledge the independence of the Confederate States. But this is a city of quickly-begotten rumors whose kaleidoscopic complexity of character serves to keep up a lively wakefulness to get at actual facts. Beauregard is near us, it is true, but he is not among us yet, and the prevailing impression is that he will not show himself among us for some time to come. As to the Edward's Ferry route there has been a good deal of surprise and complaint that the government has not defended this point. It is said by those in position to know that this place is purposely left unprotected with a view to entice the rebel troops to an attack upon the city from that direction. For miles this side the country is a level plain, and the result would be an open field combat—a combat that would quickly put an end to the confederate army.

Gen. McClellan is daily proving himself to be what was expected of him. He is reforming abuses on every side, and by the energy of his will, force of executive character, soldierly qualities, and commanding military genius is infusing new vigor and spirit among the troops. Under the new regulations established and efficient drill of the men, with what the cabinet and Congress are doing in officering the regiments and increasing the artillery force, we shall soon have an impregnable army. In all the camps the utmost order prevails. Old and new men are going through their allotted exercises with a fervor of will and zest surpassing anything hitherto exhibited. Officers are more at their encampments and less at the hotels. A most important element of improvement has been the changes in the commissariat, whereby the men are better fed, better contented, and will be better prepared to face the foe when again called into the field.

Since the smoke of the great battle has cleared away, and the extent of the losses have become pretty accurately known, the incidents connected with the conflict, as told by the engaged soldiers, have absorbed general attention and interest. Hundreds of these incidents have been written, and read, and wept and laughed over. Our gallant soldiers who have gone home are recapitulating them till now they are widely known. Prisoners who have escaped from the custody of the rebels are at present claiming the greatest attention. The telegraph has informed you of the escape of Capt. Allen, Massachusetts Eleventh; John P. Doherty, Sixty Ninth, New-York, and Orlando Bardolf, Wisconsin Second, who were taken prisoners at Manassas. Their escape possesses a marvelousness of romance and peril of adventure seldom paralleled. To the inventive genius, cunning and daring of Doherty must be credited the escape. An Irishman of the shrewder sort, quick, sagacious, self-possessed, bold and rollicking, he was sharp and speedy in devising means of escape. "I had no fear of their keeping me," he said, in telling me the story, "but I was bound not to come away alone." His intelligence and good nature obtained him the place of hospital steward at Sudley church. He was not long in giving a drink with a narcotic sprinkling in it to the sentinel. The incautiously imbibing guard fell asleep, and Doherty add [*and*] his comrades leaped from a rear window and pushed to the woods. They lay quiet days and journeyed by night. Several times they were pursued by cavalry, and showers of shot sent after them. At one time they were pursued into a small wood and surrounded. Hiding themselves in a thick tuft of bushes, they lay concealed sixteen hours. A horse of one of the searching troopers stepped on Doherty's leg. He felt like wincing under the superincumbent weight of horse-flesh, but did not. The strong necessities of appetite compelled them to stop occasionally at farm-houses for something to eat. Happily they only found women at home, whom they wheedled into the belief that they belonged to the "Alabama Fourth." One woman was suspicious, but they forbore waiting long enough to allow her distrust opportunity to reach a culminating point unfavorable to themselves. They all agree in saying that the

Potomac never looked pleasanter to Washington than it did to them. Pursued by cavalry and balls flying after them as they plunged into its cool embrace, they did not have the time to note the majestic beauty of the river and landscape that otherwise would have been gratifying to them.

The present times are not propitious to office-seekers. A few days has worked sad havoc among them, till now, like the Black Horse Cavalry so gallantly attacked by the Fire Zouaves, there are but few left to tell the tale. There is delectable strangeness in seeing the vestibules of our department bureaus empty of the horde of hungry, lean, cadaverous-looking men Caesar classes in the catalogue of the untrusty. Asking a wag at Willard's the cause of their precipitate departure, he replied: "They have been shelling out, you see, till they became disgusted, and now they are afraid of a more disgusting ordeal—being shelled out." It would be cruel to laugh at the joke, and we did not. Failing to reach that attitude of biographical greatness and heroism termed the sublime, they have at least displayed those rare Christian virtues—humility, patience, forbearance, long-suffering. Going away it ought to be consoling, however, to them to know, that their visit here has not been profitless—to hotel-keepers. It takes many long lives to learn the inutility of placing trust in princes.[35]

EDITORIAL, 3 AUGUST 1861

Major General John C. Frémont, who has been placed in command of the Department of the West, is a man in every way qualified for the discharge of the duties of his responsible office. He is just such a person as Western men will idolize and follow through every danger to death or victory. He is upright, brave, generous, enterprising, learned and eminently practical. He is a dashing soldier, and yet withal a cool and prudent commander, and before he has been a month at the head of his Division, both officers and men will learn to place implicit confidence in him, and will promptly execute his orders, animated with the belief that they will lead to the best results. Gen. Frémont has had much military experience, and has led just such men as now compose his command—brave, hardy, Western volunteers. He is a self-made man, but we have not time or space now to allude to the difficulties through which he struggled up from poverty and obscurity to wealth and world-wide fame. From a poor unnoticed boy in Charleston,

S.C., he has worked his way to his present position, unaided, save by his own genius, patient diligence, and indomitable energy. Passing over his early struggles to acquire an education, we find him at the age of nineteen years combating with great power the fatal heresy of secession, when it was first preached in South Carolina. At the age of twenty, through his struggle for the cause of the Union, he had a political character at Washington, and the then Secretary of the Navy, Mr. Poinsett, appointed him as a teacher of mathematics on the sloop-of-war Natchez. He remained on that vessel nearly three years. After his return, he was appointed by Gen. Jackson as an assistant to Capt. G. W. Williams (afterwards killed at the battle of Monterey) to make a preliminary survey for a railway line from Charleston to Cincinnati. He left this work only when it was suspended in 1837. He next joined the exploring expedition of Mr. Nicolett, to explore the Minnesota country, between the Mississippi and Missouri rivers. While on this expedition he received a commission as Second Lieutenant in the Topographical Engineers. He was next employed for more than a year in the Coast Survey Office. It was while thus engaged that he became acquainted with the since famous "Jessie," daughter of Col. Thomas H. Benton, to whom he was afterwards married in defiance of the wishes of her parents. Colonel Benton and his wife soon became reconciled, and he often confessed that his daughter was a better judge of men than he was. Just prior to his marriage he made, by order of the Government, an exploration of Des Moines river in Iowa. But we can not follow him step by step in his career of usefulness. At the age of twenty-eight years we find him ready to enter upon a career that has astonished whilst it challenged the admiration of the civilized world—ready to grapple with the geography, topography, geology and botany of the major half of the continent—ready to penetrate the darkest recesses of the Western wilderness, to encounter its wild beasts, savages and poisonous miasmas; to stem its wildest currents and wade its deepest snows; to descend into its deepest gulfs and ravines, and to scale its highest mountains; to bring to the view of statesmen principalities of which they before were ignorant; to conquer and subdue by the power of arms an Eldorado in the West; to become a Governor and Senator, and to grapple with the slave power and rescue from its grasp a sovereign State. We see him endowed with a compass of intellect, a fortitude, courage and inflexibility of purpose that lifted him far above ordinary men. He pursued science along every path of danger, and whether struggling with Indian foes, with swollen streams, with driving storms, with steeps and almost scaleless mountains, with deep snows, with hunger and with disease, he everywhere gave exhibition of dashing bravery, lofty courage and dauntless energy.

In 1846 we find him in the valley of the Sacramento in California. He found there going on three great operations fatal to American interests, if not at once arrested. These were the massacres of Americans and the destruction of their settlements; the subjugation of California to British protection; and the transfer of public domain to British subjects. And all with a view to anticipate the events of a Mexican war, and to shelter California from the arms of the United States. The settlers laid their dangers before Mr. Frémont, and implored him to place himself at their head and save them from destruction. At this time war had been declared against Mexico, but the news had not reached California. Col. Frémont felt the responsibility of his position, but he determined to put himself at the head of the people and try to save the country. He did so, and the American settlers rushed to his camp, bringing with them their horses, arms, ammunition, etc., and obeyed with zeal and alacrity the orders they received. As an evidence that he possesses skill, courage, and all the other requisites of a great commander, stands the fact that in thirty days from the time he took command California was freed from Mexican authority, independence proclaimed, the flag of independence raised, the enemy flying from the country, the American settlers saved from destruction, and the British party in California counteracted and broken up in all their schemes. He had done all this without the authority of his Government, and Gen. Kearney, who had been sent out to conquer California, found the work already performed by the gallant Frémont. Kearney, through envy, had Frémont arrested. He was tried by a Court-Martial and convicted, but the President remitted the penalty and requested him to receive his sword. This Frémont refused to do. He resigned his commission as Lieutenant Colonel in the army, and returned to California. The people were attached to him, and soon, through their Legislature, elected him to represent them in the United States Senate.

Mr. Frémont is devoted to the Union. He was in Europe when the present war broke out, and he resolved to return immediately and offer his services to the Government in any capacity that it might desire them. He has been made a Major General, and has been placed in command of the Department of the West. He has just entered upon the active discharge of his duties, and already a wonderful degree of activity is witnessed in his Division. Large bodies of troops are being rapidly concentrated at proper points, uniformed, armed, drilled and prepared for active service. Provisions, ammunition, tents, clothing, blankets, saddles, bridles, camp equipage, and all else needed to supply the wants of the army are coming forward quickly and in great abundance. Every day gives fresh assurance that the right man is at the head of military affairs in this Division, and under the lead of General Frémont we are confident that our army will soon give rebellion its death-blow in the South-west.[36]

WASHINGTON CORRESPONDENCE, 5 AUGUST 1861

On Saturday evening Prince Napoleon dined with the President.

When Mrs. Spriggins invites Mrs. Gamp to partake of her cucumbers and tea, the world pays little regard to the garrulous pair, swallowing their knives and slandering their neighbors in peace and quietness. And when Mrs. Ormolu with a hundred of her dearest friends sits down to the ghastly solemnity of a well-bred dinner, the event wakes no ripple in the placid stream of public events, and is only of interest to the ragged social philosophers who catch fleeting sniffs of forbidden fragrance over area railings. But when the veritable wearer of a coronet places his regal legs under the same mahogany that covers the democratic continuations of a republican monarch, the general public, never obtrusive, though mildly inquisitive, desires, yes *demands* that the particulars of the portentous hobnobbing shall be given. Your correspondent, recognizing the justice of the claim, stands ready to gratify it, and, as the event is one of importance to the world, *The World* shall know it.

The Prince Napoleon, who was the son of Jerome, who was the son the Corsican who was the father of Napoleon, arrived in the capital of our distracted country on Friday evening in a remarkably good humor at having baffled the provincial malignity of the Philadelphia reporters, who rashly thought to succeed where the metropolitan latest intelligence men had failed. He was presented to the President at noon on Saturday. The interview was deeply interesting and suggestive. On the one side marked by the studied courtesy and reticence that form the badge of the nation and the family, on the other by an innate delicacy of feeling and purity of heart that leaves nothing to conceal. The conversation was utterly free from political discussion. The President would not take advantage of his position, and the prince has a magnificent faculty for silence. After a while Napoleon arose, and, placing his hands behind him in the St. Helena style, bowed Napoleonically, and the accomplished Mercier bowed, and the heads of the suite inclined like opulent wheat ears in the breeze, and the imperial cortege rolled away.

At 7 o'clock they reappeared. They were ushered into the Blue drawing-room just as the Marine band struck up that impertinent finale of "Yankee Doodle" which forms the *songe* of the loafing crowds of Saturday afternoons. The party came out upon the balcony, and the eyes of the commons were blessed by a moment's glimpse of presumptive royalty. These Frenchmen always group themselves artistically. His imperial highness stood in the center, in that attitude which makes him seem like a portrait of his uncle on a temporary leave of absence from its frame, in full dress, his breast a flame of decorations, and the broad crimson scarf of a marshal of the empire traversing with great richness of color his substantial front-view. His face was clean shaven and his hair was arranged like that of the First Consul. He is a man to respect. You may laugh at him if you like; you may call him "Plon-Plon," and speak dubiously of the authorship of his speeches, but when you see the princely attitude, the cold, impassive, classic features, and the very look of this world's greatest man—the dead emperor—staring out of eyes and brow, you feel an entirely involuntary impulse of respect, and honor yourself by bowing to him. This was Napoleon, as the people gazed quietly at him from the lawn in the sunset.

Next him was Mercier, who honors his nation at our court. He is a gentleman, and that does interfere with his being a statesman. And the inscrutable, mysterious Baroche was there—the man who is to diplomacy what Vidocq was to crime—and the Lieut. Colonels Ragon and Ferri Pisani, and the bluff sailorly old gentleman who is well named Bonfils, *capitaine de vaisseau,* and young Maurice Sand, the son of the glorious Madame George Sand, who has made a *nom de plume* a proud inheritance for her children, and Mr. de Geoffroy, the very popular secretary of the French legation.

The guests returned to the drawing room, and the President entered, attended by Mrs. Lincoln, who was so charmingly dressed, and who looked so young and blooming, that it seemed a very good joke for her to introduce as her son the youth, a head taller than herself, who accompanied her. A friend of Robert's, Mrs. Grimsley, the graceful and dignified cousin of Mrs. Lincoln, and the President's private secretaries, Nicolay and Hay, completed the home party. A vigorous course of presentation was then begun, with alternate lulls of conversation, and spasms of interest when the grand form of Sumner appeared at the door, when Governor Chase came in, the most statuesque man in Washington, when the Postmaster-General entered, ever earnest and restless, with incarnate energy in his eyes and mouth, or the Secretary of the Navy walked dreamily forward, or Seward came in with his clear eye and unclouded brow, simple, noble and unaffected, in spite of fanatics and special correspondents the first statesman of the age. At last everybody followed the direction of everybody's eyes, and a sight worth coming from France to see, was in the door—*Scott leaning upon the arm of McClellan.*

It was a splendid contrast. Its suggestions transcended sense, and wandered into the domain of fancy and undeveloped possibilities. Six-foot-four leaning upon five-foot-eight! Seventy-five upon thirty-five! History waiting upon prophecy—memory upon hope! Two suns, here in actual life as in Dryden's grand absurdity, the one sinking in the glorified west, the other climbing the flushing east. How people have grown to love the old battered leonine face, with the fires of unconquerable will still blazing in the hawk eyes. And how gladly has the popular heart hailed the advent of the young general, who unites in himself the *élan* of the Zou-Zou with the cool imperturbability of the veteran strategist. He looked very soldierly this evening, the twin stars of the major-general gleaming on his shoulders, and a queer four-cornered dress rapier hanging trimly from his swordbelt. He spoke French with ease and fluency. The prince talked with him long and earnestly. Gen. Scott spoke French with Mercier; Sumner was doing the senator with successive Gauls; the President's secretaries aired their French with the Parisian importations, and everyone else was garrulous or dumb, "according to the dictates of his own conscience."

Mr. Nicolay receives a mysterious intimation from the door. He gives the President and the Prince marching orders. Mrs. Grimsley takes the arm of the Tycoon, and the white hand of Mrs. Lincoln reposes on the sleeve of Plon-Plon. Through the Red parlor into the dining room marches this hungry but disciplined army. They separate into two columns. The table is outflanked and gallantly taken. A long line of white cravats bristle defiantly on either side. Each man reconnoiters his position, and makes a remark to his neighbor. The immobile-faced waiters begin a series of light skirmishings.

I really cannot go any further with this dinner. Dinners must forever remain a myth to the public until "special correspondents" begin to be invited, or people who dine learn to write. I should have enlisted in the corps of waiters, but five hours of steady circumambiency is not a hilarious thing for a man of my habit or body. So let this dinner lie in the lap of cherishing silence. I only know that Gen. Scott said to the President that he had dined with every President since Jefferson, and that, in his mind, "the last should be first." And the Prince said that, after seeing this tremendous uprising of a great people, he will say no more of weak republics, and, after enjoying the elegant hospitality of Washington, he will be forced to confess that Paris is not the world.

After dinner the "blue room" received the refluent tide. People were more social and less formal than in the hungry pause that preceded the dinner-ward movement.

Let me mention one fact which will be the cause of endless conflicts among the middle-aged milliners and the rising shop boys who do the "habits of good society" business.

The prince, after dinner, drank Curacoa, and Mrs. Lincoln preferred the chaste colorlessness of the Maraschino.

At an early hour the prince made his adieux, and his suite followed suit. Lord Lyons soon after smiled his way urbanely out of doors, while Scott and McClellan and Sumner stayed and talked war with the President.

Last year this dinner would have been an event. Now it is only an incident. In the face of the tragic fact that a mighty nation is in arms for its own life, the adjuncts of conventional rank, which usually so powerfully affect the people, are held impertinent and unmeaning. Albert Edward Guelph, Esq. [the Prince of Wales], would have a less laborious journey now than last year. When the war is over we will go back to our toad-eating. Let us hope our enthusiasm may always be bestowed upon an object as worthy in person and association as his imperial highness, the Prince Napoleon.[37]

WASHINGTON CORRESPONDENCE, 12 AUGUST 1861

Plon-Plon has vanished from the tuft-hunting gaze that delighted in his presence. Quietly as he came he has departed. He beamed for a few days in rotund majesty upon an admiring and awestruck population. He elevated, in absorbent mood, his imperial little finger over the ground-glass eagles of Mrs. Lincoln's Sauterne goblets. The decorous creak of his Parisian shoes resounded through the audience chamber of the President, and the prince struck hands with the rail-splitter of the Wabash, the boatman of the Sangamon, the autocrat of a fierce democracy. He went to the navy yard where Dahlgren received him with a face as impassive as a wooden figure-head, and a brain as active as a high-pressure engine. He stood upon the decks of the lordly *Pensacola* and saw the 11-inch shell plunging though the central target and building monuments of snowy spray at every ricochet. (It was a happy thought of Dahlgren's to give the Puritan name of "Plymouth" to this irresistible gun, "orthodox, flashing conviction right into the hearts of the heathen.") He stood at the grave of him whose memory pervades all freedom's like sunshine, and returning, invaded a Virginia cornfield to flank a rebel abattis.

All this, as Pelissier said at Balaklava, "was very magnificent, but was not war." No Napoleon could come so near to pickets and not see both sides of the row. There was a charming and not wholly incurious society on board the *Jerome Napoleon,* and how can one answer questions, *mon cher,* when one knows nothing? It was absolutely necessary that the prince should go to Manassas.

It was very kind and considerate in Prince Napoleon to attend Mr. Seward's reception before he went. It was kind to his imperial highness, to whom his imperial highness is devotedly attached, because it enabled him to see everybody best worthy of being seen in town. It was a good thing for the limited everybody, because it showed them the man who will not be emperor of the French unless our little friend the corporal [*Napoleon III*] should obligingly conclude to die. It was considerate too, for everyone wished to see him once, and the casualties of irresponsible scouting parties are numerous. Who could know but that the rebels might think it a very neat thing to shoot the illustrious stranger as the guest of Abe Lincoln? Or they might mistake his traveling carriages for ambulances, and gaily riddle them. Then we remembered the fate of Harris and McGraw, and the vast difference between the *decensus Averni* and the *revocare gradum*—if Avernus will pardon me for comparing it to Manassas. On the whole we were glad to see him again, and to see him in a company so distinguished, so happy and so clean as that at Governor Seward's.

He and his *suite* went, profaning with their footsteps the sacred soil. They saw none of the flat-footed Virginians until within about three miles of Fairfax Court House. Several regiments were there encamped, and the lank volunteers loafed lazily under the trees and made the air as unwholesome with the untidiness of their cuisine as the light with their rags and squalor.

Beyond Fairfax the road was clear. No rebel legions were seen until they came to Manassas. Here they were received by the rebel general, Johnston, with exceeding great joy. Beautiful on the turnpike are the boots of him who cometh from afar, the touch of whose lavender kids will be the accolade of respectability to the bastard republic! To their excited fancy, recognition blushed in the crimson of his shoulder-scarf, and armed interference looked cheeringly forth from his orders. His air, his carriage, his easy *abord* seemed the harbinger of indefinite good things, and in his gay "good morning" they heard free trade, a broken blockade, and the blessings of a barbarous civilization carried up the Congo and Zambesi. They would have liked a pennyworth less of reserve, but they hopefully attributed that to his imperfect English. They would have preferred a deeper libation of the juice of the maize, but they supposed that his disgust for strychnine was an anti-Bourbon prejudice. They were willing to take much for granted. A legitimate prince is not often caught in a rebel camp, and they were glad. As the imperial cortege was going, Gen. (Col.) Stewart (he calls himself by both titles, so I give him both), whose enthusiasm had taken an exceedingly bibacious type, unwilling that the golden opportunity should pass forever without some decided words of regal promise, leaning confidingly over the prince's carriage, murmured gushingly: "Now, prince, when you get back home, you'll hurry up that recognition, won't you?" The wary Plon-Plon thrust his shoulders into his ears, in a miraculous Gallic shrug, and answered: "*Mais, mon ami, je ne suis pas l'empereur.*"

"What in h——l's that?" muttered the bluffed general, as he gloomily walked away, wishing his early education had not been neglected.

The prince's incursion into Dixie has no political significance whatever. Had he gone to Richmond there would have been a difference. It would have been very strange if he had left Washington without visiting the scene of the recent battle. He was afforded all possible facilities by the government here, and by no single act did he give the slightest semblance of recognition to the Richmond cabal; declining their invitation, on the contrary, in the most decided, though courteous terms. He has acted throughout with rare tact, prudence and discretion. His face has been an impenetrable mask. Though frank and courteous, he has never been garrulous. Though acknowledging the civilities of the members of the administration gratefully and cordially, he has always preserved the restraints of dignified reticence and self-respect.

He has left only kindly memories behind him, and some heartless but pious Americans think that perhaps it might not be a bad thing for France if angels should carry the little corporal to heaven some morning.

His sojourn was longer than he had intended, and even then inevitable engagements took him away before he wished to go. Quietly as he came he has departed. I saw the last of him, supported on one side by Bonfils, the *pere noble* of the expedition, and Maurice Sand, the *jeune amant,* doing the St. Helena attitude on the rear platform of a Baltimore car.[38]

Long Branch, N.J., correspondence, 16 August 1861

Mrs. Lincoln, the long-expected guest, arrived at 1 P.M. accompanied by a portion of her suite. The junior Lincoln and Mr. Hay, private secretary of the President, preceded her by a day.

The effect of the arrival upon the Branch was quite convulsive. It is not a vast place, being altogether composed of a spectral file of hotels, and a half a dozen little pavilions, pert and arabesque, which fringe the shore, consequently the assemblage which greeted the lady of the White House, although respectable, was not imposing in point of numbers. But what it lacked in this respect it fully made up in well-bred enthusiasm and pocket handkerchiefs. Mr. Torrey, the agent of the railway, had provided a special train for Mrs. Lincoln, and a carriage which awaited her at the depot, and in which she was driven to the Mansion House, where she will remain during her stay.

A pleasant feature of the reception was the assemblage at the station of a large number of young girls, dressed all in white. The little folks were in high feather, and the recipient of their welcome seemed to be charmed with the graceful and delicate attention.

Since the arrival the Branch, throughout its arid length, has been in a condition of buzz and flutter. The general anxiety to see the distinguished guest does not promise very well for the privacy which she desires to maintain, but it is greatly to be hoped that undue intrusiveness will be duly snubbed, and all tuft-hunters and toad-eaters whatsoever remorselessly squelched.

The programme for the present is as follows. To-morrow a cricket match, wherein the club of St. George encounter a polite Dragon with a bat in its paw—an extempore organization I believe, unlaureled as yet, but said to include batters of transcendent merit and ingenious practitioners of the long-stop. There will be fun. There always is at cricket. Abraded shins; small thin men knocked from their foundations; heavy old parties who *will* get in the way and are generally doubled up by a ball in the abdomen. Tents with an aeolian attachment (a brass band) and facilities for the congelation of cream are erected, and it is expected that the ladies, Mrs. Lincoln included, will grace the occasion and eat the ices. In the evening the cricketers dine in state, presided over by the veteran actor, Mr. Wallack, whose summer residence is not far hence. There are rumors that the heir apparent will attend the entertainment.

There is to be a grand ball some time next week, the date not yet determined. In anticipation thereof multitudes of young ladies from New York have flocked hither, bringing Saratoga trunks slightly inferior in size to the pavilions upon the shore. I regret to observe that there is a paucity of young men with thin legs and artillery whiskers (the inevitable indices of the dancing man), and that unless reinforcements arrive, the few here will be danced, polked, waltzed and schottisched into a condition of utter flatulence and imbecility. There is, to-morrow night, a "hop," a festival which bears about the same relation to a grand dress ball that a negligé morning toilet bears to the laced and stayed and jeweled and ruffed resplendence of evening full dress. There is a scarcity of masculine contortionists even at these minor festivals. It is frequently necessary, in order to complete the quadrille, to fall back upon heavy, melancholy old parties, who trip everybody up and perspire. This is not as it should be. Mr. Laird (the host) ought to keep a choice and elegant collection of young men, warranted to keep step, and converse without gasping. In the intervals of their being required they might stand about the grounds and smile. It would give variety to the landscape.

There is a pretty little cottage near the hotel, belonging to Mr. Gould of Newark, which is quite at Mrs. Lincoln's disposal, but she is said to prefer the hotel, and to have expressed her intention of dining *sans ceremonis* at the *table d'hote,* a gracious deference in the guests which will be duly appreciated and applauded.

The weather, beautiful during the day, holds out to-night cheerful prospects of impending storm. The sun went down behind a gray, gloomy bank of cloud, and the eastern horizon took on at twilight a pure green tint which is ominous. Rain at the sea-side is the most afflicting dispensation of a merciful Providence.

The drizzle seems wetter there than other wheres, the sky grayer and colder, nor is there refuge except in suicide or intoxication. The searching sea air penetrates with unearthly damp everything save the epidermis, and thereon it gathers in beaded drops. The napkin is moist; the salt humid; the tablecloth as heavy and sodden as if it were mildewed; one's garments become damp and flaccid, and there is, as the swell says, no "wemedy." None. A desolate and watery state of things. Therefore I hope, with the wildest earnestness, that it won't rain.[39]

LONG BRANCH, N.J., CORRESPONDENCE, 17 AUGUST 1861

A gray, desolate day; the sea and sky of uniform leaden tint, few bathers, a cricket match languidly played and witnessed by but few of the ladies, and night closes in upon us—a starless, desolate night without, the moon finding only an occasional joint in the cloudy armor of the sky, and the sea raving on the beach like Lear. But within the musicians are preludizing; there is a slow feathery drift to and fro of full toilettes, an undertone of conversation, and certain other alluring indications that dancing is about to begin. Mrs. Lincoln is not expected to attend. She has kept her room during the greater part of the day, and seems disposed vigorously to maintain that seclusion which can alone render her sojourn here agreeable or recreative. There are, of course, many regrets expressed, and her absence will deprive the entertainment of one of its anticipated delights. However, there are bright eyes in constellations, and airy, slippered feet without number, and music, stormy now as the Apennines in winter, anon sad and plaintive like the night wind among the pines, and again as wild as flying fingers and a rushing bow can wring from the tortured cremona. So, notwithstanding the absence of Mrs. Lincoln, there are enough delights yet left to satiate the most exigent reveller.

Nothing salutatory for me, thank you. "Those light at heart tickle the senseless rushes with their heels," says Romeo, and though I am rarely heavy in the vicinity of that organ, I am saurian in the deliberation of my movements; never dance, in fact. Therefore, as I do not participate, neither shall I take it upon myself to become the annalist of the festival. Out yonder, on the brow of the shore, just where the stormy octaves of the ocean and the wail of the band blend with each other, where the wind, rushing in from the wild Atlantic, whistles mournfully through the lattice-work of the deserted pavilions, I shall stroll awhile, smoke, meditate, exchange salutations with the belated tritons and nereids, if any of their tiny shallops sail hitherward to-night, and come back after the lamps are put out, the garlands (if there be any), dead, and while Beatrice and Vittoria are intoning musical good nights upon the piazzi.

It is a good thing now and then to be alone upon the sea shore, to monopolize, so to speak, for a season all its mysterious and alien voices; more than ever is this solitary communion with the sea to be desired in the night-time. The restless, hoary old monster gets communicative after nightfall, and lets one into its secrets; makes confessions of its own ravenousness; how it has gulped down stately ships, now and then, and wound its slimy coil about great cities and whelmed and consumed fair principalities, league by league. There is something inexpressibly weird and thrilling in becoming thus, for a season, the father confessor of the ocean—getting all its unhallowed secrets from it and then withholding absolution.

But still all its voices are not those of confession and repentance. It hath its splendid trills of passion, its minstrelsy of anger, its deep undertone of monition, and its dying cadence of sorrow, many voiced, like Shakespeare and the musical glasses rolled into one; it hath its Marseillaise likewise, its watery hymn of revolution. I have heard it many a time, and wondered, as I heard, whether Rouget de Lisle might not have been a merman who got his lieutenancy in the army of France under this false pretense of not being a fish. I have wondered, likewise, what the sea could possibly want with an insurrectionary lyric. Its normal condition is insurrectionary, revolutionary, lawless; no irreverent hand of restraint hath been laid upon it since the morning stars first sang together, nor will be while ever it chafes against its shores. What has it to revolutionize? It cannot be that any of the pea-green territories of Father Neptune have attempted to secede, or that any scoffing Pasquin among the water-gods has lampooned the imperial ruler of the seas, and called his trident a toasting fork. It is clear to me that the sea [*chants?*] this loud defiant stave out of mere wantonness; it has nothing to complain of; it may possibly regard the dykes of Holland in the light of a liberty, and the invention of steam as an impertinence. But even these limitations of its supremacy do not justify its attempt to whistle up a revolution.

Very quiet out here along the shore, notwithstanding that the wind has freshened, and the waters hiss upon the sand as if they wanted to take a twist about somebody's ankle, and pull him in, and now and then a tremulous wave of music, mingled with the patter of feet, strikes out along the night. The clouds cleared away before sunset for an hour, but they have gathered again, and only here and there a white rim of moonlight edges the somber belts of vapor which stretch along the east. In the darkness it is not unusual to come plump upon a nocturnal sea side flirtation. I interrupted one just now. Two young and impassioned innocents seated upon a bench by the pavilion. Ah me! whither are gone my own adolescent days? the days wherein beside pavilions long since gone into desuetude I may myself have sat, similarly impassioned and innocent, and been interrupted by the unpremeditated intrusion of a heavy, meditative old party such as I now am? The past holds them inexorably; they are gone eternally out, like the fire on desert hearthstones—like the flame of a lamp extinguished. No matter. There are golden days left yet; nor will I to-night give place to so paltry a sentiment as that of envy of young Corydon beside his Phyllis yonder, for that he is youthful while I am not only getting bald, but have clamorous nephews and nieces in scores. Not I, by the good genius of a healthful and rotund middle age.

Although I am disposed to admire and commend everything, I cannot but aver that the Branch strikes me as rather a sterile and monotonous resort. On sunny days the wide glare, unshaded by any trees, makes the eyes ache. For a whole league along the level plateau of coast not a tree nor shrub is visible. Back from the shore a little there are strips of wilderness, and murmuring fields of corn, and cottages embowered in foliage. But those to the transient visitor afford little relief, his sole outlook being upon the beach, the ocean and the level terrace of lawn before the hotels. Yet now and then the most sterile and unpromising localities have been suddenly lifted into consequence by the visit of great personages. Who ever heard of Biarritz till her majesty, the fair Eugenie, honored its tumbling surf by bathing therein. Vichy, immortalized by the transitory residence there of Napoleon III, is about to become a place of consequence. The Vichyans have laid out leagues of new avenues, contracted for an Hotel de Ville, and laid the egg which is to incubate a park. Possibly Madeira, whereto her majesty of Austria repaired of late in pursuit of health, may henceforth experience an important access of annual visitants. The world is so execrably given to the eating of toads and the humbug of tufts. Mrs. Lincoln's presence here at the Branch, whatever may be its ultimate influence, has had the immediate effect of crowding the hotels to suffocation. Possibly the fashion of coming hither may remain after her departure, and Newport find in the Branch a rival to its throne. But probably not.

There goes the final crash of the band; the dancing is over; nothing to do now but saunter up the walk intersecting now and then other gloomy old fellows seeking solitude and isolation like myself, and mingle for an instant with the crowds which, overpouring through the doors, washing along the piazzas, and waking a dreamy hum of conversation and a pattering drip of feet. The game is up for the day; the candle out, and so to bed before the Sabbath overtakes and finds us sinning.[40]

Long Branch, N.J., correspondence, 17 August 1861

The contest between the rival hotels of Long Branch, which threatened to end in an *uncivil* war on *National* grounds, has been settled amicably and without robbing Peter to pay Paul, albeit there be Peters at the Branch important enough to hold the keys of imperial Rome itself. Mrs. Lincoln, like her husband, is guided by the democratic law of majority, and has settled with her suite—where the majority annually settle—at Laird's Mansion House. Mr. Laird, the proprietor, had provided newly furnished rooms in honor of the visit of the "first lady in the land," and a suite, with private parlor, render the lady of the President and her friends as comfortable and secluded as in the privacy of their own home. Mrs. Lincoln has expressed herself delighted with the cool, invigorating climate, and the bracing sea breezes and ocean, which form so striking a contrast with Illinois and Washington, and the kind consideration with which all here respect her desire for quietness and rest, and the proverbial hospitality of Mr. and Mrs. Laird give every assurance that Mrs. Lincoln will enjoy her visit to Long Branch. Mrs. Lincoln drove out to-day with Mr. Meeker, of Newark, who has placed his carriage at her disposal during the visit. Mrs. Lincoln visited, about 1 o'clock, the cricket ground, where the match was playing between St. George and Long Branch, and remained for some time to witness this English game, which she had never seen before. In the evening a general reception was appointed to take place at the Mansion House, and about 8 o'clock the parlors, piazzas and grounds of the Mansion House were crowded with ladies *en grande toilette* and attendant cavaliers. But Mrs. Lincoln could not attend, owing to the severe sickness of her friend Mrs. Shearer, and sent her regrets to Mr. Laird, which were conveyed to the disappointed groups. Music and dancing, however, consoled them; and, as young gentlemen were more plentiful than usual, the young ladies were more happy than usual, and each bright particular star—by which we mean a coaxing young beauty and not a metropolitan policeman—was thrice blessed that she had seen Robert Lincoln, the President's son, hoped to see him again, to talk with him, to dance with him, and then—well, they haven't confessed openly that dread hereafter, but young ladies have been heard muttering to themselves, "Mrs. Robert Lincoln; dear, sweet name; how pretty," &c., and Byron's "all went merry as a marriage bell," with ominous fervor, breathed as a prayer, and with the fine, rolling frenzy in their eyes of a Pythoness or young lady that wants to settle in life eligibly. As Pilicoddy says, "What is life without Anastasia? Nothing. What is Anastasia without life? Nothinger." So what is life without Bob Lincoln? Nothing. What is Bob Lincoln without life? Nothinger!

On Thursday next there is to be a grand ball at the Mansion House, at which Mrs. Lincoln will be present, that evening being named by herself, and the arrangements and decorations will be on a scale of magnificence novel in New Jersey. Only a limited number of tickets will be issued, and every precaution used to make the affair agreeable to Mrs. Lincoln.[41]

Long Branch, N.J., correspondence, 19 August 1861

Yesterday being Sabbath was spent in quiet and retirement by Mrs. Lincoln and her party, who seem imbued with a deeper reverence for the day than is usually manifested at places of summer resort. Mrs. Lincoln was much fatigued by her unremitting personal attentions to her sick friend, Mrs. Shearer.

To-day a meeting of gentlemen (the dear creatures who foot up the bills and supply the itzebus or shekels on demand), was held in the Mansion House, to arrange the details for the grand ball to be given at the Mansion House in honor of Mrs. Lincoln. The price of tickets was fixed at $5, and the affair will doubtless excel in attractions everything that New Jersey has ever witnessed on that "sacred soil."[42]

St. Louis correspondence, 20 September 1861

On Monday the Benton Barracks were inaugurated. This repentant Magdalene of a city came out cheerfully to see the consummation of Gen. Frémont's rapid enterprise, and was charmingly and gushingly loyal. There are few instances on record of a change of heart more rapid and edifying than that whose good results flower in the daily deeds of this rescued community. Baltimore scarcely recovered from her April fever more rapidly under the heroic potions of Gen. Butler, when the seven-starred blotches disappeared from her face, and gave place to the healthy glow of the spangling constellations. When Gen. Frémont came to St. Louis, the cause of the Union, though gallantly defended, was the unpopular cause. Patriotism was *outré,* and treason was the style. But now the national cause is fashionable, and the man who meditates treason takes into the account not merely possibilities of hemp, but the contingencies of taboo. And social ostracism is a powerful auxiliary to the gallows, as a moral education.

So the show of Monday was a good one. That mythical presence, "the beauty and fashion of the city," was actually there. The languid, lazy-eyed magnificences with the sweet French names, who have hitherto deprived the vile Hessians of the light of their tempestuous beauty, blessed the scene with the flash of eager eyes, and the gleam of white shoulders. Creole and Yankee mingled kindly and warred not. "I am no ladies' man, as Jenkins is," and I do not mention this fact from Jenkins's stand-point. I think it important as indicating that Frémont and his heroic wife have brought loyalty into vogue, and have made treason not only criminal, but what is far worse, vulgar.

Frémont, though preeminently American in all his habits of thought, has gained in his wandering and eventful life, some valuable ideas of military state and style, from his observations of the courts of warlike nations. He has surrounded himself with those dignified accessions of high military rank which are so effective in commanding the respect of the citizen as well as the soldier. Secessionists sneer at these insignia of a power they dread, and special correspondents, who have been in the habit of rushing unannounced into the presence of brigadiers, and shouting, with jovial slaps-on-the-back, "Anything new, Old Boy?" are disgusted with this unusual self-respect, and revenge themselves for a corporal's snub by a thunderous broadside in their journal.

If a man has business that entitles him to occupy a few minutes of Frémont's day, he will go to his headquarters, a handsome dwelling in the south of the city, garden-cinctured and flag surmounted, and will be stopped at the gate by a dapper soldier, who will call for the corporal—a clean young fellow in a blue uniform, as jaunty and neat as that of a middy—and the corporal will take him to an ante-room, where he will await the issue of a complicated series of card deliveries, until a grave and reverend valet, who in the course of a long life of usefulness has borne the titles of "Peyton's Niggah," "Randolph's Chattel," "Benton's Institution," and "Frémont's Contraband," opens the door, obsequiously bows the white head, which age has powdered, and ushers him into a long, well-lighted drawing-room, whose furniture is shrouded, whose Brussels is covered with green baize, whose mortified air proclaims, in muffled tones, *inter arma silent* drawing rooms, and there, by a table, where lies a wilderness of papers that no man must touch, sits Major-General John Charles Frémont.

He is a little thinner, a little grayer than in the days of five years ago, when we fought for the good cause under him, using for our talismanic watchword the linking of his name with freedom's; but the man still is there, grown greater in the process of the suns. In the intensity of the eyes, in the lines that are furrowing cheek and forehead, and the quiet earnestness of voice and phrase, even in what his defamers call his faults, the quick, sharp tone of command in which he addresses his subordinates, and the utter ignoring of conflicting opinion, you recognize the qualities which the quick instinct of the people long ago recognized as those of a born leader, and which Abraham Lincoln—who, more than any other man, reflects the mind of the people—selected to call into battle and guide into victory the invincible legions of the West. Frémont is always equal to himself and the occasion. Whatever cabals against him may flourish and burgeon in quiet places; whatever rumors may float in the streets and tremble on the wires; though the atmosphere above him and below him be filled with the reproaches of mutinous officers and an angry cabinet; though a savage enemy be thundering on his frontier, and a rebel state be writhing under his feet like the great dragon under the heel of St. Michael, Frémont is as quiet and collected, as master of himself and his instruments, as though he sat in his office at Mariposa [*California*], giving orders for quartz-crushers instead of columbiads, and disbursing his hundreds where now he scatters his millions. If he is inaccessible, it is not a selfish procedure, for no man can see him without confessing that here is an exception to the mistakes of history—that the right man is in the right place.

There are few men but would fail in such a position. It is a difficult thing to hold a wildcat in each hand and attack a panther in front of you; and when, in addition, your own friends begin a brisk and magnanimous fire in the rear, success becomes at least conjectural. Yet this is nearly Frémont's position to-day. As fast as he concentrates his forces the enemy occupy the towns thus vacated, and the outraged Unionists besiege the general for succor. If he scatters his troops garrison-wise among the towns the country clamors against inaction, and reproachfully points to New Madrid and Columbus. While every nerve is strained for public use the ill-timed criticisms of imprudent friends endanger his efficiency; and while, with his little army of Illinoisans, he prepares to do battle with the whole southwest, he is ordered to send a large proportion of his command to defend the capital.

It seems to us western people that that order would kindle a shame in the East that would blister the cheek of every Yankee that stays at home, though it be hard as Bunker Hill Monument. If the swarming millions of the East cannot defend the capital against double any number the Sepoys can bring against it, without calling for help from Illinois, who has poured from her southern prairies the army which must singly breast the storm of rebellion rolling up the valley of the Mississippi—let us know it at once, that our children may leave school and our old men forsake their easy chairs and fight for a people, the memories of whose forefathers are dead in their souls. That is the way it seems to us western people—but what do we know about war?

Frémont says nothing of this, but receives the order, smiles grimly, and sends five of his best regiments to Washington. Whatever he may think, he says not a word that will ever indicate the slightest symptom of restlessness or impatience.

Just now all St. Louis is talking about Colonel Blair's arrest. It is a subject of deep regret to all true men. Frank Blair has been so long the honored and idolized representative of free thought in the West, that a wrong from him has seemed impossible. Eloquent, impassioned, generous and genial, with a great heart and a great brain, his name has been a talisman in every fight, and his presence as inspiring as a bugle. Yet Gen. Frémont could only choose between discipline and destruction, and Blair's best friends can only say, "Why would he row with Frémont at just this time?"

St. Louis is the heaviest sufferer by this war. Her streets are silent; her boats, which used to bear the commerce of the greatest river in the world, lie rotting at the wharves, while a ruthless and savage enemy rage on her borders and along the great veins and arteries of trade that center in her heart. None have such stake in the war as she. None know so well as she who can best conserve the best interests of the West. And St. Louis believes in Frémont.[43]

Washington correspondence, 9 October 1861

The cool assurance, and the imperturbable cheekiness with which an experienced and hardened villain sticks to a lie, and the nervous swagger and ill-at-ease rowdyism with which a green liar attempts to cover his retreat from an untenable position, always furnishes a contrast at once amusing and instructive. Robert Macaire may lie without a blush or a blink, but Jacques Strop invariably makes a mull of it, by his shuffling and hesitation. You cannot but be reminded of this upon reading the *New York Herald* and the *Washington Star* upon Frémont. The Satanic sheet, having been mercilessly hoaxed by its news-agent, and betrayed into a severity in which it never indulges unless it is sure a man is down—having turned its back upon its former idol and dragged his name through the foulness of many columns—still supports the canard of Frémont's removal by ingenious fictions and unblushing slanders. When Wool went to Washington, it exulted. Frémont was to be ironed, and Wool to take command at Jefferson City. When Wool went home to [*Fort*] Monroe, leaving the *Herald* high and dry on its own invention, the explanation was coolly given, that he had merely gone back to pack his trunk and settle with his washerwoman. Now that Mansfield has left the fortress, and the impertinent vapidity of Drake Decay's face still lingers forlorn at Willard's, and Wool prepares to settle on the Atlantic border, the *Herald* relapses into gloom. We cannot doubt, however, that it will prove equal to the emergency; and like Antaeus, gather strength with every knockdown.

The poor little *Star* shines more feebly, though more spitefully. It is disgusted beyond measure that Frémont's continuance in command spoils its predictions, and exhibits all the impotent fury that a quack feels, when after pronouncing the death doom of a patient, he finds him out of bed the next morning. It says to-day that Wool exacted degrading concessions from the Government as a condition to his acceptance of Frémont's command. This is of course too awkwardly absurd to deceive anybody.

It seems to be pretty well understood here, that no change can at present be made in the Western Department. Even were charges against the General substantiated, which they by no means are, the policy of encouraging an army on the eve of a battle by cutting off its head may well be considered a doubtful one. Further than this, I do not believe anybody can say. No action has yet been taken upon Col. Blair's specifications. When taken, it will be, every one knows, thoroughly fair and thoroughly searching.

Gen. Wm. K. Strong, the newly appointed Brigadier General, who left a delightful home and an interesting family in Florence to enjoy their vacation without him, and came over the seas to offer his time and his energies to the cause of his endangered nation, has been ordered West, as it is understood, at Gen. Frémont's request, to act upon his staff. His advent will probably be the signal of a renewal of confidence, for which his great business talents are the guarantee.

Col. De Ahna seems, in the opinion of the President, to have suffered sufficiently for having lifted his recalcitrant heel against the dignity of the General's Body Guard, and is restored to his Indiana Legion.

Yesterday morning the crowd of anxious inquirers who, as usual, besieged the doors of the Secretary of War and the Adjutant General, were quietly informed by the highly respectable and decorous contrabands who respectively keep watch and ward, like lidless-eyed dragons, over the Hesperidean officials—"that the Generals were out." Only this; it was probably all they knew. Others, who knew no more, said that Gen. Cameron has gone to Lochiel, whither his charming family this morning followed him—"he would be back in a day or two or three—better see Colonel Scott—he will attend to your business."

Nobody in this town ever knows where information comes from; but this morning all those who consider themselves particularly up to Macaboy, say with immense affectation of mystery, that Gen. Cameron had gone to St. Louis. The object of his concealing his departure is of course obvious. He desires to come unheralded, and to see the Department out of its Sunday clothes.—There is no clearer headed man on the continent than Simon Cameron. He will see the right or the wrong of this matter in spite of prejudice or fraud. He is thoroughly cool, deliberate and fearless. He fears labor as little as he does slander. He never shrinks from attacking a mountain of work from the fear that an avalanche of abuse may fall upon him. His expedition will not be barren of results.

No vigilance, however sleepless, no energy, however well directed, will ever protect departments from defamation. The restless press is already beginning its outcry against the navy for allowing the Bermuda to break the blockade, and the enemy on the Northern seaboard to fortify their coast. The navy is loaded with blame for what is omitted; it is given no praise for what is accomplished. When a dozen ships are captured by our fleet, nothing is said of it. The exploit is buried in two lines of an Associated Press dispatch.

When one ship escapes, the air is filled with querulous clamors. The voice of complaint is not silenced by the sound of a thousand hammers ringing in every navy yard, nor does the spectacle of our splendid Atlantic squadron, called into the waves in less than half a year, excite any patriotic emotion in the breast of these professional grumblers.

If there is anything to grumble at, let us grumble at the stupidity and cowardice that seem to be running riot beyond the mountains. Is the soil of Arizona so cursed that manliness withers there? The example of unutterable shame that Lynde set, when a regiment of regulars surrendered their fortifications to 300 half-starved wretches, at the bidding of a paltroonery too abject for anger, seems to be lately becoming fashionable out there. In those sandy wastes they are usually a year behind the time, and it seems that the nightmare apathy whose numbing glamour the last trembling days of Buchanan cast upon the people, is resting to-day upon the dwellers of the stony mountains and the arid plains.[44]

WASHINGTON CORRESPONDENCE, 11 OCTOBER 1861

The howling dervishes of the Forward-to-Richmond school are satisfied with the quality if not with the degree of McClellan's movements during the last few days. The Anaconda again begins to show signs of activity. Not as in July, when the torrid fervors of the midsummer stirred him up to spasmodic and unfruitful effort, by which he accomplished nothing and came near dislocating his spine [*at Bull Run*]; but in a more decorous and sensible style, gradually unwinding his coils and playing them quietly in the sun till he has them under perfect control.

Banks still rests on the eastern marge of the Monocacy, with a swollen and impassable river before him, a tight rein on his men and the balance of power in his hands, ready to strike at an hour's notice in any of three directions. He is thoroughly *en rapport* with the head of operations here. That Sunday expedition of the President and the Secretary of War was for the purpose of full interchange of ideas and plans. Smith has moved his division inland to Lewinsville, the well-picked bone over which the hostile pickets have been so long snarling, occupying Prospect Hill on one side and Maxwell's on the other. McCall, with his division, has crossed the Chain Bridge and filled the footsteps of Smith's advancing columns, and now stands silent, ready, imperturbable, the coolest and most modest officer on the field, prepared to support any point of the Union semi-circle before him which may be exposed to danger. Further south, Fitz John Porter has moved forward and raised the starred bunting on Minor's Hill, whence in the morning its shadow may fall over Falls Church, and his riflemen may make a target of the rebel pickets on Barrett's Hill. At his left rests the division of Irvin McDowell, whose soldierly heart has been wasting itself away in the sorrow that came with defeat at Bull Run, and who now is beginning to feel the springing of new life within him in the glorious promise of coming work and certain atonement.

The advance was made on Wednesday. Yesterday while everybody was waiting for news of conflict, and able and enterprising newspaper men were haunting the headquarters for latest advices, and the slamming of every door produced hysterics at Washington, Gen. McClellan and his staff were galloping through the chilly mist, over the steaming and soggy roads, looking along the lines, rectifying mistakes and filling up omissions, and, in short, finishing well what had been well begun. The discipline of the troops is very cheering. They march well and behave themselves when they halt. A few days more will be spent in taking up the loose edges of the work already done, cautiously feeling the way to other points of advantage, and the general limbering of the muscles that precedes and prepares for violent exercise. Circumstances point strongly to the probability, that at an early day next week, a strong reconnaissance will be made, whose result will, of course, be most momentous.

Amid the breathless interest with which we watch the slow, steady progress of events around the Capital, we occasionally turn, with a curiosity no less keen, to the great naval expedition now fitting out, whose size, armament, destination and purpose give rise to the wildest vagaries of conjecture. Those who loaf by the Baltimore depot see occasionally a handsomely equipped regiment moving quietly off, and the sly wink and whisper float through the crowd, "Annapolis." The wharf rats and amphibious idlers who adhere like barnacles to the piers and shore craft that lie at the foot of Spring street in New-York look with lazy wonder at the bustle and stir that agitate the stately decks of the *Vanderbilt* and her ocean sisters, while the thump of hammers and the voices of artisans alternate with the creak of cordage and the rattle of coaling. A great expedition is certainly fitting out. When it will sail or where it will strike I don't know, and certainly would not tell if I did. I am glad to know that such activity exists, and it will be well for the country when the people learn at last that a man is not necessarily an ass because he is gray headed, and that the dignified reticence of age is not always the cloak for imbecility and folly. Mr. Welles has performed most admirably the duties of his most important office, and not the least praiseworthy point in his character is his total disregard of the silly and malicious attacks upon him from ignorant scribblers, when in many cases a single word from him would have settled the matter. He prefers to speak in his acts, and of late they have had pretty clear voices of their own. He is not done yet by a great deal, as you will hear before long. If the Navy Department does not give some especial cause for devout gratitude before November ushers in the roast turkeys of Thanksgiving Day, I will resign my commission as Brevet Prophet.

> And deeper than did ever plummet sound
> I'll drown my book.

It is the easiest thing in the world to make charges. It requires only cheek, and influence enough with journalists to gain access to "half a stick" of space. Papers like to print, also, what is spicy and slashing. It is far more piquant to say the Honorable Minister of Finance was yesterday caught picking the pocket of a blind beggar, than that the estimable gentleman was as usual hard at work in his office. Nothing flashes through the journals like a case of *crim con.* against a minister, or burglary by a Bank President. It is very delightful to men of imperfect moral perception, to consider that good men are no better than they should be.

The clamor against some of the departments here has been utterly groundless. A great part of it began in the city of Washington, among that servile herd, who having longed and striven for office since they were old enough to know the nourishment of pap, have snuffed in the air the scent of a coming Republican triumph, and have become Republicans for self-preservation, and now begin to think that to the victors belong the spoils of office. A seedy soul of this class, lounging through one of the departments, sees a place that will about suit him, being conspicuous and leisure-abounding. He lays an accusation of secessionism against the incumbent, and if Mr. Potter desires it, he proves it by at least half a dozen of his friends. They can prove anything they like. They could prove Mr. Republican, that you were seen, night before last, stealing a sheep from a Union farmer at Falls Church, and presenting it to Beauregard in a set speech of eight minutes and a quarter. They delight in names and dates. If the head of department does not immediately remove the suspected, and appoint the patriotic informer, the *New York Tribune* says he is known to be an idiot, and thought to be a traitor. Potter has done much harm and very little good with his Investigating Committee. Van Wyck, who runs a similar institution, whose special gird is at army contracts, after the fullest power, and the most lavish expenditure of time and money, confesses that he has found nothing yet worthy of report. A leather dealer who came here the other day, full of righteous indignation that no contract had been awarded him, and profoundly impressed with the belief that there was cheating around the board, after several days diligent investigation, having learned that every contract had been let on lower terms than he could afford to work for, went back to his tan-yard, and has not since called Cameron a thief.

And, gentle reader, don't you do it, till you know what you are talking about.[45]

WASHINGTON CORRESPONDENCE, 14 OCTOBER 1861

There has never been an age so completely enthralled by newspapers as this. They have begun to be taken as the absolute reflex of the will of the people and the earnest thought of a nation. Their utterances meet with an attention absurdly out of proportion to their importance. This is by no means the result of ignorance, but of a careless habit that we have contracted of getting our opinions and impressions of current events ready made. You meet at a hotel table a seedy individual with dubious linen, and he airs his ideas of the situation to the disgust of all his auditors. In the morning he prints those ideas in a leaded article, and the same people who snubbed him the night before, now read him with grave seriousness, and imagine they are grasping the embodied thought of the hundred thousand subscribers of the journal. It is really the same dilapidated nuisance of yesterday.

Another fruitful source of mistakes is diplomacy. We send abroad alarmingly dignified gentlemen, who go with vague ideas that the American eagle is to flap his wings in a defiant manner before all the specimens of natural history that adorn or deform the escutcheons of other nations. Too often, the Embassador is not a gentleman at all, and being painfully conscious of the fact, attempts by a bullying independence to cover the deficiencies of culture. One of our recent diplomatic representatives to Central Europe used to invite the nobility and gentry to his house, and after regaling them upon hard apples and corned beef would use up half an hour in a disquisition upon the advantages of water over all other beverages in a moral, dietetic and economical point of view. The disgusted and thirsty guests could go home meditating over indigestion and the social aspects of the semi-barbarous civilization of North America. Even when our ministers are of the very highest mental and social caliber, gentlemen by birth and ed- ·ucation, statesmen by earnest study and natural habit of mind, like Mr. Adams, still the conventions of diplomatic intercourse necessarily so hamper the free exchange of thought and sentiment, that the guarded utterances of Envoy and Secretary give no adequate idea of the feeling of their respective countries.

To these two causes, the confidence we place in untrustworthy journals, and the inadequacy of guarded official dispatches to correct the false impressions thus formed, we may attribute much of the unjust clamor against and distrust of England, which has been for some time so prevalent among all classes of loyal Americans. Because the London *Times,* with that reckless mendacity that has made it for years notorious, indulges in daily sneers at Republicanism as a gigantic failure, and takes to its bosom the ebony idol of slavery to hug unashamed in the face of the world, and because the clear and eminently decorous dispatches of Mr. Adams contain little to refute the impressions thus conveyed, we have fallen gradually backward one hundred years in our feelings toward England, and from the sea to the mountains the people have been learning again the long forgotten lesson of hatred to unprincipled, cotton ridden, perfidious Albion.

The very best information is beginning to dispel this illusion. From sources whose trustworthiness cannot be for an instant impugned, our Government has information that only the kindest and heartiest expressions of good will and sympathy are heard in the best circle of the best class of England. Recent conversations, in the unrestrained freedom of friendly intimacy with men so high in fame, and position, and power as Earl Russell, Mr. Layard, the Under-Secretary of State, Mr. Cobden, Earl Grey, Colonial Secretary, His Royal Highness Albert, Prince Consort, and the gracious lady, Victoria herself, evince only the most cordial sympathy with the Federal Government, and show conclusively that the bearings of this great controversy between civilization and barbarism, between law and anarchy, is as fully understood and appreciated in the Court of St. James as in the Cabinet at Washington.

It is not generally known, that after the battle of Bull Run, in the exultation that followed that unexpected success, the penniless Commissioners of the rebel States called upon Earl Russell to obtain that recognition they thought due to a Government that had so fully showed its *de facto* character on the field, *and were flatly refused an audience.* If we are beaten in this contest and the tottering rebellion grows firm on its legs, of course it will meet with recognition from every nation of Europe, but I am able to state with entire positiveness that no probability is at present more remote than the recognition of the independence of the Southern rebels at the hands of the Government of England. We hear often of the hard up Commissioners basking in the Cosmopolitan light of Paris, drinking cock-tails with wandering compatriots, and, in the language of admiring friends, "speaking French like a native." But whether it is that their French is better than their English, that their morals suit the gay carelessness of France more than the rigid decorum of England, or that their diminishing exchequer feels more at ease in economical Paris than in money-wasting London, it is certain that they always hail with diffidence and leave with gloom the chalky cliffs of Dover.

It would be useless to attempt to deny that the rebel cause has sympathy in England. The more ignorant and vulgar classes of cotton spinners, oblivious of the distinction between cause and effect, see in the pinchings of the blockade only the tyranny of Lincoln. A certain class of servile parvenus think it on the whole rather an elegant thing to admire the rebellion, as barmaids and lottery dealers in the North did for a while. A few of the aristocracy whose souls, encased in insular selfishness and timidity, saw only a standing menace and danger to England, in the growth and prosperity of the Great Republic, hail its supposed downfall with a joy born of cowardice, and indulge in indecent exultation over deliverance from the overshadowing and lowering peril. But all these are not England. The telegraph last week told us that "Sir James Ferguson, M.P., and William Burke [*Bourke*] had arrived in Richmond with dispatches from the Rebel Commissioners." Sir James is a sporting baronet of the same social ill-fame with that precious rowdy Grantley Berkeley, whom no gentleman would kick without instantly throwing away his boots, and Burke, whose name is Robert, not William, and is spelled Bourke, after the Celtic style, is a briefless young barrister of Irish parentage who, like John Mitchell, has a natural inclination for rebellion and niggers. If from these crumbs the C.S.A. can extract comfort, let them have it. They surely will get no comfort from the dispatches which as they say Sir James brought over in his carpet bag.

Of course we mean to fight this thing out by ourselves. We need no help, and would accept none. We would fight it through all the same, if the nations of the earth were leagued against us, and only God, truth, justice, civilization and law countenanced and upheld us. These are allies enough in any fight, for a great nation. Still it is not unpleasant in the storm and stress of this trouble, to know that the great heart of the world beats kindly with us, and aids us, as we only ask to be aided, by its honest good wishes and prayers.[46]

WASHINGTON CORRESPONDENCE, 14 OCTOBER 1861

There is great probability that the recent general review, by Gen. McClellan, of all the troops on this side of the river, will be the last that we will have in Washington before some decisive movement on the part of one or both armies takes place. Some of the newspapers have been debating the utility of the review, and grumbling about what they call "a day lost"—although their reporters were doubtless glad enough of any movement that could be manufactured into an item in these dull times.

A grand review does not take place every day, even in Washington, and being enthusiastically partial to martial sights and sounds, I felt particularly spiteful when the friend who called for me, by appointment, drove off, leaving *me* behind to get through the day as best I might—but not by any means a patient or docile sufferer from sickness. But a short time prior to the review I took a ride out to Chain Bridge, and saw all that was to be seen in that vicinity.

Out of Washington, through poor old Georgetown, looking as if all the clocks in the place must have stopped at nine o'clock, some still, hazy Sunday morning, and the natives had been, ever since, under the delusion that every day was Sunday—along the banks of the placid canal, tinged by the thick, overhanging foliage with a sombre green; past long lines of army wagons droning along the dusty road under the rays of the departing day—the dark Potomac overshadowed by the densely wooded heights that crown it on the other side—all of which bristle with unseen bayonets—bearing us company at a distance, while the other side of the route, for nearly the whole distance, is flanked by the stony faces of high, steep bluffs—on we went, passing many groups of soldiers bivouacking on the road with stacked bayonets, some of them stretched full length on the ground by the road side, to all appearances enjoying their siesta with supreme indifference to the hardness of their unpillowed couch, or the minor inconvenience of sun and dust. Dusty, dingy, sun burned and camp-hardened—but there was not a brown, tough hand among them all into which I would not have put my own, proudly and cheerfully. Others may have seen only an unshorn, unwashed crew of very ordinary men—to me they were the defenders of the Union—and many of them will fall fighting for the flag whose stars and stripes must ever warm my heart and brighten my eye with an enthusiasm inherited through a long line of patriots beginning with the illustrious Warren.

There, too, as we approached Chain Bridge, was the masked battery, commanding one of the most important points on the river—from its exalted perch on one of the highest peaks of the bluff. The unsophisticated civilian who recordeth this matter mistook it for a *wood pile* at first glance, but presently began to wonder what anybody could want with a wood pile away up there and in that prominent position. We drew up near some earth works that command the entrance to Chain Bridge, just as a cavalry company came thundering over it. They dashed off in an opposite direction to that by which we had come, and we followed more slowly, passing the site of a fort which is in process of erection. We saw two guns, one planted on an eminence a short distance up from Chain Bridge, and which sweep the river at this point. And we saw many deserted encampments as we went along—the occupants having been ordered across the river only that day. There was one division camped not very far from us, but the lengthening shadows warned us of the distant city, and so we drove to an eminence whence we could see the white tented heights on the other side—the encampments dotting the whole view before us until concealed by intervening foliage. The Star Spangled Banner floating high over all, and the sun suspended like a great ball of fire over the top of the furtherest hill—then we turned our faces city-ward, and fled onward with slackened rein through the coolness and dew of the evening.

The troops are nearly all on the other side of the river. But their removal has been effected so quietly and gradually that it has excited very little comment.

Gradually but steadily for the last few days we have been extending our pickets in the direction of Fairfax—the Confederates as steadily falling back. The general belief here is that an engagement must take place in the course of a day or so, but this is nothing very new or original, as all Washington has been "spoiling for a fight" for the last two months. I was at headquarters Saturday, and things wore a very brisk, business-like aspect. Officers continually riding up to confer with Gen. McClellan and his aides. The former remaining in until 11 o'clock, and up to his eyes in most important business— this deponent supposes. By the way, how the initiated—those who are behind the scenes and are in a situation to trace effects to causes—must chuckle over the manifold blunders into which the "specials" of leading newspapers are betrayed and ridiculously false scents which they are so often thrown off upon. It is not to be supposed that the Commander in Chief wants to have his plans bruited over the country either before or while they are in process of fulfillment, and that simply to serve the purposes of some ravenous reporter, who is intent only on distancing all his comers in obtaining the very "latest, most reliable and startling intelligence." Neither is it to be supposed that those who are necessarily acquainted with the details of these plans are willing to forfeit lucrative positions by unguarded or indiscreet disclosures in reference to the movements contemplated by those intrusted with the vindication of our national honor. But your true sensation reporter is not to be snubbed or put down in his pursuit after knowledge. If anything unusual is going on, it is his business to be on hand by fair means or otherwise. It is his business to "nose" out all he can of every proscribed matter—to watch for the slightest word or hint that may fall designedly or otherwise, from those who are in the secret. In his own line of business your professional news monger will match any detective in the land. A word, a hint, and he has his cue. Trust to him for the *details* for he well understandeth the art of making a mountain out of a mole-hill. It does not make the least difference to him whether the information is reliable or not. He's got an item—that will serve to pacify the public appetite for the hour at least; and that is all he comes for—he goes it neck or nothing, and the important and startling intelligence is telegraphed or written and posted instanter.

The professionals of this class are often most scandalously victimized— put on the wrong scent by those whom they are seeking to "pump," from interested motives. The papers publish *their* programmes of the plans and movements of the directions of the campaign most elaborately got up, and the parties most knowing in the matter, and laugh slyly at the success of their ruse. Well, they think, the papers must publish, and it is better that they should be misled, than to parade important matter prematurely—thereby damaging the interests of Government, merely from interested motives. So you may rely on it that all the "important intelligence" in regard to the contemplated movements of Government is only "made up" and pieced out by certain fertile imaginations. Of course, a man has a right to air his own surmises in regard to the course which will be pursued by the parties in power; but he has no business to put his views into the mouth of every Government official, simply for the sake of the éclat which will accrue to oneself from having it supposed that he is in the confidence of some important personage.

When Secretary Cameron left this city very quietly one day last week, it was given out that he had gone to Pittsburgh on some trivial business connected with the Department; but when he extended his journey to St. Louis, that which had only been whispered before—that his departure was in some way connected with the Frémont-Blair difficulty—was loudly proclaimed. Not long since there was an absurd story going the rounds about a certain lady, a wife of a Cabinet officer, whose influence with the President was so great that she procured the release of ex-Mayor Berrett and Mr. Emory. If those who have the least opportunity of judging may be called good authority, we shall run no risk in saying that the mistress of the White House possesses more influence over its master than any other lady, or any masculine either, for that matter, excepting one of his Cabinet ministers. And in connection with this, there is a little bit of gossip: all have heard the current story as to how Col. Wood, ex-Commissioner of Public Buildings, obtained his appointment. Besides being a very skillful diplomatist, he is also a very courtly gentlemen, and was for a time so much of a favorite with Mrs. Lincoln that she elected him a Master of Ceremonies at the White House. But alas! that differences will arise between the best of friends! It is said that Mrs. L. thought she had a right to control the affairs of an appointment obtained through *her* influence; but the *suave* commissioner was of another way of thinking, and so he resigned, and they are not friends any more. Others, however, tell the story differently, saying that the resignation was because the appointment was unpopular, and there was nothing given him to do. The East Room at the White House is being repainted and furnished up in view of the receptions of the coming season.

My impressions of one notability: Saturday evening there came very quickly into the drawing room where I sat conversing with an acquaintance, a well-looking elderly gentleman, tall and portly, of ruddy countenance, pleasing and intellectual features, and a particularly fine head. Notwithstanding that he sat so quietly and with such an unpretending air, with his plump hands crossed over his majestic front, I could not get rid of the impression that he was a man of mark, and was not much surprised when a mutual friend coming in designated him as "Senator Hale of New Hampshire."[47]

WASHINGTON CORRESPONDENCE, 17 OCTOBER 1861

Nothing decisive yet, but many favorable straws.

The Grand Army moves steadily on, resting well after each movement, and stretching out its far-reaching antennae to determine the position and gauge the strength of the enemy. We have occupied the country as far as four miles to the right of Lewinsville, and two miles and a half towards Vienna. As we approach they fall back, precipitately at first, then returning cautiously when they find they are not pursued. The wretched excuses for fortifications that crowned Munson's Hill when the rebels deserted it are rapidly giving way to works of strength and permanence. The stove-pipe that menaced the Capitol has been replaced by very talkative "Parrotts"; and the miserable-looking heaps of clay, that looked as if they might have been designed in some maniac-dream of Gideon Pillow, and erected by a very lazy detachment of first families on a very warm day, are forgotten in view of the substantial earthworks that are rapidly rising on the brow of this commanding eminence.

The rebels are still in force at Flint Hill and at Fairfax Court House. They are unable, in their present state, to attack McClellan with any reasonable hope of success. They can only watch and wait, hoping that he may run his head into the very apparent web they have woven for him with more than arachnean skill, until the thunder of the coast expedition startles their Southern legions from their tents by the claims of a nearer allegiance, or the rude notes of the Northern artillery suggest to them that McClellan has begun his part of the fighting.

Further up the river the monotony of camp life has just been diversified by a most agreeable episode. Col. Geary of the Pennsylvania 25th, going over the Potomac to get 20,000 or 30,000 bushels of wheat, which he thought entirely too good for the use of rebels, was attacked by a force of about 3,000 of the enemy, including bodies of infantry, artillery and cavalry. His little squad, less than half a regiment, stood their ground magnificently, and pounded away with their big gun until the enemy got so close that Geary considered it personally offensive, and ordered a bayonet charge, which was executed stunningly, resulting in the capture of a 32 pounder, which Geary exultingly calls a columbiad, but which is probably a howitzer. The enemy's loss was heavy—ours very light. "We shall save the rest of the wheat and other articles of value," Banks coolly adds in his quiet report of the action. The sentiment of Washington finds vent in the language of the ribald, "bully for Geary."

About once a week for the last month, certain New York journals of the spasmodic school sensationalize to the extent of several sticks [*of print*] over the closing of the Potomac. There is at present a lamentable and most piteous howl on this subject. Its justice may be inferred from the fact that the *Mount Vernon* passed down the river today, loaded with marines, and no shots were fired from the point where the batteries are said to be placed. They very frequently amuse themselves by firing at our shipping as it passes in the line of their batteries' range, but not a single sail has yet been touched. The Potomac is not closed—nor will it be. Before our friends over the way have completed their arrangements for that purpose, there will be a sudden gathering in of scattered extremities to sustain the stricken trunk in its death struggle.

In the West we hardly know whether to say we are hopeful or not. General Cameron is expected to return to-night, and vast results depend upon his report. If the givings-out of his confidential friends can be relied upon, he will report adversely to the present administration of affairs in the Western Department. It is understood already that the orders he has transmitted from St. Louis will very seriously embarrass all future movements of General Frémont, and perhaps necessitate his retirement from that command. What results would follow such a step we, at this distance, can only conjecture. We know the enthusiastic devotion that Frémont's brave soldiery feel for their dauntless commander. We know the wonderful magic of his name on the prairies and the mountains. It remains to be seen whether the Government can afford to sacrifice such a man. There certainly has never been a matter more thoroughly canvassed. The President and General Cameron are both incapable of any personal feeling in the matter. They will decide with equity according to best available information, and by that decision all will abide. This affair has already created scandal enough. It is time it were stopped.

Of late a plentiful shower of Kentuckians has fallen on Washington. The warmth and heartiness of the Union ardor there is most delightful to witness, when exhibited in this city, where the Jugurthine maxim of *omnia venalia* is entirely applicable. It is pleasant to hear these men from the neutral ground say, "It's high time, sir, for the hanging to begin." It is refreshing to hear these slaveholders say, "Frémont was right; you must take the crops and the niggers of these rascals or you'll never bring them to their senses." It was a wonder such sentiments do not blister the cheeks of Northern men who wish to make this war such a very civil one that if your enemy smites you on one cheek, you must not only turn the other, but also courteously present him with a sledge-hammer to pay his respects effectively.

Thos. H. Clay is here, as good a patriot as his father was and as his brother wasn't, and several of the Speeds—a sterling family—and the good and brave and noble Robert Anderson, whose pale, thoughtful, kind face I never see without a rebellious murmur at Fate which deprives us of so much use and him of so much glory. I am afraid he can never command again.

He has left behind him a good man. Sherman has a very winning way with traitors. No sneak, no coward, no liar has any show with Sherman. He understands both men and tactics, which is a conjunction not always found in Brigadiers. He said a very good thing to a cowardly Home Guard in one of the central counties the other day.

The provincial dignitary coming in, said, "General, we are terribly harassed by a secession camp in our county, and we wish you would send a regiment down to us."

"What is your county? Yes. Let me see."

The General turned to his map of Kentucky upon which he had designated by distinguishing marks the Union and secession counties, and found the county of the valorous Home Guard and all the adjoining ones, strongly Union. He turned to a Secretary.

"What is the name of the woman up North who believes in woman fighting, voting, &c?"

"Abby Foster."

"Well send for her, and a regiment of girls to take care of this gentleman and his Home Guards."

A roar followed from the bystanders. The provincial brother, perceiving instantly the position of affairs, turned to the group of amused listeners, and inquired blandly: "Won't some gentleman have the kindness to kick me into the street?"

There is no doubt that disaffections are greatly on the increase in the rebel army. Virginia is, as of old, the fruitful source of dissensions and rows. Floyd and Wise are engaged in an ugly plug muss, and the whole State seems about to join in it; while the Gulf State men think this Virginia matter amounts to very little, as they cherish, and have no hesitation in expressing, a profound contempt for Virginia honor and Virginia pluck. Altogether things are not looking comfortable in Dixie, and if, as the telegraph announces, Mason and Slidell are off to Europe, they have very neatly slipped the halter. They would be still cozier if they had been able to carry a plantation and a hundred contrabands in their porte-monnaies. As it is, it is to be feared that the horrors of the "shorts" will soon attack them, and the bookkeeper at "Meurice's" has positive orders not to receive Confederate bonds except at a discount of one hundred per centum. It is probable that they have not escaped, and this item was hatched to beguile the blockading fleet into laxity at another point; but no such salt as that can ever be deposited on the tail of so venerable a bird as Secretary Welles.[48]

WASHINGTON CORRESPONDENCE, 21 OCTOBER 1861

There is nothing more cowardly than capital. There seems to be a universal affinity everywhere between rags and recklessness, between affluence and error. There could have been nothing more senseless than the panic that brought the bulls to grief and the bears to ursine glee in Wall Street the other day, when Mr. Seward's calm circular to the Northern Governors on the subject of Harbor Defense was read. Recognizing the helplessness of the nation at this time, the importance of presenting an attitude to the world, which while respectful will command respect, and the great principle of political wisdom which commands us to prevent assaults by removing the temptations thereto, he sent this circular to the North and the world. Not that any cloud is seen in any quarter of the horizon—not that any foreign dispatches breathe any ominous whisper—not that we feared the cotton-thirst of money worshipping and insolent England—not that Mr. Dayton had learned French enough to suspect Napoleonic hostility, but simply because our harbors are not sufficiently defended; our armies are occupied with engagements which it would require several months to fulfill, and it is well enough to say to any nation whom malice or cupidity would tempt, "Stand off for a while." Still, the circular was unexpected. The newspapers had not discussed it as usual for a week in advance of its appearance. Wall street stupidity combined with Wall street cowardice to give the bears an easy victory, and sent the lame ducks waddling bewildered in ruin and dismay.

I presume the Secretary's reply to Lord Lyons' insolent letter will still further flutter the brokers. This affair must create great feeling. With all the professions of amity and good will that members of the English Government and masses of the English people are continually making towards us, the Foreign Office, or Richard Bickerton, Lord Lyons himself, is eternally, with a stolid impertinence unparalleled in civilized diplomacy, laying the foundation of a first-class row with this nation. This last instance of English genius, whose inanity is only equaled by its insufferable snobbishness, reads more like a burlesque than a grave international document. It says in effect to this Government, "You have no one in Washington intelligent enough to perceive or honest enough to follow the plain requirements of the Constitution. This is all very well, you know, as long as you make your own people the victims of your ignorance and tyranny. But it won't do for you to try that game on British subjects." That, with no exaggeration, is a fair paraphrase of the language of this most remarkable document. It is the apotheosis of insolence.

The reply of Gov. Seward is equally remarkable, for clearness, calmness and temper. Eminently proper and decorous in style, abating not a particle of the dignity of his position, and treating the screed of Lyons as if it deserved the treatment of a gentlemen and a statesman, he fully explains the circumstances of which Lyons complains, exhibits temperately the attitude the Government necessarily assumes towards its enemies, domestic and alien-resident, and only at the close does he make the intimation, which many think should have formed the body of the reply, that the Government of the United States must be permitted to interpret for itself the meaning of the Constitution, unassisted even by the luminous sagacity of the advisers of the British crown.

In all this there is no promise of hostility on the part of the English Government. It is simply bad manners, such as they invariably indulge in, when they think it can be done with impunity. The State papers of all weak republics are full of these bullying epistles from the Court of St. James. They are delighted with an opportunity of serving us in this style. They do not wish a fight, and they certainly will not get one out of us at present. They will not acknowledge the rebels, or attempt a break of blockade, nor commit any *casus belli.* But they air their snobbishness and incivility to the fullest extent, as long as our hands are fastened by other work. We meanwhile will take it all returning not insult for insult, but recording everything. Some of these days, when our family quarrel is settled, we have something to say to all out-of-doors.

In the meanwhile, the Legations are very busy and diplomatically quiet. Seward and Lyons maintain their old relations of friendly intimacy. Seward, Lyons, Mercier and Tassara went on a pleasure-excursion the other day into the Virginia camps, and returning, the quartette dined with the Minister from France. There is no sort of anxiety in the west end of town about the interruption of present friendly relations, though the talk at Willard's among people who know nothing about anything in particular is very knowing and mysterious. That unclean bird, Henry Wyckoff, has smelt something in the air and has come fluttering down from New York to nose out the news. I saw the vile creature at Willard's last night, creeping around crowds of talking politicians, listening and smiling, and remembering. It is an enduring disgrace to American society that it suffers such a thing to be at large. A marked and branded social Pariah, a monstrosity abhorred by men and women, he still associates with gentlemen, and you sometimes meet him in the company of ladies. There is not such a city of contrasts out of the realm of dreams as Washington.

The dispatch stating upon the authority of the *Cincinnati Gazette* that Frémont was to be removed created little sensation here, as it was generally disbelieved. The friends of Frémont are, however, constrained to believe to-day that the report of Gen. Cameron has been adverse to his longer continuance in the command of the Department of the West. How many days longer will be allowed in which to finish work already in hand cannot now be stated. Whether the result of the final deliberation of the Cabinet would be changed by a decisive success in the Southwest is equally problematical. The opposition has been so bitter and unretiring that his administration would be likely hereafter to prove a source of endless and petty vexations both to himself and all associated with him. The matter is still further complicated by the impression so prevalent among the people that all the opposition to him arises from his proclamation of freedom to the slaves of rebels, and thus assumes the form of a persecution for righteousness sake. Another shadow in the matter is the personal element, whose admixture all must deplore. It will be impossible, in the years that will read the history of this, to keep the people from calling this trouble the Frémont-Blair imbroglio. Another evil added to what one would consider already enough is the conflict of nationalities which has partly occasioned and will, perhaps, disastrously follow this contest. The Germans, who have been attacked with equal vigor by those who have most bitterly abused Frémont, will be apt to consider themselves involved in any rebuke of him. He has stood so constantly between them and the prejudices of Know Nothing jealousy which was envy as well, that they will seem to have lost their protector when Frémont is gone.

At the least, the whole business has been a terrible one, and the loss of a battle or two would not have compared with it in disaster and discouragement.

Here McClellan is advancing at the rate of about two miles a day, doing his work thoroughly, and driving stakes as he goes. The most despondent and least sanguine admit that if he keeps this style of thing up, he gets to the Gulf in the course of a year, which is so far encouraging. The enemy are still falling back along their entire line, with the seeming intention to adopt as their base line the course of the little stream of the Occoquan up along Bull Run and Manassas Junction. Their outposts are still as far east as Centreville, and even beyond that in the direction of Fairfax Court House. It was for some time thought probable that they would only make their stand on the south side of the Rappahannock from Acquia Creek to Fredericksburg and a line northwest of that, but those best informed of the topography of the country represent those positions as entirely indefensible against a body of artillery and cavalry. It is probable that they will elect to fight where they did before, but it is not probable that Gen. McClellan will allow any such choices to be made on that side of the house. He is pushing out in a somewhat different direction, having established his outposts at Drainsville, on Saturday, and is now making steady advances in a line considerably to the north of the path by which McDowell's disordered masses straggled out to the slaughter on the week that ended in the shame and confusion of the 21st of July [*at the battle of Bull Run*].[49]

WASHINGTON CORRESPONDENCE, 22 OCTOBER 1861

Yesterday, at noon, it became generally known that General Stone had crossed the Potomac, and that a spirited skirmish was going on upon the Virginia side of the river. The enemy were taken to be the remnant of the rear guard, who were covering the evacuation of Leesburg. Towards dusk, however, the skirmish began to assume more important proportions, and people began to realize that a battle at Leesburg was imminent. The meagre installments of intelligence that percolated through admitted channels into the street were far from satisfying the eager interest of the town. McClellan's headquarters were besieged by an anxious throng, whom the bayonets of the sentries only kept outside. In the telegraph office within, sat the President conversing with General Marcy, and evincing the deepest interest in the issue of the engagement, "because," as he said, "Baker is in the fight, and I am afraid his impetuous daring will endanger his life." In a pause of the conversation, the quick clicking of the instrument attracted the attention of the operator—he listened for a moment—then seized a sheet of paper and, writing a few lines, handed them to the President. An expression of awe and grief solemnized the massive features of Lincoln as he read the dispatch, and laying down the paper, after a moment's silence, he said, impressively, "Colonel Baker is dead."

When this was heard there was little further interest taken in the affair. Baker was a man of an energy so untiring, of a vitality so intense that the idea of death seemed always incongruous with him. It was very hard to realize that that mysterious fatality, which from the beginning of this rebellion has seemed to delight in making the best and the bravest the victims of the traitors' marksmanship, had at last snapped the golden thread of his life and sent ruin and dismay into the decimated ranks of his brigade. It seemed a mere matter of course that his death should involve confusion in his command. His fall was such a disaster that there was little to rejoice over, in the fact that the right wing of the grand army had crossed the Potomac and established a firm foothold upon the soil of Virginia, that both ends of the river railroad had fallen into our power, the long day of Banks' probation was at an end, that the coil of the anaconda was closing. All of defeat, all of repulse we suffered was in Baker's fall. The object of the movement was entirely successful; we gained important positions and kept them. Yet the loss of Baker fell so heavily upon all hearts that the city was mourning as if for a defeat, and business and social routine ceased in sorrow in the Departments of Government and the Executive mansion.

His loss will be sadly felt in his regiment. He was the object and central purpose for which every man enlisted. His regiment, the largest in the service, was collected from four States, in squads, in companies, in pairs, singly. Men would come a hundred miles, who had heard him speak, who had seen him in Mexico, when after the fall of Shields he had marched into enduring fame on the bloody field of Cerro Gordo. I heard one of the Mexican volunteers speak of him once, rudely but tenderly. He was a rural Captain in the war. He said that "the cussedest man in the army was Baker, when everything was agoin' right. He was always jerking up a feller for getting things wapperjawed. Everything had to be just so, in camp and in the ranks. But in a fight it was different. Then he was as cool and quiet as a parson, and spoke slow and steady, and as pleasant as if he was in a parlor, talking to ladies. In camp we sorter swore at him, amongst ourselves—but in a battle it would have been nothing but fun to die for him."

In fervid, impressive oratory, in that peculiar ability which starts a man to his feet unprepared, and enables him to do his best in the hurry and glow of debate, Baker has not left his equal in the Senate. His mind was always entirely made up on questions at issue, his convictions were firm and ardent, and his opulence of expression and imagery was absolutely inexhaustible. His few speeches in the Senate were startlingly original and splendid. They burst into the calm and quiet of that dignified audience like sudden thunderbolts. He was utterly at home on the hustings. His ready, sparkling, ebullient wit, his glancing and playful satire, mirthful and merciless, his keen sharp syllogisms and his brilliant sophisms, whose fallacies though undiscoverable were perplexing, and the fierce splendors of his eloquence, made him one of the most popular stump orators that ever lived. In the whole range of American oratory—I may go farther and say, in the boundless field of popular harangues—there is nothing finer than that wonderfully impassioned appeal which he thundered into the hearing of the aroused and electrified thousands of New York, when the gale of alarmed patriotism was surging into the tremendous ground-swell of public opinion that began with Sumter and will increase to Montgomery. Other men, by labor and toil, produce great orations, and when they are done, the fulfillment lags sadly behind the idea. But Baker never labored and never pondered; and so powerful and ready were the processes of his mind, so rich the resources of his imagination, and so warm and glowing the fervors of his spirit, that the creations of his genius came forth in the full perfection of their finished grace and beauty, with a light, and a life and a color, fairer than he had known.

His work was so easy that he never greatly valued it, but wasted in useless triumphs and purposeless achievements the flower of his life. He never coveted position or place, though never unmindful of an honest fame. He put gracefully aside the friendly hand that would gladly have adorned his shoulder with the single, and the double star, and proudly kept the eagle to which his noble regiment entitled him. He held the highest civic post to which his nativity permitted him to aspire, and wished no higher on earth. Careless of honors, and unwilling to receive promotion, in the full flush and noon of his life and his fame, the God of battles raised him by one grand brevet, far above the orders of departments or the suffrages of peoples. Above the applause of the Senate—above the acclaim of the battle-field, he stands promoted, in the heaven of the hero and the patriot.

A king might have been proud of the simple and hearty eulogies uttered last night in McClellan's room, where the President, and Seward, and Cameron, and McClellan, and another, in deep but not unmanly grief, received the heavy news of the fate of their friend. Each had his word of earnest sorrow and honest praise. The President mourned the sundering of the dearest of those ties that connected him with the memory of a happier and more careless day. The philosopher of Auburn [*William Henry Seward*] deplored the stainless statesman, and Cameron the dauntless patriot. And McClellan pronounced his bluff and soldierly epitaph: "I would rather have lost a battle than Baker; yet no loss is so great but it can be repaired, and though many a good fellow with shoulder straps go under the sod before this row is over, the cause must triumph."[50]

WASHINGTON CORRESPONDENCE, 26 OCTOBER 1861

A short residence in this city would entirely convince the most sanguine perfectionist that the day of complete regeneration is as yet far distant, and the vast capabilities of the human race in the matter of lying are just beginning to be fully appreciated. The liveliest and most charming fictions continually unfold and burgeon in the hot air of Willard's bar-room and kindred blossoms of the imagination shed their fleeting brilliancy upon the thoroughfares. I shall not, of course, refer to those wild flights that kill McClellan with silver bullets—tumble rebel generals from their horses in absurd attitudes—take the Navy-yard—cross a hundred regiments into Maryland on a mud-scow—and indulge in all the lofty tumbling of unblushing rumor sanctioned by every variety of instrument from the "reliable gentleman" to the "intelligent contraband." These stories live their little hour and perish with the evanescent glitter of the moribund dolphin. But there are stouter and lustier lies—lies which have vitality enough to survive a day's oral criticism—chrystallize into the correspondent's report—escape the telegraphic censor's destroying pen—go over the wires to the enterprising press of the metropolis [New York]—and spread their baleful influence through the provinces. These ought to be at once disavowed, when ascertained to be false, but their fond parents will never disown the bantlings. So that telegraphic dispatches from here are beginning to have a very ill-fame.

Let me notice a handful that seem to have received general currency of late.

The *Tribune* has succeeded to the place of wonder-monger on the Frémont question, vacated by the *Herald,* and announces every day that the head of the Western Department has been taken off, and the necessary orders issued from the Adjutant General's office. Frémont has not yet been removed; whether he will be or not is known only to one man, and that man, the President. After a resultless discussion of the Cabinet it was referred to the Executive for final decision. That decision, if made, has certainly not transpired. That the campaign in Missouri may be subjected to important modification is not unlikely. The impression is gaining ground here, that Price does not mean to fight, and that his freedom from baggage and his fleetness of travel will effectually prevent Frémont from overtaking him. A better place may be found for stationing the legions of the Union than the barrens of Southwest Missouri. It cannot be denied that the demoniac howl against Frémont is dying away. The President, always true to the great instincts of honor and justice that have so far saved and will save his Administration, has hitherto refused to submit to clamor or to condemn unheard. Whatever results may come he will have credit for that.

The splendid affair of Pilot Knob, the other day, coupled with the brilliant defense of Camp Wild Cat, and contrasted with the woeful waste at Conrad's Ferry [Ball's Bluff], have had some effect in opening the eyes of people to the fact that mistakes may be made in the East, and that the West has no monopoly of bad luck.

Some Northern papers are lashing themselves into a fine frenzy because, as they say, Gen. Scott is plotting the rise of Henry Wager Halleck over the ruined fortunes of Geo. B. McClellan. It is rather small business contradicting that. There is no one who more fully appreciates the sterling virtues of our energetic young chief, than does the battered hero of all our history;

and no one looks up to Gen. Scott with more filial love and respect than does Gen. McClellan. It has been the fondest wish of Gen. McClellan that Halleck may be placed in a command in the East, commensurate with his genius and his fame. He has strenuously opposed all plans for assigning to him a station at a distant field, and earnestly prefers that he may have the benefit of his labors and counsels. The whole story is an infamous creation of the *New York Herald*.

Another *canard* akin to the last, and one which seems a pet delusion of some of the aqua fortis abolition journals, is that McClellan is anxious to make a forward movement, but is prevented by the old fogy timidity of the Cabinet. They see the General in their mind's eye as a prancing and high-mettled charger straining on the curb, and panting to be gone, while the laggard and imbecile Cabinet stand by in an agony of dread, fearing to hold and fearing to let go. Every man who knows anything knows that the most perfect *entente cordiale* exists between General McClellan and the Administration. He frequently sits in Cabinet council, and his opinion is listened to with respect and attention. He has the confidence of every Department, and perfects his plans without let or hindrance, modification or suggestion. The President and the Secretary of State, against whom these shafts of ignorant malice are oftenest hurled, spend several evenings of every week in McClellan's private study, in friendly and intimate converse, discussing the campaign, and listening to the impressions and ideas of the alert young commander. There never was a more perfect *rapport* between the civil and military authorities than here to-day. The other day, McClellan said to the President, "I think we will succeed entirely if our friends will be patient, and not hurry us."

"I promise you," said the President, "you shall have your own way."

Does that sound as if the Administration were holding the army back?

Probably one of the most singular delusions of the day is the one that the Potomac is closed. This has been often iterated and often disproved by the provoking vessels that in spite of prognosis would insist on coming unhurt by the bristling batteries and calmly folding their wings in the Navy Yard. But latterly the report gained universal credence. There was a story, full of gunpowder and peril, rough with beetling ordnance, florid with theatrical effects, of shots fired at random from passing ships, and a sudden disappearance of acres of underbrush, exposing a grinning array of eighteen guns, commanding all the waters in sight of Mathias Point. There was no reason in the world to doubt this tale. Craven believed it, Dahlgren had confidence in it, McClellan received it. We admitted the Potomac closed. The *George Page,* trusting in something akin to it, came skulking out of Acquia Creek and cruised playfully around Budd's Ferry. Hooker's Brigade went down to reinforce Sickles. Everything down the river looked lively and business-like.

How marines can lie!

Last night Capt. Fox came up from the Lower Potomac and reports our vessels lying peacefully in the tranquil stream off the dreaded Point; no sign of a battery breaking the romantic scenery of the Virginia bluffs, and no enemy near enough to come within the ken of the Captain's glass. A highly enterprising contraband, who was sent ashore in the night, his sunburned complexion harmonizing with the shadows, reports "not a mouse stirring" within the wooded slopes of Mathias.

The occupation of the Maryland shore will soon be completed and the *George Page* exposed to the fire of our batteries. Our steamers coming up to Acquia Creek can intercept her retreat, and the Potomac be effectually weeded of its vermin.

There is little cessation of the stream of armed men pouring into Washington. The finest regiment in the service, perhaps the finest thousand ever enlisted, marched by the President's house on Friday. It is the People's Ellsworth Regiment of New York, selected from every town in the State with the exception of the cities of New York and Troy. Magnificent in physique and morale, well dressed, well equipped, well armed, officered by the perfectly trained Chicago boys and commanded by Ellsworth's friend and companion, Col. Stryker, lacking the effeminacy of the Seventh and the brutality of the Fire Boys, it unites the refinement of the one with the muscle of the other, and goes into the field animated by the loftiest motives of patriotism and the highest incentives to daring.[51]

Washington correspondence, 2 November 1861

Yesterday, Lieutenant General Winfield Scott retired from the Command-in-Chief of the Army, and to-day George B. McClellan assumes command. The warning encroachments of age have for many weeks been reminding the war-worn veteran that the days of his labor are drawing to a close. Only by the solicitations of the President and the Cabinet has his term of service been so far prolonged. But at length his system, worn out in the struggles of three wars, and three-quarters of a century of unremitting toil, began to give intimations that could not be disregarded, that absolute rest was imperatively demanded for the short remainder of his life. He requested that the President should withdraw his objections to his retiring, and the President, sensible of the earnestness of the request, could no longer refuse. In these last days the devotion and gratitude of the civil and military representatives of the Government to the old hero, whose record exhausts our warlike glory as a nation, have been most conspicuous and touching. The General has been often moved to tears by the evidences of unaffected and affectionate admiration and love that these concluding hours of his service have brought to his notice. The President and Cabinet called upon him to take farewell in person, and the young General who succeeds him, escorted him to the depot this morning with his full staff and a troop of cavalry, omitting no demonstration of affectionate regard. The general order in relation to the retiring chief, promulgated to-day, is a model of manly and eloquent eulogy. Thus honored and loved he goes to his needed rest, the greatest soldier of our history. The benedictions of a Government whose existence he sustained in its darkest hour, follow him to his home and dwell with him forever. The love of a grateful people, whose liberties he has saved inviolate, rest and will rest through time upon his memory. It is no vain trick of rhetoric to call him the savior of the century. It is by isolated acts of devotion and decision that States are saved and lost, more than by the ceaseless toil of years; and had Scott not come to Washington last winter, when treason was honored and countenanced in high places, and invested the national defense with the stern authority of military law, the Capitol had been to-day in rebel hands. It was his firm and determined grasp that strangled the serpent of nullification in its inception. It was his just and equable policy that adjusted conflicting claims in the far Northwest. Our history has few studies for art, in which his form of martial magnificence is not the chief and central figure.

The nation is fortunate in its new commander. It is seldom that a man so simple and so plain in his manners, so free from the ordinary tricks of popularity, and the ordinary appliances of journalistic influence, attains a recognition so sudden and so universal. The people repose entire confidence in McClellan. He has had nothing of that frenzied impatience to complain of, that forced Scott into error and disaster. Nobody in the country has called him a traitor or a coward because he has wished to be ready before moving. His Generals have relied upon him with entire confidence that they would have fighting enough as soon as they were prepared, and the President and the Cabinet have forborne to suggest the expediency of haste, or the necessities of the waning autumn. A little knot of howling dervishes, contemptible both in number and character, came hot-foot to Washington the other day possessed with the ridiculous idea that Lincoln and Seward were holding McClellan back, and feeling an inward call to protest against further delay, and fearing some compromise was patching up in the Cabinet which would end the war without either bloodshed or abolition. They called upon the President and the Secretary and gravely made their protest. They were quietly referred to McClellan himself. They found to their intense disgust that the Administration and the General thoroughly understood and confided in each other, and not a glimmer of intrigue or jealousy could be discovered to base a respectably plausible howl upon. They went silently, like Metamers, back to their wigwams.

It is an omen of great good to see the singleness of heart and earnestness of purpose that characterize the movements of men in authority here, in relation to the war. All ancient jealousies are laid aside. All scrambles for future footholds are forborne. The claims of conflicting partisans are growing feebler in the searching light of experience that demands in sternest tones that merit shall be the test of office. The unanimity of the Cabinet in a matter of such vast moment as the investing of McClellan with supreme command, is especially significant of this state of things. And in all things else we see the same purity of motive exhibited, save, perhaps, in one case, where the busy tongue of calumny has succeeded in poisoning honest minds against the brave commander in the West. But it is simply absurd to say that political hopes or jealousies had anything to do with the action of the Cabinet in the case of Frémont. It was simply an irresistible pressure from men whose position entitled them to consideration. The Administration had two courses before them—either to distrust Frémont, or, like David, to say in their haste all men are liars. Even those who should have been his friends broke faith with him. Let me instance Col. Parson Gurley, who, coming here to plead the cause of his chief, discovered instantly on his arrival that the man he had come a thousand miles to defend was a thief and an idiot.

When I spoke of purity of purpose, I meant, of course, nothing personal in regard to Adjutant General Thomas, the loftiness of whose patriotism is only equaled by the sparkle and brilliancy of his style. I can imagine how fondly he read and re-read the luminous pages of his unparalleled report, dwelling with ever new spasms of paternal delight at the exquisite minglings of sarcasm and pathos that adorn its long-drawn sweetness, until unable longer, in justice to the world to withhold from it the enjoyment of such a model of esthetic and warlike genius, he rushed to the room of his compagnon du voyage, Wilkinson, handed the bulky gem to the beery journalist, and gave orders to the telegraphic censor to "let her gush."

Beware of your heels, my asinine friend! Perhaps the lion is not dead!

It is the earnest hope of Gen. Frémont's friends that he will allow nothing to goad him into resigning his position in the army. With youth, genius and friends (and nobody can deny his possession of the three), there is nothing that the future may not afford to a man like him. He is the second officer in the armies of the Republic, holding exactly the position which McClellan held yesterday. Possibilities of vast utility and honest fame are before him—not to be lightly cast aside, in a momentary revolt of sensibility against a seeming wrong. It will not take many months of service to remove the stains which reeking calumny has spread over his name. There is a blank page of our history waiting for Frémont's name. He should not disappoint Fate and baffle auspicious Destiny.

I was talking, when this subject of Frémont beguiled me away, of the intimate relations existing between McClellan and the Administration. McClellan's house and Governor Seward's are on the same block both fronting the same square with the Executive Mansion, and nearly every evening, the President runs away from the affectionate and disinterested patriots who haunt his doors, with no disinclination to serve their country at a paying rate, and accompanied by only a single Private Secretary, trudges over to McClellan's headquarters, sometimes picking up Seward by the way, and talks war for an hour or so. Now that there is nothing between McClellan and the Government, and the possession of undoubted position relieves him of any embarrassment, we may look for great promptitude and energy in the conduct of the campaign. The President is himself a man of great aptitude for military studies, and his suggestions are often very valuable to veteran officers. Many of the orders issuing from the War Department are penned by the hand of the President. McClellan's promotion relieves him of great annoyance and anxiety in the management of his local plans, and bringing him into direct contact with the President and Secretary of War, gives him an added freedom which more than compensates for the increased responsibility. So he now expresses himself. He is the stuff of which great captains are made. He has no bravado, and no diffidence. As to that affectation of modesty so common, with which every man tries to convince you that he is utterly unfit to be left at large, McClellan has no conception of it. He knows about what he can do, and how he is to do it. He is perfectly possessed of the idea that the Government has done a very great thing in securing him to command its armies, and we all agree with him here.[52]

WASHINGTON CORRESPONDENCE, 4 NOVEMBER 1861

We are the most sensitive people alive, and the readiest to be vexed at slight causes. While all the world is at peace, and substantially in sympathy with us, our national bristles are continually rising on account of fancied slights. Moved by the insolence of the Foreign Office, and the after dinner platitudes of played-out novelists, we are ready to renew with England the passage at arms of 1812; and forget in the vexation with which we read these exhibitions of ill breeding, the hearty good-will and sympathy with which the general English mind regards us. This, every succeeding day is manifesting. Not a mail comes over the waters which does not convey a tender of service from officers in the British army, which is already represented in our ranks by the dashing and irresistible Adjutant General of Stone's division, who veils under the pseudonym of Captain [*Charles*] Stewart the aristocratic title of Lord Ernest Vane Tempest. The last steamer brings over a youthful ally, who offers to our cause the sword and the name and the blood of the honored and loved General Sir Henry Havelock. The prosecution of Col. Rankin is no test of the feeling of Canadians, and the professions of many honest years are not yet stifled by the voice of prejudice or smothered by the hope of gain.

From the nations of continental Europe the voices of encouragement and cheer are still more decided and free. The patriot soldier of Caprara [*Garibaldi*], whatever may be said to the contrary, has expressed for our cause the most earnest wishes and prayers, and nothing but the critical attitude of Italian affairs keeps him fretting at home, with a sheathed and rusting sword, waiting and watching. Many of the most distinguished of his compatriots are here already doing good work. There is enthusiasm enough in the Garibaldi Guards alone to fire all Italy with its contagion. The spirit that goes back in letters from the camp of De Trobriand's magnificent Frenchmen cannot but have a powerful effect at home. Whatever may be the plots and schemes that lurk in the tortuous brain of the impassive and silent Emperor of the French, the hearts of his people know no cause but ours. Old officers, whose lives have been campaigns, are offering their swords every mail. That the popular feeling is with us is too plain for argument, and no better proof of the cordial sympathy of the old nobility of the realm could be found than the presence among us of the Prince de Joinville, and those splendid young fellows of the Orleans blood, the Count of Paris and the Duke of Chartres.

It goes an immense distance towards softening the Democratic prejudices of a century to see the sterling manliness and quiet good sense of these brave young aristocrats. We have had several princely visitations of late years. In token of a magnanimity and kindness which we were willing to show for the oblivion of ancient grudges, we made great asses of ourselves over the Prince of Wales. It was up hill work. The highest praise the most devoted Jenkins would give was that the young man had all the amiable stupidity of the Guelphs. There are not a dozen Americans who can swear they ever heard him talk. His morals were infinitely better than his manners. He was subject to fits of somnolence at the dinner table, and his dancing was the horror of Fifth avenue. Yet we got up over him a very passable article of enthusiasm, except in Richmond, where our polished contemporaries called him a "squirt," and advised him "to go home to his ma."

When Plon-Plon came, magnificent in heaviness, corporal and mental, we did not bore him so much. We had too much to do to be enthusiastic. Toad eating is at a discount in war times. So Napoleon looked quietly about him, and went quietly home, and future ages will only record as incidents of his visit gathered from diligent search in the files of leading journals, that he dined with Mrs. Lincoln, shot grouse in Illinois, and that Lady Georgiana Fane and N. P. Willis once assisted at his enshrinement—or some other man's.

Plain people began to think princes a bore. Fortunately for the class, at this time came our young soldiers of the house of Orleans, to redeem from contempt the princely character. Roused by a noble and glorious impulse of abstract honor and principle, they came to fight in the Western world the battle of freedom and constitutional law. De Joinville came with them—three honest, earnest and gallant men. They threw into the cause they deemed the just one, not only their lives and their swords, but the moral weight of the influence of the proud, rich, exclusive ancient nobility of France. The clustering traditions of a thousand glorious years came with them, a pledge that wherever they went, honor would follow. Fully impressed with the Republican character of the Government for which they were contending, they took off their Princely titles, as working men take off their holiday clothes, and accepted their commissions under the styles of Captain Louis Phillipe D'Orleans and Captain Robert D'Orleans.

The busy days that are opening the campaign of McClellan give proof that they will never disgrace the high glories of their names. Always at their posts, alert, intelligent and subordinate, they are the pride of the officers and pattern of the soldiers. Their fine education and general information commend them to the society of the elders of the Administration.

Le Comte de Paris, the older brother, upon whose baby brow settled the shadow of the coming crown of France, in the days when his grandfather was king, is a tall, good looking young gentleman, who seems much older than he is, with short brown hair, and whiskers of the fighting color. His knowledge of English is perfect, though marked with a singularity of accent, and his command of English jurisprudence and English history is astonishing in a foreigner and one so young. There are few British statesmen, if we may judge by their speeches, so well acquainted with the workings of the representative and federal system as this young nobleman, whose time one would imagine occupied in softer and more fascinating pursuits than the barren study of law and government. His intercourse with the magnates here is distinguished by a quiet dignity and deference combined, that marks the better days of the *ancien regime.*

His younger brother, the Duc de Chartres, is a fine, romantic figure for historical pictures and school-girl dreams. Though very young, not twenty-one, he has already served with distinction in two wars. He stained his maiden sword in the cause of struggling Italy, and fought at Solferino at the side of *Il Re Galantuomo.* He also wears his hair *en Zouave,* and a blonde moustache which gives promise of future excellence shades a delicate and sensitive mouth. His eyes are rather those of a poet than a soldier—dreamy and soft and tender. He looks more like an artist in love than a warrior in wrath. If there was any society here, society would rave about him. His beauty, and dignity, and grace, and valor, and name would be an irresistible combination, storming the heart of any lady who admires (as who does not?) the poetry and romance of real life.

There is something in this unselfish consecration of life and labor to a cause in which no personal interest can be felt, which inevitably attracts the admiration and love of a candid world. The tone of baffled malignity with which the organs of the insolent cotton-worshippers of England have attacked these two brave young men is the surest proof of the significance and importance of their mission. It adds in certain small, though influential circles of Europe, the seal and sanction of legitimacy to this contest for national life. It affords a contrast so striking to the sordid and groveling motives which affect the cowardly policy of the upstart English Lords of yesterday, that their leathern cheeks crimson with rage and shame. You might be sure somebody was hit when howls like those of the *Times* and *Morning Post* are heard. Failing to debauch the mind of Europe to the level of their own avarice and jealousy, they will not be deprived of the luxury of throwing dirt at cleaner men who refuse to wallow with them. The long list of follies and blunders of leading journals show none more glaring than the base attempts of a few English papers to cramp the mind of the world to cotton worship, and repress the sympathies which the generous of all lands must feel in the uprising of a great people against a murderous and gigantic assault upon its life.[53]

WASHINGTON CORRESPONDENCE, 7 NOVEMBER 1861

After full and free discussion in the Cabinet it was resolved, upon the 23d day of October, to relieve General Frémont of the command of the Department of the West, and to appoint General Hunter to the chief command, until such time as his successor should be designated by the Government. The order was sent to the West on the following day, by the Hon. Leonard Swett, of Illinois, and a few days afterward, an additional order was sent, the purport of which has not yet transpired, but which probably concerned the future conduct of the war in that Department.

It seems to be well ascertained that the order first mentioned was expressed conditionally. It was not to be delivered if Gen. Frémont was on the eve of an engagement or in earnest pursuit of an enemy. As Gen. Curtis seemed to think that the propinquity of Frémont's and Price's camps was not sufficient to justify apprehensions of a collision, and as the chase from the Osage to Springfield was not sufficiently ardent to be called a pursuit, he sent the orders to their destination, and that they were delivered, and of their effect, the telegraph yesterday informed us. In the quick impulse of the disappointment that followed the promulgation of that order, we recognized the love of a trusting soldiery, and in the true and manly patriotism that rebuked those friendly murmurs into peace, we recognized how worthy of that love was John C. Frémont. And here for the present the Frémont question rests.

It is a source of regret to all the earnest admirers of General Hunter, and that includes all Washington, that the ill-advised gossiping of Adjutant General Thomas should have ever seen the light. It was a conception worthy of the honorable A. G. to force an honest and truthful soldier to make grave charges against his superior officer under the seal of official confidence, and then, in a spasm of senile vanity, publish to the world the changes thus made. We, who know General Hunter to be the incarnated soul of honor, can appreciate his chagrin on being placed, by this absurd indiscretion of Thomas, in a position so delicate and embarrassing. He is a man who would scorn advancement unworthily obtained, and nothing but official compulsion could ever have unsealed his lips in regard to the faults of his superior officer whose mantle he expected to inherit. Let him be absolved from all blame therein. The record of a long and blameless life, whose every hour has been spent in the service of his country, the confidence and respect of his superior officers, the love of all who are so fortunate as to know him, the fame of good works and the halo of suffering and sacrifice that crowns the memory of his glorious labors on that disastrous Sunday in July [*at Bull Run*], are enough to rescue him from the faintest suspicion of unworthy intent. If the *baton* of command must be struck from the hand of the people's idol, the heroic Pathfinder, it could fall into no grasp worthier than that of David Hunter, the best fighting General in the army.

Frank Blair is here, oftenest in company with newspaper men. He has been so excited by the Brevet that the *Republican* recently bestowed upon him, that he talks continually of strategy and battles. He knows all about the Western army, with the exception of his own regiment. He discourses unceasingly of the situation. He says of recent events: First, that Zagonyi never had any fight at Springfield. Second, that he got badly whipped in the fight that he did not have; and third, that he deserved cashiering for risking his men in a skirmish that never took place. Blair is never mincing in his manner. He denounces Scott with the same energy and vigor with which he vituperates Frémont, and bewails the misfortune that kept the old hero in our ranks so long. It takes away much of the sting of Frank's abuse to find you are blackguarded in such splendid company.

Henry Wager Halleck, the new Major-General with whom we expect to do great things, is here, and quietly awaits orders. He is a handsome and quiet gentlemen, who dresses well and talks well. Further than that, just now, we will not say. The Administration seem to be keeping him here for the present, and silently taking his measure, that they may cut out a piece of work for him to do. The time for chance allotments of Generals, depending upon the result of costly experiments for the final estimate, is past. The blunders that have enlivened each day at Fortress Monroe, the weekly flurries of timorous incompetency in Kentucky, the disasters in the Western Department have been a terrible schooling to the directors of affairs. Hereafter, greater caution in the choice of leaders, greater attention to special adaptability for special service, increased care in the distribution of appropriate troops, will soon be seen in the war movements of the Administration.

Let me put a few rumors to bed. General Wool has *not* resigned and evinces no disposition whatever to do so. He is champing the bit at Fortress Monroe with all the energy of fifty years ago. He is a good man to have there. He is an accomplished and thorough master of the art of defense, and he holds sound and refreshing theories on the contraband question.

Halleck has *not* been assigned any command, but is in frequent consultation with Gen. McClellan. He will probably not take charge of the army of the Potomac, as the commanding General wishes to retain command himself. He is frequently spoken of for the West.

Thurlow Weed and Archbishop Hughes have *not* been sent to Europe as Commissioners Plenipotentiary, to circumvent Slidell and Mason. The Archbishop sailed to-day, and I learn that Mr. Weed will soon follow, going to the continent upon an errand entirely voluntary, which will act upon the public sentiment there entirely unofficially and without connection with either ours or any European Government.

And this brings me to state that the advices brought over by today's mails are said to be most cheering and hopeful, evincing the rapid growth and manifestation of a feeling in England and in France that will effectually surround our cause with what it has to a great extent hitherto lacked, the earnest sympathy of the civilized world. It seems that an association of Secessionists resident in England, and a number of their sympathizers, have recently projected a line of steamers to run from Liverpool to Charleston, and have applied for countenance from the Foreign Office, stating at the same time that if the Government declined protecting them, they only wished permission to protect themselves. Earl Russell answered that her Majesty's Government, so far from favoring such an illegal scheme, would utterly discountenance it, and if they persisted would turn them over to the tender mercies of the American cruisers; which was rather rough on the susceptible feelings of the bold privateers.

Another report is that Prince Napoleon has reported to the Emperor, as the deliberate conclusion derived from his visit, that the South have neither justice nor resources in their cause, and that the North must conquer. All which we knew a good while ago, but are glad for Napoleon's sake that he knows it.

I can only glance at this to-day as the mail closes. If confirmed, you will hear more of it.[54]

WASHINGTON CORRESPONDENCE, 11 NOVEMBER 1861

The air of the Capital yesterday was jubilant with the paean-strains of exulting newsboys, who piped in a patriotic treble around the corners of Pennsylvania avenue, "Ere's your extry Chronicle! Stars and Stripes a-floating over South Curliny!" It was, of course, a very pleasant thing to hear that our fleet had safely braved the possibilities of coast defense and the dangers of the surf, and had come safely to their haven. But a keener zest was added to the enjoyment of all who heard the news, by the fact that the soil of that contumacious State, from whose fell pestilence of treason spread the contagion that blasted her neighbors, was now to suffer in earnest the horrors of that dread arbitrament which her swift hands had invoked. It fulfilled the utmost demands of poetic justice, that the still proud city of Beaufort, sitting in the quiet reverie of wealth and ease upon the idle shores of the tidal river, cinctured by its net-work of guarding islands, careless of war and contemptuous of trade, should first cower beneath the avenging footsteps of the hard-handed chivalry of the North, and should bow in the bitterness of defeat before the advancing tread of the base mechanicals of our swarming cities. It was well that this crusade against the usurping divinity of cotton should first assert its invincible prowess upon the very throne and center of his power. For in the fair islands of that amphibious land, where the still waters steal lazily through the sluggish lagoons, and the clear sunlight is always propitious in the endless summer skies, the powers of nature seem united to render homage and service to this white monarch of the Carolinas. The whitest and softest, the silkiest and longest-fibred cotton grows undisturbed among these river-girdled islands, and spreads to the tropic airs the virgin beauty of its bloom. This castle of aristocratic indolence, this seat of the blackness of the primal barbarism, this chosen home and realm of the Cotton-King, now wakes from its dream of lazy years, and finds itself thrilling with the strange new life of the North. And all the people say it is a good thing to do.

Some years ago, the United States Government had some intention of establishing a navy yard at Beaufort, recognizing the beauty of the situation, the splendid harbor and the vast unimproved advantages of the site. A horror fell on Beaufort at the news. Hideous visions of creatures in red shirts, smelling of tar, who got up early and worked all day, floated before their minds' eyes. A dim premonition of the possible effects of vulgar industry upon the tone of society—a fearful foreboding of the contingencies of Yankee association, came up before the general imagination of Beaufort to haunt and harry. A stern and indignant protest was written in blue ink on rose-colored paper, whose perfume was far more irreproachable than its orthography, in which the agonizings of harrowed sensibilities mingled with the graceful escapades of exceptional grammar, and was sent to the powers that were; and the gentle seductions of the potent spirit of Cotton melted the heart of the Administration, and the blight of industry passed from the air of Beaufort. How infinitely delightful to the Democratic mind is this swift influx of invincible workingmen into the quiet of this exclusive town! There is a wild justice in history.

Not only in its poetry and its fun is this thing notable. In effect it is a great incident of the war. Here will be tested the Southern ability to defend their coast. If they fail here, where they expected us, of course they fail everywhere. If the Union troops make good their lodgment here, no earthly power can prevent the fatal cordon of fire from creeping around the whole periphery of the revolted States, and rendering resistance as foolish as hopeless.

Here, too, is to be inaugurated, or tested, at least, the great system of cotton exportation. From this port probably will first go out the peace offering of cotton to an angry world. This will hush the hungry murmurings of Lancashire and the early howl of riot in the provinces of France. And here, too, will first be seen the unknown effect of the linked shout of "Union and Liberty" sounding into the dull ears of the waiting contrabands. Will they consider the constellated banner of the kind invader the promise of a vague and traditional good, or will the incessant teachings of a degraded lifetime associate it with everything the childish mind knows of cruelty, rapine and ravage?

Of all these things we as yet know nothing at all. We build these conjectures upon the foundation of two sullen lines in the *Richmond Enquirer,* which inform us that "the Federals are marching inland from two points," doubtless to strike the railroad connecting Savannah and Charleston, at Pocolalego. A surreptitious chat with the wheelman discloses the rumor which is blanching all cheeks in Norfolk, that the Hessians have taken Beaufort, and that the Court House is quivering with high-bred indignation beneath the polluting shadow of the Federal flag. This is very nice as far as it goes. The unusual reticence of the *Enquirer* surely betokens no ill to us. We need only possess our souls in patience for a very short time, and our returning dispatches will bring us tidings of full glory and triumphant success.

Even then, the fleet is far from being *functus officio.* There must be a nice little job attended to at Fernandina. Gen. Braxton Bragg will never forgive us if we don't pay our respects to his yellow flagged fortifications at Pensacola. Galveston Bay is said to be a good harbor, and Mobile stands seducingly near our line of operations in the Gulf. These waiting peoples must not be much longer kept in suspense. Then the volcanic activity and irrepressible enterprise of the fighting lawyer of Massachusetts, General Benjamin Franklin Butler, cannot be kept under the recruiting bushel. The energy that is continually getting him into musses at home would be much better worked off by a little pocket expedition of his own, by which he could take some important island and no end of glory. That some such command is shortly to be given him seems to be the general impression at headquarters. He will give an admirable account of himself, for though in his character you may discover elements of vanity and arrogance which somewhat mar its symmetry, yet his worst enemies cannot call him unsoldierly, or deny him the possession of those rare native powers which place men at the head of armies in trying times.

It is needless to say that the expedition, if successful, will very seriously derange the plans of the enemy throughout his territory. It is too much to suppose that the gulf regiments now chafing for a fight on the border will longer remain idle at such a distance from home, when the invader's footstep is on their native heath, and nothing binds them to their place but the cob-web of federated delegated authority, opposed to the triple-twisted cable of State Rights, strengthened by the instincts of home attachment and the preservation of property. There is reason to believe that so early as yesterday, the still Sabbath-sunshine lighted the large numbers of retiring rebels on their homeward way. In front of Heintzelman it is sure that there has been a sudden and important withdrawal. Demonstrative cavalry flurries from the direction of Leesburg warrant the opinion that this seeming activity is meant to cover a retreat. The line of their Potomac batteries, which it is quite certain they expected to be attacked, have very recently suffered great diminutions of strength, as we are credibly informed by scouts that came in last night.

The coming week will probably justify the sagacity of the views of those who planned this great armada and insisted upon the logical consequences of its action.[55]

WASHINGTON CORRESPONDENCE, 13 NOVEMBER 1861

If the interests of the American Government suffer in Europe, it will certainly not be from the want of the ablest representatives. In the first place, the Ministers appointed by Mr. Lincoln are generally men of ability, even if not always of that peculiar style of education which fits men for diplomacy. Nobody can deny to Mr. Dayton the possession of great and solid statesmanship. The worst charge that can be made against the Legation at Paris is that French is a language as unknown as Hottentot, and no immediate likelihood exists of the deficiency ever being supplied, for Mr. Dayton is too busy to learn a new language. His son is a Jerseyman born, and of course is never expected to learn anything; and the Secretary of Legation, "Bill Pennington," of Newark, who was thrust neck and heels into the Legation on account of the entreaties of the "heavy father," will have to postpone his French studies till he acquires enough English to enable him to make a decent appearance in society; and that, according to present appearances, will take from now till doomsday. This, of course, is unfortunate. It arises from the strange delusion existing in the minds of fond fathers, that confuses their ideas of public offices and idiot asylums, and persuades them that a half baked youth, who was never able to take care of himself, is the very man to take care of the State, and is encouraged by the twin delusion existing in the minds of rulers, that fond fathers are to be gratified, when they carry precincts in their pockets. Thouvenel, the French Minister of Foreign Affairs, speaks no English. Our Legation speaks no French. If it were not all plain sailing in Paris now, our rigging would certainly foul.

England is a harder nation to manage, and there we are perfectly represented. There is probably not a man among all our people who is so entirely fitted by life and reading for a minister plenipotentiary as Mr. Adams. It is a happy circumstance, considering the intense English reverence for blood, that he is the third in the lineal course of descent from the first American Ambassador to the Court of St. James. Our history affords no equal instance of inherited fame and talents, as is presented by the names of John, John Quincy, and Charles Francis Adams.

To Spain, Carl Schurz has carried the learning of a laborious youth and the energy and zeal that have made him so conspicuous in his turbulent manhood. In spite of the dreary prognostications that heralded his departure, he has taken his place with quiet dignity in the front rank of our diplomatists and the active brain and unresting spirit that have always made their possessor the idol of friends and the terror of foes, will now be equally efficient in the service of his country. And Harvey is outliving at Madrid the suspicions of his former *Tribune* employers, and Marsh is quietly studying his two hundredth tongue at Turin, and Motley is delving in the libraries of Vienna, and Judd is jolly and merry, and popular at Berlin, living in the finest house in their Belgravia, and riding after the fastest horses in the star spangledest carriage in Prussia—at home and abroad, a wonderfully indefatigable and genial man. And Cassius M. Clay is chafing in St. Petersburg as in a splendid prison. He catches the roar of the distant battle floating over the sea, and his proud heart is breaking that he is not in the fray. He sends over in his dispatches piteous appeals for recall, and fears that all the bloodshed may be over before he gets here. He has great military talents. It is not improbable that he may yet, in the front rank of the lately-roused Kentuckians, renew the efforts and the triumphs of his younger years.

Everything would seem to be going well in Europe, in spite of Sandford, the inevitable and unabashed, who exhibits a wonderful facility in getting himself and others into trouble without any possible cause. You remember his latest exploit: on hearing that Garibaldi had expressed some intention of offering his sword to his former country, he posted off to Caprera to tender, on his own authority, the post of Major General in the army to the Italian partisan. He has for the present subsided on the swell of reputation that followed that luckless dash, and quietly waits at Brussels, biding his time. Events show many opportunities for persistent donkeyism, and you will hear of Sandford again.

Barring Sandford, we are respectably represented. One would think that, being at peace with Europe and morally certain to remain so, there would be no occasion for any further increase of our diplomatic force abroad. At first glance it would appear so. If we considered only the accredited Ministers of our own Government, and the appointed emissaries of the insurgent States, we would rightly conclude that no harm could come of the Southern missions. But the springs that influence public feeling in Europe are not always exposed to the light; and it is certain that the most earnest and untiring efforts are making to bring down the mind of Europe to the level of the Manchester school. Information is continually received here of this persistent effort among the capitalists and the people, even after the attempts at national recognition have signally failed. Such influences our ambassadors cannot, of course, in their official capacity, counteract. They must be met on their own ground, by private citizens whose feelings of patriotism and loyalty furnish them with motives as powerful as the hope of gain to the apostles of cotton. As long as the interests of the cotton Confederacy were confided to the awkward hands of Yancey and King, and Mason and their confreres of the ward-politician school, there was nothing to fear from their diligence. The more of such, the worse for their cause. The influences proceeding from Manchester and Lyons are far different. There is no apparent tinge of absurdity in what these hived advocates say. They make no silly appeals to principles of justice, for an utterly unprincipled cause. They make no claims to virtue and patriotism. They talk only of money and manufactures; they do not waste their time cooling their heels in the antechambers of Kings, but go to the counting houses of moneyed men and swear by their ledgers. In the social world also, these paid evangelists of rebellion are beginning their operations, toiling with the last spasm of a desperate cause to make treason respectable in Europe.

Meanwhile, the greater part of our Northern tourists have come home. Those who would have been most useful to us in Europe have hastened home to fight for the cause they deemed in danger. We were likely to be left almost entirely unrepresented in some of the most influential classes of continental society. At this juncture a number of patriotic citizens, distinguished for high character and past services, being incapacitated by age and infirmities from serving their country on the battle field, proffered their time and their energies to the cause of constitutional liberty, to be used unofficially in any capacity which was deemed expedient, and the names that appear on the passenger lists of recently-sailing steamers would seem to indicate that their offers had been accepted. Thurlow Weed speaks for himself, in answer to the infamous falsehoods of the *Independent*. Archbishop Hughes crowns a life of good works by this glorious sacrifice of ease and comfort. Edward Everett throws into the scale of truth the rich treasures of his vast erudition and experience. John P. Kennedy will go, it is said, to speak for the maligned and misrepresented Border States, and it is rumored that Bishop McIlvaine will add to this volunteer mission the saintly beauty and sanction of his perfect character. In such hands the interests of the country are utterly safe.

But before they are there the news of the Union victories will make their mission unnecessary. The triumphant thunder of artillery at the gates of the cotton islands and the shout of Western exultation at the magnificent stroke of Nelson in Kentucky will fall on the ears of the trading world, a most unanswerable argument to prevent investments in such a sinking fund as the bonds of the C.S.A.[56]

Washington correspondence, 18 November 1861

The capture of the Southern confidence men who sailed so jollily past Fort Sumter a few weeks ago, and whose escape from the grim teeth of the blockading squadron was hailed with such premature exultation by all the Southern press, has furnished to the volatile population of Washington their allowance of gossip for the last two days. No occurrence since the war began has been received with such unalloyed satisfaction as this. Previous seizures have been mainly of the smaller sinners, weakminded and indiscreet border politicians who were induced by their Southern betrayers to become the mouth piece of alien treason, or unfortunate wretches whose folly or necessity has forced them into the ranks. No one of the ring leaders of this gigantic crime has as yet been caught. They have kept themselves safely out of the reach of possible danger, and sent their deluded tools to fight and bleed on the border. A hope that Floyd would fall into the meshes of the law for a while enlivened us, but after bombarding Rosecrans for a few days from a healthy distance, he became aware of the presence of Policeman Benham, and stole thievishly away. He and Wise, the maniac spouter of Accomac, are spared to each other for the present, to indulge in a tonguey warfare in which all charges on both sides are true.

If from the whole scoundrelly calendar of infamous names which have become identified with this rebellion, we had selected two to serve as representatives of its meanest phase of criminality and to receive a representative punishment, the suffrages of the nation would have fallen upon Mason and Slidell. Davis and Stephens are doing as well as we could ask already. Floyd is disgracing disgrace, and Toombs is falling into the obscurity which has already entombed the pestilent agitators of the Sea Islands. But Mason is the best possible representative of Virginia treason. Better than Wise, for Wise is a frantic old babbler who is hardly accountable for the crimes that have their origin in congenital follies. Better than Pryor, for Pryor is not a representative of the blue blooded aristocracy of the Commonwealth, and is at best but a plebeian and a bullying coward—a man bankrupt in character and pecuniarily out-at-elbows. Mason represents everything that has entered into the structure of this rebellion. He exults in the pride of birth, for he can look back to a long ancestry, no man of whom ever did an earnest or an honest work. He looks over wide spreading acres of tobacco land, tilled by contrabands of graduated colors, and sends yearly to the South a promising drove of his animated agricultural engines. He has not been out of office for many days since he cast his first vote, and probably even yet jingles mournfully in his trousers pocket the remnant of the last installment of salary he drew from the Government he was plotting to destroy. His mouthings in the Senate were always the loudest about "my honored State," and the grey breeches and coat into which he defiantly inserted himself was the first protest entered by the rebel barbarism against the aggressive civilization of the North. Mason will do for the average Virginian.

But Slidell is a different style of man. He unites to the arrogance and undemocratic sentiment of the extreme planters the shrewdness and phlegm of the Northerner. He is a native of New England, and the largest farmer in Louisiana. He is a man of fine acquirements and vast acquisitions. He carried brains and education enough from the North to make him fit company for cultivated men anywhere, and he stole land enough in the South to support him in a style which excited all the flunky soul of Russell into a paroxysm of servile admiration. At home, in the midst of the far-stretching miles of rank fertility and luxuriance that composed his Houmas plantations, surrounded only by the cursed pariahs of a stricken race, or the more slavish Caucasian ministers of his will, his mind became filled with the fantasies of absolute command, and the dignity and worthiness of republicanism faded utterly from his contemplation. Wherever he went, the blight of insincerity that waits on great wealth followed him. He was doomed to hear no words that were not paeans to his praise. His constant attendants were flatterers and sycophants. It was not to be wondered at if, from his experience of Washington and Louisiana, he should adopt the contemptuous opinion of a barbarian prince centuries ago, and say "omnia venalia." So by his wealth and his success came the ruin of John Slidell. The fumes of servile incense entered his brain, and the grand structure of Republican Government looked mean and common to him. With his whole heart and mind and soul he entered into the scheme of destroying this simple and beneficent structure. His vast influence was inexorably used. His countless wealth was devoted to this object. In the first attempt he and his confreres succeeded. The Charleston Convention broke up in ridiculous disgrace, and the Kentucky Lucifer was nominated at Baltimore. And John Slidell and his friends went diligently to work "to fire the Southern heart." In this they succeeded. And this fire of the Southern heart will be their funeral pyre.

Senator Mason and Senator Slidell will be very good men to hang.

When the *Theodora* slipped the blockade there was great rejoicing among the ungodly. It was thought a very good joke on the blockade, and Lord Lyons remarked "that there were only three ports on the coast effectually blockaded—Washington, Georgetown and Alexandria," which was the sharpest thing that that rather dull nobleman ever said. When the rebel Commissioners got to Havana, they thought they were safe. They would have been with ordinary cruisers. But Captain Wilkes and his associates were not ordinary cruisers. They heard of the obnoxious arrival, and remembered that Fox had once said, "Men lose their commissions for cowardice and inefficiency, not for zeal and well intentioned imprudence." They were not perfectly satisfied of the legality of the proceeding, but were entirely sure of the justice of it. They thought they would happen around in the narrow channels of the Bahamas about the time the *Trent* would pass with her rebellious cargo, and take the Southern wanderers home to their uncle. They did it, and it was considered a good thing to do.

There was extraordinary rejoicing in Washington over the news of their arrival at Fort Monroe. Everybody knew them here and each had some instance of snobbishness or disloyalty to relate. Strangers who only knew them through their acts were glad that the whirligig of time was bringing round its personal revenges, and even the diplomatic body seemed pleased at the sudden extinguisher applied to absurd pretension and arrogance. The messengers at the Department who had been snubbed and insulted by them in former days, grinned irrepressibly, and Irishmen on street corners chuckled, "I'm thinkin' the dirty rebels will not be afther hangin' Corcoran *just yet*, any way." So small an affair never was so merrily hailed.

The brave fellows, who rather thought they were transcending their instructions, when they took the roving diplomatists, were not so far wrong as one might at first suppose. No right is more clearly defined by the law of nations than that of stopping *in transitu* a bearer of hostile dispatches on a neutral vessel. It may be doubted whether the *San Jacinto* would not have been justified in seizing and confiscating the *Trent,* according to the highest English authorities on neutral rights. It is a case far different from that of seizing State prisoners on a neutral vessel, when they have taken shelter there in trying to escape from their own country. Such asylum is held sacred by all civilized nations. But the English Government has already recognized the Southern cabal as a belligerent power, and placed them clearly on that footing. Mason and Slidell can therefore only claim the protection accorded to Ambassadors of a country hostile to us. In this case, English authorities are clear and explicit. Sir W. Scott says, (Robinson's Admiralty Reports, Vol. 6, page 461,) "The limits assigned to the operations of war against Ambassadors by writers on public law are, *that the belligerent may exercise his right of war against them, wherever the character of hostility exists; he may stop the Ambassador of his enemy on his passage;* but when he has arrived in the neutral country, and taken on himself the functions of his office, and has been admitted in his representative character, he becomes a sort of *middle man,* entitled to peculiar privileges, as set apart for the preservation of the relations of amity and peace, in maintaining which all nations are, in some degree, interested." In this clause, which so strongly asserts the immunities of Ambassadors, the very unqualified assertion which is made of their liability to seizure *in transitu,* coupled with the elaborations of their subsequent immunity, is the clearest proof of the undoubted legality of captures such as the one just made. Of course, there can arise no question that the proceeding was one eminently expedient and just. It is rather comfortable to learn, also, that it is entirely legal.[57]

Washington correspondence, 24 November 1861

The spirit of careless enjoyment is beginning to revive among the citizens of Washington. The gloomy aspect of distrust and apprehension is vanishing from all countenances, and the city is growing as gay, as jolly and as dissolute as in the flush times that are gone. "Willard's" is rapidly regaining its proud pre-eminence of being the most crowded, extortionate and uncomfortable of caravansaries. The Avenue is enlivened with other conveyances than ambulances, and the tiresome flood of uniforms on the pave is giving way to the increasing incursions of Northern beauty and fashion. There are sounds of revelry by night in the stately mansions of the West End. There is the jingle of coin and the rattle of chips in the brilliantly lighted and grate-guarded dens, where fortunes are lost and won, at the turn of the merry pasteboard. Round, rosy and rascally, the contractors swarm at the hotels and on the sunny sidewalks, and the churches on fine Sundays are filled with the flashy silks and the baggy broadcloth of this new-born shoddy aristocracy. Public amusements, which have languished since Abraham was President, are reviving in the revival of good times, and people are finding time to laugh again.

The melancholy little theater, whose mirthfulness has been so gloomy since the dark days of April, when the "Star Spangled Banner" was hissed, and the scared little band struck up a dreary attempt at the "Marseillaise"—when Dixie was popular and loyalty was outré—is now renewing the glories of its earlier days; its sticky actors inject patriotic gags into the farces, and its heavy females do Drake's Address to the Flag. In the revival of the drama a new star has risen here, a very beautiful girl named Josephine Chestney, a full and splendid South Carolinian, with sweet dark eyes and bonny brown hair. Everybody goes to see her, and those who go early get all the seats and leave an eager crowd outside, who speak profanely of the little theater. She is worth going a great way to see, for she looks and walks and talks like a lady, and one of winning beauty, and delicate fancy and lively wit. This is something very rare on the American stage since those evenings when Mrs. Mowatt charmed away the young heart of the Richmond irresistible, Ritchie; and Jean Margaret Davenport left the stage disconsolate, to assume the role of First Lady in General Lander's household. If Miss Chestney will study her books, and respect herself and her art, and not flirt too much with squirtose Lieutenants, you will hear of her some day.

The burnt-cork fraternity have also come down in an avalanche upon Washington. At every corner their emissaries stand distributing play-bills. The "Canterbury" of New York has a branch establishment here, and on pleasant evenings you may find the heavy Pennsylvanians in the smoke-clouded rooms spending, in this refined relaxation, the wages of shoddy. The

Knights of the Tanbark are renewing their ancient honors, and Joe King's Hippodrome seduces, with lights and music, the idlers of the Avenue to enter and rejoice in the bisexual graces of the Zoyara, whom Josephus Rex elegantly styles the Cleopatra of the Ring.

But *faciles principes* as caterers for the public amusement stand McClellan and Herrmann. There has never been seen, since wars began to be fashionable on earth, such a brilliant succession of reviews as that splendid series now passing in the suburbs of the Capital. They began in October with that magnificent cavalry and artillery show on Capital Hill, where ten regiments, in their holiday clothes, wasted a splendid day *en grande tenue.* They continued with detached reviews of Porter's and Franklin's and Smith's divisions, and culminated in that colossal affair of last week at Munson's Hill. There could have been no greater success, in this way, than that. The heavens were suspicious, a little overcast in the morning—the clouds shimmering into that sweet haze of Indian summer in the afternoon. The material was, of course, beyond all compare—sixty thousand of the best fighting men the world has ever seen. The master of ceremonies, Irwin McDowell, Brigadier General United States Army, was perfectly up in his part, and proved by the masterly skill of his evolutions that he knows how a battle ought to be fought, in spite of the damaging memories of Stone Bridge. Then there was an audience such as rarely inspires a star company. The President, who, like most long limbed men, rides well; Cameron, who looks better on horseback than anywhere else; Seward, who looks better everywhere else than on horseback; Senators, and Governors, and postmasters, and reporters, and shoddy kings; and, in the charmed circle within the square, stood the barouches of the noticeable women who are in Washington now. From noon till dusk the glittering battalions moved proudly by the reviewing party, an army large enough and brave enough to do anything, if they had for a leader a man of genius as well as energy, of inspiration as well as detail. The future will soon disclose the extent and the cost of the glory that awaits them. That they will succeed, there can be no reasonable doubt. All the cards are in our own hands. Even clumsy and careless playing cannot now lose the game, and McClellan is neither clumsy nor careless.

The volunteers having had their share of fun, the regulars come in for a little spree on Capitol Hill to-morrow. The full regular force will be then reviewed, and the volunteer officers will be there to see, and to say, "I'll back my ridgement agin any one thar for the drinks." The jealousy between the army and the volunteer contingent is very fast dying away. The insolence of the one and the sensitiveness of the other have equally felt the mollifying influences of common toils and dangers. An absurd idea is talked of, for the next session of Congress, to consolidate the volunteers with the regulars, for convenience of officering and discipline. This would be to demoralize both forces.

The war has been for a week a secondary topic of conversation in Washington. McClellan pales his ineffectual fires before Herrmann. Now that the fleet has done its work, and the Rebel Commissioners are safe in jail, the public mind falls back with ancient love for swindling, and the crowd rushes to see a man swallow rabbits, and turn a bandanna into a vase of goldfish, and tell what you are thinking about, and whistle like a blackbird, and hum like a bee, and howl like a hound. Herrmann is a genius—a bright-eyed, black-moustached, quiet, handsome and inscrutable German Jew. He evinced great power and originality in choosing a name to be known by, of such stupendous proportions that it has to be pronounced by installments. His brother, who always accompanies him, is a precocious boy about a dozen years, who, always ready and never obtrusive, is, in fact, the explanation of most of his most wonderful tricks. The physical sleight which enables him to pull Canary birds from a spectator's ear, or Guinea pigs from a lady's porte monnaie, is very wonderful, but not to be compared to his masterly feats of mathematical combinations in cards and clairvoyant vision. The other evening at the President's, he asked Gen. Mcclellan to think of a card, not mentioning it. He then gave him a pack of cards and told him to look for the card he had in his mind. It was not there. "Give me the pack," said Herrmann. He took it, and springing the cards from one hand to the other, a card came to the top. It was the one the General had thought of. He will allow a dozen persons to select each a card from a pack and return them without his seeing them. Taking the pack in one hand and one card, selected seemingly at random, in the other, he will, without apparently bringing his hands near each other, cause the single card to assume successively to each of the dozen persons the appearance of the card they had selected. One goes from his *soirees* with faith confirmed and strengthened in the father of lies, and a general impression left on the mind of the truth of those lines in which Horatio Smith embodies the substance of Byron's philosophy,

> Thinking is but an idle waste of thought,
> And naught is everything, and everything is naught.[58]

WASHINGTON CORRESPONDENCE, 29 NOVEMBER 1861

Before this reaches you, the telegraph will have informed you of the opening scenes of the coming session of Congress, and what are now surmises and conjecture will have become history. It is certain that no Congress ever assembled under circumstances so peculiar, and no session has led to such momentous results as will this. The called session [*in July*] did little more than ratify the acts of the President. The crisis was too new; events had not assumed a character sufficiently destructive to warrant any position and final legislation upon vital points.

The not very flattering result of the Richmond Anabasis, had a great effect in modifying the ardor of some of the most heroic talkers in the National Legislature, and the mountains of Pennsylvania and seashores of New England suddenly assumed new and seducing charms on the 22d day of July. Then the provender at Willard's was placed on a starvation basis; the ghostly waiters dreamily haunted the dining hall in indolence; bills became payable daily in view of the uncertainty of life and the propinquity of Beauregard; and programmes disappeared utterly in the expensiveness of printing. If possible, Willard's was worse than usual. What temptation was then to stay in Washington? Having nothing to do, the legislators did it, and went home, finding no amusement, no recreation in the city whose distances only are magnificent.

The coming session will find a very large amount of work lying ready for its action, which the progress of events has cut out and presented. The questions which are to guide and terminate this contest will come up for full and free discussion and final action. Measures involving the gravest problems of political ethics will surely arise. Financial expedients, which are to result in national deliverance or insolvency, will be submitted, and the best minds of the country are already dividing upon them. The usual amount of eloquence which is inseparable from a concourse of patriots must be gracefully submitted to, and we shall be lucky if all the political Colonels do not make a flying visit to Washington to ventilate their glories, and give Congress and the Associated Press their version of their blunders.

These are some of the subjects that seem at present to occupy the greater share of attention among prominent men.

The subject of foreign relations, although we are utterly at peace, and there seems at first glance no possibility of embroilment, yet the experience of every day shows the temptation which civil war in a wide spread republic offers to the cupidity and ambition of foreign powers. The restrictions of our blockade, the possible umbrage at the seizure of Mason and Slidell, the tripartite alliance against Mexico, all afford the liveliest grounds for concern and caution. This, of course, involves the necessity of timely and extensive coast defense.

The recognition, long and foolishly delayed, of the negro Republics of Hayti and Liberia, will form a subject of discussion early in the session. The squeamishness which our Government has hitherto shown in this matter forms a striking contrast to the common sense course of European powers who long ago recognized those infant commonwealths.

The retrocession of the Virginia side of the District of Columbia in obedience to the caprice of a partizan Legislature has proved an evil so fraught with disastrous consequences, that the attention of Congress will probably be early called to the adoption of measures looking to the renewed acquisition from the Governor of Virginia of this territory, which experience has shown so indispensably necessary to the proper defense of the Capital against domestic or foreign attack.

The action of the Secretary of the Treasury is anxiously awaited by capitalists. There is great contrariety of opinion in regard to the measures which it is thought he will propose. I believe the minds of leading moneyed men are about equally divided in respect to the relative expediency of continuing the present policy of Government loans, or founding a sort of National Bank system, the basis of security being United States stocks exclusively.

The status of the contrabands and the disposition to be made of confiscated negroes will, of course, engage the most earnest attention of both houses. No conjecture can yet be made as to the probable decision of these weighty questions, but it is safe to assume, I think, that the Government will never become a shareholder, and that all negroes, once lawfully confiscated from the possession of their rebel owners, shall become free men, leaving their future destination a matter of deliberate legislation.

Territorial matters will engage less than their usual amount of attention. The Indian tribes within the extent of the loyal territory are mainly friendly, and even among those whose chiefs, beguiled by flattery and fire-water, have transferred them to the rebellion, there are great symptoms of dissatisfaction at the exchange, and an evident disposition to resume their former safe and prosperous status under the Washington Government, which they have learned to look upon as the beneficent source of money, blankets and tobacco. The Indians of the Pembina country are growing a little insolent and exacting, but no danger is apprehended, and something is to be pardoned to the feelings of hungry men. The Government will probably avert famine and hostilities among them.

The reconstruction of the Supreme Court and the consequently necessary remodeling of the entire national judiciary system will be considered, if not decided, by the coming Congress. The circuits of the associate Judges have grown so immense in extent that it now amounts to an impossibility for them to hold their regular sessions at all points required. Judge McLean, it will be remembered, for many years previous to his death, never held Court in Illinois. To increase the Supreme Bench to a sufficient extent to accommodate the business wants of the country would be to make it too cumbersome and unwieldy for its original purpose.

Some plan must be derived, by which the Supreme Bench will still be kept within moderate limits, and the Circuit or District Courts be capacitated for performing their several functions with less inconvenience. That the President intends some such mission is evident from the fact that he has allowed three seats on the Supreme Bench to remain vacant for nearly a year, in spite of the clamorous appeals of played-out barristers, from all quarters of the Union, who thought these would be magnificent castles of indolence to dodge away the rest of their days in.

These will be some of the measures coming before Congress, if Congress assembles. The doubt is occasioned by the following fact: The whole representation of the rebellious States is of course vacant. Several will be found wanting from Missouri and Kentucky. In addition to these it is known that between twenty and thirty of the Representatives in the present Congress are engaged in various capacities with the armies now in the field.

It is too much to expect that all these will come back from shoulder-straps to common clothes, and put off the sheen of their buttons to come down to earnest work. The majority of them have steadfastly refused to resign, while holding State commissions, and no vacancy is thus created for a second election. Those causes may prevent in the first days of the session the assembling of a quorum. But the lightning will tell you on Monday, if I presage rightly or not.[59]

WASHINGTON CORRESPONDENCE, 1 DECEMBER 1861

The anomalous fact that we must get our first news of battle from the hands of our enemies produces a singular state of public sentiment whenever the tidings of conflict come up from the South, muffled by the envious and angry enemy. The presumption of victory, which our confidence in our arms and our incredulity of Southern statements always beget, is still more or less modified by the vague suspicions and distrusts that always accompany uncertainty. When the conqueror of Greytown sent up to the anxious North his graphic and modest account of the heroic and condimentory treatment with which he had received the Yankee fleet, we knew he was lying, but thought even *he* must have some foundation for it. We did not laugh at the "Turtle" for several days, and waited most anxiously till our own dispatches proved the baselessness of his gasconade. When the chivalric hosts went over to call on Billy Wilson, and caught that flower of gallant rowdies *en chemise,* we thought from the exultant yells they sent up from Norfolk that perhaps they had shorn Billy's lambs. It was very pleasant to hear that the Zouaves had not lost the old use of their muscles in the South, and that after the first trial of strength between the extremes of both sections, the Old Gridiron still waved in triumph over Southern soil.

So, when we heard from Port Royal that the Federal fleet was unsuccessfully bombarding the town of Beaufort, and that the venerable Tatnall was just getting ready to go out in his little mudscow and bag the entire Armada, although we thought very little of his discretion, we very sincerely admired his pluck. That admiration vanished when we heard how ingloriously through the aqueous back alleys of the sea-islands the frightened gallinippers fled from the threatening thunders of our navy.

Of late, however, the flags of truce from Norfolk to Old Point are wonderfully reticent. Even when we get a glimpse of the whitey-brown newspapers of the Southern cities, they are very sulky and silent. We heard never a word from Tybee Island, of the slow strangling of Savannah by the relentless fingers of the loyal army, tightening at Braddock's Point and Tybee Light, of the awakening of the contraband, of the ominous movements of the fleet. General intelligence having been proved by their statesmen to be the bane of a free people, they have resolved to withhold it not only from us but from themselves.

But at last, after so long a silence, Bragg has spoken. He says the Hessians have opened fire and he is taking it coolly—that the wretches have fired on his hospital, where there were no sick or wounded, which he considers a brutal act and a waste of powder—that the *Colorado* and the *Niagara* had been bucking at Fort McRae, and hauled off very much disabled under the protecting shadow of the Fortress. The accounts have the usual muddle of magnificent vaporing and tragical growls with which the seedy press gangs of Secessia pepper their dispatches.

Those who best understand the state of affairs at Pickens see nothing in these reports but grounds for jubilation. For several weeks the *Niagara* and the *Richmond* (not the *Colorado,* as Braxton insists) have been holding a position whose object the rebels seem not to have suspected. They have been lying on the left of the channel very near the shoals, seemingly for blockading purposes, but really observing the powerful water battery lying below and eastward of the walls of Fort McRae. The guns of the fort are deficient in range and power; those of the adjoining battery are very powerful, but the embrasures point only toward Pickens, as, when it was built, it was thought impossible for men of war to approach within range. But careful soundings at last revealed positions from which the *Richmond* and *Niagara* could pour an enfilading fire upon the battery, while all the shots that went too high would batter the crazy walls of McRae. It was the intention of Brown, as soon as these points of attack were made untenable for the enemy, to direct his fire to the Navy Yard and the town of Warrington, withdrawing the ships to guard the island of Santa Rosa against the attacks of the heavy force posted at Deer Point, who, in case of a collision, were expected to cross the narrow sound to the island, for the purpose of taking Fort Pickens in the rear, while its utmost strength was occupied in front.

From the reports of Bragg himself, it would seem that the entire programme of Gen. Brown has been successfully carried out. Not one word is said of the battery by McRae nor the Fort itself. The town of Warrington is reported in flames, and the Navy Yard destroyed. No mention whatever is made of the forces at Deer Point, from which we may conclude that they have been unable to make their services available. The only exultant passage is where he speaks of the disabling and withdrawal of the *Niagara* and her consort, which, of course, to us who know Brown's plan, indicate the entire success of their operation on the left, and their anticipated withdrawal when their work was done, to guard the Island from a rear attack. It is more than usually safe to conclude, in the absence of positive dispatches, that this first scene of the act in the secession drama assigned to Fort Pickens has been performed in letter perfect style.

The disposition of affairs at this point has always been subject to singular misapprehensions. When the present administration came into power, the very first act of the President was to give an order to the Secretary of War that the public property in the revolted States should receive no detriment, and authorizing him to call upon all departments of the Government for means to that end.

When, in pursuance of that order, reinforcements were ordered to be at once landed at Fort Pickens from the vessels in the harbor, the commander of the fleet refused to land them, because the order had not come in due form through the Secretary of the Navy. And later, through the unparalleled stupidity of an army officer, whose ideas had become fossilized by long regular service into absolute machine routine, the guns of the Fort were silent at an important juncture, through some unexplained quasi armistice of the late Administration. But the spell has been broken, at last, and the lethargy of long silence has passed from this most important post,

> And now by the waves of the Santa Rosa deep
> And deathful-grinning mouths of the Fortress, flames
> The blood-red blossom of war with a heart of fire.

I think we have reason to hope that the reverses of the Union side are about over on the sea coast. The Navy Department provides every expedition which sails against almost every possible contingency. The grey bearded Secretary himself is proving the fallacy of that ungenerous logic, that argued that because a man is experienced he must be cowardly; because he has succeeded in philosophy he must fail in action. And the assistant Secretary, Gustavus V. Fox, an incarnation of inexorable energy, is wearing out a powerful mind and an iron constitution, in relentless and unceasing labor for the cause to which he is heart and soul devoted. There is in the future a glory preparing for our Navy, brighter even than its splendid past. As I write, the narrow entrances of two Southern harbors are probably the scene of an act, simple and commonplace in its accessories, but grand in its conception and awful in its righteous retribution. I speak of the stone fleet of whaling hulks, or, as the sailors jocularly term it, the Rat Hole Squadron. It is a magnificent idea of poetic justice thus to alter the face of creation at the bidding of outraged law. To say of a place where nature designed a great city should be, and poured a mighty harbor, and narrowed its approaches for easy defense and leveled a graceful plateau for its habitations—"Here there shall be no more trade; population shall fly from the paralysis of traffic; in the years to come the white sailed ships, the evangels of wealth, shall shun the sunken death that lurks beneath the fretful ripples of the channels; for in an evil hour these cities raised their rash hands against the loving breast that cherished them, and scarred and gashed it; therefore the spirit of indignant Justice has cursed them, and they shall be cursed."[60]

WASHINGTON CORRESPONDENCE, 3 DECEMBER 1861

The appearance of the two houses of Congress is very little changed from last session. The eye is gradually becoming accustomed to the thinner sprinkling of occupants in the legislative chambers, and we are growing to recognize the fact that sporadic patriotism is superior to confluent disaffection. Few stars have fallen from the Senatorial firmament. The black-haired, black-eyed splendid Kentuckian, whose eloquence of manner went so far to compensate for his irresolute weakness of purpose and laxity of principle, is gone. I am very sorry for Breckinridge. A ridiculous weakness, which he fatally mistook for honor, snared him to his ruin. The flattery of the seditious and the cruel contempt of the loyal hastened his departure. He could not suit himself to the new state of feeling. In the town whose every pulse of sentiment had sensitively responded to his utterances, he felt lonely and strange when the advent of a new dynasty had changed that fickle populace, and he found himself not only suspected but out of fashion. He was too proud to conceal, and too weak honestly to change. He retained to the last the same stern inflexibility of prejudice, mingled and toned with that courtly grace and dignity that so often made many seem right, when he was engaged in debate, with some rough specimen of patriotism from the woods or the mountains. Even in his most atrocious utterances of disloyalty, he was always calm and gentlemanly. He lost himself once, when the ignorant mob of Baltimore were signalizing their recent return to virtue by howling at a benighted brother who was yet in the gall of bitterness. He could endure the abuse of Lane and the sarcasms of Sumner, but he raged like a maniac when a Baltimore crowd with its hands red with the April stains, told him to dry up, and called him a traitor. The spoiled darling of Kentucky could not repent, and has fallen for the rest of time. I am afraid it would be putting a premium on disloyalty to say how much more graceful, esthetically considered, is his open treason than the cowardly paltering of Beriah Magoffin, who seems determined to save his salary and cheat the hangman, and Lazarus Powell, who walked to-day as contentedly around the vestibule of the Senate as if his heart were full of loyalty and his neck had never dreamed of hempen collars. The lone grave of the slain rebel is, I think, more honorable than the mean life of these abject creatures, too cowardly to be traitors, too depraved to be true.

There is hope that Crittenden will return to the seat from which this ambitious youth lately ousted him. The Senate is hardly itself without Crittenden. The old gentleman is never quite at home in the House. They are noisy, and talk fast, and do business there. It bores the old patrician to sit with the tribunes. He ought to go back to the still sleepiness of the Senate; it is a better frame for his venerable and true old head.

Kentucky was never better represented in the House. Gov. Wickliffe made a most charming little speech to-day, which he called an obituary notice of his late colleague, Burnett, who has set up a traveling government for Kentucky, and assumed the style of a peripatetic Governor. Burnett was a very stupid rebel and a bore in the House. He was never amusing, except when he rose, as he did every day, "solemnly to protest." He was a slow-blooded, pig-faced nuisance, who looked more like a dropsical tallow-chandler of weak mind than a revolutionist. He used to sit near Vallandigham, for whom he had great contempt, and when Val. would snarl and yelp at the House, and look to Burnett for approval, Burnett, in a stupid piggish style, would snub him and proceed "solemnly to protest against the violent and irregular proceedings of the House." Then Val. would look unhappy.

Both the House and the Senate look very clean and decorous—more so than usual, as it appears to me. The members occupy their seats, instead of the lobbies, and business is executed (in advertisers' style) with neatness and dispatch. They already begin to show evidence of the preparation which has been making to render this the most important session in its results that has ever been held. Bulky manuscripts are being dragged out of carpet bags, and furbished up with brown covers and red tape. Already a light skirmishing party of buncombe resolutions have been sent forward to clear the way for the approach of the heavy artillery of bills and enactments. Mason and Slidell have been doomed as far as Congress can doom them to the same lodgings and prog which Corcoran is supposed to be regaled with, and a vast variety of gay and sprightly contraband doctrines have been displayed for an instant to the gaze of the enraptured galleries, and laid over till next Tuesday. Those do the young gentleman who originate them no harm and serve to keep them out of more mischievous employment.

Both Houses got to-day about as much thinking to do as they can conveniently execute in the President's Message. This is a document which, though at first sight it may appear unimportant and commonplace, will be found upon close inspection to be one of the most truly admirable State papers that have ever issued from the Executive mansion. It will probably be violently attacked by the extremists of both sides, and will give less comfort to Jeff. Davis than to any one else. The Reverend Owen Lovejoy and the Hon. General Lane are very much disappointed in it. They seemed to have expected that it would contain an ethnological treatise to prove that negroes are not black, and a recommendation that our citizens burnt-cork their faces and learn to play on the banjo, in compliment to the contrabanditti. Others who come from the Hub of the Universe [*Boston*] are disgusted because there is no fierce howl over the barbarism of slavery, and no canting assertions of the virtues that radiate over the North from the blarney stone of Plymouth. But all moderate men are quietly delighted with the message. It is permeated with that intense common sense and intuitive knowledge of the people, which in Abraham Lincoln rises to genius.

One singular objection which I have heard urged against the message is what all thinking men must recognize as its happiest point. Some say that its lengthy discussions of matters of administrative concern are out of place at a time like this, of public peril. It seems to me that no fact could place the stability of our Government in stronger contrast with the weak and wavering character of that dismal affair down South than this quiet interest with which the President discusses treaties, and Indian matters, and agricultural progress, and the Judiciary system, compared with the feverish hurry with which the Richmond rebel dashes through the reckless lies and special pleas of what he calls his Message to the Congress of the C.S.A.

Yesterday, when it was understood that the President had not yet finished his communication to Congress, a grave and deep anxiety possessed the public mind. Rumors of dissension in the Cabinet, of anticipated changes of policy, of startling plans in embryo, gave color to the suspicion that this morning would bring a lurid revelation with it. But the President's Message, calm, temperate and firm, soothed all anxieties and checked all doubts. Whatever happens we are sure of a strong, true hand at the helm of State, and it is probable that some high in office have learned the significance of the admonition, "*Don't speak to the man at the wheel.*"[61]

WASHINGTON CORRESPONDENCE, 5 DECEMBER 1861

It seems that the Western lawyer has been asserting himself again. General Cameron having in his report made certain recommendations, which, in the view of Mr. Lincoln, transcended the present constitutional powers of the Government, and showed a dangerous leaning to a radicalness of action which has been thus far avoided, was firmly requested to modify them in accordance with the requirements of strict law and the known views of the President. This seemed at first impracticable, for advance copies had already been sent to all leading cities of the Union, before the President had himself seen the report. The telegraph rendered an easy matter that would have been impossible a few years ago, and every copy was recalled, except the one which, as is usual of late, the *New York Tribune* had surreptitiously obtained from, say, General Thomas, or some other crony of Mr. Wilkinson [*Sam Wilkeson*]. The world may thus see how the President has modified the Secretary of War.

It is one of the most singular incidents of these odd times. It would have seemed the height of folly, last winter, to predict that Abraham Lincoln, the Abolitionist of the back woods, the *bête noir* of all the compromisers, would ever stand in a more conservative position than Simon Cameron, who at that time led the ultra-generous Republicans in the olive-branch business. How would the sight have seared the eye-balls of John Cochrane, if, while he stood, within a year, on the balcony of a Richmond tavern, speaking words of encouragement and cheer to the rebellious mob, he could have been favored with a glimpse of the future man—Col. Cochrane, of the First Chasseurs, enunciating an Abolition programme to his soldiers in a speech, at sunset, in the suburbs of Washington, while the Secretary of War sat in his carriage and quietly assented to the doctrines there propounded. It is one of the most significant indications of the overwhelming powers of that sudden revolution in the mind of the people, that has raised Butler and Dickinson from the dust where they have groveled for years at the feet of the mutinous South, and instantly surprised them into manliness.

There is no question General Cameron is thoroughly imbued with the convictions which he has recently manifested in so many different ways. The doubt in which his few brief remarks at the Chasseur's camp left his sentiments was soon dispelled by his calm and dispassionate repetition of them, over Colonel Forney's oysters and wine, and to prove that they are no mere holiday utterances to tickle the ears of the grandfathered, withal he takes especial occasion to reiterate them in an enduring and authoritative form. Admitting the honesty of his convictions and the purity of his intentions, which I think no one doubts, and leaving the substance of his recommendations to the impartial criticism of coming necessities, there can be no question of the entire propriety of the President's modification of his report. Whatever discussions may take place in the friendly security of Cabinet council, no symptom of even unimportant disagreement should be displayed in public documents. And in a matter of such vast importance and consequence as the liberation of the blacks in insurrectionary districts, no step should be taken by the administration without the fullest and freest expression of the will of the people, through their representatives, and the largest opportunity for discussion in the press and the country.

Whatever may be the impression entertained generally of the mental characteristics of Mr. Lincoln, one fact begins to be displayed most strikingly in every important act of his official career. His strong common sense guards him from all extravagances, and his wonderful intuitive knowledge of the feeling and wish of the people is at once the cause and justification of the fullest public confidence. It is derived from many sources: his humble origin and early struggles—his daily intercourse with all classes in the laborious pursuit of his profession—his purity of purpose and earnest democracy of sentiment. With none of the ordinary arts for moulding public opinion, with no attention to newspapers as the organs of popular feeling, he is always inevitably *en rapport* with the mind of the country, and when he differs with the louder and more clamorous pretenders to popular leadership, you always hear the deep, low murmur of approval coming up cordial and trustful from the heart of the people. It is this entire knowledge of, and harmony with the honest sentiment of the masses, that constitutes the liveliest hope for the future of his Administration.

This difference of opinion as to a question of expediency between the President and the Secretary of War involves nothing of personal feeling and no collision whatever of administrative policy. The surest indication of harmony in the Cabinet is the perfect freedom of discussion and liberty of criticism that seems to prevail in their councils. They are so entirely united and single-hearted in the prosecution of this business to the end, that they are careless of seeming so. There has not been a period since the Fourth of March, when it was possible to predict how the Cabinet would divide upon any anticipated question of public policy.

It is of course to be presumed that each of the eminent gentlemen and accomplished politicians that compose the Ministry has his own plans and his own schemes of future use and fame. But the future is too far, and the changes of each day are too immense, for men of their sagacity to build upon the slender contingencies of present complications. As Seward very felicitously expressed it the other day, when some overzealous friends of his were trying to warn him against the intentions of a supposed rival: "It would be as absurd for one of us to-day to spend our time in laying plans for future political advancement, as it would have been for Noah to have used up his forty days in the ark, laying out town lots on Mount Ararat."

It is one of the easiest matters in the world for people who know nothing about it, to charge the lowest and meanest motives upon men high in authority. It is the cheapest of pleasures to ordinary minds to drag down to their own level the characters of better men. Nothing less could be expected. When a man takes a high office, he should dispose of his sensibilities and clothe himself in dirt-proof apathy. The action of Mr. Lincoln's Cabinet in recent affairs seems to indicate their appreciation of this necessity. But they are quiet in the consciousness that they know, and the country *will* know, the honesty and sincerity with which they are working together.[62]

Washington correspondence, 12 December 1861

There has been for the last few days a great deal of unnecessary discussion in Washington about the statement made by old Thaddeus Stevens, in caucus, on Monday evening, that General McClellan had induced the modification of Mr. Cameron's report, by holding his resignation *in terrorem* over the head of the President.

A more silly and pernicious lie could not easily be imagined. Leaving out of view its manifest absurdities—that McClellan should know what Cameron intended to embody in his report—that he would be guilty of such an impertinence or the President of such a folly—the gravest apprehensions may well be indulged when we hear a legislator solemnly pronounce such a lie, and a portion of the press as solemnly approve it. The *Evening Post* of New York contained a remarkably temperate and well-considered article upon the matter, and was instantly attacked in the most scurrilous style by the *Philadelphia Inquirer,* whose ideas of loyalty at present consist of the most slavish adulation of the commanding General, and running a blind tilt at everything which looks like criticism.

We have had already more than enough of this. The movements of the American mind are equally absurd in action and re-action. Before the Manassas battle, the people, hounded on by the Press, clamored wildly for an advance. Absurd as the dictation was, and causeless as the blame that fell upon the General and the Cabinet, they yielded to it, and the fight was ventured and lost. McDowell quietly sunk into a General of Division, and McClellan, who had been very fortunate in a few skirmishes in Western Virginia, took command of the Army of the Potomac, and soon after of the Army. The same extravagance which marked the former blame marks the present praise. This young man, who has never fought a battle, is called the new Napoleon. Swords are presented by servile corporations so costly that even he recognizes the absurdity of giving in advance of trial that which should only be the reward of achievement. The popular mind begins to invest him with mysterious attributes of heroism, and N. P. Willis goes into well bred hysterics, and knows that the long-lost warrior with the strawberry mark is come.

This, though very silly, is not at all reprehensible. It is rather a neat thing to invest your warriors with heroic haloes. It promotes confidence, and softens the pains of the measles and the ennui of convalescence, (the only danger our armies encounter,) to think that a great man, who knows all about the matter, is caring for the soldiers and organizing victory. It is a good thing to make songs about the Commanding General, and sing them in the camp. It is a good thing for a General to dress well and imposingly, to surround himself with all the accessories of dignity and power, (if his name isn't Frémont,) and to omit nothing which will impress and even awe the soldiery. For, without unquestioning respect and obedience, an army becomes a mob. Only reverence for a commander will supply in a volunteer force the lack of that discipline that turns to machines the men of standing armies.

But it is ill for a Republic when the military arm begins to rival the civil power. The military power must be subordinated to the civil, with a discipline as rigid, an obedience as absolute, as that which binds the subaltern in the presence of his superior. Gen. McClellan has always recognized this. A brighter promise for future usefulness, than the memoirs of tactical books or Virginia skirmishes, is seen in the modest and yet dignified respect with which he has always regarded the gray-haired chiefs of the Administration, and the perfect and soldierly reticence which he has always observed in regard to political questions arising out of the present complications. He is a soldier, and knows that his duties in that capacity will occupy all the time he has. With an army of seven hundred thousand men under his care, he understands thoroughly that a proper distribution of labor will leave to the President and to his Ministers the political conduct of affairs.

It may seem to be paying too much attention to a lie so silly, to contradict it gravely; but the spirit in which it was uttered, and the spirit in which a portion of the newspapers have made their comments upon it, are indications fraught with the profound possibilities of mischief. General McClellan would never have so far forgotten the decorum of his position as to make a demand so arrogant and impertinent, and Mr. Lincoln has already shown on several occasions that however careless he may be of personal slights and attacks, he will take care that the office he holds shall never be degraded by cowardice or subserviency. When next you hear that a general has threatened resignation as the alternative to a change of policy in the Administration, and do not hear at the same time that his resignation has been accepted with alacrity, you may conclude that *that rumor*, like *this*, is utterly groundless and foolish.

Our little friend, the Reverend Colonel Gurley, was severely snubbed in the House on his motion to refer his Confiscation Bill to a Select Committee, of which his Reverence would, of course, have been Chairman. The glimpse of glory thus opened to his imagination, by which, through the stolen thunder of Frémont, he was to storm his way into fame, were ruthlessly dispelled by the House cruelly refusing to entertain the seducing proposition, and referring the matter to the usual committee.

The parsons do not seem particularly lucky so far this session. Owen Lovejoy charged gallantly on Halleck's order No. 8, which everybody in the House considered foolish and ill-advised, but no one seemed anxious to go into battle under the Lovejoy guidon, so Owen's resolution was tabled in defiance of the sentiments of the very men voting.

The Reverend Marble Nash Taylor closes my list of remarkable parsons who seemed to find politics a hard road to travel. This is the highly respectable party who recently elected himself Governor of North Carolina, and a young reporter, named Charles Henry Foster, Congressman from the Hatteras District. This young person has the greatest possible facility of venue. He lives in Washington, claims certificates of election from both Murfreesboro and Hatteras, and keeps a bright eye to the windward for any possible vacancies occurring in the southward march of the grand army. The Provisional Government of North Carolina is considered a very good joke. Imagine a half-dozen barefooted fishermen calling a moonlight meeting on Bloody Island, and establishing a Provisional Government for Missouri, and you have a fair idea of the brilliant Gift Enterprise of Mr. Taylor and Mr. Foster.[63]

Washington correspondence, 13 December 1861

The only events of the week worthy of mention in the Senate have been the two days of mourning for their dead. On Tuesday many Senators spoke in friendly eulogy of Kinsley Bingham, one of the most amiable, modest and pure of our recent statesmen. The remarks were all in good taste. There was nothing highflown or extravagant in the praises with which his friends honestly mourned him. He had done, as the most eloquent of his eulogists remarked, "if not enough for glory, too much to be forgotten." You would scarcely have expected a series of funeral speeches from Americans so full of honest sorrow and sensible reserve.

The next day there was a wider field for ornate eulogy. No man ever died in the Senate whose life was so picturesque as Baker's. No biography combines so much of drama and romance. His life will stand forever in our history a splendid lyric of patriotism. An embodied poem, complete in all its parts, a rounded idyll of the actual, a trilogy whose parts are eloquence, counsel and war. As a reward for the devotion and the fervor of youthful effort, his manhood gave him the robes of a Senator, and as if Fame had resolved to perfect a work so well begun, she crowned his death with the halo of martyrdom. It was a very easy matter to be eloquent when Baker was the theme.

There was an inspiration in the audience too. The galleries were more crowded than ever before this session. There was something about the flash and glitter of Baker's mind that irresistibly fascinated the people, and they all came to hear him mourned. And just before Senator Nesmith rose to announce the death of his colleague, the door to the left of the President's chair opened, and Abraham Lincoln entered, seemingly taller and more gaunt than of old, the lines deepening around his mouth, the first fall of the snow visible in his hair, dressed more carefully than in former days, and walking, it seemed to me, more erectly than I had noticed before. He was accompanied by the Illinois Senators and by his private secretaries, Nicolay and Hay. The Vice President rose and resigned his own chair to him, taking a seat on his left. The President sat quietly there, leaning his shaggy leonine head upon his black-gloved hand, with more utter unconsciousness of attitude than I ever saw in a man accustomed to being stared at, and listened earnestly to what the Senators had to say about his old friend.

All who said anything did their best. McDougal redeemed himself finely from the memory of former carelessnesses; Browning, in regard to whom there seems to be a constant surprise and wonder that Douglas' successor should be an orator and a statesman, fully sustained the reputation he gained on his entrance, for correctness of expression and brilliancy of delivery. I cannot imagine a more satisfactory effort of its kind than Browning's was. If a man might order his eulogist with his undertaker, a dirge such as Browning so grandly intoned over his friend is what a man of sensibility might be happy to anticipate in dying. Not fulsome in praise nor captious in censure, he fitly showed the Senate the man they had lost.

Cowan's remarks were finished and scholarly, but ill-delivered; they read well. Latham was touching and florid, and his voice full and sonorous. The galleries liked him. But there was an instant rustle, dying into dead silence when Sumner rose. There is a magic in that man's voice and manner that atones for all the shortcomings of his life, even in the minds of those who hate him most earnestly. And in the ideas of most who in these latter days throng the galleries of the Capitol, the majesty of his presence is enhanced by a halo of sacrifice, and the wonderful melody of his voice sounds in their ears like the bugle, prophetic of the victory to be. Every one listens rapt when Sumner speaks. Those who curse his doctrine listen to his eloquence, and admire esthetically what they condemn politically.

He talks more than formerly. He seems to have resolved to omit no opportunity to strike a blow at slavery whenever in season or out of season an opportunity occurs. He made a hero of Kinsley Bingham on Tuesday, because Bingham honestly hated slavery. He rode rough shod over facts, on

Wednesday, to show that Baker was a type of the civilization of the North, as opposed to the barbarism, fighting which, he fell. He called him a weaver's boy, whose father was a school teacher; he orphaned him in infancy, whose father lived to see his son a brilliant and successful lawyer, and whose mother yet mourns him. Yet he bore the sympathies of the vast audience easily on, till every heart thrilled with the passionate energy with which he arraigned, as the murderer of the dead Senator, not the General Commanding, nor his superior, but the power behind the rebellion, saying, "*l'etat—cest moi*"— slavery.

George Bancroft is here now and many other parties, eminently respectable, are here ferociously urging upon the Administration the immediate abolition of slavery as the only certain and satisfactory method of ending the rebellion. It is a most instructive sight to see the Illinois emancipationist converted into an earnest conservative, and resolutely resisting the solicitations to abolition persistently urged by those who so bitterly denounced his radicalism a few years ago.

It will be noticed that the more violent of the radicals are now composed of those who lagged further behind the age not long ago, and as a general thing the most earnest of the anti-slavery men are waiting quietly for events to justify them rather than seeking to hasten them by clamor or agitation. Of course I except Mr. Lovejoy, whose very dreams are unwholesomely permeated with the flavor of colored person.

These changes are seen no less plainly in nations than in individuals. A year ago, a man who had predicted that we would ever be embroiled with England on account of her championship of slavery, would have been instantly treated to a straight jacket and *eau glace* on the brain. Yet there are things more entirely impossible than a war with England. They are behaving very foolishly in Liverpool, and the London *Times*, though admitting that we are right, very strongly insinuates that we are not to be allowed our rights in this matter, and that now is a very good time to tackle us anyhow. I do not think we can be bullied into a war. But if I understand the old gentleman who at present lives in the Executive mansion, there will be no sacrifice of honor or principle even to avoid a war with the swaggering bully of the United Islands. As to giving up Mason and Slidell, that may be done, as [*Virginia governor Henry*] Wise observed of John Brown, "after we are done with them." If Great Britain demands them, Mr. Seward will probably reply, "send on your burial cases."[64]

Washington correspondence, 16 December 1861

Half of December is gone and no winter yet. The weather here for the last ten days has been as mild and balmy as a bright May morning. Fires and overcoats are useless luxuries; the close shaven parks, with the fallen leaves well broomed out, have quite a vernal appearance; building and every other kind of out door business is prosecuted with as little hindrance as in midsummer, and the genteel mob that crowds the city from all parts of the world except Secessia, throngs the thoroughfares in silk, feathers and broadcloth, saying as plainly a face can speak,

I'll be gay and happy still.

It is doubtful whether Washington was ever blessed or cursed with such a mighty crowd before, except upon some inauguration day. Sky parlors on the fifth floor, are at a great premium, and quiet, retiring gentlemen are glad of a chance to be hustled into a seven by nine closet, to sleep with a strange bedfellow. The principal hotels have no spare rooms for several days, and chance vacancies are pre-engaged a week beforehand. The publicans and shopkeepers are having a glorious time and reaping a golden harvest.

The great topic of thought and conversation in Washington at present is the chance of a rupture with England on account of the Mason-Slidell arrest. The British lion has roared, but "gently as a sucking dove," or more like the angry growl of a kicked cur, for, in the very hurricane of her passion at the fancied insult to her flag, she acknowledges all that we claim, the right to do just what we have done. There is no excitement here upon the subject, and no serious apprehensions are felt with regard to the result. When England is ready to live without corn as well as cotton, it will be time enough for her to stir up a quarrel in opposition to a principle she has advocated and practiced for centuries. The dastardly course she has pursued for the last few months, secretly gloating over our misfortunes, speaking friendship to us and acting sympathy for the rebellion, "willing to wound yet afraid to strike," places her in a position of antagonism to the sober sentiments of her own subjects.

The whole inventive genius of the American people is now centered upon a single object, and if they do not work out some miracles in the use of iron, lead and "villainous salt petre," they will belie their past history and all the idiosyncrasies of the universal Yankee nation. Machines and inventions for facilitating industrial pursuits and all the mechanical arts are lost sight of for the time being, and the whole inventive spirit is working night and day to discover new and improved methods of slaughter. But few models of new inventions in agriculture and the mechanic arts make their appearance in the Patent Office, whilst the "War Department" in the same building is crowded to repletion with deathdealing instruments. Farmers, mechanics, dairy maids and sewing girls must content themselves with such facilities as they have at present, for the genius of America is absorbed just now in contriving improved methods to carry on the great work of human slaughter.

Of all the "infernal machines" lately come into vogue, none has struck me as more admirably suited to its purpose than the "volcanic rifle" and the pistols of the same pattern. The rifled carbine of this class is about three feet in length, including the stock, much lighter than a Sharp's rifle, and much more efficient. Underneath the barrel is a magazine, in the shape of a cylinder, which will contain twenty-five cartridges, the charge and cap being both inserted in a cavity of the ball. The simple movement of a lever throws one of these balls into the rear chamber of the barrel, at the same time cocking the piece. The whole magazine can thus be fired in little more than a minute of time. To replenish the magazine requires about the same time as to charge a gun with buckshot, and you are ready again to deliver twenty-five rifle shots. This gun carries accurately a distance of five hundred yards, and its calibre is a little less than that of the Enfield rifle. Twenty thousand of these guns have been ordered by the Government, and several regiments are already supplied.

There are three sizes of the "Volcanic Pistol" manufactured by the New Haven Arms Company, upon precisely the same principle as the rifled carbine, and their magazines will contain, respectively, six, eight and ten charges. They are manufactured of the very best quality of material, and with the nicest adjustment of the parts, and the whole affair is a beautiful as well as a most effective instrument of death. The smallest, or pocket pistol, will carry two hundred yards to kill, and the largest, or cavalry pistol, almost as far as the carbine. The mechanical arrangements of this pistol are more simple than those of the revolver, and less liable to get out of order. I should also mention that the pistol barrels are well rifled, and carry the ball with great accuracy. I learn that a depot for the sale of these arms is about to be opened in St. Louis, and the "soger boys" will have an opportunity to test the correctness of my remarks.

As admirable as this volcanic carbine appears, it is being excelled by another arm on the same principle, called Henry's repeating rifle. This new gun is now under inspection and trial at the War Department, and is pronounced by officers high in position, and by experienced sharp shooters, to be the *ne plus ultra* in this department of invention—the best rifle in existence. Its magazine contains fifteen of the improved cartridges, and its range is both effective and accurate at a distance of one thousand yards. The whole piece is an example of beauty, symmetry and strength combined, and it is equally adapted to cavalry or infantry service.

Yesterday I spent a pleasant hour at the Washington Navy Yard, now under the superintendence of the brave and talented Captain Dahlgren, whose fame is being thundered from a thousand iron and brazen throats. His practical genius has achieved wonderful triumphs in the construction of cannon and projectiles, and the Dahlgren gun is allowed by all to be one of the most effective instruments of destruction ever invented. Upon entering the Yard I found keeping watch and ward at the gate a couple of French "war dogs," whose history has a spice of interest in it. They consist of two long eighteen pounders, cast of bronze and beautifully ornamented. They were cast at the same foundry in 1740, and bear, amongst other inscriptions, the old kingly motto of "*ultima ratio regum.*" These twin children of Mars were separated for nearly a century. One of them came into our possession with the purchase of Louisiana, and the other with the capture of the city of Mexico. The fates have brought them together again on the banks of the Potomac, and as modern improvements have thrown them into a state of desuetude, they can spend a green old age in memories of former prowess. A very large force is now employed here in manufacturing almost every instrument and appliance of war, from a pistol cartridge to a twelve-inch rifled cannon, but I will defer my notice of the mechanical wonders of the establishment until another time.

Whilst here I was kindly invited to witness the operation of bridging a portion of the east branch of the Potomac. Colonel Murphy, of the Fifteenth New York regiment, conducted the experiment with his newly invented Pontoon bridge. The sustaining or floating power consists of buoys anchored at proper distances from each other. Each buoy consists of a cylinder of india rubber twenty-five feet long and about eighteen inches in diameter, resembling, when inflated, a good straight saw-log. Three of these are placed together, inflated and anchored at a distance of eighteen feet from the shore.

The string pieces or "baulks," as they are called, are then placed on, and the whole is covered with plank. Whilst one party is completing the covering of one section, another anchors a second buoy, and the bridge grows at the rate of fifty or sixty feet in a minute. In less time than I have taken to write this rough description, the bridge had stretched across a cove three hundred and sixty feet, and a regiment of soldiers, four abreast, was gaily marching over the flood.

Amongst other inventions designed to smooth the horrid front of war and add some grains of comfort to the life of those who are fighting the battles of their country, the newly invented houses for soldiers deserve to be specially noticed. The grounds in front of the War Department are filled with patented contrivances of this kind, each inventor apparently striving to reach the highest point in the combined qualities of comfort, convenience, lightness, economy and care of construction. I noticed one house built in sections and designed to accommodate fifty men, which can be taken down and loaded into wagons in less than five minutes, and be reconstructed in the same time. Another house, somewhat smaller, is constructed of single planks, each being properly numbered and fitted to its place. The walls and roof are made of inch pine plank, put as in weather-boards style, the posts, studding and rafters being supplied with hooked staples to receive the edge of the planks. All these houses are so furnished with hooks, staples and other contrivances for holding together the posts, that they are designed to go up like Solomon's temple "without the sound of a hammer."

The utmost confidence is expressed here by those who are high in authority as to the naval expeditions, that are either gone or going to operate upon the Atlantic and Gulf coast. Cunning Mr. Yancey and his confreres in rebellion thought they had their plans nicely fixed up, to throw the burden and desolation of the war upon the Border States, which had no part in its inauguration. But the terrible blows and more terrible fright now falling upon Palmerstondom [*England*], the very head and front of the treason, show that those plans for preserving the cotton fields from the devastation of war were not quite perfect.

A curious feature in these coast expeditions is the Stone or Rat Hole fleet, as it is called. It goes around and makes no warlike demonstration, but silently drops into its appointed place and seals up forever the rebel ports. Nearly a hundred of these stone laden hulks have already gone on their mission, and when they have done their work in front of the most refractory and contumacious of the rebel ports, the blockading ships can be spared for more active operations. If this system of perfecting the blockade was designed to cut off access to the whole Southeast coast, it might be regarded as a barbarous proceeding. Instead of that, the stone fleet is designed to mete out a righteous retribution by stopping up some "rat holes" along the coast, closing such harbors as Charleston and Savannah, and opening far better ones at Port Royal, Brunswick and other points. Charleston merchants desired to be princes, and Palmetto politicians to be Presidents, and so they clubbed together, hoping to gratify their ambition by stirring up this infernal rebellion. Could a more just or terrible punishment be inflicted than to let her stand for future ages the scorn and scoff of true hearted patriots, and the silent, unpeopled and gloomy monument of parricides? To such a fate for such a city, the nation would say Amen! and even the conservative secessionists of the border States would have no tears of pity to shed over the ashes of Charleston. And poor old Virginia! The proud mother of States and of Presidents. After living in happy wedlock three-quarters of a century, with her children settled all around her, then to turn wanton and sell her virtue for the gilded bauble held out by King Cotton! Once the largest, richest and most populous State in the Union, she sees her whole territory desolated as by fire, her patrimony about to be partitioned out amongst her loyal neighbors, and the whole prestige of her former power and glory passed away forever. Whether the act of partitioning Virginia, by reconstructing the boundaries of this and the adjacent States of Maryland and Delaware, should ever be consummated, and it is hardly probable, she will never again rule the American Republic.[65]

WASHINGTON CORRESPONDENCE, 17 DECEMBER 1861

In spite of the ferocity of the recent growls from over seas, there is little excitement and no trepidation in Washington. Those who have for so long a time foreseen the complication which has now arrived could not have hoped that the people could have received so calmly the news of a possible rupture with England. Yet, while every one discusses reasonably the probabilities of the case, there is never heard any expression of dread or foreboding. Some are delightedly contemplating the prospect of another passage at arms with the venerable bully, out of whom we have already twice taken the conceit; but most conclude that an open rupture is improbable, and that it is not much of a show after all, and turn with renewed interest to ask if Butler has really landed at Ship Island, and what is the position of Schoepf and his Wildcats. A subject so momentous has rarely been treated so cavalierly by those whom it so vitally concerns.

This indifference arises from several causes. In the first place England has rendered herself so obnoxious to all right-minded people by her insufferable impertinences ever since the beginning of this trouble that a quiet contempt has taken the place of the intense sensitiveness which formerly responded so promptly to every manifestation of hostile feeling from England, and we now look with no emotion whatever upon every expression of public feeling from the British masses. The hypocrisy, which swung so rapidly from Exeter Hall fanaticism to aiding and comforting a proslavery rebellion, was so bare and reckless of decencies, that it readily cured us of any lingering respect we might have had for the moral sense of England. Having ceased utterly to think anything of them, of course we are entirely indifferent to what they think of us.

In the next place we do not believe there will be any war. Nations are very rarely struck blind, either by passion or cupidity. We do not think that English rage at the loss of two passengers would interfere with English views of interest and hopes of future gain. You cannot fire the British heart without security to the British pocket. And a man with no more brains than Palmerston can see at a glance that a war with us to-day would be, financially, the ruin of England. While her poor are growing gaunt and turbulent with hunger, our granaries are filled with an opulence of harvest unparalleled. However strong a temptation free cotton from the South may tempt the watering mouth of John Bull as he thinks of the silent mills of Lancashire and Manchester, the pinched blue faces of the famishing poor strike to his sinking heart a dread which warns him to stay his hands.

Besides, the British commerce is the most extended and unprotected in the world. Within twenty-four hours from a declaration of war our privateers would dash from every inlet of the Northern coast. Every merchant vessel, seeing no safety for ordinary traffic, would run into port, and taking a couple of pieces of brass ordnance on board, would push out to prey on the rich shipping of the enemy. In every sea would be re-enacted the drama that was played in the early years of this century, when the long hoarded wealth of British merchants poured lavishly in to enrich enterprising and undaunted merchants of New England. So universally in all the navigable waters of the globe did the spoils of traffic reward the valor of the Yankee privateersmen, that the boast of Britannica ruling the waves became a doleful and melancholy farce, and the distress that our sea guerrillas carried into the warehouses of London contributed more to bring the Government to reason than all the precious blood shed at Niagara or Lundy's Lane, or before the baffling bulwarks of the Louisiana cotton bales. All this may be in a week's time renewed. Many seem to be laboring under the impression that privateering is a relic of the dark ages. So, for that matter, is war. Both are barbarous. But "all indispensable means," as Abraham the First, says, "are to be used against our enemy." Nothing estops the United States from privateering. We declined the eminently wise and humane proposition for its abolition proposed by the Paris Congress, because at that time we did not wish to deprive ourselves of so powerful a means of defense. Subsequently, however, we renewed the proposition extending it still farther to cover all innocent ships and cargoes, and the Great Powers declined our proposal in turn. So that matters remain in this respect in the same situation which they held last century.

It is not improbable that this consideration may have its weight with the irascible British Cabinet, and warn them not to go too far in their well-meant endeavors to seem plucky and defiant to their constituency in the rural districts, who are roaring with stupid, rustic wrath at what they call the insult to their flag.

Another nice little glass house that England possesses in view of the world will probably keep her from any very serious exercises in stone throwing. Above our northern boundary stretches a fine extent of country, running to seed for want of Yankee thrift and industry to work up its resources. Its people have lived so long out of the atmosphere of home, that they have learned to regard England only as a sort of vague tradition rather than as an actual and visible sovereignty over them. They have inhaled so much of democratic freedom floating over the lakes that they have suffered their minds to run dangerously upon the subject of pure republicanism. Now, although we have grave objections to losing any of our territory, we have long since conquered any scruples we might have had against acquiring it. And as all the land between the Gulf and the North Star ought to be ours anyhow, this would be as convenient a time as will soon offer for extending to our waiting brethren over the border the privileges of the American eagle and Presidential electors.

It is needless to say that this is a possibility which has already engaged the gravest consideration of the English Government, and which will go far to inspire a spirit of moderation and discreet reserve in their counsels.

There is another thing which we may mention, since it is never out of the mind of England. Just across the channel lives a quiet, cool-headed Emperor, who never omits an opportunity. The only skeleton in Louis Napoleon's closet is the unlaid ghost of Waterloo. An English-American war would be too fine an occasion for a Bonaparte to lose, to balance for all time that unequal account. But the Emperor, who never does anything from impulse, will find his interest in breaking with his arrogant friend. France is starving. Hunger pinches in Paris and the provinces. America laughs with fatness. Here is a situation. Louis may say, "I feed my people. I avenge my ancestor. I defend the right."

It is impossible that the British Cabinet should not think of this. They are filled with gloom and doubt. Their thought finds utterance in the lines of their poet laureate:

True that we have a faithful ally—
But only the devil knows what he means.

With these sleepless French eyes watching her at home, with plain manifestations from Russia of friendly sympathies with America, with the whole world arrayed morally against slavery, and the long record of pharisaical years patent against her present position, England cannot afford to be very insolent and exacting about his matter. It is not apprehended that she will be. A growl—an explanation—more growl—more explanation, and the thing will be forgotten.

On the part of our Government, there is no disposition to yield one jot of what are our just rights in the matter. While all negotiations arising out of the complication will be conducted with the most entire candor and careful courtesy, there will be seen no unmanly subserviency, no cringing and no insolence. There is nothing to dread. We shall not lose honor—retaining which, all losses are slight.[66]

Washington correspondence, 19 December 1861

Gen. Jim Lane has at last gained the title he has so long used. He will no longer be reduced to the necessity of "playing Brigadier with no commission—betting high on small cards," to use his own graphic language, at Leavenworth. He will immediately depart for the West and take the command assigned him by the War Department. The General has not been entirely magnanimous in regard to his Brigadier's commission. He was about to accept it and vacate his seat in the Senate last summer, when discovering that Governor Robinson, thinking he had resigned, had appointed Mr. Stanton to succeed him, he instantly withdrew from the glittering bait he was just swallowing, and went back commissionless to his men. Stanton remained in Washington, while James was burning rebellious villages, and acting in Missouri like an ill conducted patriot of imperfect lights, and tried to operate upon the candid minds of the eminently respectable old party that formed the committee on his claim. Yesterday morning they reported, the majority being favorable to Stanton's pretensions. The gallant Brigadier protested earnestly against being buried before he was dead, and contended for his place as earnestly as if he had not made up his mind to resign it the next day to accept the commission from the President, whose nomination, even while he spoke, was lying sealed upon the Clerk's desk.

I do not think Lane entirely magnanimous in these matters. There has been a very old feud between Lane and Governor Robinson, existing for years. The acrimonies engendered in old political battles were carried into recent contests, in the Legislature of Kansas, and in the ante-chamber of the President. In all these, Lane has been successful. He went to the Senate; he strongly influenced Kansas appointments; his friends were rewarded and Robinson's were slighted. The President has treated him with very remarkable kindness. It would have been graceful in him to have retired from the Senate when he first received his commission, and to have allowed Governor Robinson to fill the vacancy thus created. But he has thus far maliciously deprived Stanton of his place, and even now shows a disposition to defeat him utterly by retaining his own seat until January, when the Kansas Legislature, I learn, will meet, and as Lane hopes, will elect a Senator more friendly to him than to Robinson.

Your Missouri Senator, Mr. Polk, seems also to have gotten recently into bad repute among his compeers. Mr. Sumner yesterday introduced a resolution of expulsion of that worthy, recommending its reference to the Committee on the Judiciary. He read the letter, which you have heretofore published, to Wilkes, in regard to the *States Rights Journal* [*Equal Rights Gazette*], in support and explanation of his resolution. Mr. Saulsbury, of Delaware, rose and with his manly bosom heaving with generous rage at this unprovoked attack upon an innocent and saintly absent one, indignantly stamped the letter as a forgery, because, as he said, "Trusten Polk never could have used the expression '*ante up.*' He wasn't that kind of a man." Then Mr. Sumner said impressively, "Why is he in Memphis when he should be in Washington?" And Mr. Browning said that reliable gentlemen in St. Louis assured him the letter was genuine, and Mr. Bayard, who seemed to think that any reference to the infamy of gambling must be meant for him, blundered out a few leathery sentences, and the resolution was referred. Your State is so far wholly unrepresented in this most important crisis of national affairs. There is no State in which a deeper interest is felt in Washington. The condition of Missouri has been a subject which has very deeply occupied the mind of the President. He received yesterday a delegation of very respectable gentlemen from the Southwest section, who wished to hear some settled plan of action in respect to the conduct of the war in slaveholding regions. There is very great difficulty in announcing at present any settled forms of action which shall be the guide of our generals in every part of our wide spread field of operations. The reason is manifest. The circumstances are never entirely alike in any two localities, and they demand the exercise of a sound discretion in the General commanding as to the course proper to be pursued.

A few of the noisiest and most turbulent of the Congressmen here, resolutely refuse to see this fact, or to make any allowance for the existence of these necessities. They clamor for an emancipation policy at Beaufort, forgetting that even if the negroes obeyed a proclamation which they could not read and came into camp, a week would exhaust completely the commissariat of the army if we were to feed and take care of the millions that according to their showing, would flock to our banners; it would compel an instant indefinite multiplication of our transportation and stores, and a corresponding additional agony in Mr. Chase to furnish the money to pay for the board of this cloud of hungry locusts. There is nothing more wildly unreasonable than this little handful of earnest impracticables, who would cause the sky to fall, if they could, to catch the lark they have wished for so long.

They have been very bitter on McClellan lately, but his popularity as yet knows no wane. The other evening at the President's levee when the General entered with his beautiful young wife, an instant rush of sincere admiration which warmed into positive nuisance attested the reality of the popular confidence in him. The sweet, bright face of his wife became the centre of attraction, and she reigned thenceforth Queen of the Blue Room. Wherever McClellan goes, the hearty welcome of the people proves how ineffectual have been all attempts to write him down, or drown him with faint praise. This is the more remarkable and significant, because the recent attacks upon him have been so grave and dignified in tone, and so able in matter and theoretical discussion. There are few Generals whose popularity could survive an attack so vigorous and so calm as the recent pamphlet of Charles Ellett, of Georgetown, which some over zealous friends of the General attempt to deride as the vagary of a madman. It is a very profound and well-expressed essay. I consider it very much to Gen. McClellan's credit that he regards it calmly and without resentment. Not on account of anything he has done, but on account of many things he has not done, many more things that he will do, do the people love and honor and praise George B. McClellan. And the people are rarely wrong.[67]

Washington correspondence, 23 December 1861

There has not been in Washington of late years an administration so provokingly reticent as the one that now holds counsel in the President's room. In the bad old days when James [*Buchanan*] was President and the reporters of the New York *Herald* attended Cabinet meetings, there was some comfort in being a newspaper man. Able and enterprising correspondents would stroll unabashed into the very presence of republican royalty, and confidently demand an item, or wait with quiet dignity in their sky-parlors until heads of departments should come to traffic latest advices for puffs, well seasoned and peppery. But our new President, who is too busy to read about himself in the newspapers, and our Secretary of State, who has received puffs enough in the first half of his life to last for the rest of it, exhibit none of that craving for journalistic applause which is so charming to those who "write for it." They seem to consider inchoate action an improper subject for public discussion, and prefer to take the course which seems proper to them, uninfluenced by the myriad voices of those whose opinions, however sagacious, are not founded upon that basis of entire information necessary to a complete understanding of political movements.

So the souls of reporters have been troubled within them, and their hair begins to grow gray and their brows furrowed, in the vain attempt to discover what Her Majesty's messenger gave to Lord Lyons—what Lord Lyons said to Mr. Seward, and what Mr. Seward replied to Lord Lyons. So far, they have discovered nothing. Mr. Seward exhibits a charming faculty of holding his tongue, and Lord Lyons, who talked very garrulously when he had nothing to say, has suddenly discovered the virtues of prudence and discretion. They seem to be on the most cordial possible terms—the Secretary and the Ambassador. They have frequent conferences, which, to all appearance, end in nothing, and a bewildering flight of white envelopes fly like carrier doves between the British Legation and the Department of State. As the position which our Government is generally understood to hold is a very plain and simple one, this apparent inaction and oscillation can but be accounted for by concluding that Lord Lyons' dispatches from his home government having been founded upon an entire misapprehension of facts, his Lordship finds himself a little at a loss what course to pursue in the matter. It may possibly result in his sending home for renewed instructions. He is not a man of a great deal of sprightliness of mind or readiness of spirit. His intercourse with our Government has thus far been marked by a singular combination of sluggishness of purpose and seemingly unintentional impertinence of expression. He forms in these respects a most striking contrast to his predecessor, Lord Napier, who was wonderfully successful in adapting himself to the habitudes of American thought and sentiment. He is most kindly remembered by all those with whom he came in contact, and the universal expression now is, that if Napier were here, he and Seward would talk this matter into shape in an evening's interview.

The delay in this matter is of course only ominous and at the same time productive of good. It shows very clearly that there was nothing peremptory in the demand of England, and no intention on the part of either Government unnecessarily to precipitate matters to the last arbitrament. It cannot but result in good to the disturbed spirits of our anxious brethren over the sea. The aspirations of exaggerated rage are dying fast away in the streets of Liverpool and the tap-rooms of Manchester. Time for reflection is showing them the folly of a causeless war, which will bring in its train gaunt hunger and slaughter, and what is worse to an English mind, bankruptcy. The shippers of the United Kingdom will cease clamoring for a war, that being begun for an idle assertion of the rights of neutral bottoms, will end in sweeping from the seas the entire commerce of England, in the wasting path of the Yankee privateers.

The gnawings of famine will quiet the howls of rage. And in the palaces of the rulers, where the destinies of nations are woven in the tangled web of ministerial discussion, the awful peril that lurks in the quiet watchfulness of the silent Emperor over the channel will have its own terrible weight in counseling the peace in which alone safety dwells.

In connection with this last aspect of the foreign question, the brief telegram which this morning announces that Gen. Scott is off Cape Race in the Arago is invested with a strange and startling interest. We may be sure that no ordinary motive has brought the battered warrior back from the rest so long desired and so gladly hailed. Many indications conspire to prove that the American question has excited the gravest and the profoundest interest in the councils of France. The visit of Prince Napoleon, undertaken ostensibly for mere recreation, it is now quite certain was made at the express command of his imperial cousin to ascertain by personal observation the exact state of affairs in this Republic. His discreet reserve while here—his avoidance of any assertion by which his sympathies could even be suspected—his visit to Beauregard at Manassas so curiously regarded and violently blamed, proved conclusively that he had come resolved against any committal. His report, immediately on arriving at home, of the certainty of the final triumph of the Union cause did, of course, credit to his sagacity, but its publication was a most significant indication of the feelings of the Emperor. Since that, the passing weeks have not been barren of incidents, all pointing one way. It is impossible to resist the conviction that the clear headed and patriotic despot of France is watching an opportunity to attack with entire certainty of success the arrogant and insolent power that cordially hates him and his people. Men frequently say that Louis Napoleon lusts for revenge for Waterloo. This is absurd. Men like the Emperor of the French are not governed by impulses, such as rule school boys and prize-fighters. If nothing but feelings of personal pride and national spirit called for war with England, it would be long before the guns of Cherbourg opened, or the black bulk of "*La Gloire*" steamed sullenly into the straits of Dover. But far deeper considerations than any derived from national antipathies, or the cankering memories of old battle fields, influence Napoleon in his suspicious attitude towards England. The necessities of intact existence and the peace of a continent demand that that arrogant and greedy government shall be scourged and humiliated into a decent respect for the rights of others. Her career of unblushing oppression and insolence has continued so long unchecked, that it has at last become an article of her national faith that her will shall be the only law upon the seas, and the London *Times* shamelessly asserts "that we shall not permit others to do what we once did ourselves." America, alone of all nations, has met and contested these vexed questions with her. In the day of our strength we defeated her, once in arms and once in diplomacy. She esteems this a happy opportunity to humiliate us in return. But the interests of all civilization imperatively demand that this shall not be done. When a power grows strong enough and shameless enough to substitute its will for international law, the safety of the world demands that it shall be outlawed and hunted down, as pirates and slavers are.

Louis Napoleon is too sound a statesman and publicist not to recognize the pernicious consequences of allowing an outrage, such as his insolent ally proposes, to be perpetrated in the light of day. He feels that if a great nation, sorely troubled by domestic treason, is to be sacrificed for the cowardly greed of this overshadowing tyranny, hereafter there is no safety for any people, in the just restraints of decent honor and international comity.

It is unlikely that General Scott would return except upon the gravest business. And I have reason to believe that what I have said of the disposition of the Emperor of the French is not altogether unconnected with his appearance.[68]

Washington correspondence, 26 December 1861

There are very few observers who have not been startled at the strange and unexpected response which the tocsin of threatened war wakes in the hills of Ireland. It has always been our custom, speaking loosely of the chances of the future, to say that Ireland would some day rise again, when the feet of the Saxon pressed a little less heavily on the neck of the prostrate nationality. We have so long been accustomed to the sweet and melodious extravagance of Irish poets, who, ever since the conquest, have so musically apostrophized the golden coming time when the Deliverer should appear, with mighty surges to rouse the dreaming people into life, to dash off the chains from the fair form of the spell-bound Erin, and to startle from their stony sleep in the caverns of Killarny the drowsy horseman of O'Neil—that we have fallen gradually into a colorless habit of thinking, that only the shock of actual war could rouse from her trancing lethargy the soul of Ireland. Vague ideas, also, of the vigorous power of English public opinion, and the stringency of English treason statutes, seemed to preclude the possibility of the real spirit of the people obtaining authentic utterance in print or in convention. But to our surprise, no less than to that of England, we find that the souls of the National Irish are all aglow with the quiet inspiration of the future deliverance. A public meeting most numerously and respectably attended is held in Dublin, at which resolutions expressing the most unreserved sympathy with America, and the most undisguised expressions of joyful hope that now is the time for all who have longed for the unity of Ireland to watch for the opportunity, surely coming, for a blow to be struck for freedom and independence. Two reputable and widely circulated journals contain the reports of these proceedings, adding commendatory comments, and bear words full of calm, determined, earnest hope—the hope that flowers into action. Smith O'Brien writes a letter full of honest blunders and generous untimeliness, in which he has no hesitation in avowing his certain confidence in the future of his land. And all over the emerald valleys of the beautiful island goes the significant whisper, counselling patience and inspiring hope; and the hearts of the down-trodden are lifted up, and a strange new light goes into the eyes of youth, and new words are in their mouths, and the happy foreshadowings of the coming time of struggle and glory float half confessed over

The fair hills of holy Ireland.

All this occurs seemingly by the connivance of the British government. Either they blindly underestimate the deadly peril of the time, or else they fear, by strict judicial action, to excite to still ruder demonstrations the enthusiastic and untamed populace. So the preparations for the coming struggle go on quietly. Even when this cloud with England blows over for a little while from our sky, the heavens are not clear over Ireland yet. It will not be many years that the most pacific administration can keep our justly incensed people from settling at once, on land and sea, all these accumulating scores. The arrogance of England must be distinctly met and tamed, and I think Providence has specially detailed the United States for that particular duty. And when the time comes that England is occupied in defending from our sea-militia men her costly cargoes and garrisoning her cities against our swarming veterans, then will the sublime resurrection of Young Ireland begin.

Although parted by an ocean swelling between them, the leal hearts of the Irish Americans beat most warmly for their waiting brothers at home. You have heard, of course, of that mysterious and powerful organization whose ramifications extend through every county in the Union, whose members are pledged to the sacred cause of liberty as against all other causes. In this mighty army, whose *esprit de corps* is nourished and sustained by the purest fervors of an almost fanatical patriotism, Michael Corcoran, it is said, holds the position of Major General. An army so composed, so banded, so inspirited, and properly commanded by men of themselves, would be well nigh irresistible on the sod of their long desecrated homes. If England should persist in the incredible folly and suicide of forcing a war upon us, what a shout of exultation would go up from the downtrodden and long suffering Celts! How brightly, through the roseate mists of slaughter, would gleam the distant sunshine of liberty, and an independence cemented by blood and hallowed by glorious memories!

When the time comes, their Generals will not be wanting. It is to be hoped that long before any such necessity can arise, the gallant Corcoran may be restored to his friends and companions-in-arms. But if led by an insane and murderous cruelty the rebels should take that precious life, his indignant shade would float, a palpable presence, before the serried legions of his countrymen, devoting to the infernal gods the shrinking and panic-stricken enemy. Shields is on his way here from the Pacific shore. He brings with him the prestige of success in everything which he has thus far undertaken. His courage and his military ability were removed above the sphere of discussion, in the best-contested battles of Mexico, and his power of moving masses of men is known to all who ever heard one of his chain-lightning speeches, toward the close of a hot campaign. He accepts, with patriotic alacrity, the post of a Brigadier-General, though he honestly thought that his services and acquirements deserved a place where increase of rank would bring increase of labor and responsibility. Had it not been for the malignant jealousy of Jeff. Davis, General Shields would now have held a high position in our regular army. What better hand could be found to raise the star spangled banner side by side with the gold-bordered verdure of the Irish flag on "the fair hills of holy Ireland?"

Another Irish thunderbolt is Thomas Francis Meagher. He has made fame enough for ordinary ambition since this fight began. But he left in the island home of his love a name approached by none other for fervid and impassioned eloquence. He, more than any other, was worthy of being styled the fiery tongue of the Irish revolution. His industry and energy have been unsleeping. His oratory has caught anew the unction and fire of his wonderful youth. He became the idol of his men as a Captain in the Sixty-ninth [*New York Militia*]. But his modesty has been as distinguished as his merit. To all the entreaties of his friends he has steadily responded that he preferred the brigade which he had called into being should be commanded by a man more technically capable than himself. He only yielded when further resistance would have seemed like obstinacy, and a disposition to avoid responsibility. His very name will be worth a host in any field where the strong magic of nationality is to be used to harden the hearts and stiffen the sinews of his clansmen.

Altogether, it seems that there is more of reality and less of romance than ever before in the dreams of Irish patriots. We can imagine the drugged troopers of O'Neill stirring uneasily in their drowse, and the tramp of the coming deliverer mingling cheerily with their breaking dream. It is no longer a wild fancy to hope that the eyes of men now living shall see Ireland free. The morning already begins to grown gray. It may not break without its dawn flushing red with the haze of battles; but that is no more than its early prophets have foreseen, as poor Clarence Mangan, many years ago, so tenderly sang, typifying his nation under the delicate shadow of the Dark Rose:

> Oh! the Eire shall run red
> With redundance of blood;
> The earth shall rock beneath our trod,
> And flames wrap hill and wood;
> And gun-peal and slogan cry
> Wake many a glen serene,
> Ere you shall fade, ere you shall die,
> My Dark Rosaleen!
> My own Rosaleen!
> The Judgement Hour must first be nigh,
> Ere you can fade, ere you can die,
> My Dark Rosaleen![69]

WASHINGTON CORRESPONDENCE, 28 DECEMBER 1861

Some of the earnest Republicans in Congress find themselves placed in the most embarrassing situation by the present state of affairs. By every consideration of honor and duty, they are pledged to support the administration of Mr. Lincoln—and the wise and prudent patriotism that has thus far marked his course, forms another most powerful incentive the same direction. Every motive, both of duty and interest, would seem to lead them in the same path, but the habit of opposition, acquired and cherished through long years of a baffled and struggling minority, is too powerful to be so suddenly overcome. Mr. Trumbull, who has been accustomed, for the last six years, to watch with the eyes of Argus for any symptom of glaring dereliction in a corrupt Administration, and to hail with transports of avenging joy any irregularity or recklessness that could leave an opening for the shafts of his remorseless logic, has been fidgety and nervous ever since his honest old friend went into the White House, and dried up the source of his perennial and hitherto exhaustless fault-finding. He has been sitting sadly and silently at his desk, mourning over the decease of the good old days of Covode's researches, when you could not beat an official thicket without scaring up a lively covey of frauds and thefts, and when patriots in the minority might cry aloud and spare not against the minions of a pampered despotism, and put the galleries to sleep, while rousing the hoarse murmurs of the rural districts. What was the use of being honest, and acute, and brave, he thought, if you did not pitch into somebody? Such a train of reflections led him into that hornet's nest that gathered around his astonished ears the morning he charged so valiantly on Mr. Seward and the President, for shutting rebels up in castles by the sea, without benefit of counsel. He was handled so roughly by even his best friends that he will not be likely to repeat that act of indiscreet and unconquerable patriotism very soon. The only man who came to his rescue (save those sheepish, semi-secessionist recruits that, hearing the bugle of onset sounded against the Administration, came up to his side to be in at the death, not seeming to mind it particularly if their leader were the most opaque of Republicans, while he fought against the Government)—was John P. Hale. The fortune of this worthy gentleman has been especially hard. All the reputation he has ever gained in Congress has been through his ceaseless and merciless attacks upon the party in power. Given an Administration measure, you are sure to have a witty, caustic and unavailing speech from the New Hampshire Senator against it. He has been fighting so long for the rights of the down trodden minority, that he has fallen in love with the very idea of hopeless championship. And now that the minority has come into its possessions and needs his arm no longer, he turns from it in disgust and sets diligently about making another little minority to fight for. He has made several little dashes in that direction, but he really had hardly the heart to go any noticeable lengths in his denunciations of his friends, and all the Republicans in the Senate liked Hale so well that any acrimony of debate has hitherto been avoided. His last manifestation of spleen on Thursday was most singular and only not surprising because it was his. Nothing could have been imagined more inopportune or ill-chosen. While the echoes of the Christmas bells were yet sounding in the air, and the memories of the yesterday's lessons of peace and good will were yet lingering in the minds of all good people, the Senator dyspeptically rose and railed without sense of discretion against the Government for not immediately declaring war against England. It amounted simply to that. When everybody knew that the honor of the country was safe in the hands of men so thoroughly American as the President and the Secretary of State, while everyone appreciated the awful consequences of undue rashness or unmanly subserviency, it was little short of madness for a Senator of the known patriotism and rugged honesty of Mr. Hale, to make a speech at once so silly and so pernicious. It was easy enough to see why a sneaking reptile like Vallandigham should, in a cowardly attempt to serve his Southern owners, try to bully the House into some expression of hostility to the power which has the power and longs for the opportunity to embarrass us dreadfully in crushing the rebellion. His animus was so plain and so contemptible, that a quiet snubbing disposed of him. But Hale every one recognizes as honestly devoted to the Union cause. To see a man of his calibre engaging in a course so absurd and so perilous was a most melancholy illustration of the extremes to which a one-sided fanaticism and a mere reprehensible and causeless grumbling will carry a man who has given himself completely up to such influences.

It is a promising symptom that he took nothing by his motion. There was no movement of cohesion in the Senate chamber. The few dignified remarks that Sumner made, in reply to the vociferous and heated harangue of Hale, expressed clearly and tersely the sentiment of the Senate and the country on this subject. His remarks were most timely, and happy in their effect. He spoke with a certain authority, as Chairman of the Committee on Foreign Relations. His earnest confidence and the unreserved expression of his conviction that the affair with England would have a termination both honorable and peaceful, has not been without its healthful effect upon public sentiment. The panics of last week are over now, and the public mind seems settling into the conviction that the quarrel, not of our seeking, is in skillful and prudent hands, and that in some honorable way, so great a misfortune as a war with England is to be avoided. Combined with this new born hope is the old steadiness of purpose and resolve. If a war with England should come, we will do as we have done twice before, in similar cases.

Altogether, the rampant patriotism with which this Congress began its session seems happily going out, and a more sensible course of work will probably begin with the new year. The Investigating Committees, which are to be, I suppose, standing nuisances, from this time, are flickering out. There has not been enough fraud discovered, or money saved, to pay half the hotel bills of the peripatetic pilgrims of the committee. Wherever they have gone, they have been confronted with the unwelcome apparition of honesty and good management, till they actually began to be ashamed of their business. Real abuses, like those of the medical and the pay bureaus, inefficiencies of systems, and shameful slavery to traditions of service, are left untouched, while these virtuous ferrets of political rat-holes are wasting their own time and the Government money, in travelling over the country on a wild goose chase after impossible villainies. The easiest way in the world to get a reputation for integrity is to prove your neighbor no better than he should be. This principle our budding Lycurguses have worked *ad nauseam*. It is to be hoped that we are to have next month more work and less indignant virtue.[70]

3

1862

MCCLELLAN'S ILLNESS, WHICH AT FIRST WAS CALLED AN ORDINARY cold attended with slight fever, seems to be hanging on with that vague pertinacity which characterizes every disagreeable visitation of Washington society, from office-seekers to ague. Every day the sensationalizers represent him as in *articulo mortis,* and immediately after, the hopeful and kind-hearted optimist of the Associated Press says that he will certainly be in the saddle in a day or two. Yesterday the President spent the greater part of the afternoon with him. There has been no one in Washington who has exhibited more intense anxiety than the President that an early and effective movement should be made against the enemy, at a time like this, when our army has reached almost the highest point of discipline attainable in camp, and the forces of the rebels are beginning to feel the pernicious effects of idleness and a general lack of organization. His constant supervision exercised over all the departments of the Government has been a constant rebuke to indolence and spur to activity. He appreciates fully the vast importance of every moment of passing time. McClellan, I learn, informed him yesterday that his illness was not serious—that he considered himself convalescent, and that only the warnings of his physician kept him in doors at present. If he remains indisposed many days longer, his place as Commander of the Army of the Potomac will be filled by another, and his functions as Commander-in-Chief will be assumed by the President.

Symptoms of the vague uneasiness that last summer culminated at Manassas are beginning to make themselves manifest at the hotels and in the lobbies. Congressional grumblers, who have been thus far in the session placed in the background by the earnest and self-sacrificing patriotism evinced by the people and the press, who have so generously abstained from censure or criticism of the Administration, are gathering strength and position for new attacks. The tendency to finding fault is evinced in many ways. Some have mounted the discarded "Onward to Richmond" hobby of the *Tribune* and clamor with a very fair show of reason for an immediate advance. Others go groping around among the details of contracts and finance, smelling with the diseased appetite of vultures for any indications of fraud or peculation. Still others, more insufferably mean and hypocritical than all, are striving to gain a little cheap popularity at home, by cutting and trimming at the pitiful salaries of department clerks. Foremost in this crusade against the daily bread of the hardworking subordinates of the departments is John Sherman, whose passion for cutting down other men's salaries and saving his own amounts to a monomania. There has not been a session of late years in which the honorable gentleman from Ohio has not made a nuisance of himself by impertinent intermeddling with somebody's pay. The Government has been paying him at the rate of ten dollars a day, to pitch into abuses amounting in the aggregate to a yearly waste of five hundred dollars. Van Wyck is another foul bird. His constant effort is to prove somebody a thief; the sight of an honest man is to him an abomination. He is playing the united roles of a Colonel and a Congressman, and playing both badly. In his seat in Congress he never sinks the Colonel, and in the Camp he never forgets that he will be a candidate for re-election to Congress. His Investigating Committee is an absurd fiasco. It has been used chiefly as an engine to ventilate personal animosities and prejudices existing in the minds of the incorruptible committeemen against better people. The exquisite passages detailing the researches of the Committee in St. Louis are supposed to be the handiwork of Elihu Washburne of Illinois. As well by the gross and palpable absurdities which deform every sentence of this division of the Report, as by its silly attack upon Marshal Lamon of this district, is the authorship of this specimen of modern statesmanship discovered. It is to be hoped that the House will at once administer an effectual rebuke to such shameful exhibitions of private envies and jealousies under the cloak of rampant patriotism and indignant honesty.

Horace Greeley, who has come down here apparently to marshal the hosts of the grumblers for the fray, is a different style of man. No man denies his honesty, no man questions his disinterestedness. He is not a candidate for any office within the gift of the people or President. He grumbles because he is an honest old fanatic, and does not agree with the Administration; and all honest people honor him for his integrity, though they may differ by a world's width from his views.

Frederick Conkling, of New York City, is another stern crusader against the President, the Cabinet and all others in authority. He is a thoroughly honest and impracticable man. He is for cutting down his own salary, his own mileage and that of his compeers, which his incorruptible friends don't like. They are willing enough to take the bread from the hungry mouths of the children of over-tasked clerks, but propose to touch their own three thousand a year, and, to use the language of the ribald, "they don't see it." Conkling is a man of wealth, of high character, of fine social position, of handsome and commanding presence. He is the cleanest of the fanatics in the House.

There has recently been a most amusing and suggestive love-feast among the brimstone radicals. Old Thaddeus Stevens, and the little knot of Pennsylvanians who have not received contracts, have been abusing the Secretary of War with every ingenious epithet of objurgation, since the Fourth of March. Thaddeus himself said on a public occasion, that "Cameron naturally followed Floyd in of homogeneousness of succession." Andrew Curtin, the gentleman who occupies the Gubernatorial chair of Pennsylvania, was equally severe upon Simon, and answered Seward's Defense Circular in the most impertinent terms, merely because he thought the Secretaries of State and War were friends. But the assumed difference of the President and the Secretary of War upon the contraband question, reconciled all those family jars, and Cameronians and Curtinites fell on each other's necks and wept. The delighted and melted Stevens in a gush of guileless confidence exclaimed, "A man who is right on the nigger can steal to all eternity, and I am for him."

General Cameron, who never is vindictive, reviews with a quiet smile these new-born congratulations, and wonders what he has done to merit them. There has never been the slightest unkindness or distrust between him and the President. He modified his report readily at the suggestion of Mr. Lincoln, and recalled the copies sent to the Press. Those who hoped to see discord in the Administration will have to wait for a future occasion.[1]

WASHINGTON CORRESPONDENCE, 11 JANUARY 1862

There have been two seats vacated in the Senate since the falling of the leaves. The halo of a patriot's martyrdom lingers over one, which lost its occupant [*Edward D. Baker of Oregon*] on that day of unavailing glory at Ball's Bluff. A stain of treason and basest ingratitude deforms the other, whose fugitive owner [*John C. Breckinridge of Kentucky*] is still pursued by the loud voice of public scorn, forever repeating, like a bellman advertising an absconding apprentice, "ran away from his duty."

Could a more striking contrast be imagined than between the dead hero and the lost traitor? Through all time our history will cherish the memory of the grand, gray-haired Senator, standing undismayed in the presence of the death that was certain, earnest to throw an honest lustre upon the close of a day that folly not his own had made disastrous, and counting life and honor and fame as little worth in the achievement of this bright but cruel sacrifice. Not less pointed and suggestive will be the scene of the lost Kentuckian's flight to the future historian. He fled by night, away from the memories of his old fame, the connections of an honored ancestry, the love of his countrymen and the honorable place to which their partiality had raised him, into the beguiling embraces of a mad and ruinous rebellion. There is nothing more mournful than the spectacle of that wandering and vacillating man, plunged by weakness of will and desperation of wounded vanity into endless disgrace and moral suicide. While the sunset glow of Baker's life brightens the hills and valleys of Oregon, the smirch of Breckinridge's treason dims sadly the white loyalty of Kentucky.

Destiny, which seems to delight in startling contrasts and unforeseen circumstances, has given as the sequel of this incident a picture, whose lights are as bright, whose shadows are as dismal. The magnanimous recoil of Kentucky from the incubus of hidden treason, has thrown into the Senate, the wise, sagacious and incorruptible Garrett Davis, and the Governor of Oregon, taking an infamous advantage of the decree of God, which left the seat of Baker vacant, has dared to pollute it by forcing into its occupancy a semi-secessionist named Starke. This would have seemed impossible out of Oregon. When every heart from the Ponobscot to the gold-sanded Fraser's River was bowed in sorrow, ennobled by pride, for the death and the glory of Baker, did it not seem impossible that any man could be found to gratify a cherished malice by the awful opportunity of the hour, and to take a hideous vengeance on the hated name of the glorious dead, by dishonoring the place his genius had illumined, by the presence of his and the country's detractor? It is too contemptible for anger, too sad for ridicule.

I am glad that the *personale* of these two men carry out so faithfully the impressions of their antecedents. Garrett Davis is a gentleman, slight in stature, elderly, quiet, grave. A fine head—thin white hair, the baldness of the brow giving prominence to the benevolence and energy indicated by the phrenological development—clear bright eyes, a Wellingtonian nose—a firm, straight mouth—a complexion untarnished by dissipation, and an expression of feature honest and steadfast, without concealments and without fear.

If the new Senator from Oregon is a true man, he should sue his face for libel. He has a long, evasive countenance; shiny, sandy hair; narrow forehead; white eye-brows; colorless, pale eyes, nearly closed, which watch furtively, felinely; a mouth whose expression is hidden by mahogany whiskers and moustaches. I should think he would feel ill at ease in Baker's place. I should think the ghost of the dead patriot, murdered by the treason that Stark has smiled upon, would rise before him and discomfort him. He is not to be envied in his honors. The tool of a disaffected Governor, the misrepresentative of the honest sentiment of his State, the successor of a man whose glory dwarfs him, he is to be congratulated only on his pay, and his ample mileage. Perhaps he is satisfied with that.

Anyhow, the halo of past worth still sanctifies the name of the young and loyal State. In spite of the trick of little men, and the presence of their agent, in the hearts and minds of the people, in the tender memories of Senators and the eloquent suggestions of history, the seat of the Senator from Oregon is vacant, or only tenanted by the august shade of Edward Dickinson Baker.

The modest and loyal Kinsley Bingham is gone forever from his place, and Mr. Howard, a good man, formerly a Representative from Detroit, takes the vacated desk of the honest farmer of Michigan. The Senate, in an unusual attack of virtuous indignation, is threatening the expulsion of your two Senators, those flowers of statesmanship and loyalty, Trusten Polk and Waldo P. Johnson. They have been for several months pining for the light of their presence, and not seeing the propriety of the great State of Missouri longer remaining unrepresented by the *laches* of her elected Senators, they propose to make room for better men. Stanton will probably in a day or two step into the boots of the Bombastes of Kansas [*Jim Lane*], while the brave Brigadier goes forth conquering and to conquer. And that will for the present close the changes in the Senate.[2]

WASHINGTON CORRESPONDENCE, 14 JANUARY 1862

Cities and communities have their peculiarities and proclivities as well as individuals, and to the mere dreamer, or the speculator in the science of ethnology, these distinguishing characteristics are as interesting as surprising. Boston is famous for notions, Lowell for factory girls, and Lynn for cordwainers; Wethersfield smells of onions, and Newark of paint and varnish; Pittsburgh is so grimed with smoke, soot and cinders that the sun at midday looks like an unsnuffed tallow candle; and Cincinnati is so intensely porcine and oleaginous that, since the perfecting of the river blockade, hog's grease is cheaper than daylight, and some of the merchants close their shutters and light their lamps at noon day.

Washington is most remarkable for political corruption and curious horseblocks. The former characteristic is pretty well known to all news readers, but the latter, though quite as noted a feature of the Capital city, has not yet been embalmed in old rags and lampblack. Ancient Troy was immortalized by a single wooden horse. Washington has done better, and must live in history on account of its whole regiment of stone and wooden horse blocks. These horse-blocks, or carriage-blocks as you please to call them, deserve to be noticed, for they are the most prominent objects in the fashionable streets. There is an originality and simplicity in the contrivance which reflect as much credit upon the inventor as upon those who, for long years, have followed the fashion. The first impression upon a stranger is surprising, not to say disagreeable. As you pass along the wide *trottoir* [*sidewalk*] of one of the fashionable avenues, the first idea is that a fleet of steamboats has just departed, leaving their stage planks lying higgledy-piggledy, with one end upon the pavement and the other extending out into the sea of mud, for these patent horse-blocks resemble nothing in heaven or earth so much as a twelve foot section of a steamboat's staging, one-half lying upon the pavement and the other half over the gutter. This and other singularities, in which much labor and money have been expended to produce showy inconveniences, lead one to conclude that Washington was originally settled by a bad cross between the Virginia Tuckahoes and the Pennsylvania Quakers, and that they have managed to perpetuate the follies and eccentricities of both classes without the virtues of either. But a change is coming over the spirit of the dream. There is a vast irruption from Yankeedom, and the spirit of utility and speculation is rife everywhere. Magnificent shingle palaces, with open fronts and gingerbread architecture, are looming up on the business streets; the Capitol basement has been turned into a huge bakery, and if the worst should come to the worst, the Rotunda may answer for a cotton factory or grist mill.

The popular pressure upon the Government and upon the military leaders is becoming more intense every day. The people cry out for something to be done. They say, give us at least one live General who will stop proclaiming and go to fighting. They see immense armies and fleets collected and a monstrous public debt accumulating, and yet nothing accomplished at all commensurate with the means employed. Half a million of men are now in the field, well armed and equipped, being supplied with every implement and appliance of successful warfare. For months past all the public and private armories in the country have been working double time, and producing immense quantities of the most approved patterns of cannon and small arms, as well as death-dealing projectiles, and every description of war munitions. On the sea and rivers we have more than three hundred war vessels of all descriptions, manned by twenty-five thousand sailors and marines, and armed with more than a thousand heavy guns. With this immense land and sea force, we have done some things most creditable to ourselves and injurious to the enemy. We have at least preserved our soil from invasion, and have retaken at Hatteras one post that was seized by the insurgents. Is this all that was promised or expected? and if not, where lies the responsibility of the failure? Such questions as these are propounded by the people in every section of the country, and the clamor is growing louder every day.

The Secretary of Finance has displayed wonderful zeal and ability in filling a bankrupt treasury and supplying the sinews of war. In this respect, Mr. Chase has accomplished a herculean task, but all his plans and efforts will end in ruin unless followed by wholesome legislative enactments and decided military movements. Already the treasury notes have commenced to depreciate, and with a few months of Congressional and military inaction, they will sink to a level with the old Continental Scrip or the assignats of the French Revolution. In the meantime Congress blatherskites over the nigger, and the army remains *in statu quo*. Nothing but a series of decided successes by the Union arms, seconded by such legislation as will provide for the prompt payment of interest on the debt, can save us from financial evils of the gravest character.

Will this legislation and these military triumphs come in time? I think they will, especially the latter, and the more important of the two. It is true, that we have been promised from time to time some grand demonstrations, most of which have fizzled out in smoke, or the impatient commander, after striking the first blow, has returned home to be glorified, instead of following up his success, blow after blow. The present indications are that the country is no longer to be disappointed, and the first month of the new year will yet put a new face upon war matters.

A great difficulty has been that the war was commenced and prosecuted on the Union side with the intention that "nobody should be hurt." The first plan was to choke the rebellion to death with a big snake; but that snake is long since dead, even to his tail. Then came the plan of the fabled iron dungeon with its collapsing walls, which, as they approached each other, were to squeeze Jeff. Davis and his crew into something less than a cocked hat. This device is partially given up, and the general notion prevails that there must be some hard fighting. In this connection, the question naturally arises whether, if this war is to cost fifty thousand lives, it would be better to lose them at once in battle and end the strife, or to continue it through a series of years in a sort of border-guerrilla practice, in which most of the lives would be lost by camp diseases. This last plan would utterly exhaust the resources of the whole country, demoralize a million of men by years of camp life, destroy the institutions of the South, and render it a barren and almost unpeopled desert, at the same time so intensifying sectional animosity that no union of heart could ever exist afterwards. This, however, is the plan of the ultra Abolitionists and the army contractors. Oh, for one day of the old Napoleon, who would hang or banish enough of these miscreants to save the country!

The war has reached a point now where compromise is not dreamed of on either side, and there is a general conviction that somebody must be hurt—in fact, that somebody must be whipped, before a permanent peace can follow. When it becomes necessary to have two suns and two moons in one hemisphere, it may answer to have two great republics on the main body of the American continent; until that time shall arrive there can be but one. This great country, which Providence designed as a home for the lovers and martyrs of liberty from all nations, must absorb others instead of disintegrating itself. The South has waged war upon passion instead of principle, and the concession of her demands would open the way to nothing but anarchy, for which secession is a perfect synonym. In this contest one or the other party must go under. May God give victory to the right.

A committee of Bank Directors is here at present, in conference with Secretary Chase and the Finance Committee of the House, respecting the best means of sustaining the credit of the Government. The bank men wish to impose some new conditions upon the Government, which would ultimately give us a moneyed instead of a military despotism. Congress inclines to the plan originally proposed by Mr. Chase, and the main features of this will, in all probability, be adopted.

To mete out justice and fairly divide the expenses of the war amongst those who would have it, an important bill has been reported by Mr. Blair, from the House Military Committee, the main features of which are as follows: The apportionment of the proper amount of the national tax amongst the seceded States, and the collection of each seceded State's portion from its real and personal estate—the appointment of Commissioners to sell the landed property for the benefit of the United States, allowing a right of redemption to all loyal citizens—the confiscation of the property of rebels who refuse to pay the tax—the emancipation of rebels' slaves who come within our lines—the employment of these emancipated slaves for the use of Government—arrangements for the colonization of the emancipated slaves—the accumulation from the sale of rebel property to be used to indemnify losses to loyal citizens, pay the expense of colonizing manumitted slaves, and assist in discharging the National debt. The bill is long and somewhat complicated, but these are in brief its main features.

Messrs. Isaac H. Sturgeon and Adolphus Meier, of St. Louis, and Mr. Craig, ex-member of Congress from Northwest Missouri, are here to look after the interests of the Missouri railroads. Their great object is to relieve the Hannibal and Pacific roads from the condition imposed by the grant of lands, to transport troops and war munitions free of expense to the Government. There is so much justice in the matter that I am not surprised to learn that they are likely to succeed.[3]

WASHINGTON CORRESPONDENCE, 15 JANUARY 1862

It would scarcely have seemed possible to a careless observer that a change in the Cabinet could have been accomplished with so little stir and excitement as that which has sent General Cameron to St. Petersburg, and called Edwin M. Stanton from the cobwebs of his office to the head of the greatest department of the Government. The present Administration, surely, is nothing if not discreet. There was no whisper of anything about to happen, until Mr. Nicolay had sent to the desk of the President of the Senate the sealed envelope containing the new nominations of the late Secretary and the late Attorney. A few of the Senators loafed quietly up to the desk, according to their custom, to look at the nominations, and saw what before there had been no hint of, a change in the Government.

During the last week there has been an earnest and unceasing opposition to General Cameron in quarters whose representations are entitled to respect. No charges affecting his personal integrity have ever been made except by the ignorant and the reckless. But, like Frémont, he has been in very many instances unfortunate in those whom he has trusted. Many indications of a dissatisfaction, founded on palpable and tangible evidences of malversation among the employees of the Department, came daily to notice. The unfortunate affair of his report, while it affected no change whatever in the cordial and friendly relations between the Secretary and the President, gave rise to much of sinister comment. In spite of all charges, however, he retained the kind feeling and the sincere friendship of the President, and closed the controversy in regard to his incumbency by abruptly resigning his office. The President at once appointed him Envoy Extraordinary and Minister Plenipotentiary to the Court of the Czar, in place of Cassius Clay, who has been for two months clamoring for a recall.

In the selection of a successor a great many qualifications were requisite, most of which were found in Stanton. Harmony with the present Cabinet was secured. He is personally friendly with every member of it, and in entire unity of feeling and thought with the two leading spirits of the Government, Chase and Seward. He was a Pennsylvanian, and his selection satisfied the jealous State pride that placed General Cameron in the Cabinet. He was a Democrat, and his nomination furnished a triumphant vindication of the professions of leading Republicans, that former party politics are to be ignored in this great struggle for the National Life. He is a man whose laborious and successful career in the pursuit of his profession has made him few enemies, and removed him utterly from the bitter partisanship and prejudices of political campaigns. He is an energetic and efficient worker, a man of initiative and decision, an organizer, a man of administrative scope and executive tact—a very good pattern for a Secretary of War.

There is one ugly thing about this matter, which is almost sure to give rise to false impressions. Some weeks ago the Legislature of Kentucky passed a set of very impertinent resolutions, calling upon the President to dismiss Gen. Cameron from the Cabinet. The seedy and chivalric Kentucky Unionists—who, instead of staying at home and fighting for their State, are hanging around the bars of hotels, and the anteroom of the President, blowing their little penny-trumpet of patriotism, and modestly asking to be made Consuls and Paymasters—have continually echoed the insolent demand of their Legislature, and filled the foggy air of Washington with denunciations of the Secretary of War. They will, of course, claim the recent change as a victory. It is absurd to imagine that they and their legislation influenced the matter a feather's weight. A State whose politics fluctuate continually with the rise and fall in the price of negroes is not exactly the point from which an Administration would expect reliable indications of public sentiment.

Many appointments would have been more popular and more in accordance with the fancy of the multitude. The magnificent eloquence and the unshaken loyalty of Jos. Holt have endeared him to the hearts of the people, and created a vague impression that if ever a change were made, Holt would go back to the place his occupancy has already made so honorable. General Dix was unquestionably the choice of a very large and respectable class, although his often quoted order in relation to shooting on the spot the man who should attempt to haul down the flag, has not been the rule that has guided his gentle sway, in his duties of conciliating Baltimore and conquering Accomac. The very best man for the place was Nathaniel P. Banks, if circumstances would have allowed the appointment to be made. But Banks is of late an Illinoisan and that taboos a candidate for office under our sensitive President, who thinks when he gives an office to an Illinoisan that some other State is swindled. Taking everything together, though, we may be glad we have gotten so good a man. I hope our incorruptible Congressmen will not blackguard him out of his place before he is fairly seated in it; and

I hope that the newspapers will not make a policy for him before he speaks for himself, because if they do, they will go many degrees astray. For it must not be thought that because he is an earnest and hard-working Democrat, and because Gen. Cameron, who is gone, was an abolitionist, that Mr. Stanton is going to fold his hands in the defensive style, or show any greater solicitude for rebels than for loyal men. He is one of those straight-thinking and honest men, who believe in the realities of principle and the earnestness of war. He carries behind his gold mounted spectacles a far-seeing eye and an active brain. He goes into his place untrammeled by promises, unfettered by hungry friends. Where he sees the rebellion strong and defiant he will strike blows to stagger it. If it staggers, he will mercilessly strike blows to finish it. So say Mr. Stanton's friends, who know him best, and we, who do not know him at all, say, if it be true, then the President knew whom to select for his new Secretary of War.[4]

WASHINGTON CORRESPONDENCE, 20 JANUARY 1862

The spouting wretches at the Capitol are still wrangling over little things, and shamefully neglecting great ones. It seems hopeless to look for further efficiency from a body of men selected in peaceful times, who are unable to forget the old traditions of their craft, and to come up on the level of the altered time. You will find in either chamber the same old cringing to the fancied wishes of the constituency of each particular district, regardless of the paramount claims of the endangered nationality. In a time like this, a legislator should lead his people out from the mists of old political dogmas into the clearer light of the changed expediencies. Old things have passed away, and legislation should be renovated. It is melancholy to see, at a time like this, members of the National Legislature talking the old bosh of campaigns, and working with one eye always open to the contingencies which may affect their reelection. This indolence and timidity is most outrageously apparent in the conduct of Congress in relation to the needed tax bills. When the whole country is crying for an early, vigorous and effective scheme of national taxation, you may find in the Capitol only an assembly of shivering and timorous wretches, standing in deadly fear of their seats, and each one nervously solicitous to have the required bills pass without his vote. They have wasted in vain and unprofitable discussion the golden moments of December and January, without one single effort to relieve the stricken and faltering finances of the country. And still the lamentable farce goes on. Still they waste the long days in senseless disquisitions on the status of the colored person; still they discuss the finer points of international law, and pass resolutions of inquiry to embarrass and hinder the work of the overcrowded Departments of the Government, while public credit lies fainting and gasping before them, although in the very plenitude of life and capability, like a muscular giant under an exhausted receiver. This is pure and simple cowardice. Indolence is not an apology. Childish vanity and the lust for printed reports of speeches are not alone at the bottom of all this silly and deluging talk. They are afraid to tax the people, who are begging to be taxed, for fear that in the revulsion of re-awakened avarice their tenure of three thousand a year and mileage will be endangered.

The more a man knows himself a coward, the louder is he sure to be in bluster and gammon. A bully who has shown the white feather in a street row is very apt to blackguard some good natured person who laughs at his disgrace. These spouting wretches in Congress, who have not the heart to place a necessary tax upon the people to whom they are looking for popularity, endeavor to gain a little cheap reputation for courage by attacking in a dastardly style the President, the Cabinet, and the General-in-Chief of the army. The amount of Billingsgate lavished in the last few weeks on men in authority by these timorous creatures is sufficient to set up some future Pierce Egan in a dictionary of slang.

One of the special objects of their wrath is Ward H. Lamon, the Marshal of the District of Columbia. A great deal of useless eloquence had been lavished on the condition of the "men and brothers" incarcerated in the dirty little District jail, and it became so fashionable to visit the jail, that the Marshal's Deputies had little else to do than to introduce the idlers of Washington to the male and female factors in the donjon keep. To keep out the thousand strangers who thronged there, Lamon issued an order admitting members of the Senate and House upon a certificate of membership from the President and the Speaker. Mr. Grimes, a bushwhacker from Iowa, strolled around the jail one fine afternoon, to have a little congenial conversation with the thieves and runaway negroes therein abiding, and was asked for his pass. He told the jailor that he was a Senator, and blasphemed the pass. The jailor, after scanning him attentively, concluded that he did not look like a Senator, nor talk like a Senator, and logically concluded that his Senatorship was a convenient myth for gaining access, with a pocket full of files and bedcords, to his friends inside the doors, and very properly ordered him off the premises. In a decided state of snub he went to the President's to complain, and found that this functionary was closeted with General Mc-Clellan and the Cabinet, and was not visible, even to Senatorial optics. In a frame of mind bordering on frenzy, he went to the Senate and blabbered forth his griefs to a sympathizing world.

And the mild and gentle Hale thought it was too bad, and John Sherman thought it was a fine opportunity to cut down the Marshal's salary, and altogether it was a very nice opportunity for Ethiopian buncombe and an attack upon the President.

With such exceptions as these Congress does nothing at present. Their mournful little attempts at retrenchment and reform are very melancholy, and not destitute of fun. Instead of devising and placing on foot some effective scheme of financial reform, which will meet this tremendous strain of a million a day, the energies of their minds seem completely exhausted by such gigantic achievements as cutting down the President's gas bill, forbidding the keeper of the Congressional conservatory to buy any more guano for his dahlias, ordering the discontinuance of the only work of science that ever resulted in any great national advantage—the coast survey, which has made the many networks of our shores an open book for science and for war, which has shown us the way to attack, and which alone can be relied upon to show us the way to defend. Then they have made spiteful little digs at the appropriations for public grounds, the pitiful salaries of half starved clerks, and the scanty earnings of worn widows and children, who make a scanty living by copying documents and clipping Treasury notes. All this sounds impossible, but it is the saddest truth.

Among their cuttings and parings, their own salaries remain intact. Not only that, but with an effrontery which reaches sublimity, the recent "Bill for Robbing Department Clerks" expressly retains the old mileage abuse of ten cents per mile for travel, which never costs but three or four, the full round salary of three thousand a year, and (climax of impudence) *adds a hundred dollars per year to pay them for their abolition of the franking privilege.*

It seems reserved for this Congress to end the succession of partizan Legislatures of the past school with a blaze of folly and inefficiency.[5]

Washington correspondence, 22 January 1862

The happiest man in town all day yesterday was Andrew Johnson, United States Senator from Tennessee. Early on Monday the welcome news of the victory at Somerset elated him. Exultation checkered with doubt filled up the afternoon. He went to bed thinking that a great thing had happened if the news were true. At midnight, a dispatch from the President, announcing the official confirmation of the news roused him from his bed at the St. Charles, and he indulged in a *marche de triomphe* over the certainty of success. He considers the victory most cheering in character, most important in results. The moral loss involved in the total and indiscriminate dishonor of the precipitate flight is not less crushing to the cause of secession in Tennessee than is the material ruin involved in the capture of their Quartermaster's and Commissary's stores, and worst of all in that country of hard travel and heavy roads, the abandonment of the very thing our troops most needed—their transportation. It is this item, the loss of the eighty wagons mentioned in the beginning of the dispatch of Thomas', that in Johnson's mind renders probable the inference with which he concludes that the rebels have dispersed.

Johnson is in Washington a noticeable man. The population of this sprawling village is not, as a general thing, noted for either honesty or enthusiasm. Holding a comfortable office is not the best preparation in the world for a career of vigorous effort and earnest enterprise. In the departments of Government, and in that better epitome of the political society of the country—the tavern bar-rooms—you will hear very little of hearty hate or eager malice against the traitors who are troubling us so. The general expression of feeling is one of regret for their errors, of mild condemnation of their leaders, and a hope that they may see the madness of their crime before they are utterly ruined. In Congress there are two spirits abroad. One full of sympathy with our misguided brethren, which finds utterance in the stuttering common-places of Bayard, the defiant insolence of Bright, and the spaniel snarls of Vallandigham. The other extreme lost all sight of the Southern treason in the intensity of the bitterness with which they are attacking the conservatism of the Administration, and the earnestness of their desire to make capital for re-election by a mad tilt at everything the Administration proposes, short of declaring in so many terms that black is white, and shall be white considered from this time henceforward. Among those growling factions an honest man, with singleness of purpose, is a most refreshing spectacle. And such a man is the Senator from Tennessee. He does not stop to discuss the niceties of constitutional law when the constitution itself is attacked. He does not bully the pilot when the ship is on the breakers. He sees no enemy but the rebel in his front. He has forgotten what is the difference between a Democrat and a Republican. He sees in the President and the Government the only power through which this rebellion can be crushed, and he gives freely up to them the whole unquestioning energies of his mind and heart.

The conduct of Johnson is not less remarkable than noble. It is in striking contrast with that of many earnest Republicans. There is no question that John P. Hale and Lyman Trumbull far more nearly sympathize with the President on all questions of National concern than Johnson can; yet they are always captiously criticizing or factiously opposing his movements and his plans, while Johnson supports him as earnestly as he ever opposed him. Belonging to the straightest sect of Breckinridge Democrats, he shook the trammels of party allegiance from him like cobwebs when he found their slight restraint hindered him in his duty to the Government. He is a shining example to those worthy gentlemen who seem lately inclined to use the weapons of partizan warfare upon the President of their choice and the exponent of the very principles whose indiscreet advocates are so bitterly attacking him.

Not only in his attitude to the Government but in feelings towards "our misguided Southern brethren" is Johnson unique. The genuine fire of honest and personal detestation which he feels for them would be worth many battalions if felt in our army. He has lived among them; he has seen and appreciated their grasping ambition, their sordid greed, their brutal ferocity. He has seen his neighbors driven from their homes, scourged and insulted for no crime but loyalty. He has seen murder become commonplace, and rape and robbery mere incidents of campaigning, in the reign of beastly savagery that followed the mock secession of Tennessee. In his own soul he has felt the treason forged iron. His family has been proscribed, his goods spoiled, his head made merchandise, like a wolf's.

If Andy Johnson is a little severe with our misguided and chivalrous brethren; if he calls for war, sudden, sharp, overwhelming; if he stands by the

Administration that is struggling with the grim earnestness of self preservation; if his loyalty is tempered and toned by honest, hearty righteous hate of the sin he is battling, let us remember there are reasons for it.

For Andrew Johnson is not a cavalier of the South. He is one of the people. In every fiber of his being, every pulsation of his heart, he is a Democrat. His clear, sharp mind sees that the glory of a Democrat is not necessarily founded upon the arrogance of a tyrant; that liberty is not a mere adjunct of slavery. All his boast and all his pride is in the truth and dignity of the Democratic principle. He has always held the suffrages of his equals a higher title to consideration than the ownership of his inferiors. So with those swaggering traitors whose treason is now revealed, he never was popular. The better time of the country, redeemed from this arrogant despotism, is the better time for him. The thanks of a people, on whom we hope the sun is already rising, after a night of darkness and storm, will reward him best, for his devotion to the principles which have swayed his life, in the time that tested the material of all men's natures.[6]

WASHINGTON CORRESPONDENCE, 27 JANUARY 1862

The principal amusement during the summer and through the mellow days of the Indian Echanasia of the autumn, when every genial influence of earth and sky seemed to be wooing our men-at-arms to seize occasion by the hand and march conquering against the listless enemy, was derived from reviews. Bright was the gleam of epaulettes on the heights of Smallytown, and by the rolling waters of Goose Creek; thunderous was the report of blank charged ordnance on Arlington; and valiant and intrepid were the charges of innocuous cavalry on the level plateau of Capitol Hill. Every day the long wagon train of the commissaries rolled slowly over Long Bridge, to feed the robust and vigorous inhabitants of the tents beyond the Potomac. All night the overtasked Treasury clerks signed Treasury notes to pay the rapidly growing dues. Each month the stalwart officers charged on the Paymaster, and retreated in good order with their unearned stipend.

The President and the Cabinet sat taking counsel together, relying with a generous confidence upon the vigor and the alacrity of the General commanding, forbearing to blame, unwilling to embarrass. The press throughout the country, schooled by the dreadful lesson of Bull Run, were silent, refusing to add one tittle to the troubles, or take away one iota of the responsibility of the General-in-Chief, by words of blame or criticism. The people, always generous and readier to praise than to carp, sung endless paeans to the brave young gentleman, whom no one knew anything about, and called him the new Napoleon, and waited for great things to follow his ready assumption of the reins that had dropped laxly from the time stiffened fingers of the grand old hero of a hundred battles. Never was there such an opportunity. Never such a conjunction and occulation of favoring stars.

Combined with the allurements to enterprise and energy were the warnings against idleness and delay. Over the sea there were clouds gathering, vague and undefined, yet their presence darkened with a sense of insecurity the political atmosphere. The despots of tradition, the tyrants of usurpation, who had so long watched us with an eye of jealousy, now gazed with a sullen satisfaction at the perils that environed us, and from contemplation of our listless attitude began to cherish the hope that all life and spirit had deserted the enormous frame of the Republic, that had cast a shadow over them so long. They began to dream of taking counsel together and administering upon the estates of the sick man. Each day of delay set the rebel cause firmer upon its legs; giving to them confidence, courage to their timorous friends, and casting the shadows of distrust over the spirits of all who loved liberty the world over. Meanwhile commerce languished in the suspense of war. The sea, though almost utterly free of pirates, was haunted by the presence of the uncaptured few. All our relations, social, political, commercial, were unhealthily affected by the pestilent presence of the uncrushed rebellion. The universal thought abroad in every civilized nation which watched us was, "If you have the power, why don't you exercise it?" and our own hearts answered the inquiry with the vague echo, "We have the power; why don't we exercise it?" And from the headquarters of the army no answer came.

"Wait till the leaves fall, and we can see the batteries unmasked," said some, anxious to find a reason for delay. The leaves fell, and the armies rested on stripped hills, under the bleak boughs. The frosts of the late autumn fell from the inclement skies, and the damps of the chill evenings crept fatally up the bared hill sides of the Potomac borders, and many a Northern man lay shivering in his tent, or still in his shallow grave. And all they waited for, longed for, sickened for, was a fight. When the long roll sounded one night in the camp of the Ellsworth Boys, fifty sick men started up from the hospital tents, their weak limbs strong for the fight, the light of battle in their hollow eyes; they stood in their places till the disappointment laid them on their backs again. There never were seen better fighting men. One day, at Drainesville, Ord's brigade met an equal number of the enemy, who had come out to take them bodily. It was a fair stand-up fight—four regiments on a side. In less than an hour's time the enemy were routed and running for life. Ord was called back. His brigade stamped Drainesville on their banners. The superiority of our soldiers was made manifest. If any result was attained, I have not heard of it.

You will have noticed that these matters have not been much spoken of in the North. We do not wish to destroy confidence in our generals. In Richmond they are not troubled by any such scruples, and they, in the extremity of their astonishment at the inaction of our army, invent all sorts of wild and absurd explanations. They say that McClellan is a Secessionist at heart; that the President and Cabinet wish to prolong the war; that our soldiers are afraid to fight—all which theories are simply absurd and ridiculous. There is no truer patriot than McClellan; there is no man more eager for a fight than the President, and the men who are to do the fighting are equally so.

The bad weather is ending. The sky is looking like the sky and not like dirty sheet lead. The roads are getting to be no worse than roads usually are in Virginia. Cameron is on his way to St. Petersburg. Members of Congress are allowed at the War Department but one day in the week. Contractors are seeking fresh fields and pastures now. The brand-new Secretary of War is a quick, ready man, with a keen eye, a sharp voice, and a tendency to speak his mind. Things are not as bad as they might be. And I have omitted to state that all is quiet along the lines.[7]

WASHINGTON CORRESPONDENCE, 30 JANUARY 1862

Whatever else the first six months of this anomalous war has brought forth, it is very evident the heroic element has not shown any particularly violent outcroppings. Whether the march of improvement has substituted correct sighting and careful loading in place of hard fighting and daring exposure, making silence answer for valor, and shells for chivalry, or whether in a war arising from fancied wrongs, neither side feels the intensity of rage which prompts reckless deeds, it is sure that very few men have appeared, in any personal sense, noticeable and picturesque. The artists of the illustrated papers are hanging hungrily around Washington, waiting for somebody to do something dramatic and give scope to their well-trimmed crayons. But in the dearth of more exciting material, they fall back on the shooting of deserters and (subjects of kindred melancholy) Mrs. Lincoln's receptions. There is nothing suggestive to an artistic mind in the silence of camps, and the pilgrim's progress of baggage wagons through the mud of the ruined roads. And that is all the war is now affording them.

The man who, in a greater degree than any other, has succeeded in impressing the minds not only of his troops, but of the people, with the idea of personal force and merit is General Ambrose Everett Burnside. While he was in the army, he was noted as a careful and honorable soldier. He carried into the business of railroading great administrative scope and ready judgment. His training in a railroad office was the best possible for his present position. A man who can successfully manage a railroad has qualities for commanding that must distinguish him in war. A strikingly large proportion of our soldiers come from such pursuits. McClellan, Halleck, Rosecrans, Banks, Stone, and others. While Burnside remained in command of the Rhode Islanders, he lived constantly in the public eye. His regiment was a very fair one, the flower of the little State that sent them. Men from the richest families of the State served unostentatiously in the ranks. Their Governor added the official sanction of his presence and the moral weight of the renunciation of his well known anti-coercion doctrines. The men soon became passionately devoted to their Colonel. His regard for them was something beyond that of good officers for their men, amounting to a nervous sensitiveness in regard to their comfort and convenience. Yet on occasion he asked and received great efforts from them. He made, with those delicately nurtured young men, a march of twenty-three miles, one day, over ruinously rough Maryland roads, expecting a battle at the end of the journey. When he was made acting Brigadier, they felt a sort of jealous dissatisfaction that any other regiments were to share their Colonel's attentions. At Bull Run very much was expected of Burnside. I do not believe he wholly fulfilled the expectations which were formed of him. The jealous regard for the men under him, without which no man can be a good General, is disastrous when carried to excess. I have heard that Burnside had too much of it; that his anxiety to guard his men from injury rendered him careless at times of great advantages to be gained by judicious expenditure of life. Every one admitted his personal bravery, but many thought him too sensitive to the sight of the blood of his boys. Yet, even this, endeared him to the soldiers.

There is a dash of the dramatic in everything Burnside does. His dress is always peculiar and generally picturesque. We hear of him during the late storm off Hatteras, working for the comfort of his men with an utter disregard of fatigue or exposure, dressed, *en Garibaldi,* in a gray shirt, breeches in boot-tops, felt hat, and general air of b'hoyishness. The picture drawn by the letter-writers is graphic and evidently true of the muscular General, standing like a sea-god on the prow of his vessel, insensible to discomfort or danger, working harder than any private there—never for himself, always for others.

He is one of the best men in the world for the very work he has gone to do, which requires energy, combination, patience, administration. If he fails, it will be from only one reason: an intense desire to do his work without sacrificing his men. He will find himself inside of Hatteras Inlet, with a fleet damaged and men fatigued by the storm. He will be tempted to wait for reinforcements and more perfect organization before moving up to attack the finished and well garrisoned fortifications on Roanoke Island. The success of the attack demands perfect accord between the military and naval forces of the expedition. Goldsborough must pound away in front with his heavy guns, while Burnside goes behind the island and struggles along through swamps and sand in their rear. The enterprise is one of difficulty and danger. Unless the rebels run, (which seems rather likely from the great panic reported at Norfolk,) there will be many valuable lives lost in the undertaking. The vast advantages which would follow success will pay for them all. It is to be hoped that we will soon hear of a success complete, even if not bloodless. It is scarcely possible that the expedition will rest contented with the occupation of the island. That once secured, there is nothing to prevent an easy capture of Newbern, which, in its turn, will give us Beaufort, and the well armed Fort Macon, and with very little delay the whole eastern half of the old North State.

That the rebels themselves entertain little doubt of the success of the enterprise appears from the dismay and confusion apparent in Richmond and Norfolk during Friday and Saturday, as reported by Mr. Taylor, a released prisoner, who came up on Saturday from Fortress Monroe. They carefully concealed from him the newspapers of those days and prevented him from buying them. He infers that there must have been something unpleasant in them.

They are beginning to appreciate the tremendous force of the power opposed to them. An army which can keep an overwhelming force idle and ready at the base of operations, and detach columns so powerful as to be irresistible, from time to time, to threaten and even cut off the enemy's communications, are inevitably sure of victory sooner or later.

Everything indicates that this happy consummation will be reached before long, perhaps in time to fulfill the prophecy of that undaunted optimist, Mr. Seward.[8]

WASHINGTON CORRESPONDENCE, 6 FEBRUARY 1862

Yesterday, just as the gas began to be lighted in the Senate, the vote upon the resolution relative to the expulsion of Jesse D. Bright was taken, and the resolution by a large majority, passed. Everybody was glad that the thing was ended, whether for good or evil.

Which of the two, good or evil, it will result in, remains yet to be seen. I think, and say frankly, that to me the precedent thus set, seems a bad one, and prolific of evil. The expelled and disgraced Senator himself has not been injured. In fact he had no rights in the case. He could ask no consideration from the body whose privileges he has abused, no sympathy from the country whose noblest aspirations he has endeavored to crush, and whose most strenuous efforts he has persistently maligned and ridiculed. He came to a grossly partisan Senate, with informal and illegal certificates of election, and was admitted to a seat to which he had no sufficient title by the votes of political friends, most of whom are now in arms against the country. His character is not such as to be readily blackened by any aspersions which, at this late day, can be cast upon it. It would be gilding refined gold to try to sully the record of Jesse D. Bright. He has been true to but one aim, and that is self-aggrandizement. He has been faithful to but one principle, and that is a blind and unquestioning devotion to the wishes of the South. In a long Senatorial service there is no light cast by the history of his labors. Where anything brave or manly was to be advocated, he has ever been silent. When an honest man was to be slandered and bullied into silence, he was very often the chosen instrument. He has never been a leader, but has been the most faithful and reliable of all followers, at the beck of that coterie who now are wrangling, as of old, in Richmond.

There is nothing about the man Bright to attract the sympathy which the record of the Senator Bright repels. He is essentially coarse. Hardly above mediocrity even in political information and intrigue, he is very far below it in all else. His mental poverty is not concealed or relieved by social graces. The indefinable air that always surrounded poor Breckinridge, of courtesy and gentleness, was never observable in the Senator from Indiana. There was always vaguely connected with Breckinridge, the associations of refined and honored ancestry, and the charm of personal beauty and mental clever-ness, that redeemed in the minds of those who knew him, a portion of the stigma of treason. He was not wicked or malignant—only weak and vacil-lating. He had been petted and spoiled from boyhood. He lacked courage and nerve to do right against the solicitations of his flatterers and sycophants. He gave way, and fled by night into disgrace and danger. Bright was de-praved, without excuse or palliation. He represented a loyal constituency. He was a Northern born man. He had never breathed any air but that of free-dom. His hopes, his treasure, his interests were all with the North. Yet he was stubbornly and sullenly disloyal, against interest, against honor, against light and knowledge.

I am far from wishing to palliate Bright's fault. It was very great. I think his writing a letter to Jeff. Davis, a rebel in arms, and styling him President, was enough to stamp him with indelible infamy. It was enough to sink him forever into the depths of public scorn and forever incapacitate him for pop-ular suffrage or popular honor. If that act were not enough to complete his condemnation, his conduct since can only be taken as the enlargement and complement of his crime. He writes a letter to his friend justifying his let-ter to his rebel friend. He looks with open and undisguised contempt upon the magnificent resurrection of loyalty which his own State shows him. He goes like an evil genius among his people, scattering the ill seed of discord and discontent among them, striving with devilish ingenuity to check the spirit of patriotism that was growing so strong, and quench the burning flame of devotion that blazed so clearly on the altar. He saw legion after le-gion of his fellow citizens march away from the soil of Indiana, in the holy crusade of Freedom, and they gained nothing from him but sneers and ridicule. Wherever Indiana men labored or fought or died; in the chill and lonely nightwatches; in the toilsome marches, in the red storm of battle, in the weary torment of the hospitals, or in the dreamless rest of the soldier's rude grave, they never heard a "God bless you" from Jesse D. Bright.

Even when his disaffection was patent, and trumpeted to the world, and all decent people thought he would resign and save scandal to his State and to the Senate, his wonderful and impassive impudence still sustained him. He came and sat stolidly in the place he had disgraced, and when charged with the unseemly thing that he had done, he rose and said that he would do it again without hesitation.

Such a man as this surely deserves no consideration at the hands of the Senate. They were only to consider what was due to themselves in the premises. The question presented to them was, whether it were better to free themselves from the contaminating presence of a man, who was at heart, if not disloyal, at least indifferent to the welfare of his country, or to preserve the dignified attitude which has been theirs through all time, and leave him to the condemnation of the people and the infamy of history. They judged and decided, as was their right. I cannot help thinking them in error.

It is at all times most disastrous to set a precedent which can open the door to future license. It will rarely happen that public interests demand the prompt ignoring of technicalities and the stern assertion of equities. This is not one of those occasions. Bright in the Senate was powerless for evil. He is a man of sluggish mind and indolent habit. There was no party with him, no people behind him. His term was soon to end, and with it his political career. Why should he not have sunk quietly into obscurity without further notice? Why was it necessary to send the creature home with material to weave for his narrow forehead the crown of a martyr? If Bright could be invested with dignity, this expulsion will do it.

There is a grave consideration in this case, which it will not be well to overlook. In after times when the excitements of war give place to the mimic battles of politics, and a remorseless majority may have it in their power and in their hearts to free themselves from the truthful tongue and troublesome argument of some bold leader of the opposition, how dexterously they will twist this case of Bright's to suit their tyrannical and outrageous purpose. And who knows but in the heated convulsions that mark our Western campaigns, this creature, so ennobled by the august sentence of the Senate, may come to the top of the political cauldron again, and be ready, with all the malice of a low nature, to revenge the infamy of yesterday by voting to expel a Senator whose eloquent denunciations scored his callous sensibilities not twenty-four hours ago?

It is an improbable and a disgusting suggestion. I am sorry that the Senate have made it a possible one.[9]

WASHINGTON CORRESPONDENCE, 10 FEBRUARY 1862

There seems to be a sudden awakening of the Anaconda. Under the most unpropitious weather, he stirs his immense bulk and loosens his monstrous coils. From the far South we hear of a movement upon Savannah. The Federal gunboats are slowly weaving the web of destiny around the beleaguered fort on Cockspur Island, and threatening with a ruin slow and irresistible, the doomed city of Oglethorpe's pride [*Savannah*]. The avenues of communication lie open to Sherman's [   ] whenever the dyspepsia leaves him leisure to advance.

Already Burnside is thundering at Roanoke Island, the key of Albemarle and Pamlico Sounds, the point of observation for all operations along the Middle Atlantic coast, and the back door entrance to the city of Norfolk. Burnside's expedition has not been expeditious. It has wasted a good deal of time beating about the sand banks at Hatteras, and lying by to refresh its weary virtue in the lee of the Inlet. All kinds of absurd rumors have characterized it. There seems to be a general impression that on account of the development of the original plan to the enemy, the destiny of the expedition has been changed. This is untrue. The thunder of Goldsborough's guns in front and Burnside's musketry in the rear of Roanoke Island is the first echo and fulfillment of the original plan, agreed upon by General McClellan and the President.

The dispatches of this morning, from Norfolk, state that the attack has already been made, and the Federal forces twice repulsed, but add, that two rebel gunboats have already been sunk. We remember the earliest reports that flashed over the wires in reference to the Port Royal affair; how the Yankee fleet had been driven ashore by the irresistible dash of the Mosquito admiral; and how Tattnal hoped to bag the whole Federal navy, if his luck held out and the weather was fair. Applying to these first news of Burnside the usual co-efficient of rebel lying and we have a perfect and brilliant success. The public taste in victories runs very much to capture of cities. It is hard to make people believe that it will not pay to take large towns. Points neglected by the popular fancy are those seized upon by the eye of a General. The little strip of rocks and barren sand on the sluggish stream through which the waters of Albemarle creep into Pamlico, in the eye of the strategist, is worth far more than a dozen Charlestons.

After they have taken Roanoke Island, a good deal of discretion is left to Goldsborough and Burnside. Newbern may tempt them. It lies invitingly open at the head of the hospitable Neuse river, and its capture would result in the certain fall of Beaufort and the surrender of Fort Macon. This is a point of no very great importance just now. There are one or two railroad centres in that vicinage that afford a fine opening for an enterprising and energetic young general, if the weather favors and the mud is dry. Weldon would not be hard to take, and [*the town of*] Goldsborough is delightfully suggestive to the weather beaten Commodore of the Expedition. Wilmington is in a terrible state of perturbation, but I think she is in no danger. Her insignificance protects her. But the most elderly and unattractive virgins are usually most fearful of the amorous regards of lawless youth. However, all these matters will probably be decided before you receive my lucubrations. It would be rather staggering to your correspondent's claim to omniscience to have my letter appear side by side with a dispatch that Lynch had sent Burnside and all his men to the bottom of a new Dead Sea.

General Wool quietly bides his time at Fortress Monroe, occasionally demonstrating Norfolk into paroxysms of fright. Banks is vigilantly observing the enemy from Frederick. Lander has been beguiling the tedium of the rainy days of last week by taking Romney and frightening into precipitate flight the queer, blundering, thick-skulled, honest dunce, General Jackson. Of the doings of our men-at-arms in Central Kentucky, what need to speak? Nor has fame of late been silent in regard to the Department of Cairo. There is resurrection in Tennessee for the true hearts that have sighed so long for deliverance. Beautiful upon the hills of their Northern border, floats from the flagstaff of Fort Henry the constellated banner of their fathers! Let General Halleck look to it, that his proud promise be fulfilled, and that that flagstaff "flap its tethered flame" to every breeze that blows from the South or the North, till victory brings peace and tranquillity again.

The West is still troubled with feuds, and the craft of demagogues. I believe no good thing will come out of Kansas until Jim Lane has retired to private life and the cormorants that surround him see no prospect for further plunder in his train. The man and his history form a marvel of unmerited distinction and utterly baseless success. Low, vulgar, and coarse, he has gained the plaudits of the polished fanatics of Boston. Illiterate and narrow minded, he retains a seat in the Senate of the Republic. Tricky and unprincipled in politics, he has somehow gained a reputation for bluff honor and frankness. With no military ability, he has succeeded in impressing the public with the idea that he is a thunderbolt of war. Crafty, cruel, remorseless, and only half civilized, he has fostered the idea in the mind of his deluded adherents that on him alone rest the hopes of endangered civilization, and that in his success are contained the grand possibilities of aroused and regenerate humanity. Since Joe Smith, the lazy loafer of Albany, became a prophet, priest and king, no equal delusion has fallen upon the people of our country.

It is pitiable that such a man should have such power for evil. By a steady course of low animal cunning and consummate trickery he fastened in the toils of his chicane that most soldierly of commanders and most generous of men, General Hunter, and by a system of unblushing and incessant falsehood created in the mind of Hunter and of the President respectively that what he wished was most agreeable to the wishes of the other. Hunter, whose zeal for the common cause overrode all considerations of private interests, made no complaint at the enormous assumptions of the crafty demagogue, until forbearance gave way to the continued assaults of arrogance and insubordination, and the dignity of his position forced him to [*clap?*] an extinguisher upon the flame of the Brigadier's vanity.

There is no saying what will be the issue of this matter. It is, however, most probable that the fox-like Jayhawker will be run to earth; that he will be forced to make his election between being a Senator and a Brigadier General; that he will be taught that insolence and petulance are not the best qualities for a subordinate commander, and that no amount of political influence can shield a man from the consequences of insubordination and duplicity.[10]

WASHINGTON CORRESPONDENCE, 11 FEBRUARY 1862

One would think that the arrest of a Major General of a Division, on charges amounting to a direct allegation of disloyalty, would be a sufficient stimulus to the gossip of a quiet little town, without the necessity of any further augmentation of the statement. But people think different in this *blasé* village. No rumor is able to stand alone long. Popular fancy begins to add a lively series of supports and amplifications to the original story, until the nucleus is lost in the extent of the periphery.

When it began to be whispered on Sunday night that General Stone was under arrest, the statement fanned into the liveliest action the imaginations of all the Washington gossips. General Stoneman was added to the list of the proscribed, probably from that love of alliteration that pervades all literature. The old disgust against General Thomas's Frémont fiasco revived, and there was a lively story afloat about his having absconded with the spoons belonging to the "Soldiers Home." Then somebody remembered what a mean looking hang-dog expression of countenance Starke of Oregon wore when they last saw him, and said on the spur of the moment that he was lying in irons in the military jail. Some indignant patriot, whose wish fathered his thought, next announced that Vallandigham would certainly be hung on Friday, if the weather was favorable. Thus the air was thick with rumors, and most of them were more or less probable.

Morning, however, came, and the stories vanished with the day. Starke came brazenly into the Senate, and sat there caressing his mahogany whiskers, a white eye browed abomination to all true men; Stoneman galloped over the river to his daily duties; Vall—(I really haven't time to give his real name)—went currishly snarling to his place in the House. And the blameless Lorenzo, the faultless Adjutant, the Pecksniffian Thomas, fluttered like an elderly seraph around the War Department, smiling and busy, giving assurance to a doubting world that he would never, while Treasury Notes were a legal tender, forsake the service and the salaries of his own, his native land.

The thing was bad enough as it was. It is not a light matter to take a popular commander from the head of his army and clap him into jail, charged with crimes the foulness of which appals every soul. The Administration deserve some credit for courage and decision in this matter. It remains to be seen whether they deserve any for discretion and sound judgment. For a crime so monstrous and so in opposition to all reasonable probabilities, must be most irrefragably proved, or an irremediable wrong will be done.

The case is most strange and peculiar. Stone was born in Massachusetts, drank in with his mother's milk devotion to his country, and learned nothing from earliest youth but lessons of patriotism and honor among the New England hills. In the dark days that closed the ill-starred reign of Buchanan, there was not in all the District of Columbia a man so earnest, so active and so effective in defense against the anticipated attacks of the traitors, as Charles Stone. Gen. Scott repeatedly said, that more to Stone than any other we were indebted for the safety of the Capital. On the organization of the additional regiments to the regular army, he was made Colonel of the Fourteenth Infantry, and three days afterward, on the 17th day of May, he was made a Brigadier General of Volunteers. At West Point, he bore a fine character for scholarship and good conduct. When he resigned, he carried into civil life a reputation for energy and ability. He was taken back to the army with the universal consent of all who knew him.

Independently of any suspicions of disloyalty, I am inclined to think him a failure. At Alexandria, he frequently exhibited strong fits of petulance and passion. He had a great facility of getting into trouble with quiet people. He distinguished himself on one occasion, by putting in the guard tent and threatening to shoot an unfortunate reporter whom he caught in camp. While in command of the Corps of Observation on the Upper Potomac, he did nothing well. His administration was crowned by the tragic and pitiful blunder of Ball's Bluff, by which we lost nearly two regiments, our glorious statesman soldier, Baker, who was worth many regiments, and prestige, which was worth all.

He gave great offense by his needless officiousness in catching fugitive slaves, by the senseless and petulant spite which he exhibited in his correspondence thereanent with Sumner and Andrew, and by his flippant impertinence when summoned to give evidence before the investigating nuisance in Congress. (No one can blame him for despising such a committee, but he should have had the discretion to conceal his contempt.) He never could lose the slang of his former politics. He still talked about Southern chivalry and Northern fanaticism in a very silly and indiscreet way. These and many other things prejudiced good people against him, and no man is strong enough to resist prejudice.

It is very certain, he has been arrested on trifling grounds. Stanton (whose exclusive act the arrest is supposed to be) was very intimate and friendly with him in the days when they worked together for the capitol. He thought well and kindly of him, I know. He would not have arrested him had he not thought that grave reasons existed for such a course. We will know all about it when the Court-Martial begins.

As if to form a farcical ending to this tragedy, another arrest was made yesterday, which is generally regarded as the best thing of the season. Dr. Ives, of New York, one of the editors of that virtuous and consistent daily, the *New York Herald,* who has been for some days reorganizing the bureau of correspondence for his newspaper, was to-day arrested as a spy and a general nuisance, and sent to Fort McHenry. The newspaper men are at a loss whether to deplore the attack on their professional privileges, or to rejoice in the scrubbing of that frightful old snob, the venerable harlequin of Plum Gut. The *Herald* has so persistently and indecently insisted on being recognized as the organ of the Administration and the special champion and protector of the President's family, that great curiosity is felt here as to the spirit in which the canny Scot [*James Gordon Bennett*] will receive this slap in the face. The prevailing opinion is that he will quietly swallow the insult, disown Ives, and leave him to his fate, and say, "Served him right! To jail with him, and let Greeley and Raymond go with him! I'm for the Administration." Consistency, of course, is nothing to him. He gasps for social recognition. He thirsts for that society which can heal the wounds of a battered reputation, and thinks that servility and adulation will carry his point. Perhaps so. But it seems a dear price, to barter manliness and self-respect, for cast-iron smiles once in a year, and a bi-monthly square inch of lettered card-board.[11]

WASHINGTON CORRESPONDENCE, 14 FEBRUARY 1862

We received this morning the authentic reports of the Roanoke battle. The remorseless style in which the plain statement of Burnside pricks the swollen bubble of rebel boasting is most amusing and suggestive. The early accounts taken from the Norfolk and Richmond papers represented the fight as the bloodiest of modern times. The rebel hosts were enveloped in a halo of devoted daring that half redeemed their fate, and plucked bright honor from the thorns of disaster and defeat. The dingy little *Day Book,* which I saw the day after the fight, though in its disheartened and seedy appearance most plainly proclaiming that the pinching days had come, still tried to be gay and plucky in its defeat, and mingled its wails for the lost with paeans for their valor. In the light of the slaughter it relayed, its whitey brown columns grew absolutely luminous with gore and glory.

I am sorry that treason fosters such a tendency to lie. I am rather glad that the rebels do not fight any better, albeit the picturesqueness of history suffers by the lack of valor. There were not "a thousand Yankees laid cold on the polluted soil," but something less than fifty fell. The Confederates did not lose "whole hecatombs of their best and bravest who gladly offered up their lives upon their country's altar." There were only a dozen or so who preferred death to defeat. The Richmond Blues did not stand to their guns "fighting with the united incentives of patriotism and despair"; but they very meekly laid down their arms as soon as Lincoln's minions asked them to. The

Confederates from beginning to end of this business have nothing from which they can extract the slightest suspicion of comfort. In the beginning every advantage was on their side.

They had full and timely intelligence of the force and destination of Burnside's Expedition, and all possible facilities for strengthening their position. The very elements seemed to fight for them in the beginning. For many days the Northern fleet was buffeted about the shallows of Hatteras and several of the transports were lost, some of the last regiments being forced to go back to Annapolis. The boats in the war and naval departments of the expedition were equally frail and unreliable, and every hour of their progress demonstrated the avarice of contractors and the careless haste of purchasers. Finally, when Goldsborough and Burnside steamed up to the frowning island, the whole advantage of situation was on the rebel side. Yet after a fruitless cannonade of all day, Burnside landed his fighting Yankees at night and they walked in a quiet New England fashion up to the batteries and took them. The chivalry left with all convenient haste, and after holding a hurried town meeting on the north end, they concluded that death was cold and moist and damnation unpleasant, and they might as well be decently clothed and plentifully fed in a Northern prison, as shiver and starve in a Southern swamp; so they, with what surly grace they could, laid down their arms and walked, with the precision of soldiers and mildness of lambs on board the Yankee Transports.

This is a very tame and unromantic ending of an enterprise begun with immense flourish and flutter, and assisted to a point of wonderful inflation by Southern gasconade and Hatteras squalls. The maniac Wise was carried from Nag's Head in an ambulance crazier than usual, and his hopeful son, Obadiah Jennings, was caught in his flight by a bullet swifter even than a retreating Virginian, and lamed for the rest of his life, as he himself had lamed Sherrard Clemens a few years before. Of all the plumed and caparisoned warriors that marched so gaily out of Richmond to beat back from the threatened shores of Roanoke the vandal hosts; the heroes of many a run in Western Virginia, the riff-raff of the mountain counties; the clay eating chivalry of the pine woods, none will come back to tell the tale of Southern valor and Yankee fright. Three thousand hungry heroes will come North to cultivate an appetite for human food, and a taste for civilized life, and to undergo a course of training to be missionaries to their kindred heathen in the good time coming after the war.

Burnside has done very well. In other expeditions the navy has so completely distanced the army that the undivided glory of the enterprise has lit upon the war ships, and illumed the transports only by proximity. But this time the plan of attack was fully and completely carried out. I learn from a source whose accuracy is absolute, that in every particular the account of the achievement agrees with the original plan of the expedition. While Commodore Goldsborough was occupying the attention of the batteries in front, and amusing himself by blowing out of [the] water those forlorn little gunboats that poor Lynch had brought down for the purpose of bagging him, Burnside landed his men, and, in the teeth of the entrenched enemy's fire, took every position from them with scarcely a struggle. The achievements of the army and navy were both splendid and both complete and satisfactory. While Burnside took the batteries, and his brave Yankees saw the twinkling heels of the fleet footed Virginians disappearing up the Island, and young Wise carried off in a blanket by sympathizing friends, Goldsborough was quietly "seizing, occupying and possessing" the navy of Albemarle Sound, sending his blue jackets to make visits of ceremony to their rebel peers, and making the truculent hero of the Dead Sea Expedition take to the water, and swim like an elderly grampus for dear life to the shore. The taking of Elizabeth City and of Edenton, which Goldsborough lost no time in doing, was merely clinching the nail which had been driven, and neatly finishing the work.

So far the success of this business is absolute. The object of the expedition is accomplished. The Island of Roanoke was considered a position of very great strategic importance and worthy [of] a great effort to obtain. It is the key to the Sounds, and the back door to Norfolk. It is a most valuable base for future operations in that vicinage. It is one very essential link in the chain which the fingers of the loyal army are weaving for the rebellion. When it begins to draw, the rebellion is strangled beyond recourse.

There would be little advantage in the capture of three thousand hungry wretches, while bread is so high, were it not that this gives us an opportunity of dictating terms to the rebel chiefs, whose insolence has grown so insufferable upon the presumption that with the name of Corcoran and Lee, they can frighten us into all possible concessions.

The Roanoke prisoners, as you will have presumed from the fact that they ran with such ease and alacrity, are members of the first families of Virginia and Carolina. Their friends and relatives are prominent conspirators.

They will never expose their aristocratic weasands to any danger of retaliation by hanging Col. Corcoran, or any other of our gallant and unfortunate soldiers now in their hands. You have already seen that they refuse to allow Bishop Ames and Governor Fish to catch a glimpse of the horrors of Southern jails. We may now hope that those horrors may soon be ended by the liberation of our imprisoned heroes.[12]

WASHINGTON CORRESPONDENCE, 21 FEBRUARY 1862

The clamorous crowd of news-devourers that haunt the bar rooms and street corners of this idle town, seem for once to have gotten as much news as they want. They have passed no less than two days in comparative quiet, and have not grumbled for a battle nor insisted upon the taking of an island. Fort Henry gave them an idea of how things were managed in the West. Fort Donaldson [*Donelson*] carried out the impression thus felicitously conveyed, and the chase of Price into Arkansas filled out the demand of the week neatly and agreeably. There is a general lull of public eagerness and a quiet anticipation of great work to come at Nashville, if we accept as true, last night's rumour, that Clarksville has moved there. There is none of the listlessness of a few weeks ago. Every one is satisfied with the Government. Every one is convinced that the welfare of the nation is in safe hands. The war is shrinking rapidly in its proportions, and the events of the next weeks are to begin its end. So we all think at Washington.

Another thing which we hear very often in Washington is "Who is entitled to the credit of these achievements?" To which the prevailing answer is,

First—The officers and soldiers who stood in battle array around the trenches in the Tennessee mud, and fought and faltered not. These are entitled to the highest honor of all. Then General Halleck is praised for wise precautions and sound strategy. Then Abraham Lincoln, Commander-in-Chief, (by Constitutional provision, and by actual assumption of the power,) of the Army and Navy of the United States. This high functionary for the last two months has never ceased, with the energy of a restless purpose and the authority of absolute command, to hurry to the utmost limit of expedition, the two enterprises that have culminated in Roanoke Island and Fort Donelson. His mind looked beyond the mere requirements of strategy, and foresaw the vast political significance lying wrapped up in these enterprises. The welfare of the nation is in safe hands, when the Chief Magistrate has at once a genius in conception and a talent in execution that renders him at once independent of Generals and of politicians. Such a man, people are growing to believe, we have for President to-day.

The study of geography has excited a new and peculiar interest in the minds of people who read newspapers and talk about war lately. With recent improvements in transmitting intelligence and conveying means of campaigning, war has approached the nature of an exact science, and moves almost exclusively in geometrical lines. Strategic points in this war are, to a certain extent, changing their relative values. Points of railroad conveyance have become valuable only to the belligerent who holds behind him the conveying lines of road. We cannot, as a usual thing, use a railroad track to pursue a retreating enemy, as it is so easy to break up and destroy either track or bridges, involving great delay for reparation. This makes of vast importance for such purposes the possession of all water courses. It would seem that those two wandering rivers, the Tennessee and the Cumberland, that stroll so aimlessly down from their mountains, and meander vaguely—the one over the boundary of Alabama, into Tennessee, through which it rolls quietly into Kentucky, to empty itself into the tranquil Ohio, and the other, issuing from the cool snow-thaws of the Cumberland Mountains, and pursuing a wild or vagabond journey through Eastern Kentucky and Northern Tennessee, into the rich plantations of the centre, then turning its face to the North Star, like a runaway contraband, to lose its identity in the same blue waves of the Beautiful River—were created for the special purpose they have served and are serving: to bear the loyal thunders to the haunts of sleeping rebellion. How wild must have been, to the astounded Florentines last week, the vision of that spectre flotilla lying at anchor on their banks in the early sunrise, and fluttering at the fore of each gunboat the curling and rippling beauty of the old starred and striped banner! That was the first time, probably, that the fact had been brought home to their senses that their river ran into a region of civilization and law, and that from that section, where they used to sell their tobacco, the avenging Nemesis of an outraged sovereignty could come and go at will.

It is very difficult for us, with our present lights, to see what chances are left the poor scared creatures now huddled at Columbus and Nashville. If the garrison of Columbus even succeeds in getting away with their worthless lives, they must forfeit so very large an amount of war material that it will be equivalent to a defeat. If Breckinridge and Hindman have been silly enough to be cornered in the little triangle formed by Bowling Green, Clarksville and Nashville, no power on earth can save them from capture, and the edifying spectacle of the ex-Vice President [*Breckinridge*] pendant may soon swing in the Northern air, a grisly warning to rebellious youth. But with all the force that the rebels can concentrate in Nashville, it is scarcely possible that any positive stand can be made there. They have wasted so much time in the fortification of their Northern outposts that they seem to have neglected the more important points on their interior. Nashville may safely be assumed to be less strongly intrenched than Fort Donelson, and means will be employed against Nashville of vastly greater destructiveness than any that were used at Donelson. The immense mortar boats just beginning to be completed at Cairo will rain from an inaccessible distance a tempest of death upon the heads of the enemy, who have nothing whatever to oppose to them. The "*Benton*," also, the masterpiece of your St. Louis builder, James B. Eades, will be ready for service in a day or two, and will be an army in itself in the narrow stream of the Cumberland.

When these people are thoroughly whipped at Nashville, there is very little recourse for them. That of course closes the campaign in the West, and it goes very far to close the rebellion as well. Their forces are in this way broken in two without a possibility of integration or communication. They must disperse. In all points where they can mass, we can handle them with perfect ease. Along the level country and on the river sides, our superior means of transportation make us easily victorious.

They talk, sometimes, in their inebrious leaders and pamphlets, about retiring to their mountain fastnesses and carrying on from this vantage ground a war of extermination against the hireling oppressor. This is indeed the final result of all unsuccessful rebellions, but is very ridiculous and absurd when predicted as the closing scene of this. In the first place the leaders are not made of the stuff that forms Marions and Schamils, and the rank and file will be glad enough to get back to their allegiance after this year's bedevilment. And in the second place, in contradistinction to all other rebellions in the world's history, the mountain districts are thoroughly and completely loyal.

I think this is a better opportunity than usual for Mr. Seward to make a speech and utter his usual three months prophecy of peace and victory.[13]

WASHINGTON CORRESPONDENCE, 21 FEBRUARY 1862

The friends of General James H. Lane, of Kansas, are gathering their strength for a new attack upon the Government. They think it an intolerable outrage that this innocent creature should be thwarted in his plans, that this pure hearted reformer should be deprived of anything to reform, that this enterprising child should have the costly expeditionary toy taken from its hands, with which it fondly expected to play soldier the rest of the year. They are laying pipe for serenades and remonstrances and protests, and freedom-shrieking eloquence, and *Tribune* ravings. They say, "Lane is coming—let slavery apologists and West Point grannies stand from under—the man of the people is on their track!" This, with other great nonsense of the kind, is daily uttered in the streets and the bar rooms of dollar-a-day hotels, by long haired and malodorous disciples of the Jayhawker, and the poor devils really plume themselves on believing that to them alone is given the vision of the revealed glory of James Henry, the apostle of the new political gospel.

It is an encouraging sign that Lane's adherents are gradually being narrowed down to a class so contemptible both in numbers and character as that which continues to swear by him so reverently in Washington. Every school teacher who has gone mad on the woes of slavery, every bran eating philosopher who mistakes dyspepsia for brotherly love, every unclean theorist who believes that white linen is a sin and good clothes an abomination unto the Lord, seems to look to Lane as the embodied ideal of all his prayers—the coming Savior, the sword of the Lord and of Gideon.

This would not be so strange if Lane were himself an honest maniac like his followers.—There is no insanity about Jim Lane save that which always springs from a depraved and malignant mind. He is thoroughly and grossly animal in feeling and impulse—an untamed savage in rage and cruelty—but cool, quiet and crafty as any serpent in the prosecution of his purposes. There are no designs too dark and sinuous for him. No enterprises bloody and cruel enough to shock him. There is no public virtue so white but that he will regard it accessible to corruption. There is no intellect so honored but that he regards himself its match in trickery and finesse. He has succeeded in tempting men that were thought far above the reach of such allurements. He has fooled and deceived men far his superiors in mind and experience.

His course of action in regard to this war has been most singular and characteristic. He recognized of course the great political capital that could be made by a successful general in future canvasses. He therefore used his position as a Senator to have himself appointed a Brigadier General. Finding that his successor in the Senate was not likely to be a creature of his own, he refused his commission and held on to his seat in the Senate as a surer and more valuable means of influence. Still feeling an itch for military rank, he managed to gain another tender of appointment under pretense that it was the earnest desire of General Hunter to have his cooperation. He next went resolutely to work to identify himself and his name with the radical theory of universal armed and forcible emancipation. He saw that no respectable officer would undertake the carrying out of an idea so absurd and monstrous, and he saw that a large number of people throughout the North believed in that principle. He announced it as his own and became the rallying point of that scattered fanaticism.

Knowing that the Government had resolved upon a Southwestern expedition under the leadership of General Hunter, by an almost inconceivable course of duplicity and falsehood he deceived the War Department and Gen. Hunter till each believed that the other was earnestly in favor of Lane's connection with the expedition. This may sound absurd, but I am assured by persons who know whereof they speak, that it is true. Previously to his leaving Washington, he caused an Abolitionist clerk in the Treasury Department to write out and take to the several newspaper correspondents in the city a pretended conversation between himself and the President, in which the President was made to utter the most unreserved Abolition sentiments and suggestions as Lane's future rule of action. The *New York Tribune* printed them. The other papers refused to touch them. The President authorized an emphatic denial of them.

Receiving orders to report himself to General Hunter, at Fort Leavenworth, he started upon what resulted in a triumphal journey. At every prominent stopping he held a levee, to which the long-haired disciples thronged to shake hands and wish him God-speed. The most ludicrous exhibition was at Chicago, where the editors of the *Tribune* attended his *matinee,* and stood obsequiously at his elbow, learning his policy of the war. It was a sight long to be remembered, to see the editor of a paper, so powerful, so able, and, were it not for its wild vagaries, so earnestly patriotic, standing by the side of that cunning and wily rowdy, taking the crude and ungrammatical utterances that dropped from his lips, as flashes of strange and novel wisdom which were to result in the healing of the nations.

When he came to Leavenworth his game was up. Gen. Hunter is not a man whom he can fool, or bully, or cajole. He is pre-eminently a soldier. He knew that Lane was not, either by nature or by education. He was an open, frank, manly dealer with men. He would not meet Lane on his own level of chicane and fraud. He was so thoroughly in earnest, feeling in his inmost heart the conscience of the war, that he instinctively recognized in Lane the impostor and the charlatan. He was a gentleman born and bred, and Lane's manners were not such as to impress him with either respect or esteem. Gen. Hunter soon stripped the lion's hide from the shoulders of the insolent masquerader.

Finding that in Hunter he had met his superior, he began to clamor for the interference of his friends at Washington and in Kansas. It never for a moment seemed to occur to him that he could obey the orders of the War Department, report to Gen. Hunter for his commands, receive them and execute them. He insisted, in defiance of all discipline and decency, on making his own orders, giving himself his own command, and being a law to himself, self-poised and self-centered. He wanted General Hunter to abdicate in his favor, to give into his hands the whole Southwest expedition, and to remain in Leavenworth for the purpose of sending on Quartermaster's and Commissary's stores to him. These were his demands. Whether he really wished them acceded to is another matter. It seems more probable that his object is not to be placed at the head of an enterprise for which he, of course, must feel himself incompetent, but by raising this storm and tumult over the matter, to call public attention to himself as a persecuted and distressed martyr in the holy cause of emancipation. With this he can come back to Washington with a whole skin and with any amount of material for future speeches at serenades, and lay his plans for future elections and present jobs, free from the risks that attend the lives and reputations of those that go forth to do battle.

I think James Henry is very nearly played out in Congress. The Senators are getting tried of the continued presence of a man they have twice confirmed as a Brigadier, in the vain hope of being freed of him. If he appears again in his seat in the indeterminate condition of buttons and toga, which has so long marked him, there will be very great disposition to repeat to him the question to which Gen. Hunter was so anxious to hear the answer, "Are you a Senator or a General?" In the House his adherents are getting very sparse and very quiet. Mr. John Covode still stands by him, as honest and true a man as lives, but one with very little knowledge of men and things, and deluded by the appearance of anti-slavery that Lane puts on. In Congress James Henry is of the things that were.

A dreary little abolition paper, printed here by a bilious youth who has gotten no office of the ten he has applied for, still exalts James Henry as the Coming Man. It has fallen recently, however, into such a melancholy frame of mind that its early demise is anticipated, and Lane will be left without an organ. Let us hope that he may sink into respectable common-placeness when his friends all desert him.[14]

WASHINGTON CORRESPONDENCE, 25 FEBRUARY 1862

A very ridiculous row seems to be growing up and gathering form and proportion between the friends of General McClellan and those of Mr. Stanton, the Secretary of War. It is very absurd that anything of the sort should take place at this period of good feeling. It is certainly very surprising that the first symptoms of disagreement should appear between Gen. McClellan and Stanton, who is, like him, a Democrat in politics, and thoroughly in sympathy with his views, and was before his entering the Cabinet the peculiar confidential friend and advisor of the young General-in-Chief. In fact, it is not perceived that any ill feeling exists between the Secretary and the General. There is nothing to show that their cordial relations have suffered any change. It is, however, very evident that the friends of the parties have taken up the cudgels in dead earnest on each side, and an open warfare will probably before long be inaugurated. The *New York Tribune,* the especial champion of the Secretary, has opened its heavy artillery upon McClellan. The *Herald,* which is generally on the side of the Administration, whatever that may be, has been grieved away by the unmerciful snubbing it received in the person of its trusted representative, Dr. Ives, and espouses with great energy the cause of McClellan. The *World,* a cool, quiet, conservative paper, also defends McClellan with great earnestness, and the *Times,* as usual, trims. It is a very pretty quarrel as it stands.

In the very beginning of Stanton's administration of the War office, he seemed to become aware that our system of subordinating the whole operation of a campaign to the command of one General was in itself wrong and pernicious. This fact, which had been previously recognized by others in the Government, he began to act upon, issuing orders in the name of the President and without consultation with the General-in-Chief. General McClellan was a man of too much good sense, and too clear a perception of soldierly duty and responsibility, to take the slightest exception to this, but fully approved it, as in all respects more fitting and relieving him of a good deal of useless care. Many of his friends, however, regarded it as an infringement of his prerogative, and an audacious innovation upon the established traditions of the service. This was the beginning of the discussion which has continued ever since. There can be no question of the justice of this view, for which, by the way, Stanton is not at all responsible, but if the general impression be true, the Commander-in-Chief of the Army and Navy himself first recognized and acted upon the principle for which ill-judging friends of General McClellan are complaining.

The authority of the President and of the Council of Administration is, and ought to be absolute in determining the general plan of campaign and policy of war. General McClellan himself, who adds to great military skill a clear and accurate perception of war to Government, has always plainly enunciated and governed his action by this principle. There can be nothing more absurd than the senseless clamor of exultation raised by the crack-brained fanatics in Congress, and out of it, at the supposed discovery they had made of the decline of McClellan's power and influence. The assumption of power by the President and War Department proceeded from no diminishing of confidence in General McClellan. They were the result of the clearly recognized views of the President, and were in entire harmony with the ideas of McClellan. Whatever the indiscreet friends or the silly opposers of the General may say, it is true that no relations now exist, or have existed between the President and McClellan but those of the most cordial and even affectionate nature. There not only *is* no misunderstanding, but there *can* be none between men whose relative positions are so clearly defined and understood by each, and between whom there is so much of mutual confidence and esteem.

One matter has given rise to a great deal of discussion. After the battle of Fort Donelson, when everybody was exulting over so magnificent an assertion of the awakened power of the Republic, and no thought of private glorification entered into any mind, the *New York Tribune*, instigated by Dana, that demon of discord whose excess of bile always makes him most miserable when others are most happy, took it into his head to throw an apple of contention into the feast by ascribing the sole merit of the victory to one man. He gave the award—not to Generals Grant and McClernand and Smith, who led our soldiers through the deadly storm to victory—not to Foote, who anchored his frail boats in the very mouth of hell—not to Halleck, who directed the storm from his office in St. Louis—not to McClellan, who had watched for months the progress of that enterprise—not to the President, whose farseeing sagacity had long ago seized upon that great idea, and who had cherished and fostered the scheme since the last summer—not to any of these, but to Edwin M. Stanton, who had come into the Cabinet after the expedition was organized, and who had recovered from a sick bed just in time to write a star-spangled and ringing order of the day, in honor of the magnificent achievement.

The very absurdity of this praise defeated its object. The madness of the malignity deranged its aim. Everybody laughed at this ascription of undeserved palms. Stanton himself saw the absurdity of it, and rushed hastily into print. You have seen his letter to the *Tribune*. It is in scarcely better taste than the article which called it forth. He denies that he is entitled to any particular praise for the achievement, but instead of giving honors to whom honors are due, and when they would have been acceptable to the sensitive and ambitious spirit of hard-working soldiers, he generously divides the credit of Fort Donelson between himself and Heaven. If Heaven were working for a brevet this would be all very appropriate, but I question the propriety of taking all credit due to human effort and toil, and throwing [*it*] into the boundless ocean of Divine beneficence.

A short while ago at a railroad meeting, the Secretary of War made some remarks. The reporter in transcribing them introduced a paragraph complimentary to General McClellan, who was sitting near the Secretary. The *New York Tribune* foamed at the mouth about it, and Mr. Stanton with very unnecessary emphasis denied having made any allusion to the General. If he did not, he might have done so with very great aptness and good taste.

These things have produced a little coolness between the friends of the distinguished parties and have given rise to much silly and useless talk. The reckless haste with which the *Tribune* and Tribunites have argued themselves into the belief that Mr. Stanton holds with them the opinion that black is white, and that the highest privilege of the Caucasian is to burnt cork his face and learn the banjo, is very amusing and instructive. They will change their tune some morning when Mr. Stanton writes an "order" with twice the usual amount of the American eagle in it, complimenting Gen. McClellan on the occupation of Manassas, or issues a rescript for the imprisonment of Wilkinson, *Tribune* correspondent, as a nuisance and malcontent. I do not know what else will bring them to their senses.[15]

WASHINGTON CORRESPONDENCE, 28 FEBRUARY 1862

The tendency of all things to fight against repression has been strikingly illustrated in the recent result of Secretary Stanton's rescript, silencing the sensationist telegrammarians. Before twenty-four hours had elapsed after the promulgation of the order, announcing that the telegraph would hereafter be closed to the transmission of all news of any movements, a most plentiful crop of startling tidings and spasmodic rumors grew up and blossomed in the streets. The House of Representatives was the nursery of a most promising collection of these exotic flowerings of lively imaginations. One excited lawgiver rushed into the lobby and announced that Daniel E. Sickles had been shot at the head of his Brigade by a corporal whose wife had smiled upon her husband's general. "You don't say so," said another. "Yes, I am sure it is so," adds a third, "for Ben Wood says it is a lie." This, of course, settled the matter, and the married men talk of voting a silver whistle to the nameless avenger of domestic peace.

Before the bottom falls out of this story, another appalling rumor gathers shape and substance. Banks has crossed the Potomac, and has fallen in with the enemy in force, who have driven his command into the river and probably crucified the General. This obtains general evidence and gives rise to sage comments on the fallacy of entrusting important commands to political generals. Soon somebody who knows nothing about the matter contradicts the rumor in a firm, loud tone, and it falls dead as Caesar on the floor of the Capitol.

An enthusiastic and red faced person, whose wish stands in the parental relation to his thought, rushes into Willard's and announces that Hooker has crossed the lower Potomac and occupied the entire range of batteries. He is instantaneously surrounded by a sympathizing group, to take his largess of news with open mouthed eagerness, until overcome with the thirst of much oratory, he hides his glowing countenance behind a Santacruzian flip.

In the midst of the shower of rumors, you should note with what composed dignity of demeanor the Government Directors of Telegraph walk through a gossiping crowd. The sublime indifference manifested by Eckert, who looks more like a Major General than McClellan does, and the easy unconsciousness of anything mundane that sits upon the placid forehead of Captain Stager, is most exhilarating and inspiring to the soul of the news hunter, downcast and heavy hearted at the rain of canards. If people must talk about war movements, it is probably as well to let them talk within a mile or so of the truth, for falsehood seems of late to gravitate inevitably towards despondency. The system of Government telegraphing is now most simple and efficient. The Government is, without delay, placed in the possession of all news of importance, and is thoroughly in relation with the whole scheme of operation along the immense line from Ship Island around the coast, and inland to where the volunteer levies of Col. Canby stand ready to meet the ragged plunderers of Texas, at the disgraced and betrayed walls of Fort Fillmore.

It is to be hoped that the evil caused by the Secretary's peremptory order will be remedied by a timely arrangement, furnishing to the press all proper intelligence received at headquarters. There is little now to conceal. The rebels have learned by a more outspoken teaching than any that newspapers or spies can give them, the plans of the Government. It was thundered into their ears by the cannon of Dupont and Goldsborough. They read it in the glistening of the Union bayonets. It was revealed, in no equivocal terms, by the hurried flight of the ragged legions that escaped the penalty of treason at Donelson and at Bowling Green. The despair that followed the full understanding of our plan may be seen in the doleful utterances of rebel papers and the hollow bravado of rebel chiefs. The madness of men who feel that a wicked cause is falling may be discovered in the barbarism of the fugitive Governor of Tennessee, who advertised his desperation in the blaze of burning archives, and in the devilish savagery of the wild and desperate wretches whom Curtis has hunted to the death, who seem driven by an agony of fear and hate, to an infamy at which cannibals would shudder.

While the President pursues his present course of energetic and unresting pursuit, while our Generals with sleepless vigilance and incessant toil carry out the great schemes of national restoration, the Secretary of War need not hope that the rebels can be kept ignorant of our plan.—Let them know what it is: active, unresting war, until the supremacy of the Constitution and the laws is re-established. The more they know of it, the worse for their cause.

There seems to be no question at present of the great and rapidly increasing dissatisfaction of the rebels with those conducting the war. Their recent astounding reverses seem to be exciting among them a great deal of original thought and discussion. They are driven naturally to inquire into the cause and the explanation of what seems to them incomprehensible. Mingled with the gravest apprehensions as to capacity and energy of their government, are vague doubts as to the long received belief of the Southerners, that each one of them is equal to five Yankees. The extravagant assertions of rebel newspapers in regard to feats of valor which the mortality lists do not confirm are beginning to be coolly dissected, and indignant skeptics resort to figures.

Here is a portion of a most remarkable note printed in the *Richmond Examiner* last week, which indicates the spirit of sullen unbelief that is beginning to sap the foundation of the rebel rule:

> The Roanoke affair is perfectly incomprehensible. The newspapers are filled with extravagant laudations of our valor—the annals of Greece and Rome offer no parallel—whole regiments were defeated by companies, and we yielded only to death. Our men finally surrendered "with no blood on their bayonets," and what is the loss? Richmond Blues, two killed and five wounded; McCulloch Rangers, one killed and two wounded; the other four companies lost in all two killed and eleven wounded. Comment is needless. The whole army had better surrender at once, for it will eventually come to it.
>
> I am, sir, &c.,
> AN OFFICER

Please note the spirit of these words and read in connection the letter of poor Maury to Commodore Lynch. The unintentional tone of melancholy in that remarkable epistle is most significant and suggestive. The tide has turned. Southern people are beginning to think. And it is bad for a baseless cause when the native hue of resolution begins to be sicklied o'er with the pale cast of thought.[16]

Washington correspondence, 9 March 1862

There have been at least three memorable Sundays since the beginning of the war for the Union. One came on the 21st of July, when the joy of assured victory gladdened every heart until midnight and the crushing certainty of disappointment came in with the dusty and bedrabbled soldiers that straggled mournfully over the Long Bridge, on Monday. Another Sunday not to be soon forgotten was that which closed the fight at Donelson when Gen. Buckner acceded to the unchivalrous proposition of General Grant. But no day has been more checkered in its manifestations of public sentiment, than this in whose grey evening I write. Early this morning the news came to the War Department that the ironclad steamer *Merrimac* had come out of James River and sunk the *Cumberland* and captured the *Congress*. Mr. Stanton at once ordered the news to be made public, as it affected commercial interests, and he thought it due to the merchants of the North that they should be immediately apprised of the extent of the danger. For a while the news looked very badly. From Gen. Wool's first dispatch there could be drawn no inference, but that the invincible monster, after destroying the remainder of the fleet there, would go out to sea and take her choice of sacking Washington, New York or Boston. For a great part of the morning the panic at Willard's was intense. Nothing was too wild to be believed in the way of theory and suggestion. I saw one old gentleman, who has a son in Burnside's expedition, turn purple with fright on hearing it said that the *Merrimac* would go down to Roanoke Island and sink Goldsborough's fleet. He recovered on being reminded that it was inconvenient for a vessel drawing twenty-one feet to sail in eight feet of water.

To guard against the smallest possibility of danger the commandants of the harbor defenses at Boston and New York were ordered to stand to their guns, and Captain Dahlgren went cooly to work at our Navy Yard here to make the proper preparations to receive the bold rover courteously if she decided to visit the Capital.

General Wool's second dispatch looked more cheerful. The camp at Newport News was intact, the *Minnesota* was unhurt, the *Merrimac* had gone back to Craney Island, which last was a piece of most unaccountable fatuity, since it lost them the opportunity of sinking the *Minnesota*, a magnificent specimen of naval architecture. The tide once turned in this way, it continued turning. After a while we learned that the *Monitor*—better known as the Ericsson Battery—had arrived and was ready for action. Then at four o'clock we learned that the cable was laid from Fortress Monroe to Cherrystone Point, and we could talk with the Fortress face to face. The mystery being taken from the danger, half the danger was gone.

The evening dispatches made people as jolly as those of the morning had made them glum. It really was a magnificent fight, that the little *Monitor* made with her redoubtable enemy. It was one of the pluckiest things on record. Instantly on arriving at the Fortress, the *Monitor* was sent up to guard the huge and defenseless hulk of the *Minnesota* against her invulnerable enemy. In the early morning the rebel flotilla—the *Merrimac, Yorktown* and *Jamestown,* and several tugs—came down to what they supposed would be an easy prey, the unwieldy frigate wallowing on the sand, unable to turn, unable to fight or escape. They seemed to treat with supreme contempt the little nondescript lying quietly by the side of her disabled friend, until they saw her suddenly leave the *Minnesota* and bear down upon them like David on Goliath. The frigate and the *Monitor* began to fire, and the wooden rebel gunboats began to remember an engagement they had further up the river, and the *Monitor* and the *Merrimac* were left to fight it out alone. I believe the annals of sea fights show nothing like this. From early morning to high noon these two ungraceful creatures hammered at each other. The *Merrimac* had vastly the advantage in size and metal, ten guns of great calibre, against two eleven-inch dahlgrens. The *Monitor* had the advantage in perfection of machinery and rapidity of movement. On the *Monitor,* too, was Lieutenant Commanding Worden, who fought with all the coolness of a Northern sailor, and all the stern determination nursed by half a year's solitude in a rebel dungeon. They pounded at each other, their adamantine sides grinding each on each, their flags mixed in each other's smoke, "hot gunlip kissing gun," until the rebel monster, thinking she had seen enough of that style of thing, hauled off and clawed her way back to Craney Island, bruised, battered and beat, leaving the plucky little *Monitor* unharmed, and victor of the hardest fight on record.

The end of these proceedings at Hampton Roads is not yet, of course. The *Merrimac* is not so disabled as to prevent her from doing a great deal of harm if she is able to get out. It will require very careful management on the part of our artillery and naval officers there to keep her in check or destroy her. The events of to-day show most conclusively that these armored boats are the only efficient means of river and harbor defense. They triumphantly vindicate the thoughtful providence of the Government who hurried the construction of the *Monitor* with an almost feverish impatience, and have the satisfaction of knowing that a gain of twenty-four hours has saved the fleet in Hampton Roads. There is cause for special gratulation in the fact that the *Minnesota* is saved. She is a splendid frigate, one of the best in the service of the Government. The *Cumberland* and the *Congress,* which the *Merrimac* victimized, were of little value, and their loss is itself considered no special misfortune. The loss of their crews is of course deeply to be regretted.

But as if the stars in their courses fought for us, even in our seeming disasters, the news of this afternoon extracts all the sting from our misfortune. It has been for some time known in well informed circles that attacks were to be made at once on the batteries of the Potomac and the fleet lying at Fortress Monroe was relied upon to furnish the most important assistance in that enterprise. But at the very moment when we are so singularly deprived of the assistance of the fleet, we find compensation in the fact that the enemy have fled from those dreaded batteries, and have left nothing for Hooker and our flotilla to do, but to land at Cockpit, Freestone and the other points, and take possession of the deserted forts and half-spiked cannon, and raise the Stars and Stripes over the entrenchments.

We are having such an uninterrupted series of undeserved successes that it may be well for us to lose a frigate or two on the principle in accordance with which the Grecian prayed, "Send me, O Zeus! some slight misfortune that I may escape the dreadful envy of the gods!"[17]

Washington correspondence, 24 March 1862

The progress of ideas in a revolution is more rapid than in any of the chartered colleges or universities. Cannon balls will beat new notions into thick noodles where birchen twigs have failed to develop superior intelligence. A great revolution is like an overgrown mob; every one in the crowd seems to know what was the original design, but no one is wise enough to tell where the violence and lawlessness will cease. One year ago the most loyal men in the border States were anti-coercionists, and the strongest seceders were not ready to take up arms to defend their opinions. Now an anti-coercionist is only another name for a rebel, and the theoretical secessionist has put on his armor and sworn to perish, if necessary, in defense of his supposed rights.

Last year Wendell Phillips was hissed and almost rotten-egged in Boston for making an Abolition speech—last week in Washington, with the Father of his country looking down upon him and his country's flag floating above him, he announced to an applauding multitude that he had no interest in the existing war prosecuted with the Lincoln policy, and that he had labored for thirty years to dissolve the Union.

Last year at this time Commodore Buchanan was commandant of the Washington Navy yard, making show and profession of true loyalty—to-day he is dead of a wound received in his mad efforts to destroy the country that had heaped honors on his head. So we go. The lines of demarcation are sinking deeper every day. There is no middle ground left, and every man is a true loyalist or a sworn traitor. The extremes, too, instead of meeting, are still receding from each other. The unquestioned loyalty of last March is denounced as open treason to-day.

Whither do these things tend, and what is to be the result? One thing seems plain to every reflecting mind. If this bloody strife continues six months or a year longer, it will degenerate into a pure anti-slavery war, and end in the utter devastation of the whole South. All honor to Abraham Lincoln for the noble stand he has taken upon this subject. Dentatus like he planted himself with his back to the rock of the Constitution, and for the last year has fought bravely and successfully against the whole crowd of radicals. But through Congress and the abolition press, they are becoming masters of the position, by climbing and stealing behind him, and sooner or later he must succumb. When that time comes, God help us; for without such aid, the country will be ruined for a generation to come.

Under these circumstances, what should every honest man in the South who has still some love of kin and country left, pray for? The immediate and complete success of the Union arms. This is all that can save the country from a desolation as terrible as that which sweeps a whole nation from the face of the earth. With the capture of New Orleans and the opening of the Mississippi, the Southern mind will certainly reach the conviction that they can be overcome, and if you please, subjugated. But with a war of utter subjugation, what pictures of horror haunt the imagination! Blood and carnage on a hundred battle fields, impoverished millions, slaughtered and exiled thousands, immense throngs of liberated slaves wandering about, a curse to themselves and the white population of the North, towns and cities destroyed and whole regions of fruitful country turned to a barren waste. This is a faint outline of what must happen if the war continues another year. Let us hope that the President in his wisdom, after another great triumph of our arms, shall proclaim to the deluded people of the South, that if they will desert their leaders, lay down their arms and return to their allegiance, they shall receive friendly protection for the future, instead of punishment for the past. Such a proclamation might leave the rebel leaders without an army and with no chance to save their necks except by voluntary exile. But if such a proposition should have no effect, except to increase their insolence and audacity, then—well then let the "abomination of desolation" take its course.

This bloody revolution was brought upon the country by the slavery propagandists of the South and the radical abolitionists of the North. They can divide the honor and responsibility of the matter in such proportions as they like. The latter party are most anxious, at present, for the continuance of the war. Its speedy close would not half accomplish the work they desire to have thoroughly done—the emancipation of the whole negro race in America. They believe, and with good reason, too, that if this war is continued for six months or a year, the country will become so exasperated with the loss of life and the burden of taxation, that it will insist upon devastating with fire and sword the whole slave region of the South. They understand the fact which has been present and urged in your columns a hundred times, that slave occupation and military occupation of the same country are utterly incompatible and impracticable. They see, that in consequence of the secessionists having forced this state of things upon the border States, even for a few months, slavery in them is doomed, and they pray for the war to continue long enough to extend the expansion of the same [*cause?*] quite down to the Gulf of Mexico. Whether their prayers are answered in curses upon their madness and folly, a few months will tell.[18]

WASHINGTON CORRESPONDENCE, 27 MARCH 1862

A history of the rise and downfall of that illegitimate offshoot of the Republican party whose forlorn hope is headed in the North and West by the big and little *Tribunes,* would be, perhaps, not altogether uninteresting to an appreciative public.

Now, in unraveling the tangled skein of causes and effects which led to the conspiracy against McClellan, which so lately culminated to an outburst in the columns of the *bigger Tribune,* the first deduction is this: McClellan's growing popularity overshadowed that of Frémont, whom they were endeavoring to foist upon the people as the greatest, the ablest, and the most persecuted man of the day; and secondly, there was not the most remote hope of the prosperity of their party, so long as such men as McClellan on the Potomac and Halleck in the West occupied the places of power. Two very strong incentives to the course which they have so faithfully adhered to in accordance with the laws of self-preservation and self-defense.

So long [*ago*] as last fall, in remote corners and secret places of conclave, and within earshot of the Executive Mansion, were heard, here in Washington, murmurs of discontent from the exasperated expectants and tag ends who go to make up this party, and who had hitherto been loudest in their adulations of Lincoln as "our" President.

"*We* elected this man," said they, "and now he ignores our existence. *We* put him where he is now, expecting to find in him a pliant tool for our own purposes, and now he takes the reins into his own hands and coolly orders us out of the way. And now we begin to find out that we are not to rule the nation after all, and that the loaves and fishes are not to flow into our hands. We are tired of this man," said they, "and we want another in his place. *We* put him up, and *we* will pull him down." Thenceforth the President and his Cabinet were black-balled with the foulest charges, the vilest insinuations, the most malicious aspersions—attacked in open field, or from some sly ambuscade by this disappointed clique. Then came Frémont's famous *Missouri splurge,* in the shape of a proclamation. Eureka! The malcontents had found a man after their own hearts. The proclamation came just in the nick of time. To be sure it was not very judicious as a *war* measure just at that particular time. But what matter? It was a grand political hit, and showed in what particular province its originator was most likely to win laurels; and the clique of malcontents, hitherto nameless, organized themselves as Frémont men.

There were blustering menaces of a revolution—the dispossessing of the present Administration of its power if it did not act up to the expectations of the new party on the emancipation question—a provisional government and Frémont at its head. This may sound like mere matter of moonshine at this late day; but nevertheless I assert that the notion was maintained seriously by certain public individuals whose senses on this subject were "clear gone," but who had discretion enough to reserve such rank treason for secret assemblies and private conclaves. A revolution! A revolution was the day-thought and the night dream of this sect. That they used every covert means to bring this about has been clearly proven. But the people wouldn't rise! They were not strongly enough imbued with radical enthusiasm. Not even when all the stage accessories which were so industriously gathered around the removal of Frémont were brought to bear upon them—even then they would not rise! In vain the seeds of treason and dissatisfaction were sown broadcast throughout the land. In vain the stealthy attempts to undermine the confidence of the people in the Administration, and the open censure lavished by them on the conduct of the war; and the envenomed malice which went even into the family precincts of the White House to find some shadow of blame upon which to arraign the loyalty of the servant of the people. Frémont's removal from Missouri, before he had altogether succeeded, not in earning, but in securing the distrust of the nation which still waited indulgently, and hoped for "better things," was a glorious addition to the scanty capital with which his party had started out on their operations. Never was the role of martyred worth more skillfully acted! Never the protests of generous indignation more loudly mouthed! And the hope was that the party would be strong enough to rise and proclaim Frémont as their nominal head, in defense of all existing authority. That hope failed, and another resource was put forward. Now begun the preconcerted attacks upon McClellan, who, with his friends, formed one of the chief bulwarks against their aggressions. "Let Frémont but head the army," said his friends, "and we shall yet carry the day." The hope was that such an enormous pressure would be brought to bear upon the Administration that they would be intimidated into giving Frémont McClellan's place. And as the investigation before the Military Committee drew to a close, the note of preparation was sounded. The *Tribune's* attacks upon McClellan became frantically savage; then Frémont's apology (misnamed defense) "drew its slow length along." Shanks and Colfax opened cry in the House of Representatives; and our friends flattered themselves that they had gotten affairs into a very prosperous train—so they had—but Uncle Abe very quietly put his foot down upon the apex of this delicious scheme and squelched it by giving Frémont an appointment, the exquisite fitness of which was recognized by an assenting public; while the Chief's followers, struck dumb with consternation at this unexpected "move," dared not complain of it. They tried to cheer it—they tried to regard it as a very handsome compensation, and to make people believe it was a great triumph and just what they had expected, they tried to draw some scanty consolation from the mistaken idea that their old enemy McClellan had been "snubbed" as well as themselves. They very magnanimously told people that they had "never wanted McClellan's place for Frémont, because he could be next President if he wanted to," and finally slunk off with drooping crests to hide their ill-concealed defeat, while the man on whom their hopes are hung goes to his post a General without an army, a soldier without an enemy! The struggle has been long and desperate, and has lasted throughout the winter. It has been waged in the columns of the *Tribune;* in the Senate and in the House; at the Smithsonian, where "the Washington Lecture Association" had things all its own way; up at the Capitol on Sunday by the fanatic Cheever; and the result is, that extremists are worsted. They can twist very little consolation out of the President's Emancipation Message; less yet out of the fact that McClellan is no longer Commander-in-Chief of the armies, since the change is a merely nominal one, and he still enjoys the confidence of the Administration. The President has said very plainly and unequivocally that he is not of them, and that he will "none of them." But they do not yet despair of so working upon the people by false representation as to bring to bear upon the Administration so strong a pressure as shall induce it to oust McClellan and put a man of their choosing in his place.

Of Frémont, personally, we have nothing to say, except that he proved himself not the man for the crisis—that he rewarded the mistaken devotions of the people of Missouri by sending abroad the impression that St. Louis was out and out a disloyal city. And if he knew of the unworthy machinations made to centre around him—and which were treason to the established authorities, then he was trebly unworthy of the high position which he occupied—and it is to be hoped that in his new department he will find some nobler occupation than in conniving at the conspiracies of a discontented faction, or the selfish casting of lots for the raiment and the spoils of a torn and bleeding nation, which while standing up to face its foes in front, is stabbed from behind by that arch Judas—that party which, to reach the heart of an enemy, would not hesitate to strike through the bosom of its dearest friend.

But the party which raised the hue and cry against McClellan has failed— "combinations to the contrary notwithstanding," as Mr. Shanks (of Indiana,) says. Frémont for the Presidency! is again the darling idea of the agitators;

but across the path that leads up to the Presidential chair looms a shadow which never grows less but increases daily; and the blackness of that shadow upon the hopes of the newly organized party is cast by the brightening prospects of George B. McClellan.

No wonder the big and little *Tribunes* abuse him.[19]

WASHINGTON CORRESPONDENCE, 29 MARCH 1862

The minds of the people are, just now, in a singular state of suspense and nervousness in regard to what is coming next. The study of geography, which has so long been a favorite pursuit of those who read newspapers[,] has taken a more general and discursive character within a few weeks. Imagination, and that logic which inevitably leads to absurd conclusions, lend their assistance to the earnest geographer and flower into most brilliantly impossible campaigns. The admirers of Frémont have indulged in some of the most florid of these imaginary campaigns. Their feverish fancies have been filled with wild mountain expeditions, desperate Thermopylaes, St. Bernard marches, Utopian communities in the hills on the contraband basis, and all the poetry and color of an Alleghenian empire. Burnside, too, has been the theme of many variegated dreams. Although none have reached the height of sublime ignorance attained by the English Solomon of the *Saturday Review* who landed him, flotilla and all, on the Western slope of the Blue Ridge, the victories which the public have been discounting for him in advance are as brilliant as they are impossible. Leave him the glory of Roanoke Island and Newbern, and call his work nearly accomplished. His men fought very well there. They have silenced the insolent slander of the whipped rebels of the Mississippi Valley, "that though Western men can fight the Yankees can not." It is not the *State* that sends our soldiers to the field that fills their hearts with fire and nerves their arms as with steel. It is the banner of the Union that floats over all alike, the representative not of an accidental league or discordant association, but of a nation, one and indivisible.

Still the Western troops have certainly been far luckier than the Eastern. Not only strong in their arms and in their cause, but in their leaders, they have alternated more frequently than any other Department the quiet labor of the camp and the fierce joy of battles. They have been less cursed with the strict requirements of military science than any others. While the long bulk of the Potomac army lay wasting in the wintry moisture and the biting frosts, chafing with inaction and longing for advance; while the army under [*Thomas West*] Sherman loafed lazily among the cotton islands by the inland seas of Carolina, watching the gentle coming of the Southern spring, and amusing themselves only by shooting the straggling picket and chaffing the frequent contraband; while the guns of Pickens lay silent on the barbette, looking harmless defiance at the still camps opposite, while soldiers and seamen wondered if there was war in the land and why the guns had nothing to say about it, and Billy Wilsoneers shot and strangled each other in peace, on the silent sands of Santa Rosa Island; while Phelps was too busy inculcating the elements of political economy into the wool-defended craniums of the adventurous darkeys that came over by night from the deserted huts of Biloxi, to think of marching on Mobile or picking up New Orleans; while over the whole vast circle of operations, everybody seemed Micawberishly waiting for something to turn up, those Western men were going steadily at their work, letting results take care of themselves.

The nation delights to honor these Western men. Throughout the East they are spoken of in a tone of generous enthusiasm as the heroes of such fighting as the world has not lately seen. The Legislature of Maine, the farthest East, has passed resolutions in praise of the magnificent achievements of the Western troops, "and to the troops of Illinois especially, for their heroic conduct at Fort Donelson, the country owes a debt of gratitude which cannot be acknowledged too heartily, and which can never be repaid." Those Eastern Legislatures exhibit in these ascriptions of praise to distant soldiers, a rare and beautiful unselfishness and patriotism. Seeing their own sons and brothers restrained from the glorious fields where laurels are to be had for the grasping, they yet are loudest and sincerest in applause for those more fortunate, though not more brave, whose hands are free to pluck the chaplets of enduring fame.

Even here where any fighting is allowed by the politeness of the enemy, there is sure to be a very strong if not predominant Western element. It is rather Hibernian to class among Westerners, General Shields, a gentleman who was born as far east as Ireland, but all his fighting qualities were matured and nourished in the West. At the head of a Western brigade he fought in Mexico, and a very considerable shaft of Western sunlight shone clear through his body in the path where a Mexican grapeshot had preceded it. In the first considerable fight of the Potomac army this broth of a Western boy was in command. And being as usual in the immediate vicinity of the vagrant shells and bullets he came in contact with a shell. His arm was broken, but he did not seem particularly to mind it. He still directed all the operations of the battle with the greatest coolness, until General Banks coming up took command in person, and pursued the beaten and disheartened enemy beyond the hills of Strasburg. And Banks, you know, is another Illinoisan. It is rather cool to name as one of the Suckers, the most prominent politicians of Massachusetts, but we will leave the East the politician and remember that Banks, the fighting-man, was taken from Chicago.

Gen. Richardson, of Quincy, has also a right to be named among prominent western men who have done well for their country. He has had the moral courage to decline an appointment as Brigadier General, to which he thought some of the fighting Colonels of his State were better entitled. For a prominent politician clearly to apprehend and confess that he would not make the best possible Brigadier General, proves a degree of self-knowledge and correctness of perception as rare as it is admirable.

It is very interesting to observe the readiness and almost magical distinctness with which a man's former life flashes into view in the light of new achievements. A year ago who remembered anything of the Baden Revolution? If it was ever mentioned it passed before the mind dimly as a dream, colorless, void of life; the actors stood as representatives of heroic and unfortunate endeavor—nothing more. But in the fires of this war, those fading characters come out clearly revealed, like the warmed manuscripts of invisible ink.

Since the great day when Sigel retreated from Carthage, leaving his path red with the blood of a baffled and defeated enemy, the days of the Baden Revolution are coming more clearly into view. The glories of those Southwestern battles shed a clearness and distinctness upon that memorable contest for liberty, which it never had before. Its history comes out with embarrassing distinctness sometimes. Gen. Blenker sees no possible occasion for the disentombing of Sigel's celebrated order denouncing Col. Blenker as a marauder. Blenker has been in great trouble recently, but his troubles seem nearly over. On Sigel, the brave and blameless, there has never rested the shadow of a stain.

One more Westerner sails to-day for usefulness and glory. David Hunter, late Major General Commanding the Department of Kansas, goes to take command of the Southern Atlantic coast. Wherever he goes there will be seen the evidences of the fresh revivifying Western spirit. The soldier that led the only division that did its whole duty at Bull Run—the honest and clear-minded patriot that saw beneath the mask of the cunning jayhawker and sent him back harmless and ridiculous to the Senate, will always, in whatever position, do all that is asked of him. He is an old army officer, into whose mind the dream of divided allegiance never entered. With all the energies of a vigorous manhood, and the calm experience of sixty laborious years, he goes to the arduous duty to which the confidence of the Government has assigned him. He is surrounded by a staff like himself, firm, honest, brave, Northwestern. There is no doubt but that you will hear of him. He has always been fortunate, for he is one of the men that compel success.[20]

WASHINGTON CORRESPONDENCE, 6 APRIL 1862

General McClellan seems to be determined to keep up the succession of fighting Sundays. This quiet spring morning when all of the population of Washington who fear God and wear clean shirts are on their way to church, the work of death and slaughter goes on in the Peninsula. It is scarcely possible that the fierce contest of yesterday conquered the entrenched enemy. From McClellan's position escape is impossible to the beleaguered rebels. If they ever intend to fight at all and not to become the laughing stock of the world, they must fight today. And probably at this very hour the shock of arms reddens the turf that years ago felt the tread of the humiliated and heart broken British General. Yorktown is a good place for a battle. We established constitutional liberty by a success before its walls. It will be a neat thing if the crusade for its perpetuation also inscribes upon its torn banners the glorious name of Yorktown.

And there exists no good reason why it should not. The Army of the Potomac is qualified by numbers, by equipment, by drill, by material, to arrogate to itself by this time the proud title of invincibility to anything that can be brought against it. It cannot fail before Yorktown. In the absence of authentic news we may safely assume that Yorktown is ours, or soon will be.

On Friday morning, General McClellan, at the head of the Army of the Potomac, took up the line of march for Yorktown. This is a very important point, commanding the navigation of the York River, and furnishing the best possible situation for an entreport of stores. The road from Fortress Monroe to Yorktown, a distance of twenty-four miles, is, for the most part, good.

It consists of a finished turnpike, much superior to the usual style of Virginia roads, which had been obstructed by the rebels only when it wound through forests, by the felling of trees, and in the fording places of the brooks where the shallows had been filled with the sharpened branches and boughs of the trees that lined their borders. About ten miles from the Fortress they came to the ill-fated battle field of Big Bethel, where through the folly and inexperience of some older officers was lost two glorious young fellows, Winthrop who had, if ever soldier had, the hand of iron in the velvet glove, the soul of the poet in the frame of the warrior; and the brave and good-looking young artillerist, John Greble. Still proceeding north, the monotony of the march became alternated by frequent skirmishes, where the activity and enthusiasm of the Virginians' attacks were only equaled by the unanimity and alacrity of their retreats. Towards evening one great object of the first day's work was successfully accomplished. The Union skirmishers succeeded in turning the rebel batteries at Ship Point, and our cavalry occupied them about sundown. This was a very fine piece of luck in the first day's business. If you look on your map of Virginia you will not see Ship Point. But if you will write that name just north of the mouth of Poquosin river, and south of the debouchure of Cheeseman's Creek, your map will be ever after more valuable. The importance of the place consists in this: that the Poquosin river and Cheeseman's Creek afford great facilities for landing troops, and that vessels not drawing more than seven feet of water can land at the very dock at Ship Point, and those of still heavier draught find no difficulty in running along side the abrupt banks at the head of Cheeseman's. It becomes a matter of great importance to economize transportation of supplies as our vast army moves inward, and it seems as if Providence threw this piece of singular good fortune directly into our laps. Ship Point battery, with its two dozen guns, is a "good thing to have in the country."

The General's advance halted for the night at Cockleton, a little crossroads settlement, about five miles south of Yorktown. Saturday morning a combined attack was expected to be made upon the works at this place by the army and the navy. Up to a late hour last night, no trustworthy intelligence from the scene of action had been received. We received dispatches from the operator at Cape Charles, who was in a profound state of bewilderment at the extraordinary sounds and noises that the soft spring breezes bore to him from the main land. Of course, the only things in his mind connected with fighting, were the Rip Raps and the *Merrimac*. So he cocked his ear for the reports that he was sure came from there. He utters not a suspicion of Yorktown. Yet the deep bellowing thunders that rolled so sullenly above the peaceful waters to the quiet promontory were all the fading remnant of the deafening roars that shook the sky and hills of Yorktown. Some hint of ancestral fight inspired them perhaps; some notion of the old feud between two English-speaking peoples, nearly a hundred years ago. We await the full returns of this fight with perfect confidence.

The army of the Potomac, as it moves upon this expedition, will make clean work of it. There will be no loose stitches—no slovenly ends raveling out. Gen. Wool, it is expected, will occupy and hold the rebel batteries along the James river as the army advances, not giving up Newport News or any other important place. There will be no danger of attacks in rear or flank. Nothing but the sea was behind them when they started. No enemy can flank them for some time to come. The left will be thoroughly protected by Wool's attending corps, and the right will be defended by the York river and the gunboats there. The campaign promises absolute success. With McClellan's industry and Wool's experience, things will be handled in refreshing style.

And yesterday morning the President gave us two new Departments. Banks takes command of the Valley of the Shenandoah, and shoulders the entire contract of the abolishment of Stonewall Jackson. McDowell takes command of the Department of the Rappahannock, giving him all the country outside of McClellan's path of proposed march, and a magnificent opportunity to retrieve that sad and mournful 21st of July. No one who knows McDowell doubts that he will do that. Fame, who was terribly disappointed at not being able to crown McDowell then, has been saving his chaplet for the surely coming time when, worthier than ever, he shall reap the reward of his labor and his sturdiness of heart.[21]

Washington correspondence, 20 April 1862

There is enough of the "Onward to Richmond" fervor in the army at present to satisfy the most clamorous of the progressionists who have shouted that battle-cry. It seems as if the President, tired of waiting to see the rebel capital taken through any one instrumentality, had decreed a sort of scrub race, giving each of four Major Generals permission to enter Richmond by one or another door, and dispatched them with the inspiriting injunction "the devil take the hindmost." McDowell, when last heard from, was at Fredericksburg, having made a splendid forced march thither from Catlett's Station, on the Orange and Alexandria Railroad, and scattered the few remaining rebels without so much as a skirmish. Banks' last dispatch was dated at Sparta, in Rockingham county, adjoining Augusta, whose Court House is at Staunton, and in whose mountains swarm hundreds of stubbornly loyal Union men, who having fought against secession with all their might for the past year, have taken to the hills to resist unto death the recent conscription of drunken John Letcher. Just across the Shenandoah Mountains, at Monterey, is the force of Frémont, perfectly equipped, thoroughly drilled, compact and resolute. If Frémont and Banks come together at Staunton, they can experience very little difficulty in the capture of Charlottesville, a point of great importance. It places them directly in the rear of Gordonsville, and gives them their choice of two open railroads. They can either go (in the words of the Virginia poet) "along down, to Lynchburg town," and hermetically seal that most convenient back door of the rebel army, which affords their only outlet to the Southwest, or they may march directly upon Richmond, and quietly bag that bone of contention of the past year. It is not probable that having sent to the peninsula the immense force which is reported to be lying in McClellan's front, they have retained sufficient troops at home to make any very protracted resistance to the splendid legions of Banks and Frémont.

Everywhere there are victories and omens of victory, wherever the sheen of the national banner dazzles the wondering eyes of the disheartened treason—everywhere—but in the peninsula. The reports that we receive from there are so meagre and so unsatisfactory that flourishing crops of rumors spring continually from the graves of daily hopes. The telegraph is silent, or dwells only with abject tremors upon the strength and numbers of the enemy. Nothing breaks the tension of suspense from day to day but voluminous reports of petty skirmishes, and "highly successful reconnaissances" which result in nothing. Shrewd old fellows with a fancy for statistics grin with deep intelligence at the reports of the swarming myriads of the enemy, and obtrude embarrassing queries as to how the rebel army can be in force at half-a-dozen places at the same time.

Yet no one speaks unkindly of the brave young General who commands the magnificent army lying before Yorktown. His industry and energy and pluck and fine soldierly bearing so won upon all hearts while he worked in Washington, that everybody suspends censure upon him, and waits with full confidence for the report that he will give of himself. He has been the darling of the people. No such generous and unsparing confidence was ever given to a General before. He has deserved it, so far, by hard work and earnestness of endeavor. If he fails, it is the fortune of war and his own misfortune. He has been fortunate in all things but one; he has been cursed with wrong-headed friends and indiscreet advocates. Good people have shrugged their shoulders when Biddle and Cox have fought for McClellan in Congress. They have asked, "What treason has this man done that Vallandigham should praise him?" The blatant young whelps who have passed their time airing their epaulettes on the sidewalks at Willard's, or cursing the Administration in the bar-rooms and brothels of Washington, have invariably with the most insulting assurance assumed the especial championship of the General. The wives of semi-secession officers, whom their rank and pay have kept in the army, too loyal to quarrel with their bread and butter, have publicly reviled the Cabinet and Congress for their supposed intentions in the war, and said if they were only General McClellan they would send a file of soldiers up to the Capitol and turn the miserable rabble into the street. And worst of all, the staff officers of the General have not been discreet in their utterances.

For all these things, of course, well informed people hold General McClellan utterly blameless. He is too busy attending to his over onerous duties to know how ill-judging are his noisy advocates. Yet these things explain much of the opposition to him. Indifferent people tired of the clamorous and defiant championship of contractors, parasites and semi-traitors, speak slightingly and unjustly of the man that these persons so noisily praise. They call for results instead of assertions. They say they would prefer a victory to a volume of eulogy. They say impatiently: "Leave off your damnable faces, and begin."

The climax of folly and ingratitude is reached in the malignant attacks that these creatures are beginning to make upon the President for what they call his persecutions of McClellan. To no man in the world, not even to himself, is Gen. McClellan so indebted as to the President. He has had from him, more than justice, affectionate and generous indulgence. The President, even since the days of the astounding disclosure of the unsuspected evacuation of Manassas, has steadily protected and defended him against a pressure which can never be known; for if McClellan succeeds, no one will ever have been against him, and if he fails, no one will have the heart to blame him or to say—I told you so.

Already his friends are throwing anchors to the windward to provide for any possible mishap at Yorktown. They say it is unjust to expect success from a General whose plans have been thwarted, whose troops have been taken from him, who has been deceived and outraged. I am not going to run the risk of Fort Warren and subject you to the suppressionary vengeance of Mr. Stanton by telling you what everybody in Washington knows about these things; but I may venture to say without leave of the Government censor, that *General McClellan has everything he has asked for, and more than his original requirements.* Having begun his active campaign, after mature deliberation, with everything deemed necessary, even those members of the Administration who most strenuously objected to the proposed movement determined to forbear all opposition, and sustain him most heartily and unreservedly in every way, and to the full extent of their several abilities. This has been done. No single requisition has been disregarded. No one connected with the Government has had the insane malignity to thwart one purpose of the General. Everybody who knows him well is his friend personally, and the President and the Cabinet know him well.

It cannot be possible for him to fail. Sustained by the hearts and hands of all the loyal millions of the North, backed by the finest army that ever went to battle, opposed by the dejected wreck of a waning and wasted rebellion, defeat is too absurd a dream for any one to contemplate for him. Still more absurd is it to imagine that in the North there exists any jealousy so fiendishly malignant as to rejoice in his downfall, in whom are now reposing the hopes of civilization.[22]

WASHINGTON CORRESPONDENCE, 21 APRIL 1862

The usual monotony of the Senate has been agreeably diversified for a few days by a highly entertaining discussion between McDougal, of California, who appears as counsel for General Stone and general challenger of the Administration, and Ben Wade, of Ohio, who stands as the champion of Wade and the Government. The discussion, though disfigured at times by unseemly displays of partisan malice and personal acrimony, has been in the main conducted with propriety, and cannot but result in good, in giving to the country correct ideas as to the action of the executive department of the Government in matters of high public concern.

In the debate of last week, McDougal's charges were rather vague and indefinite, consisting mainly of accusations of tyrannical and inquisitorial assumptions of power, and they were answered by Wade with a like lack of definiteness. He defended the course of the committee in general terms, and inveighed against the course of those gentlemen who are always found so ready to invoke the protection of the Constitution in favor of traitors, and so slow to exact its rigorous requirements against them.

To-day, however, the debate was more to the point. McDougal, in very bitter and intemperate language, attacked the Secretary of War by name, and for many acts of his official career, specifying them in detail. He made the most ingenious use of the few facts that he had as foundation for his remarks, and pieced his speech out with fancy and distorted inference. He was particularly eulogistic of Gen. McClellan whom he seemed to use as the embodiment of all the virtuous antagonism to the Administration. His most earnest endeavor was to disjoin Mr. Lincoln from the Administration, to represent Gen. McClellan as a persecuted hero, and Gen. Stone as a martyr for opinion's sake. This style of thing is growing not uncommon with the Vallandigham Democracy. They never in plain words attack the President. They fire away their little batteries at the members of his Cabinet, blaming them for acts for which he alone is responsible, and lashing with their invective-and-water the blameless agents of his tyrannical will. They will unmask some of these days when the skies are fairer and it becomes safe, because harmless, to talk treason.

Wade answered McDougal more coolly and deliberately than last week, when he lost his temper in the suddenness of his indignant surprise. He very calmly and quietly reviewed the positions of McDougal, and with a discretion and dignity unusual with him, exposed their fallacies and absurdities, and dwelt severely upon the evident design of this new conspiracy of reckless partisans to break down the Administration, careless as to how the Government should suffer in the process. The final point in the speech was when, after referring to McDougal's highly wrought eulogy on Gen. McClellan, he sent to the Clerk's desk to be read the passage from the Committee's record, stating that General McClellan first suggested the inquiry into the case of General Stone, and requested the summoning of Stone himself before the committee.

When the two principal debaters had freed their minds and subsided, a swarm of little speeches came upon the Senate, but there was nothing worth mentioning in them, except an angry episode between Chandler and McDougal, which afforded a striking argument for the adoption of the Main

Liquor Law. McDougal himself made a little speech at the conclusion of every other man's speech, and interjected two or three little speeches into the body of every one's remarks. His usual average is six speeches a day, but he overdrew to-day largely.

The result of the talking was valuable, as it elicited facts in regard to the action of the working of the Committee on the Conduct of the War, which will be of service when generally known, and which ought to have been made public before. The Committee has suffered under very unjust, and as it appears, utterly unfounded aspersions, from its very inception up to the present time, which a simple explanation, such as Mr. Wade made to-day, would at once have dissipated.

It appears that operations of this Committee have been conducted with marvelous discretion and caution. Composed of men of every shade of politics it was incapable of serving a partisan purpose. If any one man objected to the summoning of a witness, or objected to any question being put to a witness already summoned, the witness was not summoned, or the question was not asked. In no case has any evidence tending to criminate any one or even subject him to suspicion been elicited, but that the person thus inculpated has been at once sent for, the evidence submitted to him, and his own statements and explanations taken as rebutting testimony. The most delicate consideration has been paid to the rights and the feelings of every one. In no case has any evidence been divulged except to the head of the Government to guide him in his action in the premises. The committee have submitted to the most ungenerous suspicions and insinuations, in silence, from the conviction that the public interests would not be subserved by the publication of their action or the explanation of their operations.

Their action in this respect offers a most striking contrast to the despicable proceeding of such engines as Van Wyck's committee. This, originally instituted with a deafening flourish of virtuous trumpets, has degenerated into a machine for the gratification of the pettiest personal animosities and local spites. But in no case has the action of the Committee on the Conduct of the War been used for any purpose but the good of the country and the glory of our arms. With such earnestness of purpose, such self-denying purity of intention has it been conducted that it has materially modified the first impressions even of its own members on questions of public policy, and softened to a perceptible extent the asperities of political feeling in their minds. They have been of very great service to the Government, to the Army, and to Congress. The attack of McDougal has thus resulted in great good. The committee tried in the ordeal of this bitter onslaught has come out brighter than even its friends had deemed it.

I referred above to an attempt sedulously made by the enemies of the Administration to disconnect the President from his acts, and to laud him while abusing his ministers. It proceeds from a shrewd idea that the best way to conquer is to divide. The attack upon Mr. Cameron, the other day, by Pierce Butler; upon Mr. Welles, recently, by the Avenue grumblers; the threats against Mr. Seward, and the assaults against Stanton, are all parts of the same programme. The message which the President to-day sent to Congress will, perhaps, throw a little light upon this matter. He distinctly avows the act of Mr. Cameron and unhesitatingly assumes the responsibility of his imprisonment of Butler. He is not a man to shrink from the consequences of his acts. His recent exhibitions of pluck and determination, and more which are to come, and which are now dimly hinted by his ministers, prove that the time has come when the President can exercise the full measure of the powers which the Constitution confers, and which for many years past have slept unused; while the Chief Magistrate has sat in his chair of state, like

A painted Jove,
With idle thunder in his lifted hand.[23]

WASHINGTON CORRESPONDENCE, 22 APRIL 1862

Blessed are the Poor in Pocket, for They shall not be Taxed. This beatitude is not quite canonical, and is somewhat restricted and partial in its general application, yet its relative truth is quite apparent. The people of America have hitherto known nothing practically of taxation for the support of the General Government. By the sale of public lands, and a moderate tariff on imports, which the poor man never felt, and would scarcely have known to be in existence if he had not been told of it by some demagogue, the machinery of this Government has been kept in motion nearly a century without imposing any burdens upon the people. We have only known that we had a Government by the rich blessings it conferred upon every man who took shelter under its protection. The wicked effort to break it up has proved two things. First, that we have a Government strong enough to defend itself against the secret machinations of scheming traitors and the open assaults of armed rebels; and second, that this war for the Union will teach us how to appreciate it, as every one values highly that for which he pays a round price. Hitherto its benefits have come to us free as the blessed light, the summer showers and falling dew, about which some people quarrel with Providence if they do not come in the exact time and measure to suit their individual caprice. The scene is changed now, and every man must pay his share for that which protects and prospers all alike.

I have been led to the selection of my subject by the examination of a most formidable Congressional document entitled "An act to provide internal revenue to support the Government and pay interest on the public debt." It is a quarto of 137 pages, and contains the Tax bill, as it is popularly called, as it lately passed the House of Representatives. As the Finance Committee of the House spent months of labor in its preparation, and its provisions underwent long and careful scrutiny in Committee of the Whole, it is not likely that any radical changes will be made in the Senate, and this may be regarded as substantially the Tax Bill of America, for the next few years at least.

A first inspection of this formidable document is very trying to a man with weak nerves or doubtful patriotism. A simple list of the taxed articles, with the rate of taxation, would fill more than a page of the *Republican* and it seems to touch everything that can minister to the comfort or happiness of man in a civilized state. Apparitions of the tax question start up at every turn and seem to haunt a man in every condition and avocation of life. Like the English tax system, it begins with the baby in the cradle and never leaves him for a moment until he is nailed down in the coffin, and "sleeps with his fathers to be taxed no more."

A more careful examination of the Act shows that it has been framed with the special purpose of touching as lightly as possible the poor man's purse, and gathering the great bulk of its revenue from those who can pay without any real detriment to themselves. The poor farmer who owns his quarter section on our Western prairies, and lives by the sweat of his brow, may continue to live on for years without receiving a visit from the national tax collector. His farm and his products, his house and its furniture, his horses, cattle, hogs, sheep, and farming utensils, are all exempt, and he need scarcely know that there is such a thing as a direct tax for the support of the General Government. The increased price in the groceries, and manufactured articles used in his family may increase his expenses two or three dollars a year, and if he is able to indulge in a fine watch, piano, or carriage, he will have to pay a trifle for the luxury. In many of the articles taxed, the burden will be borne by the manufacturer, the prices remaining unchanged from what they are at present. In illustration of this remark take the newspaper, the great lever of civilization, and which is very properly becoming almost as much a household necessity as bread and bacon. Although the tax bill reaches the proprietors in a half dozen different ways, it is hardly probable that the great leading journals of the country will make much change in their terms of subscription. The same may be said of magazines and books, so that the food for the mind is likely to remain as cheap as it was before. The very poor man will know no difference between the past and future; the man in moderate circumstances will have to pay just enough to keep up a lively recollection of the fact that he enjoys the protection of the best government in the world, and the little pittance required from him is well spent in rescuing it from the hands of knaves and traitors; whilst the millionaire, who has to dig deep into his plethoric purse to pay his income tax, will think the annual payment of thousands an excellent investment, as a good government is all that can make his capital worth possessing, and it will also induce him to go to the polls to assist in placing honest men in positions of honor, trust and power. Under these circumstances, let the man possessing but a horse, or moderate competence take courage, for the tax, instead of eating out his substance, will scarcely be felt at all by him; and let the man of wealth who groans at the annual "tithing" of his income, take comfort from the fact that without such a government as he pays liberally to sustain, his title deeds, bonds, mortgages, and stock certificates, amounting perhaps to millions, would not be worth the paper on which they are written.

National debt is not the worst evil that can befall a country, if it has the resources to pay the interest without oppressing the people, and ultimately to extinguish the debt itself. The public debt of Great Britain, amounting to four thousand millions of dollars, has formed a solid foundation on which the English throne has rested securely during the political upheavings of Europe for the last century. The reason for this seeming paradox is simple enough. Almost every Englishman who possesses a money income owns more or less of the Government stocks, and is directly and pecuniarily interested in the stability of that Government. Whilst it would be bad policy for the American Republic to become so deeply involved as our British cousins, it cannot be denied that a few hundred millions of Government six per cents, owned by the wealthy as a permanent investment, would leave but small disposition for revolution or disloyalty amongst that class of citizens.

Yesterday there was a stormy debate in the House over the "Man of the Mountains [*Frémont*]," and his administration of the military affairs of the West. Mr. Blair pitched into the Pathfinder quite savagely, and held him up as a proper mark for scorn and ridicule, whilst performing in the *role* of Xerxes *redivivus* on the western bank of the Mississippi. It being well known that Abraham is fond of a little quiet humor, it is well understood here that Frémont's appointment to the "Mountain Department," where he reigns supreme a general without an army to command or an enemy to conquer, is one of the President's practical jokes. In the meantime, the radical Abolitionists still hang to him as the best timber they can get, out of which to hew a President. That they may continue to cleave unto their first love, should be the wish and prayer of every patriot.

Whilst the present war has already developed a large amount of latent heroism, and conferred many a star and eagle upon those who have won their honors by the highest exhibition of soldierly merit, there is no doubt that some sad mistakes have occurred from which the country has already suffered. Promotion is one of the things the soldier lives for and is willing to die for, but if honors are scattered at random, and given before they are earned, they become worthless as a fool's cap or a child's bauble.

Speaking of a gun reminds one of shooting. I see that the editor of the *New York Times* adopts and advocates the suggestion I offered in the *Republican* a month ago, that Commander Foote be created first "Admiral of the Red, White and Blue." He is not yet advanced even to the post of Captain, the highest rank known in our naval service, whilst his genuine heroism and great success with the Western Flotilla, entitle him to the gratitude of the nation and the highest honors it can bestow.[24]

WASHINGTON CORRESPONDENCE, 23 APRIL 1862

One thing we have certainly gained by the fierce convulsions of the past year, if nothing else, and that is the power of discussing the question of slavery in a practical, common-sense way, without any of the former captiousness and irritability that has marked all disputations upon this delicate subject. The rude friction of war and legislation has taken from the matter a great deal of the nervous sensitiveness that characterized it, and it is canvassed dispassionately in quarters from which it has ever been jealously excluded. The people of the Border States are beginning to talk of it in a tone of resolute calmness, as a matter in which they are vitally interested, and which it would be the height of reckless folly to ignore. The people of the North are discussing it, not with the heat and fervor of former fanaticism, but with the practical perception of economic and political influence which forms the normal and legitimate rule of action of the Anglo-Saxon mind. It is true that Vallandigham and his compeers sing the same old refrain of "don't touch the nigger"; it is true that the philosophers of the Hub of the Universe [*Boston*] still talk of the Oppressed Type as a Man and a Brother, and call down Heaven's vengeance on his wrongs, but the mass of the people are beginning to talk and think of slavery as an ugly question, to be discussed and settled coolly and not, as in all former years, to be shelved quietly out of sight, or only kept as a "wooly horse" of the hobby breed, to ride into place and power upon.

The most striking instance of this new disposition in the discussion of this vexed question is found, not in Congress, though Frank Blair in the House of Representatives and Senator Henderson in the Senate have talked with eminent appositeness and gravity upon this matter, but as the people are invariably before their leaders in this country, and Congress reflects (not illustrates) public opinion the most significant indications of this new and dispassionate consideration of this vastly important concern, is found among the leading Conservative citizens and presses of the Border States. Especially in Maryland is this becoming evident. In this, the most conservative and dignified of the old Colonial Commonwealths; in this home of the only true aristocracy of the English emigration in this State; which more than any other preserved unbroken the mould of social and religious caste, the exercise of the soundest and most progressive common sense is being brought to the consideration of this weighty matter.

And it is natural that it should be so. The war brought on by the intolerable insolence of the peculiar friends and apologists of the slave power has torn and desolated Maryland sorely. She has seen her soil occupied and devastated by the footsteps of a far-brought soldiery. Her civil officers, recreant to their trust, have in many instances, to her and their disgrace, expiated their wrongs in Northern dungeons. Many of her young men, poisoned by the deadly heresy bred of slavery, and strengthened for its protection, have fled from her borders and used all the power of their arms and hearts to strike dead the Government to which she is loyal. Her chief city has languished in the paralysis of trade. The fact that the aggressions of the Abolitionists have been bitter and galling, in no respect changes the aspect of the matter. They have been a small and insignificant band, powerless for active mischief, unknown in legislation, undecided in politics. Yet their agitations have always shaken Maryland. The pestilent heresies that have had their headquarters and home in the city of Charleston, never infected the political atmosphere of Maryland. The demon of State's Rights never led away her statesman into madness. Yet Maryland suffers from South Carolina's follies far more than South Carolina. These considerations suggest inquiries as to the cause of the trouble.

The most recent manifestations of the general opinion indicate that a great change is coming over Maryland, that men of great conservatism of political views, of life long devotion to the interests of the institution of slavery, are coming to the opinion that the highest wisdom of the border States is to look out for themselves, whether slavery stand or fall. The old sensitiveness, the old devotion, has vanished in the miseries of a war springing from slavery. They are discussing the economic bearings of this question, regardless of patriarchal suggestions and ethnological chimeras. They believe that slavery has received its death wound in the house of its friends, and the allegiance of the States of the border is absolved.

As long as there seemed to be danger of the Government entering upon a fanatical and unconstitutional raid against the institution of slavery, no opposition could be bitterer, no denunciations more violent, than those of the Maryland conservatives. It was only when they became convinced that Congress meant no evil, and the President would permit none, that they began to consider calmly of the situation. There is now little fear in the minds of candid people that any violent action will be taken in the matter of emancipation.

The President has clearly enough defined his position, and there is not enough of reckless radicalism in Congress to override his wishes or nullify his acts. The single sentence in which he expressed his approval of the act for the release of the slaves in the District of Columbia, saying that he was gratified at the incorporation of the principles of compensation and colonization, has been of great value in settling doubts in the minds of nervous people.

I cannot but think that the recent speech of Frank Blair in the House has been of use. He is said to have indicated the feeling of the President. There is this much of foundation for the remark. He indicated the sentiments of his brother, the Postmaster General, and it is usually conceded that the President is more in *rapport* on the question of slavery with Blair and Edward [*Bates*] than with any other of the members of the Cabinet. The important points in his speech were that there was no danger of forcible interference with slavery in the States; that the President's object, according to *his* conclusions, was to limit slavery as a governing power, and not violently to annihilate the rights of the slaveholders; that the Government favored an extensive and liberal scheme of colonization. The speech has had a good effect among border men, who neither admire the President nor the Blair family, because it gave a clear and definite answer to many of their fears.

I cannot better illustrate my meaning than by appending an extract from a careful editorial of the *Baltimore American* of yesterday, a newspaper of great respectability, and the largest influence in Maryland, which has hitherto exhibited a jealous disrelish to any discussion inimical to slavery. These are its last significant utterances in regard to Blair's speech:

> Taking this carefully elaborated speech as an authoritative exposition of the policy of the President and his Cabinet, the slaveholding interest of Maryland is left to consider at leisure what it may expect under all the circumstances. That no hostile movement is to be expected from the Government with reference to the institution is a safe conclusion and yet, with the agencies set in motion to break it down everywhere—the wealth of the loyal States a formidable reliance amongst these agencies—how long will it survive in the now unfavorable locality for the institution—the Border States. It is much to know the worst that threatens it here, it is something to have fair warning of what we may expect. Had South Carolina never challenged the world at large to a conflict with it, it would have been as secure here to-day as at any time since it was established; but when we behold causes at work which must daily make greater inroads upon it and the plans for the extinction, especially in the Border States, complete, it is madness to attempt to ignore the situation, unless we can consent to see it slide from our grasp with nothing to compensate for the sacrifice.
>
> To those who still affect to admire the policy of South Carolina in involving herself and us in these disasters, we say: Behold the fruit of your own doings! She cared nothing for the dangers in which we were to be involved; it is even possible that she exulted at it, when one result would be, probably, to drive our whole black population, at a diminished valuation, to the cotton region; and if in so doing she has provoked an enmity to slavery that will never be extinguished except with its extinction—

sooner or later—she may thank herself and those in the same interest who have so determinedly seconded her movements. Understanding, at length, the "policy of the President," we at least know what to expect from that quarter. Comprehending the *insecurity* of slavery here, now, let Maryland determine upon a course suitable to what is undeniably a grave emergency.

It is not probable that words so pregnant with sound sense and sound policy will pass unheeded.[25]

Washington correspondence, 27 April 1862

It has become a habit with Washington people to hold their breath on Sundays for news of victory. They learned it early in the campaign, and the occurrences of the past few months have confirmed them in it. Either battles have persistently been fought on that day, or the news of successes have obstinately insisted on coming to hand to the chime of church bells. The series of Sunday advices did not show, at its beginning, the brilliancy of color and correctness of principles that have since distinguished it. Rather ashen and sober were the first of the Sabbath pictures. The displaced flag of Fort Sumter came down, after that bloodless siege, from the unscathed battlements on Sunday. The battle of Manassas, of which you have doubtless heard, took place on Sunday, and although on that occasion we received until four o'-clock in the afternoon news of a splendid and signal success, we must in all candor confess that subsequent advices did not confirm the flattering tale told by Hope and McDowell.

Sunday, feeling itself a little under a cloud, after Manassas, bestirred itself right lustily to win back the forfeited regard of the American Eagle. And the feathers of the incensed bird, we must say, have been charmingly smoothed by such emollient applications as Somerset, Fort Donelson, Winchester and the *Monitor,* whose names are all linked with the first day of the week. Sunday tripped a little at Pittsburg, but everything was righted the next day, and Monday's sun went not down on our wrath. And one of the neatest pieces of news that any Sunday has brought us has been the intelligence to-day of the capture of New Orleans by Porter and Farragut. This furnishes one most important link in the chain which we have been drawing around our revolted provinces, and fastens, to use a played-out metaphor, one more coil of the anaconda around his doomed victim. As Foote is still hammering away above Memphis, and the forces of General Halleck seem to have taken through tickets to the Gulf of Mexico, it cannot be long before the army-worm before mentioned begins the interesting process of swallowing his own tail, the final exploit which is to close his performances.

This taking of New Orleans is a good thing to do. In the first place, the rebel boasting in regard to the impregnability of the city had grown to be a bore. Mansfield Lovell's constant iterations of the entire safety of the city had grown to be as great a nuisance to readers of newspapers, as the cheery monotony of that Arctic operator, who nursed the sickly Atlantic cable, and who insisted on chirping "All-right, De Santy," when it was all wrong. Pierre Soulé also seemed to be ending his days as a sort of special policeman and Grand Inquisitor into other people's business. He wrote too many general orders, more by half than the Secretary of War, and brawled loudly in public places. He needed putting down. Then money had grown scarce. Coin had disappeared from view and Confederate rags were growing too bulky in proportion to value. It took a scuttle-full of bonds to get a scuttle full of coal. A New Orleans chiv could not take his pint of vitriol-and-water without disbursing a pound of Confederate currency. The young men had stopped enlisting, and the fair daughters of the land were taking their places in the ranks. A recent New Orleans paper chronicles the departure for the wars of a company of captivators, one hundred and three strong, who went north, and before this probably have been "found in arms." (Any one who travels in that country in years to come will find a class of population, strong as the North and ardent as the South, with characteristics as strongly marked as the great Grenadier Guard of King Fritz impressed upon the coming generation in the favored town of Potsdam.) Murders grew common and vulgar in New Orleans. The decent restraints of civil law were swept to the winds, as relics of the Northern tyranny. If a man respectfully asked his neighbor to settle "that little bill," he was instantly reported to the Committee of Safety, as a devotee of Lincoln and a disciple of the Yankee school of low and debasing economy. They were having a great time in New Orleans, just as Capt. Dave Porter came up, and he came in very good season to prevent a relapse into absolute and primitive barbarism.

It is a very great position for us to have and to hold. Its importance as a strategic base can with difficulty be over estimated. This becomes more and more important in view of the increasing probabilities that the war will be finished in the Southwest. The keenest observers have for a long time predicted that the battled and beaten conspirators when completely vanquished in the East, will make a desperate endeavor to cut their way out into Mexico, and try to find in that unhappy country a rest from the dangers of treason and the toils of war. That avenue is now forever closed to them. "Bear-like, they must fight their course."

The capture of New Orleans will have a greater effect abroad upon the public mind than any other advantage that we could gain. The certainty of our success, and the absolute refusal of all respectable Governments, and England also, to interfere with our blockade, or to recognize the rebel emissaries as Ministers or Commissioners, have combined to render this a consideration of less importance than it would have been at a time when our position was less assured. Still, it has a significance of its own. New Orleans is to foreigners our best known Southern city. It stands to them as the representative of the wealth and power of the rebellion. They have joined in pronouncing it impregnable. When we have promised to take it before the spring had fully burst its blossoms, they have smiled incredulously, and shrugged their shoulders. Mercier himself, who is usually very candid, said a very few days ago that he considered the expedition against New Orleans a wild enterprise, in which success was impossible. Perhaps this will show them that the New World has capabilities which will teach them to remodel their conceptions of impossibility. The fall of New Orleans will have, in Europe, an influence, if possible, disproportionately great.

We await with great interest the fuller particulars of the affair. We hear that cotton and stores were extensively burned; that many boats were destroyed; and that only enough were retained to carry off their coin and ammunition. As we have ammunition enough, and the prospect of free loot among the treasuries of the Gulf was never peculiarly brilliant, there is nothing to mourn over in this statement. The Mississippi river must now be to all intents open from Memphis to New Orleans. All boats found between the descending flotilla of Foote and the ascending navy of Porter must take their choice, and either burn or surrender. It is nearly all one to us. We have boats enough now. All that we want is to crush out this unnatural and wicked etc., etc., (You know the Congressional formula,) and we are not Mr. Morgan, that we should care for old river-craft. If the poor devils wish to impoverish themselves, and deprive themselves of all power of prolonged resistance, by burning their houses, their boats and their cotton, we may pity their folly, but cannot regret it. The gods evidently wish to destroy them. Why should they not make them mad?

What consternation this startling news must spread through the camps of the stricken rebellion: in Yorktown, where the beleaguered enemy is silently watching the web of death woven around him by the cautious and imperturbable McClellan, and in Corinth where Beauregard is marshalling his wasted and disheartened legions for one last struggle against the flushed and invincible army of the West! How can they avoid seeing in this last great disaster to their cause, the visible foreshadowing of its coming downfall? How can the trickery of their leaders, and the arts of their betrayers, longer close their ears to the awful warnings that speak the irrevocable purpose of the just and avenging fates?[26]

WASHINGTON CORRESPONDENCE, 11 MAY 1862

A more magnificent or a more undeserved run of luck never came to a cause than that which has been ours for the past fortnight. Those who reason upon the known principles of strategy, and take into account the ordinary range of probabilities, have been very fearful of the issue of our last great enterprises. The unparalleled gallantry of the officers and seamen of our Gulf Squadron and the mortar fleet before the guardian forts of New Orleans accounted very satisfactorily for the brilliant and astounding victory there. When officers direct and men fight like Porter and Farragut and the blue jackets under them, probabilities are out of the question, and the possibles become the practicable. But our wonderful successes on the Peninsula have been won in spite of ourselves. Our armies sat down before Yorktown and entrenched themselves. It would have been hard for an ignorant observer to have said which was the besieger and which the besieged. But one night, the enemy, as Sut Lovengood used to say, "sucked in a big skeer," and, "folding their tents, like the Arabs, they as silently stole away." General McClellan, discovering that the works of the enemy were unoccupied next morning, went in and took them. This was our first victory—one utterly without an effort on our part, yet leading to results of vast importance. The General, pursuing the enemy, caught up with their rear guard at their inner line of defence at Williamsburg. The hunted fugitives turned on their eager pursuers and a sharp skirmish took place in the evening. As night fell the Union army held their ground, and its General wrote a dispatch, stating that the enemy, in largely superior force, was in front strongly entrenched, and meant to fight, and added lugubriously, that he would do all he could with the force at his disposal. While he was writing these melancholy words the dreaded enemy was scampering as fast as fear could drive him over the hills of the Chickahominy on the road to Richmond.

In the morning, another unasked and unexpected victory—empty entrenchments—a routed and panic-stricken enemy—deserted ammunition, and all the evidences of utter and ruinous flight. These things the General recounts, and adds, "We shall have more battles before reaching Richmond." Nobody questions the energy, industry, loyalty, bravery and good conduct of General McClellan. All honor to him for his services in training and grooming his superb army. This is his work. By this he may stand. It is glory enough for one man. He will only tarnish his laurels by seeking to add to them the praise of a great thinker and military genius. His every prophecy has failed, his every prediction fallen to the ground. For this I never hear him blamed. It is the curse of high position to be surrounded by flatters and sycophants. These creatures seem lately to have had constantly the ear of McClellan. They have sedulously endeavored to inculcate in his mind, ideas of the vastness of his enterprise and the insufficiency of his army. If it were not so sad it would be ridiculous to hear their constant croakings about the slenderness of the General's force. With an army whose fighting force approximates one hundred and fifty thousand, they have pretended to fear (I say *pretended* in charity) a wretched, disheartened, ragged and forlorn mob of less than half their numbers, and saddest of all to the hearts of those who love and admire him, they have succeeded on one or two occasions in getting the signature of General McClellan signed to those unmanly repinings. I have confidence in McClellan. I know him to be brave and honest. I shall not believe that he wrote that tremulous dispatch dated before Williamsburg until he avows it himself. A General, in the hour of action, is too busy to write those communications. They are hurriedly scribbled by a nervous Aid, and signed by the General. Let us not lose confidence in our brave young soldier for one such lapse.

For long and weary months we have been waiting for the taking of Norfolk. This nest of the cockatrice has been lying under our very feet for nearly a year, breeding in the hot sunshine its venomous blood, to sting and slay us. Thence went the armament of the whole wide-spread rebellion. Thence came the *Merrimac,* that ungainly portent of ruin and revolution. It lay open to our approach, a morning's march from Lynhaven Bay—undefended by land, the petty batteries of Craney Island and Sewall's Point alone defending it by sea. The President has always been most anxious that it should be taken. Burnside has begged till he was tired, for men to take it with Commodore Dahlgren, the greatest brain, so far that the war has produced, offered to take it with little loss, and showed that he could do it. The venerable Secretary of the Navy sang of Norfolk in the ears of Secretaries and President, until he became the Cassandra of the Cabinet, presaging of coming dangers unregarded. Still the Army of the Potomac was kept intact. The President stood by McClellan, saying, "Hands off, gentlemen. Let the General control his force while it is his." So the Army of the Potomac bided its time, and Norfolk hatched murder in open day. One morning the *Merrimac* came out, and had not the Navy been there to meet her, she would have made short work with our Potomac army. The *Monitor* sent her to bye-bye, as Henman graphically observed; and she went back to Norfolk. Again the capture of Norfolk was urged, and again it was said that fifty thousand men could not be spared for that service.

The end of all this seems really funny. Gen. Wool and Secretary Chase went over from Fortress Monroe, yesterday, escorted by five regiments of soldiers, and took Norfolk. The *Merrimac* lay off Sewall's Point, and when she saw the fate of the city, instead of steaming up to the wharf and wrapping victors and vanquished in a shroud fire, instead of rushing madly down to the frowning walls of the Fortress and perishing nobly amid the wrecks of a sinking navy, she meekly and ignobly turned upon herself, like a vexed rattlesnake, and took her own life. The nursery of the rebels' inventions, the workshop of their lethal machinery, is ours; and the bugbear of the seas, the first born monster of rebel wrath, the awkward foundation of all their hopes of naval supremacy has gone up in smoke and flame, useless and desperate, in sight of its birth place.

The trifling expenditure of blood and time, the insignificance of the means employed, the ease of accomplishment, the absolute absence of defensive courage or skill with which these victories were attained are most astounding. It seems as if the rebellion, sailing the seas defiantly and rejoycing in its strength, suddenly—like the ill-fated ship in the Arabian tale, which lost in one instant every bolt and bar and rivet, by the mighty and irresistible compulsion of the Loadstone Mountain—had gone miserably to pieces, scattering its sundered and sinking fragments wide, the sport and pastime of the merciless waves.

History will record this as a wonderful war. Undertaken without cause, carried on without resources on one side, without conscription on the other; a war in which there were no Generals, but in which strategy was dictated by a Cabinet, and victories won by soldiers.

[We give a good deal of latitude to our correspondents—frequently permitting them to advance opinions in which we do not concur. Such is the case in the present instance. McClellan has had a good deal to make him indignant at the treatment of the member of the Cabinet most directly connected with the war, and if he has fretted and chafed under the neglect no one will feel much surprised that he should give expression to it. Richmond will, in all probability, be in his possession this week, and then it will be time enough to discuss the correctness of the Military policy which he has adopted. That the country will sustain him, we have no doubt.][27]

WASHINGTON CORRESPONDENCE, 19 MAY 1862

There has been little talked of in Washington for several days but the emancipation order of General Hunter. Every shade of opinion in regard to it finds representatives in political circles. The more earnest Republicans and Abolitionists hailed it with great gladness as the natural result of the progress of events and the sunrise harbinger of greater things to be. The members of the Vallandigham party rejoiced at it equally, as promising indefinite dissensions. But, in general, it was not favorably received. The great bulk of both political parties in Congress thought that it precipitated an issue which ought to be at present avoided, and exhibited also an unwarrantable exercise of power in a General Commanding a Department. Discussion on the subject was, however, confined to private and unofficial circles. It was not made a subject of Cabinet consultation, and members of the Senate and House who visited the President for the purpose of giving their views and eliciting his own on the matter, soon found that they had touched upon a subject which was not to be entertained by the President as a proper one for conversation. Wade and Lovejoy and Grow were said to be very earnestly in favor of the movement, and argued that as the President had permitted Generals Halleck and Hooker to act in the interests of slave-owners in a manner very repugnant to his sentiments and feelings, he should balance that concession by allowing to General Hunter the privilege of trying in his department an experiment which if he did not approve, he might pass over in silence. Others, who have never shown any particular respect for the President or his authority, by word or deed, were suddenly struck with the impression that there was something dreadfully disrespectful in Hunter's order, calling for instant recall and disgrace, to vindicate the outraged honor of the Executive.

The President possessed his soul in patience and kept his own counsel. From the first moment that he heard of the General's order, his mind was determined on the course he should pursue as soon as he was convinced that the reported order was genuine. Although, as the world knows, the dearest wish of his heart is to see the whole broad continent of America peaceful and free, he could not approve any such rash and violent measures for closing the war and slavery together. Although his personal regard for General Hunter is more sincere and warm than that he entertains for any other General in the field, he would sacrifice his best friend for what he deemed the best interests of the country. He decided to nullify the order of the General commanding the Department of the South. The manner of this act is also rather remarkable. Instead of a private admonition, issued to the General himself, followed by an order modifying the General's order, as in the case of Gen. Frémont, he issues a proclamation to be seen and read of all men, declaring with a solemnity and emphasis which there is no mistaking, the ground upon which he makes utterly void the work of his subordinate.

I cannot but think this proclamation, written in the silence and repose of a Sunday morning of spring, without consultation of any, however intimate advisers, promulgated without revision or criticism will have a great effect upon the country. In the border States men not utterly perverted by the enervating and contracting influence of a life long devotion to one idea and institution, must recognize the purity and honor of the Magistrate who against all the impulses of a life's antipathy, against the persuasions of his best and most earnest friends and adherents, almost, I would say, against the seeming current of uncontrollable events, stands in his lofty place to guard from illegal and injurious attack an institution he abhors, and to conserve and protect an interest which he would rejoice to see equitably blotted forever from the face of the earth. The utmost fanaticism of the Abolitionist

264

North cannot but respect the motives and the action of the man who takes this position of moral grandeur before the world, and pleads with the States to destroy in their own sovereign discretion, what he will protect with his own life against unlawful harm. And the great mass of the earnest and candid people will hail as a new evidence of safe and good government this manifestation of undaunted integrity and unassailable honor, and renew their confidence in the government and its cause.

The message is of course addressed primarily to the Border States. It is to them that the President chiefly looks for effectual strength and co-operation in his great work of pacificating the storm-rent republic. To their candor and calm good sense is of course finally to be submitted the question of what is best for the future of the country. It is a plain and simple problem, which, if men were cool, could be decided by a day's study of the census tables and the treasury reports. When the passions of these few last tempestuous years have ebbed away, this momentous question can be settled as easily as a matter of police or finance.

There are indications each day that seem to show the time for dispassionate discussion is at hand. Some of the most intelligent and honest citizens of Florida have recently made known their disposition in favor of gradual emancipation. In Maryland the subject is discussed with clearness and decision by the most prominent and respected of her politicians. The bitter malignance which Kentuckians formerly displayed in speaking of the question is rapidly going away, and they talk of the matter as a thing to be discussed and decided in the light of reason and common sense, not of passion and prejudice. And from the State of Missouri, which has stood firm amid the sorest temptations that virtue ever resisted, and has held her honor unsullied amid the tumult of a long year's harrowing and desolating war, has taken to her heart the dear-bought lesson of experience, and now only waits to be convinced of the true path of safety and prosperity to walk determinedly in it. If, after due discussion, it is thought that slavery is beneficent in its moral and financial aspects, to retain it; if injurious and hurtful, to devise means for best relieving herself of it. This is the most momentous epoch of her history. On her decision rests the contingencies of vast empire and opulence, or penury and ceaseless turmoil. Only blind and reckless action now can blast the splendid promise of the fairest future that the coming years have destined for the most favored of the sisterhood of States.[28]

NORFOLK, VA., CORRESPONDENCE, 18 JUNE 1862

The American mind accommodates itself to sudden transitions with a facility that borders upon apathy. A town changes its allegiance between sunrise and noon without violence to its feelings or bloodshed in its alleys. Districts of country, which were yesterday filled with all the dim and mysterious interest of alien possession, seem to-day as commonplace and familiar as our paternal fields. The sacredness of soil does not prevent its easy occupation, and the mythical ultimate ditch still is looked for in vain. I have walked through Norfolk to-day without the possibility of realizing that a foreign army had haunted its streets for a year; with nothing to remind me of war or revolt but the straggling soldiers and the fluttering banners waving in the air as for some high festival.

I have been in Norfolk in other days, and there is little change. The same crowds of idle boys lounged on the wharves, and flashed the sunlight from their bare brown backs and shoulders as they swam around the decaying piers. The same lazy specimens loafed around the little shops, pine-whittling and tobacco ruminant. The same rickety old carts rumbled though the narrow, grassy streets, like an ill-constructed dream of an old wagoner's brain. Here, too, formerly shuffled through the town, as now, the antediluvian Uncles and Aunties, with white wool and ashen-gray cheeks, bent forms and questioning looks. It was always a dreamy old town that had outlived its usefulness. Nobody ever entertained the lunatic idea that Norfolk ever was young. It was a fine Old Castle of Indolence.

A pleasing land of drowsyhed it was—
Of dreams that wave before the half-shut eye.

There are some changes, of course. War cannot walk through a town without crushing some life and kindling other, by the power and friction of his trampling hoofs. There is a strange activity of army wagons, breaking the repose of the shady streets. There is the frequent tramp on the sidewalks of the well shod soldiers of the North. There is the quick, eager glance of the coming men; and the sharp question and loud reply of those who learned to talk by a wilder coast and a noisier sea than this. There is an infusion of vigor little less strange than if it were utterly foreign. Norfolk is beginning to be Yankeeized.

This has come and something has gone. The Southern beauty, that in Norfolk's flush days, before the deluded old town went sillily off after the beguiling Lothario of rebellion, used to be seen on the fine afternoons of the splendid summer days, wandering up and down the shaded sidewalks of Brandon and Free Mason streets and the quiet avenues in that well-bred neighborhood, is there seen no more. The dark eyes in which the imprisoned sunlight of the tropics burned are no more the dream of the stranger at his hotel. The easy, languid elegance that turned the common garb to grace in the twilight of the past years, along those paves, are as utterly gone as the forms of the Naiads from a settler's clearing. The bright eyes are losing their beauty in the shade of lonely chambers, or reddening with weeping for the skedaddling brave who will not soon return. The milliners of Norfolk all went into liquidation many dreary months ago, and who can walk in the evening without a hat? General Dix has not yet opened the blockade, and how can they go out in the gowns they have worn since Sumter was taken? In the coming days when Yankee officers have gotten their moustaches under better cultivation, and silks come down from New York, and a hat that is not a fright can be had for love, or money, or both, and the Confederacy is clearly, as Mrs. Davis observes, "played out," perhaps they will condescend to be charming again. But at present there is nothing feminine in Norfolk visible to the eye of the stranger that might not be duplicated among the Lazzarone of Naples or the witches of the Brocken. I saw a good many women on the street, of different degrees of optical obliquity and dental integrity, but if Phidias had tried to paint a pretty woman from their aggregate charms, the Great Eastern would not have held his models. Some of perfectly nightmare ugliness would shoot out contumelious tongues, curve scornful lips, and elevate contemptuous noses till they pointed skyward, when Union officers passed by. Some ancient virgins carried faded parasols, which they spitefully thrust between their mature charms and the profaning gaze of the wide-awake Yankees. But most sat quietly in their rooms, pursuing the favorite rebel policy, of awaiting the foe, behind their breastworks. It was a grim satisfaction to the uncommonly good-looking Captain who walked with me, to see the furtive interest displayed in the passing invaders by dark eyes glancing through the treacherous lattice that betrayed the eager watcher within.

There can be nothing sillier than for Norfolk to be a rebel town. The singular madness of secession was nowhere more ridiculously displayed than in the mad leap which these infatuated people took into the arms of the beguiling ruin that tempted them. They have been always pensioners upon the bounty of the nation. They have eaten the crumbs that have fallen from the rich man's table. If gratitude had no place in their hearts, that does not make their folly less evident. The blackened and smouldering ruins of the Gosport Navy Yard—the tottering and shattered structure of the Dry Dock—the desolation and destruction that lies like a spent curse upon all the scene of former life and activity, is the strongest and most irresistible argument which can be commended to this deluded people, against the heresy that has scathed them so, for the present and for all time. It can hardly be that the time will ever come for rebuilding these places, so wantonly destroyed. Of course the idea of vengeance never enters into the calculations of a Government, but the causes of this present waste must be considered as powerful objections to any future appropriations for this vicinity.

I spent a part of the morning at the Headquarters of the Navy Yard. The fine old house, so long occupied by the commandant, was one of the few that was spared by the torch of those furious young maniacs who, with Frank Sinclair at their head, flew to Gosport, on the approach of Wool's five thousand from Willoughby Bay, and wrapped those splendid structures in a cowardly conflagration. The house and grounds of the commandant were spared. They are really very pleasant and picturesque, and, standing as they do, in the midst of that wild scene of scorched and crumbling desolation, there is something almost magical in their appearance. Winding paths of box, riotous clusters of roses, deep green masses of evergreen, the rich scarlet wealth that loads the cherry trees, and above all the glorious magnificence of the magnolias, the long, glossy leaves hiding the luxurious milk-white petals that guard and clasp the golden heart of the regal flower, make this garden a patch of fairy land in a desert of desolation, a protest of loving and kindly nature against the surroundings of man's ravage and ruin.[29]

WHITE HOUSE POINT, VA., CORRESPONDENCE, 19 JUNE 1862

In the still and lazy days when Virginia dozed away the hours within the protecting arms of the Union, the region where I now stand must have been full of a strange and unusual beauty. Even had I been fortunate enough to come up the Pamunkey in the front ranks of Farnsworth's Illinois Cavalry, when they first startled the echoes of this ancient domain with the clatter of abolition hoofs, I would have seen a landscape hard to surpass in any of the elements of attractiveness. Along the banks of the broad and winding river, gentle slopes run down to the water's edge, green with summer bravery, and luxuriant with the pink and pale clusters of the mountain laurel. A water power such New England cannot show from the Ashburton line to the shores of the Hudson, runs riotously to waste over hundreds of miles of fertile and untenanted country, where there are none but fish hawks to improve it and none but red deer to admire. The air is fresh and bracing, the hills are far and blue, the sky this fair June day is clear and frank and genial, without the muttered threat of the tropics, or the low hanging haze of the northern plains.

There are few scenes richer in memories than those which have lain for the last century uninvaded and half-forgotten in a circuit of a hundred miles from this bluff where I scribble to-day. Williamsburg, Hampton, New Kent, Yorktown—each name rouses its swarm of heroic and revered phantoms. We think of Lafayette, the brave young Frenchman whose glory makes every page of history that bears his name read like romance, and whose bright example has floated down to the passing days, and inspired the two brave young captains of the blood royal of France now camped with McClellan on the thither side of the Chickahominy. We follow him in his exciting chase of the spoiled child of rout and fashion, Cornwallis, over the hills between the Chickahominy and the James, until at last the splendid game is safely run to earth behind the entrenchments at Yorktown. But most enthralling of the legends that make this ground sacred forever are those that have come down to us, grown faint through the lapse of less than a century, which contain the name of that august shade which gives to our early history the largest portion of its dignity and halo. For Washington's life was always picturesque. The angularities of pioneer life are never seen in his history. As if the lavish fates had resolved to fashion absolute perfection, his life was made to satisfy the moral, intellectual and aesthetic sense.

In these pleasant groves and hills linger those memories of Washington which are most widely dissimilar to the grand pictures of war and council which make up the bulk of his later life. Just beyond the declivity that now is vulgarized and deformed by the weather-stained tent of that Pennsylvania sutler, Washington crossed the swollen torrent of the Pamunkey on his way to Williamsburg after the bloody horrors of Braddock's rout. There he was accosted by a hospitable shape, who forced him to go with him to the plain little mansion that crowns the hill and looks over the river and over the woodlands into the dim blue corona of hills in the farthest east. Here the invincible soldier met with his first conqueror, here the unconquerable chief surrendered. For here he met the fair and debonair young widow who lives in all the history of our land as the worthy wife of our worthiest, Martha Washington.

It is not such a house as a General lives in now-a-days. Unless you reverently bend your head as you enter, the low doorway will resent the disrespect by knocking off your hat. The rooms are low and small—now utterly devoid of furniture, and, generally, like Virginia, going to decay. In the garret, where unconsidered trifles were lying scattered profusely around, you see more proofs of Virginian occupation than elsewhere. A worn-out and tawdry side-saddle lies in one corner; several grotesque likenesses of the earlier Lees deform the walls like permanent nightmares; a pile of okra lies heaped upon the floor, an inexplicable puzzle to Northern visitors, who never dream they have often eaten in soup the seeds of that rough and nettling husk; and there, sneaking furtively out of a corner, like a rebel spy, glides a grey cat that looks old enough to have been worried by the dog that was tossed by the cow, that gave the milk that made the egg-nog, that made merry the hearts of the assembled gentry on the eve of Colonel Washington's wedding.

The grounds around the White House (called white because it is brown) are pleasant and well kept. There are some pretty roses flourishing uncared for, some such rural flowers as Lyringes and Asters, and one or two forlorn little attempts at Magnolia, which I really felt sorry for, my memory being full of the gorgeous blooms of the Gosport Navy Yard. Altogether, a fair specimen of that most singular of all delusions, the home of a Southern gentleman, which any one of the Lee family will swear is for magnificence, grandeur and spaciousness as far superior to the country palaces of the Yankee millionaires as Windsor Castle is to the summer residence of the King of Timbuctoo.

There is one thing observable which sometimes gives rise to discussion. These grounds have been scrupulously guarded against intrusion or harm. If you should go in at the rickety old gate, a sentinel's bayonet would prod you into respect for the memory of the mighty dead and the sensibilities of the skedaddled living. Mrs. Lee until within a day or two, was still supreme in these premises, and at last was carefully sent to Richmond with information which the next day her son used with deadly effect upon unarmed teamsters and stevedores, in the audacious dash of the rebel cavalry at Tunstall's Station. It is singular that vipers had that eccentric habit of biting the bosoms of idiots who folded them in, as long ago as Aesop's time. I don't blame the vipers. Compare this with the treatment of Union ladies in East Tennessee; Maynard's wife turned out of doors, [*Andrew*] Johnson's family insulted and half-starved—weaker and more helpless women whipped—and worse. These contrasted pictures make a terribly one-sided record. God forgive them!

And God bless those noble ladies that glide like angels of mercy and love through the hospital tents and the sanitary steamboats. If it were not for the impulsive, unsought charity of the North, the suffering and death among the sick and the wounded soldiers here would have been frightful. While for want of a more perfect organization the Medical department of the army has lain on its back helpless and paralyzed, these great hearted men and saintly women have done all that could be asked, and still are straining every nerve to supply the deficiencies of the army staff. Names that in other days were the watchwords of the ball-room and delight of society, have become the music of the sick tent, and mingle in the prayers of the dying. I saw two ladies this morning, whose career has ever been that of fashion and gaiety, doing work in hospitals that many men would shrink from, and another delicate creature whose life has been more like a dream of luxury, than a reality of exertion, cooking and sending out from her tent a thousand rations of gruel to the thirsty sufferers from the bloody field of Fair Oaks. This war is not without its compensations.

To-morrow for Yorktown.[30]

YORKTOWN, VA., CORRESPONDENCE, 20 JUNE 1862

We left the White House early in the morning and steamed quietly down the Pamunkey. To one who in his journeying seeks rather the picturesque than the useful, there could be few rivers which present more scenes of natural loveliness. For country in the raw—country finished and ready for the population which ought to be there—country which is a daily temptation to industry and a daily reproach to sloth—or to quote Bishop Heber, "Where every prospect pleases, and only man is vile"—commend me to the rolling plains, the sunny hills and shadowy intervals that skirt the winding shores of these wasted rivers. The air is balm—the soil laughs with fatness—rivulets plash and dance in the valleys—and vast watercourses roll their gigantic volumes of power idly to the sea, and no man tickles the genial earth with a ploughshare, or frets the silent waters with a wheel. Nature reigns here triumphant yet after two hundred years of man's occupation. The only evidences of human neighborhood which we can see as we gaze on the sunlit shores that look the view on either side, but show more strikingly the inferiority of man to his circumstances. Everything is old and tottering. Most of the houses are brown and weather-stained. The fences are eccentric in build and in a state of imminent dissolution. Old hats are the fashionable glazing for windows. Gates have a languid and dejected hang. The few wharves are rotting and weedy. Age here is not even dignified and respectable.

Things which are new are worse. Some new houses which I saw had begun to tip over, and were held sturdily up by fence rails leaning at a sharp angle against them. Several were built on hillsides, the upper side upon the sod, the lower on stone foundations, and were making frantic efforts to fall up hill. In one or two places the rebels had manifestly extemporized a hurried Navy yard, and had lazily begun the building of light draught gunboats on the river side. The dreary abortions that lay half charred on the banks attest the futility of their efforts. One can imagine the delight and relief with which the skedaddling ship-builder applied the torch on the approach of the Union gunboats, to the ungainly monstrosity that never would have floated anyhow.

I am sure I am not prejudiced. My own ancestry have lived in this country. The ashes of our greatest moulder here. It is the cradle where was rocked the infancy of the child whose strength now shakes the world. But no one can float down the Pamunkey river, with his eyes open, and not see that this land is sleeping the sleep of torpor and moral death. All labor seems to have been spasmodic and fitful. Rest seems to be apotheosized. A pall of densest indolence and sloth rests palpably on the face of this unparalleled richness of nature.

Anywhere but here these fields would be opulent with grain; those hill sides would be fragrant with fruit and picturesque with vineyards. The benediction of this genial sky should rest upon a country strong with toil and happy with plenty. Along these gigantic rivers trade should set into revolution her myriad spindles and her clattering wheels. Commerce should whiten these broad waves with sails, and fret these placid waters with the rushing keels of steamers. In all the starved extent of New England there is no such land as this, yet plenty tinkles in the sheep pastures, and content goes singing with the reapers. From the vast waters of the York and Pamunkey you might take the entire volume of the Seekonk and the Blackstone rivers, and these estuaries would be scarcely shallower; yet along those narrow threads of water a factory village is humming and toiling every hundred yards, and not one drop escapes into the cleansing bosom of Narragansett Bay until it is wearied with toil and blackened with laborious contact. What good reason is there why this region should not be as rich, inch for inch, as Rhode Island?

There may be many answers to this question, but only one suggests itself to me. It will suggest itself to you, if you sail down this river. There it stands now in the front door of the negro quarters with no shoes on its feet—its white tow breeches held up by one suspender—its black face agrin with childish delight—its shock head bare, while it waves its old wool hat as a banner in welcome to what it considers the Abolition invasion. It is the oppressed type, as Brother [*Wendell*] Phillips calls it—the man and brother as Exeter Hall hails it—the impending crisis as Helper names it—the contraband as General Butler styles it—the image of God cut in ebony as Fuller phrased it—the *what-will-we-do-with-it?* as the earnest spirit of American patriotism must regard it.

I have heard of patients, in the dead hopelessness of collapse, being roused and brought back to life by copious injections of warm, thin fluid into their flattened veins. A rosy glow courses through the ashen grey of the cheeks; the light revisits the dim, glazed eyes, and the currents of life beat again, feebly at first, but swell at last into the full, steady music of strength and health. I believe that the State of Virginia lies in this state of deadly peril; I believe that immigration—the infusion of the firm and wakeful element of a more temperate climate—will alone save her from death and decay. This can, and I believe this will. When this mighty army goes back to its home, how much of it will come back in a refluent tide over these rich and sunny plains? Enough, I believe, to save the State, and to turn its vast resources to the best account, for the sake of themselves, of civilization and the world. The faded glories of the Old Dominion will receive fresh coloring when the tide of activity and honorable effort sets again to her shores, and the restored flag of the beneficent nationality again blesses her cities and protects her fields.

Yorktown fills a large[r] space in the world's history than on its surface. It is a huddled and scrambling little village with that intense air of seedy gentility that many Virginia towns present as their only title to the respect of strangers. There is one principal street which the patriotic invaders have named McClellan avenue, and which is crossed at right angles by another which some enthusiastic Abolitionist has christened Hunter Place. In the center of the village stands the Gubernatorial mansion of Gov. Nelson, whose claim to our attention is that it was the headquarters of Lord Cornwallis during the siege of Yorktown. His lordship must have had a realizing sense of Yankee impertinence when the solid shot struck the walls and made that ugly scratch that still remains on the north side. The town is very forlorn and very dirty. All the white families have left it. The only wonder is that they lived there so long.

It makes upon my mind to-day a general impression of old houses and old darkies—big guns and little niggers—dull skies and bright mulattos—complex uniforms and complexions not uniform—piccaninnies and *Enfans Perdus*—and a general flavor of Colored Person.

The system of fortifications around the city is very extensive, and the labor of erecting them must have been enormous. The summit of every bluff is crowned with a work of great strength, and at the base of each nestles a water battery, provided with furnaces and magazines constructed with great care, and which have not yet been explored by our soldiers, as the delay lessens the danger from infernal machines. The world knows the barbarous skill with which these hideous implements were concealed; but one needs to see the narrow and convenient passage way, where they were found in greatest profusion, to understand perfectly the fiendish calculations of wholesale slaughter which the rebels had made. Had their plan succeeded a thousand men might have been butchered in the narrow court by which our forces entered the works from the level plain before the town.

A few minutes' walk from the walls in the open fields you come to the stone marking the spot where Cornwallis delivered up his sword. It stands midway between the rebel works and McClellan's parallels. The proximity of these two lines is absolutely startling. They lie in full view of each other, scarcely more distant than the bounds that mark a friendly game of foot ball. The only objects lying between their rifle pits and ours are a crumbling chimney, relic of a recently burnt dwelling, that used to change hands as often as once in twelve hours, being a stake for pitch and toss between the rebel marksmen and the Berdan Sharpshooters; and a venerable tulip-tree whose tall branches have waved proudly over two successes of the starred and striped banners whose early flutterings have hallowed this air. In the hollow of this tree the rebel *tirallieurs* [*skirmishers*] for a while took shelter until the Berdan Inevitables found them out and learned to send their peremptory summons straight into the populous cavity.

Gen. McClellan's advanced works are far nearer the town than those of Lafayette. But the reason that Magruder evacuated while Cornwallis surrendered was that the Williamsburg road, which Lafayette closed, was left open by the Army of the Potomac.

The Past mingles strangely with the Present on these fields. These long, low barrows, green with turf and gay with barberry bushes, that marked the advancing parallels of an accomplished Revolution, will be hard to distinguish in a few years from those now red and fresh and bare, which have played their part in defending the Union thus established from the mad assault of reactionary rebellion.[31]

Washington correspondence, 26 June 1862

The Senate resolved itself this morning into a High Court of Impeachment, for the trial of West H. Humphreys, Judge of the United States Courts of Tennessee, charged with the crime of treason. At the termination of the morning hour, the Senators took the seats that had been provided for them on either side of the President *pro tempore.* Mr. Foot, of Vermont, and the House of Representatives appeared at the door, preceded by the managers of the impeachment on the part of the House, Messrs. Bingham of Ohio, Train of Massachusetts, Dunlap of Kentucky, and took the seats arranged for them in the body of the Chamber. The liberal and spacious spirit of our public architecture was never better exhibited than on this occasion. Both houses of Congress were comfortably seated in the Chamber built for the use of the smaller branch.

The Senate chamber never before was so well filled. The Conscript fathers ranged along the wall formed a dignified and noticeable contrast to the younger and less distinguished assembly on the floor. There are few black-haired men in the Senate, and the fine bordering of silver-grey relieved the more youthful *personale* of the House, as a sprinkling of snow on the top branches of a cedar heightens the glossy brilliancy of the dark green leaves below. President Foot, who, in the absence of Mr. Hamlin, occupies his chair, presided with that mild and benignant authority which has its foundation more, I think, in personal presence than anything else. He is a man of very striking and patriarchal beauty. His colleague, Mr. Collamer, one of the soundest and clearest heads in the Senate, resembles him somewhat in appearance. Seward once said, with that dry humor which in earlier days was oftener employed than now, "that Collamer was a man of very fine parts, but was ruining himself by trying to look as handsome as Foot."

To the right and left of Mr. Foot are seated the Senators, against the wall, in roomy and cane-bottomed benches, looking like a highly respectable jury who appreciate their responsibilities. Contrary to the traditions of earlier days, there is no political distinction between the two ends of the Senate Chamber. Gentlemen, who in debate are in the habit of calling each other perjured traitors and insane fanatics, in hours of ease steal each other's pens and expectorate in jointly-held spittoons. Here to-day is Saulsbury sitting by the side of Jim Lane, united by a common bond of bad temper and bad manners, and verifying the adage about extremes. Near them sits Fessenden, the cool though irascible, candid though prejudiced, firm though crotchety, always brilliant and always patriotic, bundle of paradoxes from Maine, in friendly converse with the graceful, refined and honorable Kennedy of Maryland, who is everything we could wish, except a Union man—and is that in his way? I was going to couple as antithetical propinquities Cowan and Powell, who are sitting together on the left of the Bar, as one was elected as a pronounced Republican and the other has been in danger of expulsion as a secessionist. But one has gone so far forward and the other so far backward in the year past, that I do not know but that they stand about as near politically as they do at this moment personally.

On the other side of the President are seated in queer companionship, Chandler, of Michigan and Garrett Davis, the one the representative of the bloodthirstiest spirit of anti-slavery zeal, and the other the last lingering relic of a class of little great men, who cannot, in their minds, disentangle the interests of good government from those of slavery, and in whose troubled dreams mingles always unwholesomely the flavor of the unresting contraband.

There is the venerable and universally respected Father Simmons of Rhode Island, who has moved for many years through the Capitol, surrounded by an atmosphere of marked honor and purity, clad in a visible garment of unyielding integrity, which at last (*horresco referens*) has parted in twain, and disclosed to the jeering world a contract jobber, "of the large gray kind." The fine old gentleman will have a hard time of it going back to private life again with a smutch like that on his shield. It is well his time is so near an end. His lapse is enough to reconcile us to the election of his successor, the infant governor and ready made hero, Wm. Sprague.

Separated from him by Morrille [*Morrill*], who is honest enough to secure any one from contagion, sits old Ben Wade, on whose rough face a smile never comes, out of whose firm lips little praise ever issues. But in his ill-conditioned life there is much of the daily beauty that makes ugly the smoother ways of scoundrels, and through his careless grammar and tangled rhetoric often struggle gleams of a light inspired by a devotion to his country as real as it is unreasoning. Though we may not once in a year agree with him, his words have this claim on our respect—he thoroughly believes them himself.

There is Doolittle, who will be one of the greatest politicians in all our history before he dies—and Anthony, beloved of many ladies—and Trumbull, whose mind is as clear as his spectacle-glasses—and Latham, who taught the East that there were gentlemen and orators on the Pacific shore—and McDougall, who didn't do anything of the kind—and nearest the wall, filling a whole bench, the ponderous bulk of the glorious old Senator Preston King—and at the end of the line, the giant statue and leonine port of Charles Sumner, whom New England presents to the world as *her* idea of the results of civilization.

Mr. Train opened the case. The articles of impeachment were read, and he stated briefly the grounds upon which they were founded, and what they intended to prove. Mr. Bingham then began the examination of witnesses. The first examined were the Clerk and Deputy Clerk of the Confederate Circuit and District Courts of Tennessee. The coolness with which they announced their occupation, and the studied respect with which they spoke of the bogus government, was very refreshing. There was nothing noticeable about the men or their testimony. It simply established the fact of the charges in the impeachment, which were patent to all men.

But there was a very different style of thing when the name of Wm. G. Brownlow, witness for prosecution, was called. He came forward, facing coolly the glance of a thousand curious eyes, a tall, slender man, dressed in black clothes, like any Southwestern parson; long, black, straight hair, carelessly combed; sallow complexion, beardless cheeks, black sunken eyes, high cheek bones, and an unmistakable expression of fight on lip, cheek and eyes.

His examination was very racy and characteristic. After a few preliminary questions from Mr. Bingham, he went on in a steady stream of narrative diversified by comment, which excited the crowd in the galleries to a tempestuous murmur of assent, bringing into frantic activity the President's gavel, and relaxing into a pleased grimness the countenances of the honorable court. The questions of the managers acted merely as spells to rouse the demon of witty reminiscence which would not down at their bidding. Their suggestions could start the fountain of his spicy remark, but could not shut off its stream or repress its bubbling. It was a perilous experiment, one fraught with danger to the dignity of the Senate, to call the fighting parson to the witness stand. But it was not disastrous. Brownlow, though severe, was not blackguardly—though witty, was not scurrilous—though earnest, was not boisterous. He could not resist the opportunity of giving his impressions of the bedraggled and moulting bird that is now fluttering its vulture life away in the Southern marshes. He looked unhappy and unsatisfied when the President released him from further examination, and his arrows of denunciation were forced to slumber in their quiver until another time.

The Senate then voted upon the question of the guilt or innocence of the accused; upon the first article of the impeachment, every one voted "guilty." Saulsbury, of Delaware, following his traitorous instincts as far as his heart would allow him, stated in an insolent tone and manner that he did not commit himself by his vote further than to express his disapproval of an officer of the United States Government accepting an office under a foreign power. The puerility of the plea is not less striking than the dastardly malignity that dictated the insinuation which it conveys.

The succeeding votes were not unanimous. At four o'clock the Court reassembled, and voted that West H. Humphreys be removed from office, and forever disqualified from holding any office under the Government of the United States.

So ends the first case of impeachment under the rebellion.[32]

WASHINGTON CORRESPONDENCE, 13 JULY 1862

One of the most important and least talked of measures that have been submitted to the consideration of the present Congress is the Mexican Subsidy Treaty. This has been the pet measure of Minister Corwin, and has also very strongly excited the interest of the Government here. In any other time but the present, it would not only have been ratified at once by the Senate but would have secured unbounded fame to its authors and greatly enhanced the popularity of the Administration under whose auspices it was accomplished. But in the anomalous state of things in which we at present find ourselves, the Senate treats the matter with indifference, heightened by timidity; the Government suffers its own work to fall dead for want of encouragement, and the passionate entreaties and solicitations of Minister Corwin, who is so thoroughly convinced of the necessity and practicability of the scheme that he cannot look with any allowance upon an opposite opinion, have fallen upon heedless and inattentive ears. The Senate will adjourn without acting upon the matter.

By the terms of this treaty the United States were to loan to Mexico the amount of $11,000,000, payable in small and frequent installments. This debt was to be secured to us by the pledge of the public domain and the church property of Mexico. It was thought that by giving Mexico this present assistance, she would be able to buy peace and immunity from the greedy and rapacious powers that are threatening her coast. It was further thought that she would be unable to repay to us the amount lent. We would then fall back upon our securities, which are most ample. If the property, on being sold, brought a high price, we would the more easily get back our debt; if a low one, we would buy still more of rich and needful territory. It was a most advantageous treaty, one for which Mr. Corwin deserves all praise, even if it fails.

By it, besides making a firm friend upon our Southern border, whose friendship will be always of advantage, we would prevent the machinations of an ancient and treacherous enemy. It is generally understood that if we fail to make the treaty spoken of, it will be made by England. Such a lever for future mischief upon this continent should not be placed in the hands of that arrogant and unscrupulous power.

It is almost impossible to overestimate the importance of keeping so far as we can this continent free from the footsteps of European absolutism. Our own safety imperatively demands the perpetuity of Republican institutions on our borders. If we suffer any portion of our extensive boundaries to fall into the possession of a widespread and grasping European dynasty, at that moment we lose a great element of national security, and introduce into our own politics a fruitful source of trouble and tumult. All our statesmen, from Washington and Monroe down to Webster and Seward, have declaimed in the most earnest and impressive terms against the policy of allowing upon this continent the intervention of European politics. Peace is the normal condition of Republics, as war is the everlasting temptation and the first resort of despotisms. The peace of this continent demands the exclusion of European politics.

To whom, if not to us, should Mexico look for shelter and for aid? We stand in our power and strength, by virtue of continental supremacy, the guardian and parent of every hard-pressed and struggling republic. It will do much towards shaking in the minds of the weaker States about us, the impression of our beneficent power, if they are forced to resort to Europe for sympathy and aid in the time of their trial.

In view of a great question now rapidly gaining form and proportion in the public mind, a hold upon the domain of Mexico such as this treaty gives us will be of vast and well nigh incalculable benefit to us. There are now, already within the lines and in the service of the United States armies, a very large number of liberated negroes. Many more will fall into our hands, freed by the operation of the law of Congress, which gives freedom to slaves owned by rebels, who have been employed in the service of the insurrectionary army.

The slaves freed by the act of emancipation in the District of Columbia are wanting new homes. We cannot keep this ignorant and unenterprising population among us, especially if the Border States, as it seems not improbable, conclude to accept the generous offer of the National Government and to lift from their long-burdened shoulders the dreadful incubus of slavery. There must be a home provided for these unhappy people. There is but one civilized nation on the face of the earth where they can be received by the inhabitants without any prejudice, on terms of entire social and political equality—only one place where they may find the whole future open to them to work out their destiny under God, untrammeled by caste or ethnological hatred—and that country is Mexico. This is the place for the great experiment. Here the negro may learn if he is capable of self government, or whether slavery, with its countless evils, is necessary to his proper development. This treaty will give to us the opportunity for the great decision. It is to be feared that if we neglect it now, it may not come to us again.

Yet, great as these advantages appear, the treaty will not be ratified this session. Many considerations seem to influence Senators. Some object to any outlay of money for any purpose. If they could buy Heaven for a sixpence, they would call for the ayes and noes on the appropriation of the sixpence. Others think it not consistent with our friendly relations with France to give material aid to a nation with which she is in a *quasi* state of war.

It is to be hoped that a better aspect of Mexican affairs is presented by recent advices. The Emperor of the French seems to be reconsidering his project of conquest, and has countermanded the embarkation of the greater part of the troops he had intended for that service. He has a long head, and will consider well before he embroils himself in a row of which the beginning is easier seen than the end.

If the bad fortune of the French had continued at Orizaba, the Emperor would already have gotten enough of the losing conflict. But the unparalleled stupidity of the somnolent Mexicans, who suffered 150 French to surprise 4,000 of them on the heights of Cerro del Borrega, may revive the drooping spirit of conquest and silence the bold denunciations of the opposition, who, led by Jules Favre, have lately been indulging in a style of criticism and comment in the Chambers, that sounds more like America than France.

Until we finish the present business on hand we will probably keep out of other ventures. But few American fingers do not tingle with anxiety to dabble in this Mexican pie.[33]

Washington correspondence, undated (ca. mid-July 1862)

It is very pleasant one of these bright summer mornings, to escape from this great political sweat house, with the eternal dust and din of the National Capital, and breathe the fresh, free, unpolluted air of the country; to turn your back for a while upon the flooded sewers and sink-holes, where the sun's fiery fingers are already stirring up the seeds of a summer pestilence, and from the moral miasma that floats in the social and political atmosphere just above, and go forth to rejoice amidst the green fields, under the shade of whispering trees, and listen to the music of flowing waters; to linger where every sight and sound is full of the sense of beauty, and the very air you breathe comes loaded with the sweet odor of flowers and the sweeter songs of birds; where

Joy smiles in the fountain, health leaps in the rill,
And the ribbons of silver unwind from the hills.

Happier still if you make such a rural excursion as the guest of a politico-military expedition, bent upon a grand moral reconnaissance of re-conquered rebeldom. Put this and that together, and you can imagine the pleasure of accepting a courteous invitation to join a Congressional delegation, just starting on a visit to Norfolk, Portsmouth, Yorktown, and the neighboring portions of the late *terra incognita*.

A fine government steamer is at our disposal, with gentlemanly officers and a stalwart crew, a ten-inch rifled Parrot on the bows and a stack of Springfield muskets in the cabin, to say nothing of abundant commission stores and a first-class steward to prepare them, not forgetting a good supply of Boston ice and various fluids adapted to melt it. Thus provisioned and equipped, we say good-bye to the unfinished domes and monuments of the Capital, and "steer our bark" for Dixie's Land.

Down the broad river we glide, through fleets of steamers, tugs, transports, ships, schooners, sloops, smacks and skiffs—water craft of all degrees, propelled by muscle, wind or steam; and as we descend, the receding shores and broader expanse of water tell how true was the christening of the "majestic Potomac." As we pass, the last rays of the setting sun are gilding the tree tops of Mount Vernon, and we glide past this Mecca of human liberty, as beneath "the shadow of a great rock in a weary land." Sleep on, thou noblest of all our kind, for, though thy country is drenched with fraternal blood, not even the fierceness of civil strife shall desecrate the home or tomb of Washington! We may slaughter each other, and divide or destroy our blood bought heritage, but thy glory is indivisible and imperishable—it belongs to no state or nation, but is the heritage of all who love liberty and hate tyranny throughout the world.

A moonlight voyage takes us past a dozen points that have become historic in their connection with the late blockade of the Potomac, and the first light of the morning comes gleaming over the broader expanse of the Chesapeake.

A smart breeze has changed the surface of the bay into short, chopping, white capped waves that give an unpleasant motion to the vessel, and produces a singular effect upon politicians who happen to be on their first sea legs. What a company of pale faces is here. How the steward runs here and there with broken ice and various medicinal fluids. It will not all do. Old Neptune's spirit cannot be laid with doses of ice and vulgar whisky, and those men who thought they ruled the world are given up to sorrowful faces and most painful retchings. How they whine and feel like a poor sick girl as the ice and whisky goes overboard. If there was sea sickness for a politician's conscience(?), how some men would heave their very hearts into the "great deep." But they are free from such maladies, and men who have swallowed, without a grimace, daily doses of nigger wool, feel unnatural qualms at the first lurch of a ship. This is doubtless one of the compensating arrangements of a kind Providence, and we thank that Providence that our nausea comes from the wool instead of the sea moves.

Another virtue of salt water is to harmonize conflicting opinions and smooth down the acerbities and perturbations of excited minds. These men, who were fighting like cats and dogs, at the Capitol, a few hours ago, have become mild and gentle as sucking doves, and fraternize as if they belonged to the same brood. Here is every shade of political opinion, from suspected treason to rampant abolition; but for once politics are ignored, and they chat and hobnob together in the most cordial manner, showing that

One touch of nature makes the whole world kin.

Wonder if Abraham and Jeff could not be brought to smile and shake hands on such a floating platform as this?

But yonder in the dim horizon loom up the granite walls of the Fortress [*Fort Monroe*], and close by the huge stone pile of the Rip Raps, surrounded by an immense fleet of ships-of-war, gunboats, steamers and transports, and, floating over all, the bright flag of freedom. A half hour's steaming brings us to the wharf, and our first greeting upon the shore is with the fifteen-inch "peace-makers" that tried its powers of pacification by sending a few shells across the four-mile strait into the rebel camp on Sewall's Point.—After a brief but cordial interview with the veteran commander of the Fortress, and an hour's stroll through the casements and over the battlements, accompanied with the conviction that nothing but the "Confederate" powers of hell, aided by the lightnings of heaven could make any impression upon this American Gibraltar, we embark again for a short cruise up to Norfolk.

On the trip, and three or four miles out from the Fortress, two objects are pointed out, insignificant in themselves, yet full of interest in the world. On our right, and in the neighborhood of Newport News are the protruding spars of the hard fated *Cumberland,* standing like a gloomy monument of an exploded system of naval warfare, while just to our left, surging up and down upon the ebbing tide waves, lie portions of the charred hulk of the iron coated sea monster [*the CSS Merrimac*] that has set the whole maritime world to thinking, planning and reforming. The first went down in the midst of a fierce but unequal contest, but still left her proud flag flying above the engulfing flood. The last committed suicide and went down amidst the smoke and thunder of her own magazine, lighted by the rebel commander. A true but melancholy emblem of the madness and fury of a cause that defends itself, only by tearing out its own vitals. Who, but the rebels, will be poorer on account of their sunken ships, bursted cannon and burned cotton? Who honors or courts the fate of the fire girdled scorpion, stinging itself to death in sheer madness?

Norfolk and Portsmouth—there they stand—twin cities, fair as the green shores of the beautiful bay on which they are built.

"'Tis green, but living green no more."

Deserted wharves, gloomy houses, unpeopled streets. Has a pestilence swept over this paradise, blighting all its beauties, or is this only the spirit of the devil incarnated in the doctrine of secession? The contrabands are the only ones that grin, and theirs is a ghastly smile for they seem quite uncertain yet whether it is better to be vassals or vagabonds. The townspeople are submitting to the new order of things with a kind of sullen protest on every man's part. Say what we will of latent and undeveloped Union sentiment, there is underlaying all a feeling of sectional hate that generations can scarcely eradicate. If it was nothing but the mortification that fathoms defeat, it would soon die out like the sobbings of a fractional child whose good mother has administered an extra dose of palm oil. But this is a deeper and more incurable disease and though Madame Columbia has already blistered her hand in applying the remedy, the moment she ceases "to lay on," the sick child turns to a rebel trooper. And this is thus far the sad history of this sad war. If we have reclaimed territory we have failed to conquer rebellious hearts. This does not proceed from any lack of loyalty amongst the masses of the Southern people, but from their undying hatred of Northern fanatics. Fanatics and fire-eaters are striving for the violent extinction and the other for the indefinite extinction of slavery. Both equally mad and equally criminal. They have brought all our troubles, and if a hundred of the leaders on each side could be hung in pairs over oak limbs, the tumult would subside and the peace of the country be restored. The leaders of both parties are equally traitors in the sight of heaven, and both shout "liberty" for their battle cry. "O, Liberty! what crimes are committed in thy name!" Think not from this that I am willing to give in to a broken Constitution, a dishonored flag and a dismembered country. We have been dragged into this bloody strife by traitors North and South, and now that the life of the nation, and not the condition of the nigger, is at stake, we must fight it through.

A day on the Peninsula, in sketching the deserted works of Yorktown, and the battle fields of Williamsburg and West Point, closed our brief reconnaissance, and the Sabbath morning twilight found us again steaming up the Potomac past Fort Washington and Mount Vernon. And what lesson have we learned from the voyage? Does yonder, half-finished obelisk, gleaming in the moonlight, or that huge but yet uncovered dome, tell of a great temple of Freedom destroyed in the course of its erection by those who laid its foundation stones? Must the prayers of the world be checked, and the hopes of oppressed millions be crushed, by putting out the sun of liberty in this sea of blood? The hour is gloomy; but never despair. We pass through an ordeal of fire, but this heritage—this last resting place of freedom—shall never perish! And the evening gun from the ramparts, as its booming went over the waters, echoed back to our hearts—"never!"[34]

WASHINGTON CORRESPONDENCE, 27 JULY 1862

A Major General used to be an elephant rarely witnessed by the most assiduous explorer into the social life of our country. For many years, Gen. Winfield Scott was the only one whom our army list exhibited, and the most ambitious of subalterns rarely aspired to die with higher insignia on their shoulder straps than the regimental eagles. But this little shindy of ours with our dissatisfied fellow-countrymen has changed all that. If it had done nothing more, it has made the public mind familiar with the idea of high military rank, so that there is no longer any magic in the name of General. In old days, the name of Consul Romanus was enough to frighten a province withal; but after Spartacus and his contrabands had killed some half-dozen Consuls, the idea lost somewhat of its grandeur.

I used to hold my breath at the sight of the twin stars on a warrior's shoulders. But this morning I took my breakfast at Willard's at the same table with four Major Generals, and suffered no diminution of appetite in consequence.

(Don't understand me to say that I enjoyed my breakfast. Eating with satisfaction is to the dweller at Willard's a vague and impossible dream of what flits though memory, or flashes through hope sometimes, but has no fulfillment in the actual. Even the late change in the color of the waiters—whose faces recently darkened from dirty to black in the space between dinner and tea—fails to add any hilarity to the form of that inconceivably wretched caravanserai. Miraculous in meanness; contemptible in cuisine; execrable in extortion, it holds the proud pre-eminence of being the worst kept and most profitable hotel in America. If Ellsworth had only let it burn last year when the flames attacked it, every one would have sighed with heartfelt relief, "Peace to its hashes!" Pardon this little ebullition of spleen, for which, if discovered, I shall be made to drink Prussic acid glacé in my cold tea, and let me go back to my Generals, or, to speak irreverently, "return to our sheep.")

One of them is a little man, as his tailor and his photographer consider him, but history, more comprehensive in her view, will regard him as a giant. With those near-sighted eyes, by whose aid he can hardly recognize his son, who sits opposite him at table, he has gazed far through the still depths of the trackless ocean of ether, and numbered the heavenly fleets that swing at their moorings on those tideless shores. He has broken to pieces the absurd idea that men of thought fail in action. The boldest servant of American science, he has proven himself the most restless and irrepressible of soldiers. Coming at the call of his country from the still retreats where through the long nights of the slowly passing years he has sat as patient as the stars he conned; with no heartbeat but for science, no thought lower than the skies, he has burst at once into a career of splendid and [*startling?*] activity. The enemy has had little time for slumber when opposed by the earnest vigilance of this unwinking star-gazer. To one who knows him, the charges invented by Col. Norton, and celebrated by the *Louisville Journal* and the *Cincinnati Commercial,* seem no less ludicrous than wicked. A man more just and kindly than Gen. Mitchell never breathed. All his sympathies are quick and generous. He is pre-eminently merciful. I believe that, like Uncle Toby, he would be sorry to hear of the hopeless perdition even of the Devil.

Where, by the way, is Colonel Norton? Let me commend to him the lesson of a somewhat musty old saying about the usual consequences of digging a pit for one's neighbor.

Near General Mitchell sits a good-looking young gentleman, who seems very much at home among these constellated heroes, and if it were not for his plain and scrupulously neat and fashionable citizen's costume, one would take him for a soldier, there is so much of off-hand dignity and authority in his style of doing things. He has a round head, solidly built, and well padded with brains evidently. A clear, fine complexion, a bright though quiet eye, a short, straight nose, which he carries in the air as if it were a good nose to follow, which it is, I believe; a mustache and heavy whiskerage, which prevents us from seeing his mouth, and compels us to believe, without seeing it, that it is not coarse, nor cowardly, nor mean. It is a good head, set firmly and in a workmanlike manner on his broad, square shoulders, at a distance from the ground of about five feet and eight inches; shorter than Scott—but taller than either of the Napoleons—the big one, named Bonaparte, or the little one, named McClellan. He looks like a man who can work hard, think fast, strike quick, and not care particularly how hard he hits. He speaks in a quick, easy way, not abrupt, nor gruff, nor insolent, as some gentlemen who wear uniforms do. He looks like a gentleman, but I suppose we will have to admit he is a soldier, for Burnside has just called him "General." The rest of his name is "John Pope, Major General Commanding the Army of Virginia"—the Coming Man, his friends think, of the army.

Burnside, who sits near him, lets his buttons shine before men. Washington people rarely have a sensation, and he thinks it a heartless swindle to deprive the innocent populace of the gratification of seeing him in his war-paint. Burnside has been photographed so often, with such inevitable fidelity that the country has grown familiar with his Mexican whiskers and his noble brow, which, by the way, extends to the nape of his neck. He has all a true soldier's fondness for dress and glitter. He gets into attitudes which charm the artists of the illustrated papers; he says things which are the delight of "our own correspondent." He injects what actors call "gag" into the body of his dispatches, and is a little apt to take the color of Time and his surroundings. Yet he is a glorious fellow and a splendid soldier, with heart enough for a dozen generals, and sense enough for one—which is saying a great deal.

But when you begin to talk of sense you come naturally to Halleck, who finishes my quarto of major generals. There are only four here now, as McDowell is well of his wound, and Sigel has gone to the mountains—the bold, generous, confident, fortunate "Flying Dutchman"—who can't be caught and who won't stay whipped, no matter what the odds against him may be, or how well the enemy may fight; who compels coy victory to his sturdy wooing in her own despite, and snatches glory from the dreadful front of defeat. Happy the man whose name is found on the list of Sigel's corps. For him the cup shall foam—the harp shall twang. The world will some day learn the proverb that the Springfield fight made common in St. Louis: "You fights mit Sigel—you drinks mit me."

Well, as I was saying, General Halleck is sitting there amongst the boys. As a Western friend graphically remarks, "he is like a singed cat—better than he looks." Still he looks well—not as to uniform, for it is growing a little white at the seams, and seedy at the button-holes with the wear and tear of the Western campaign; not as to bearing, particularly, for he is very unassuming and quiet, with a stoop and a downward glance. But he has a splendid head piece on his shoulders. A great head, squarely furnished, and perfect in symmetry, with any assignable amount of sense stored away in it—"great chunks of wisdom," as Captain Cuttle says—vast stores of learning, which have drifted in from the assiduous reading of a quarter of a century—the culled and digested maxims of many ages—the wide and varied impressions of human nature, gained by the laborious practice of law in the sharp and busy Pacific world—the garnered treasures of an experience which has been singularly catholic and many-sided in the life that has sounded all changes of citizen and soldier. He is a cool, mature man, who understands himself. Let us be glad we have got him. The soldiers call him "Old Brains."[35]

WASHINGTON CORRESPONDENCE, 12 AUGUST 1862

The news of the flight of the enemy from before General Pope affects people here this morning like tidings of a victory. So important have we come to regard the success of the overland expedition to Richmond, and so strongly is the public confidence settling down to the conviction that Halleck is safe to plan and Pope sure to execute it, that the greatest anxiety is felt that no untoward accident shall baffle or delay it. It seemed for a while on Sunday that the enemy had begun to look upon the matter in the same way in which we regarded it, and had concluded to block our game by overwhelming numbers and celerity of movement. It was a good idea, and that it was not carried out was not the fault of the rebels, but of General Banks, who obstinately refused to be whipped.

The plan undoubtedly was to send Stonewall Jackson and Ewell over the Rapidan, who were to march hurriedly upon the outposts of General Banks' army, between the Rapidan and Culpepper Court House, and destroy them; then beat in detail General Sigel, who was lying twenty miles distant at Sperryville; McDowell's forces now reduced by repeated detachments to one Division, under the command of Gen. Ricketts, lying near Waterloo and Warrenton, and then if any advance were made from Burnside, fight him, and destroy the last defense of Washington. Success in this enterprise would have left the way entirely open to the Federal capital. Thus, while a part of the rebel army beleaguered General McClellan at Harrison's Landing, another part might have flaunted the rebel banner over the dome of our Senate House, in short though splendid triumph. It was certainly a bold and a seducing idea to a man of Jackson's character, flushed with constant success, and fanatically sure of his cause.

It came near being a success. The advance of the enemy was very rapid and, as usual, entirely unsuspected by our forces. The first hint of it was obtained by Gen. Bayard's cavalry, who saw them crossing the Rapidan in force. He detained them as long as he could by bold and skillful skirmishing, and the advance guard of Banks' Corps, consisting of Crawford's brigade of Williams' division, moved rapidly forward to meet the enemy on the high ground, between the Cedar Creek and Crooked River, about three-quarters of a mile north of the towering height of Slaughter's mountain or Cedar mountain, as it is called in the maps, a bold detached spur of the great thoroughfare range. Here the battle took place. The enemy had rather the advantage of position, as their batteries ranged in a deadly semicircle along the wooded slopes of the mountain. But our troops were sustained by their own discipline, and admirable conduct of their officers, the indomitable courage and coolness of their General, the calm, capable and energetic man of Waltham. Through the long hours of a summer's afternoon and evening, Banks stood his ground against many times his number, and held the ferocious enemy at bay. They dared not leave the cover of the wooded hill, to attack a front so firm, a line so unwavering, as that which confronted them on the lower grounds beyond. It was a fight against time. All Banks could wish to do was to hold the enemy in check until the scattered detachments of Pope's army could appear upon the field. If he could hold the ground until McDowell came up from the East, and Sigel from the West, and King from the South, the battle was won and the bold game of the rebel partisan was irretrievably lost. For this opportunity once passed would never again return. If he stopped here, the swarming legions of the North would make the renewal of this fight impossible. Let the different squads of Pope's little army concentrate on the banks of Cedar Run, and no power could pass them without deadly peril, and before many days were gone, an army would be marching to the Rapidan, which nothing could withstand, not even if they beggared their rebel kingdom and left *le faineant* McClellan to walk into the deserted streets of Richmond. This Banks knew, and this stubborned his energies for the struggle.

It was a fight against time, and Banks won it. They fought through the sunset into the twilight, and the Northern soldiers did not give way an inch; and later till the deepening shadows made musketry useless, and only the deep thunder of the artillery, the fierce red flashes from the mountain side, and the quick replies from the defiant batteries in the plain, told that the battle was not over. But the peril was over and the day was won, when about nine o'clock the tramp of McDowell's men was heard on the left, and as they marched to the front, the tired soldiers of Crawford's Brigade fell back to the rear and rolled into sleepy squads on the soft, moist carpet of a cloverfield. Later in the night Sigel's men came up fresh and hearty at the end of a twenty-mile walk from Sperryville, in the cool of the evening, and the next morning the regular and well-ordered columns of King's division were descried in the far southeast coming up to strengthen the living wall of Union defense for Virginia.

The game was finished. The attempt of Jackson was a failure. Pope's whole force lay massed in the solid and intrepid column before him. He skirmished through the day in an aimless and desultory manner, and under cover of the following night ingloriously abandoned the attack and went back to Richmond.

So ends our perils of preparation. The only danger to be apprehended during the period which intervened between the close of one campaign, which we must confess was a failure, and the beginning of another, which we hope is to be a success, was the very one that has now passed harmlessly by. The only way in which the coming campaign could fail, was for Jackson to beat in detail the scattered detachments of Pope's little army before the reinforcements destined for it arrived. This has not been done, and we may now wait with confidence the development of present plans.

Every hour that the final struggle is delayed weakens the enemy and strengthens us. His army is at its maximum; ours will be nearly doubled in the coming season. His supplies are growing scanty and communications uncertain; we still rejoice in the boundless acres of the peaceful North. His armies are suffering raging pestilences—our surgical bureau was never so thoroughly and successfully administered as now. These things are mentioned merely as causes of congratulation, not as excuses for delay. For not one hour will be wasted in useless preparation, and not one opportunity of success will pass by in the listless pauses of inaction and indecision that have formerly paralyzed the army, in the days when the spirit of Wilkins Macawber was at its head, "waiting for something to turn up."

In the coming days, when Richmond is ours, and the promise of peace blesses the land, let us remember that Nathaniel P. Banks, the civilian General, was the man who saved the campaign on the day of deadly struggle at Slaughter's Mountain, and let his name be remembered with that of Worden, who saved the army of the Potomac on that gloomy Sunday when the blood-drunken *Merrimac* came forth for another day of easy carnage among the unresisting transports and wooden walls of Hampton Roads.[36]

WASHINGTON CORRESPONDENCE, 17 AUGUST 1862

Another quiet Sunday—one in the series that is now intervening between the busy days that opened the summer and the bloody ones that will open the fall. General Halleck is steadily and coolly getting the reins into his hands to manage this matter according to his liking, and, singularly enough, the enemy is permitting him to do everything very much in his own way. There have been several occasions—since those opening days of July that established so clearly the fact of General McClellan's failure to effect his purposes—when a well organized and vigorous effort of the enemy might have carried confusion and temporary panic into the National Army. But they have suffered them to pass by, and they will not come again. What causes have conspired to produce this singular laxity and apathy, we can as yet only conjecture. Doubtless the fiery hail of slaughter that rained upon them from the battle clouds of Malvern Hills served as a powerful warning to them against following too closely in the footsteps of an enemy which even in defeat was unconquered; and the splendid retreat which Banks made from Winchester to Harpers Ferry was to them the presage of the coming disaster which would result to the rebel arms in case of any rash attack upon his front. We know that their transportation was limited and not of the best quality. We know that their fear of an interruption to their railroad facilities prevented them from exposing themselves to ruin by any sudden dash of Pope. We have always contended that their own boasts, and the apologetic spirit of McClellan's Staff, have exaggerated the number of the enemy before Richmond; and now that their armies are filled by the late sweeping conscription to the maximum number, the majority of the new recruits are utterly untrustworthy, and cannot be trusted even by their own commanders. These things together have prevented the accomplishment of the great purpose to which opportunity seemed specially to point them, the demolition of the army of Virginia, the sack of Washington and the invasion of Maryland.

That they fully appreciated the importance of these movements there can be but little doubt. The clamors of the more youthful and fiery portion of the fighting men—the unceasing assaults of the newspaper press which called continually for this forward movement—the appeals of Maryland traitors, who were constantly coining the "rivers of Babylon" business, and singing in Randall's song of mingled beauty and pathos the woes of "My Maryland," and the murmured growlings of discontent that always rose from the infatuated idolaters of Beauregard, at every repeated snub which that nervous little Creole received from their bilious Chief, who they said only opposed the Napoleonic policy of invasion because it was Beauregard's. All had this effect upon the Richmond cabal, and impressed the fact most powerfully upon the minds of Davis and his fellow rebels that their brightest hope lay in the mountains of the Shenandoah, and the true path of glory led to Washington. For with the possession of that cherished but dusty city came the hope of recognition from abroad, sympathy from the cowed scoundrels of the North, and active cooperation from the wavering masses of the Border slave States.

The last campaign of Stonewall Jackson shows how this project was cherished, and its result shows the end of that avenue of hope to the rebel cause. His movement was planned admirably. But his soldiers dashed themselves in vain upon the solid legions of Banks, and ran precipitately away upon the unwelcome appearance of our prompt and ready reinforcements. This was the end of that business; if attempted again, it must fail again.

It may be a second time essayed. It is a matter of too vast and controlling importance to be lightly given up. There are some advantages which the rebels formerly lacked which are now in their possession; and these may induce them, overlooking our enormous gains, to try the game again with livelier hopes of success. They have withdrawn for this service their transportation from the army besieging McClellan at Harrison's Landing; they have infused into the unmanageable masses of raw conscripts a large proportion of the last year's veterans; they have gathered together from scattered posts a well seasoned army, much better appointed than that which ran away from Cedar Mountain last week. They hope with the forces which they have taken away from the now useless service of watching a waning camp on the James river, to crush the growing army of Pope that is standing to arms in the passes and by the fords of the North.

If they think there is no hereafter, they had better try it. Every day since that splendid one when the Iron Man of Waltham stood like a wall of adamant in the perilous breach through which the insolent rebels hoped to rush to glory and success, regiment after regiment of our best and bravest have been quietly pouring in from every quarter to share in the honors of the coming day. Four or five new regiments come daily filing into Washington with bright clear faces and untarnished buttons, whose energy and unwasted strength will be better than discipline on the battle field. If discipline be a good thing we have enough of that, too, for the brown and hardy soldiers of the peninsula campaign are coming up daily in magnificent brigades, that look like superb machines, and walk as if fatigue were impossible and panic an absurdity with them. If our lively and enterprising contemporary, Stonewall Jackson, comes again with swollen ranks and reinforced commissariat, he will find a warm and hearty welcome, and a committee of reception, whose numbers, at least, will surprise him.

The best possible man for getting the greatest amount of training out of green troops, in a short time, is the old gentleman who is now drilling our fresh young fellows in the vicinity of Washington—General Silas Casey, from whose name the Government has wiped the stigma fastened by that hasty, ill-considered and unjust dispatch of General McClellan, at the battle of Fair Oaks, by assigning him to the arduous and important service of organizing and drilling the new troops as they arrive. Under his admirable management days do the work of weeks, and well behaved reserves are ready whenever called for.

The campaign of General McClellan having been finally modified and reconstructed by the more synthetic mind of Halleck, we may hope for speedy and cheering results. Before this reaches you, the splendid though ill-handled Army of the Potomac will have been extricated from its present dangerous and useless position, and assigned a very important post in the great work soon to be accomplished by the renovated armies of the Union, the liberation of the South.

The omens with which this great duty is begun are most cheering. The sound of threat and bluster is silent in Europe. The enthusiasm of the North is again awakened, and now tempered by the sound discretion and experience of a fruitful year. The armies of the Republic are glorious in numbers and superb in spirit and purpose. The enemy is weak and wavering between the gathering apathy of defeat and the lunacy of desperation. The vacillating loyalty of the Border is grown firm and unyielding; Union is seen there to be worth more than any institution but Freedom, and to-night comes the cheering intelligence that the Governor of Kentucky, finding his State so far before him in every element of patriotic progress as to render his position embarrassing, has gracefully resigned his seat to a man in harmony with the new and ardent spirit of unconditional loyalty that rules the hour.[37]

WASHINGTON CORRESPONDENCE, 20 AUGUST 1862

One of the most encouraging symptoms to be met with just now is the awakened confidence and firmness of the business people. If the new order of things at Washington had produced no other effect, it is as good as a victory to have a man in the office of Commanding General, in whose good sense people believe so firmly. The halo of idolatry which formerly hung about General McClellan invested his name with a singular potency in the imaginations of Wall street, and the stock market rose and fell with the varying changes of his moods. If he was snubbed, Government sixes declined. If he issued a stirring address to his troops, their applauding cheers were echoed in the Broker's Board. But now, when General Halleck, after mature deliberation and consultation with the President and the Secretary of War, decides that General McClellan's plan of campaign on the Peninsula was a failure, altogether inexpedient and impracticable, and orders the Army of the Potomac to evacuate their present position and repair to another point, to share in the danger and glories of a different campaign, the country breathes a deep sigh of relief, and rests contented that the right thing has been done at last. On the very day that the New York papers formally announced that the Army of the Potomac were moving northward, United States bonds sold in Wall street at a premium of one-and-a-half per centum, and 7.30 Treasury notes brought 105 cents on the dollar.

To-day this same cheering confidence in the military administration of affairs is seen. Gen. Pope is reported as falling back from his advanced position on the Rapidan, through the whole extent of Culpepper county, and taking a defensive position on the hither bank of the Rappahannock river. Lee, at the head of 150,000 rebels, is said to be at the Raccoon ford of the Rapidan, and his entire army advancing in divided columns in the direction of Fredericksburg and Washington. Yet there is no tremor of apprehension on the streets; no anxiety, no fearful forward looking for the battle that is to come. Every one seems thoroughly satisfied that the Union army is strong enough to whip any enemy, if rightly handled; and that, this time, it will be rightly handled.

This movement of Pope, though one that, in view of his pyrotechnic order on taking command of the Army of Virginia, will be severely criticised and possibly laughed at, is a very sensible and proper one. He hurried forward to the Rapidan to engage the attention of the enemy and distract his force, in order to give Gen. McClellan time to evacuate Harrison's Landing unharmed. He was successful in that, and now when the enemy begins to recognize that his only hope is in hurrying up the fight in the north before the Union army is concentrated in an available position, it is of course incumbent upon Pope to delay the fight for the little time that is yet necessary for the concentration of the whole efficient strength of the armies of the Atlantic shore. At the Rapidan he would be in an awkward position. His communications with Washington were unnecessarily extended, and with Fredericksburg. A wide and rapid river rolled between him and the mouth of the Estuary, where needed reinforcements could most conveniently be landed. He, therefore, retires to the Rappahannock and "takes a strong position," though with many wry faces doubtless, after his hearty abuse of the phrase a few weeks ago, and waits for the enemy at a point where his force can be best used, and where he is within supporting distance of every considerable detachment of Union troops now in Northeastern Virginia.

What the enemy means by his present maneuvering is rather problematical. Whatever other great qualities our generals may have shown, they have not distinguished themselves by any system of espionage. The movements of an enemy within a score of miles is as puzzling a subject of conjecture as the internal policy of an undiscovered island in the Southern Sea. He will probably develop his plans by actions before this letter can be published. I therefore magnanimously cork up my guesses, shrewd and exhaustive though they be.

Curious people, who want to know the reasons of things, will not cease asking why it is that the enemy, if they possessed the extravagant numbers that popular superstition has ascribed to them, permitted General McClellan to leave Harrison's Bar so quietly. Perhaps they felt the mark of his heavy hand laid on them with fury when they stood at bay on Malvern Hills, and thanked God, like Dogberry, that they were well rid of a troublesome knave. More likely they only waited to see him surely moving, that they might hasten to overwhelm the Army of Virginia before he could form a junction with Pope.

It will not do to say they were unaware of his moving, for it was advertised in the Richmond papers before it began. Anyhow, they are swarming like bees now on the southern side of the Rapidan, occasionally throwing out scouting parties like the feelers of a scorpion towards Fredericksburg and the West, but as yet not crossing the river. The unquiet ghosts that wander mournfully around the gory slopes of Slaughter's Mountain warn them in language of awful eloquence of the peril of rushing blindly upon Northern steel. The names of Banks—wedded forever to the glory which comes to iron fortitude and heroic endurance—of Sigel, sound of terror to the rebel legions of the West, and destined yet to be the thunderbolt of ruin to the hordes of the Eastern shore—of McDowell, who will yet make an unfortunate name glorious if Fate is not inexorably against him—and of Pope, who frightened them into blackguard barbarism by his early energy, may well give them pause. When to these you add the brown and bearded warriors of the Peninsula, who come with the fruits of a year's patient drilling in their well-ordered battalia, and with the fire of an earnest purpose in their hearts to be avenged of fate and treason in one bloody day, you may imagine what are the chances of the coming fight when loyalty meets rebellion—discipline meets mutinous conscription, plenty meets starvation, civilization meets barbarism. If there ever was a fight where God and the heaviest artillery, truth and sound wagons, justice and a fat larder, a righteous quarrel and three fold armament were all on one side, it would seem to be this, that soon will waken the slumbering echoes of the Rappahannock, and, we hope, settle by a glorious arbitrament the fight for constitutional liberty in the Western world.

But let not him that putteth on his armour boast like him that taketh it off.[38]

Washington correspondence, 24 August 1862

The stars in their course fight against rebellion and treason. If there was anything wanted to ensure the triumph of the national armies in Virginia, it was simply the gain of a week's time from the day when Pope fell back to a stronger position than that on the Rapidan, to wait for reinforcements. And the surest defense that would possibly be thrown between him and the advancing enemy was an unfordable stream of water, which, having no boats, they could not cross, and having no pontoons, could not bridge. Until within two days, however, the Rappahannock rolled sluggishly between its low flat banks, with scarcely water enough in many places to varnish the pebbles in its bed. At every ford the enemy could cross it without wetting their cartridge boxes, and at every ford the swarming grey legions were gathering. Now was their time, or never, to whip the little army of Pope, before the veterans of the Peninsula should join him, and finish the campaign by the mere force of numbers. It seems that the enemy was not unmindful of this view of the case. They came in great force upon Reno, who was encamped on the south side of Kelley's Ford, and he had barely time to save his detachment before their heavy columns appeared on the opposite heights. Higher up, at the Sulphur Springs, their demonstrations were still more serious and threatening. It seemed for a while that Pope would have to fight and conquer them singly, and without waiting to share the dust and glory of the fight with his old friend McClellan, ex-Lieutenant of Topographical Engineers. Friday night was filled with apprehension, which cleared up as the heavens clouded, and was washed away by the kind and beneficent rain that came down before the morning. It was a splendid rain. Not a halfway apologetic shower to lay the dust and clear the air, not an ornamental aspersion to jewel the cornfields and polish the withering leaves, but a whole-souled, hearty rain storm, with pyrotechnic accompaniments that lit up the Virginia hills, and thunder that bellowed till Pope's Parrotts grew ashamed of themselves, and felt like crawling out of sight under their caissons. The Rappahannock is a highly susceptible stream, and the next morning, as the reinforcing torrents came dashing down from every mountain and hillock into her lap, her volume increased with such celerity and ease that her banks lost themselves in her vagrant waves, and her slender and graceful form bulged into lakes and muddy inundations. Fords were washed out of existence. Bridges yielded to the imperious necessities of the situation, and floated down the current, and our pious and exemplary young friend, Stonewall Jackson, was so overcome by the prospect yesterday morning, that a highly intelligent contraband, just in from Culpepper, (who had escaped by going around the river,) declares that in his ejaculations the Reverend rascal was little better than one of the wicked. The game of attacking Pope in a hurry was played out obviously. The two generals could sit and glare at each other at the sociable distance of half a dozen miles, but they could not lock horns until the Rappahannock got over its bender. "There was something between them," and, singularly enough, they could not fight till that was settled. So Stonewall may sit down and establish on his a side a dis-"Union Prayer meeting," while our young fellow citizen Pope (I was going to say Pio, but thought No, no!) can possess his soul in patience, and prepare a cordial welcome for his good friends, who, in coming to see him, bringing good cheer with them, with whom he can prepare for the merry and gentle games of the coming week.

It is a good lot of fellows that is going to picnic with Pope on the shelving shores of the Rappahannock river. Fitz John Porter, as handsome as brave, with a square solidity of head and intellect that makes success a necessity, has gone already. Heintzelman has gone from Alexandria, a quaint old gentlemen, in whose form the fires of valor and energy have burned out all but the merest framework which still is rugged and sinewy enough to last in activity through a hundred battles. And with him goes Philip Kearney, the thunderbolt, the one-armed demon of battle, the incarnate bravery, who hacked in desperate fury the lintels of the Bellham gate till a shower of grape blew his horse to fragments and shattered his left arm, a man who would any night leave a banquet for a battle, as better fun; and Hooker, who now wears the twin stars on his shoulder-strap, whom the accolade of the admiring Commander-in-Chief has named brave among the bravest, and other stout-hearted fellows, young and old, who are panting to snatch a glory from fate that no fault of theirs has delayed so long; men of courage, and intellect, and experience; men of a renown that has been and shall be. And Pope can now afford to wait for them.

I doubt myself when I find that I disagree with General Halleck, but it does seem that no good purpose can be subserved by keeping the loyal people of the North in ignorance of the state of their armies in Virginia. I can see the justice and propriety of exercising the strictest surveillance over the press, and punishing, in an exemplary manner, any premature or malicious publication of pending movements. But when a movement is safely accomplished, why should it not be known? When a crisis of danger is passed, and the army is free from an overhanging danger that had clouded all loyal minds, why should not the lightning's flash be permitted to dissipate that cloud from the hearts and hearthstones of the soldiers' friends? In New York yesterday, when the army of General Pope and the Government at Washington were rejoicing in the good news of present safety and speedy victory, a pall of panic terror hung over New York, and Government stocks went down with a run. Why should not General Halleck authorize a statement that all is well?

Newspapers are dumb and speechless over the arrival of the splendid new regiments that come in every day from the North. We people in Washington, who live near the Railroad Depot, alone enjoy the satisfaction of knowing that so much effective strength is added to our armies. They are coming in a strong and unceasing stream—the best men of the country. The rowdy element—all of them that would fight—went in long ago. The starving poor, the floating loafers, the excitable and shiftless, enlisted far earlier; but the men who are coming now are the sober, reputable citizens whom a stern sense of duty, long struggling with family and business cares, but at last triumphant, has drawn from their farms and their workshops to put down this accursed treason as soon as possible, and bring back peace to the land that war has so torn and desolated. I cannot help thinking the press should be allowed to make the most of this good news and these most cheering indications. General Halleck thinks differently, and the reason that the telegraph is silent about them, is that I am not a Commanding General and he is.[39]

WASHINGTON CORRESPONDENCE, 31 AUGUST 1862

You could scarcely find a gloomier city than Washington is to-day. The pleasurable excitement produced by the brilliant news of yesterday has given way to a feeling of despondency and gloom most depressing and universal. As unfounded as were yesterday's gratulations is to-day's panic. These volatile people swing like a pendulum from the extreme jubilation to that of despair in the shortest possible time. The rumored capture of Stonewall Jackson, yesterday, set the street wild, and the rumored defeat of Pope this morning caused every hotel and awning to hum with the dolorous utterances of frightened patriots, who dried their drenched umbrellas and croaked over the situation, careless of passing time and scornful of the church-inviting bells.

The news is certainly not the most hilarious that could be devised. On a fair day, perhaps, it would not create a very deep impression, but on a day like this, when every patch of sky has its own ominous and vaporous weft of boding cloud, when the last winds of summer sob audibly in the dim, damp air, and the rain falls in weakly and dispirited sprinklings, soaking and permeating all clothes and spoiling all tempers, a temporary reverse like that which has come to Pope is sufficient to cause a most disastrous seeming fall in the social barometer, and transform the jocund news-hunter into the lugubrious Cassandra.

At the end of three days' hard and incessant fighting, the enemy being heavily reinforced, and pressing on his left wing with irresistible fury, his men worn out with hard work and hunger, General Pope deems it proper to withdraw from the battle for a brief period, and halt his wearied columns at Centreville. He executes this movement with perfect success and safety, without losing a wagon or a gun. His men come off in good order. Not a straggler is reported on the road between here and Centreville. This is the whole extent of the reverse which has so terrified the town. Mr. Secretary Stanton, who seems of late to recognize as clearly as newspaper men have always done, the importance of letting the people know what their soldiers are doing, at once sent to the Associated Press of the country the official dispatches in which this new posture of affairs is announced, rightly judging that nothing would so soon and effectually allay all fear and excitement as the truth, however unwelcome or unpalatable it might at first appear.

To-day no firing is heard from the field of battle. This may indicate that the two armies are so worn out with the labors and toils of the last three bloody days that they are willing to lie quiet and breathe a little space; or it may be that the enemy, beginning to appreciate the determined valor of his opponent, is concerting means to go back whence he came through the Thoroughfare Gap; or he may be planning schemes of attack or surprise, the result of which we will soon see. The fear that fills most minds in Washington to-day is that while Pope lies at Centreville, a detachment of the enemy large enough for the purpose may hurriedly dash across the country to the Orange and Alexandria Railroad, and cut off Gen. Banks and his little force, who have not as yet joined the main body. Still, they have hitherto been willing on most occasions to give a pretty wide berth to the iron man of Waltham, and we hope that his usual energy and sagacity will save him now.

Meanwhile the army corps of Franklin and Sumner are marching steadily up to the support of Pope. These are the flower of the Potomac army—the very best fighting men we have. They have proved their metal on the bloody fields of Fair Oaks, and the enemy learned to fear them in that terrible slaughter of Malvern Hills. These will soon reach Pope, and will do yeoman's service in any contingency. Besides these we have in Washington, still in reserve, a very large quantity of fine fresh troops, in whom spirit and material will supply the place of experience. These are being prepared and sent rapidly forward.

Our hypothesis of yesterday's fight is most encouraging. An Aid-de-Camp of General Schenck, who accompanied the wounded General into Washington, reports that among the prisoners taken by us, the unwavering testimony was that the whole rebel army was engaged. There is nothing in the ascertained facts of the case to make such a statement improbable. In the second day's fighting it became necessary for General Pope to concentrate his forces as much as possible to prevent the risk of their being crushed in detail. This, of course, took Sigel and McDowell from the duty of watching the approaches to Thoroughfare Gap. Lee and Longstreet might thus easily have entered through that neglected avenue, and added their fresh troops to the tried masses of Jackson and Ewell. This would account for the temporary success of the enemy yesterday, and would also be a promise of the most favorable character to us. For if Pope, reinforced only by Fitz John Porter, was able to fight all day the whole rebel army of Virginia, it will be at once seen that when joined by Franklin and Sumner, he will have little difficulty in completing the work he has so well begun. As this supposition rests, however, upon the statements of rebel prisoners, a seasoning of allowance will not be out of place.

Whatever has been as yet gained or lost in this furious slaughter, one thing has certainly been demonstrated: the pluck and endurance of our army. They have fought against fearful odds, at a disadvantage of position, with insufficient subsistence, and not in one instance have they allowed the enemy to attack them. In every case they have begun the fight. It marks a new era in the war's history. The time of Shiloh, of Fair Oaks, and Somerset is passing. The time of audacity, energy, enterprise, initiation, is come. Let us honor the man who has inaugurated it in the East, even though in his character appear the blemishes of arrogance and pride and reckless daring. Let us mark with especial appreciation the day on which this warfare begins, even though it looms in history vague in the dense mists of blood and slaughter, and dark with the trailing shadows of disaster and defeat.[40]

WASHINGTON CORRESPONDENCE, 3 SEPTEMBER 1862

This morning witnesses a very lame and impotent conclusion to the campaign whose beginning was lately hailed with so proud acclaim when General Pope marched into Culpepper, with a proclamation of stirring eloquence and a prestige of uninterrupted victory. This morning the army lies on the other side of the Potomac stretched in a seedy-blue expanse from Upton's Hill to the Chain Bridge. They lie there, those tried heroes of a dozen battles fought in the last week, the relics of the firm and full battalia that so lately marched out of Washington, and the sadly thinned remnants of the Peninsular regiments who have renewed on the sod of the Bull Run Valley, the bloody enterprise that has consecrated the banks of the Chickahominy. They lie there this morning, but not the men who marched away with Pope, not the men that followed their tattered banners from the wasteful slaughter of the White Oak Swamps. Many, as yet only God knows how many, sleep well on the trampled turf of the frequent battle fields. The wide stretch of country from Warrenton to Fairfax Court House is one vast graveyard. Each foot of earth has its sanguine history. It has been the arena of a fight such as the world has not before seen, where the most warlike race of earth met and reveled in the ecstasy of fraternal homicide, and wreaked, each faction upon the other, the hate of the accumulating years. It is startling to survey the course of this recent fighting. For every day since the middle of August, this army of Pope's has been constantly fighting and maneuvering, and since last Wednesday, a week ago this morning, they have never been out of the immediate presence of the enemy. During this terrible week success has been variable, though generally with us. On Saturday, after a brilliant success the day before, their new reinforcements came up and handled us pretty roughly, but we recovered from it on Sunday, and on Monday were ready again to meet the rebels as coolly and confidently as ever.

Monday's battle seems to me the most extraordinary. The town had become considerably excited about the army by the incoherent and tremulous stories related by the cowardly poltroons that came into Willard's after the earlier battles, and believed the army was in a state of perfect demoralization and would fall to pieces on a vigorous attack. But on Monday a dispatch was received from General Pope, stating that he suspected the enemy of an intention to attempt to turn his right flank by a march on Fairfax Court House by way of the Little River turnpike, and adding that he would attack them as soon as their intentions were further developed. This had the true ring, and we waited with some anxiety to hear the result of the movement. The enemy appeared to move with very great caution, but as soon as he had fairly taken up his line of march for Fairfax Court House, Pope dispatched Reno after him. Reno met his advance at Chantilly, a little village on the turnpike, some three or four miles from the junction of the Warrenton and Little River pikes; and a sharp, short conflict took place about dusk, which raged furiously till nightfall, at which time Reno had driven the enemy back fully a mile, and had entirely baffled the purpose of his movement, which was undoubtedly to gain possession of our vast commissary and ammunition stores which were at Fairfax Court House, and at the station on the Orange and Alexandria road. This, considering all the circumstances, was the most remarkable battle of the week. It was fought under depressing circumstances; our army was somewhat dispirited by hard work and heavy losses; they were in an unfavorable position and much exposed; they were hungry, and wet, and tired. Yet they attacked their fresh and powerful enemy on his own line of march, and beat him.

It was, however, at a terrible cost. We are said to have lost 1,600 in killed and wounded, and what was equivalent to the annihilation of two small armies—we lost Isaac J. Stevens and Phil Kearney.

Stevens was a man of great brain and great physical energy. Thoroughly educated and accomplished, eloquent and persuasive in oratory, courteous and affable in manner, of cool, calm and determined bravery, he was a man of whom his friends prophesied great things, and all who met him believed in his future. He was unfortunately placed under the command of General Benham in that useless slaughter on James Island, and the recriminations that grew out of the wretched business have to some extent unfavorably affected his reputation. But the Government exhibited its appreciation of Stevens and its opinion of the merits of that particular case in dispute, by ordering General Benham to duty as Major of Engineers, and placing General Stevens in command of the division which was brought from the Department of the South to take part in the overland trip to Richmond. He did well here as everywhere. Sometime when his life comes to be written, you will see what manner of man the country has lost in him.

But Kearney everybody knew, and everybody admired as the incarnation of desperate and splendid valor. In every fight on the Peninsula his form flashed superbly through the battle scene—a one-armed Chevalier more splendid in his maimed grotesqueness than any other in his perfection—holding the bridle reins in his teeth and brandishing his saber in his only hand—an object of intense interest and fear to the enemy, and of admiration, in which awe was mingled, to his own men. For though Kearney was idolized by his men, they feared him as well. "There was no straggling in our division"—one of the soldiers said yesterday, "I pity the skulking fellow that fell in the way of that blood-hound Kearney. He would whip them into the ranks with the flat of his sword." The soldiers say that in the wild rage of battle he laid open the skull of a mutinous coward who broke out of the ranks and ran from a bayonet charge.

Kearney was one of those splendid fighting men, whom all ages produce rarely and grudgingly, who love fighting for its own sake. In every clime he has fought, and every where he was the same magnificent personification of the very spirit of battle. In Algiers he fought as a private: he, the opulent proprietor of a princely income. When Garibaldi drew the sword for the liberation of Italy, Kearney flew to his side and served upon his staff. When our wars began he left the pleasures of Paris, which in peace he never slighted, and came home to throw his sword into the scale of the endangered nationality.

Kearney never impressed me as a man that would be killed. It seemed to me always that the invisible powers that guard the bravest in battle would never let him be marred by another bullet. I have never believed the frequent rumors of his death. I could not to-day, till the rumor faded in the fact. But, strangely enough, the surgeons say that no wound appears upon him. He lies in proud repose, unscathed by treason. In the moment of his finest triumph his great heart burst in grateful and patriotic joy, and his virile soul sped up to its God, where, let us hope, it may rest! It never rested here.

If there be found those who would tear the decorous veil from the dead hero's private life, let them forbear. He is Freedom's now and Fame's. His robust faults were better than the weakly virtues of those who would malign him.

304

After the fight of Monday, our troops were not further troubled in their march to Washington. Late last night they arrived within our lines of fortifications, and at once began the work of reorganizing and preparing for the battles that are soon to come.[41]

WASHINGTON CORRESPONDENCE, 7 SEPTEMBER 1862

This is positively the last Sunday under the old order of things that Washington shall ever see. We have gotten into the habit of saying that the capital cannot be taken, of referring to the impregnability of those ungainly earthworks that deform the circumference of the town; and from the constant iteration has come a sort of languid assurance, which has never been more manifest than now. When the enemy were maneuvering against Pope on the Rappahannock, and further back, when Stonewall Jackson was rushing invincible through the Shenandoah, driving the army corps of Banks under the guns of Harper's Ferry, there was some little uneasiness as to the safety of Washington. Timid men began to send their wives to the North, and shortly after to follow them, and the throng of office-seekers began gravely to consider that there was better work in the world than hanging upon the favor of great men, and that they had better go back to their neglected business and affectionate families. The plethora of the hotels was thus depleted, and people worked for a few days undisturbed by the swarms of these ravenous and most unlovely creatures.

This time, however, the exodus does not seem to follow the announcement that the enemy is at our gates. No one seems to think the city is unsafe, though Jackson and Johnson lie in force at Frederick, and the road is open and unobstructed to Washington. Perhaps the sight of the truculent looking fleet of gunboats that sit so calmly confident upon the river's breast below the city has something to do with this unusual fortitude. Perhaps the Northern people have had their sensibilities so blunted with the disgraces and humiliations of the past fortnight, that they are past sensations, and the Southern people don't care who rules so long as their rents come in and "profits do accrue." Some desperate patriots loudly hope that Washington may be destroyed. Our interesting young friend Mr. Wendell Phillips, in a recent convocation of long-haired and dirty-shirted brethren at Abington, expressed the Christian aspiration, that in the coming bombardment some stray shot might take off the head of Lincoln and place in his stead the more progressive and more liberal Hamlin. "Progressive," in the lunatic New England phrase, meaning "hopelessly wedded to old superstitions," and "liberal" meaning utterly bigoted and narrow, and incapable of seeing good outside of your own sphere of thought and action. At this sentiment, all the long-haired and dirty-shirted disciples applauded, and the hall was filled with the enthusiastic bouquet of Weathersfield onions.

Other wild maniacs have a vague and indefinite idea that the sack of Washington would unite the North; that on its fall will come the renaissance of public spirit; that from its ashes will flutter with wings new plumed the regenerate form of the American eagle. Many loose talkers say this, and some possibly believe it. It is a very good instance of the absurd vagaries into which an indolent and unchecked habit of sentimentality will lead masses of the people. It must be admitted, that from the beginning of this war, Washington has been to us a great element of weakness. It has kept thousands of good men at work, excavating trenches and piling earthworks, and thousands more watching them when excavated and piled, while the enemy had no such incubus upon their energies. But this drain upon our strength has been at the bidding of strong necessity. Whatever other disasters might arise, might possibly be repaired, the loss of Washington never could be. It would be virtually the beginning of the end of the war. With such evidence of strength and muniment of power, how could the enemy fail of recognition and friendly alliance abroad? We would find the whole world about our ears. The jealous hate of England would be changed into the bitterness of contempt, and she would at once prepare, in her cowardly joy, to put out of the way the nightmare of her evil imaginings for eighty years. France, though not malignant, is selfish, and will not hesitate to insult a falling nationality and greet kindly a rising one. We shall find no friends in the Congress of Nations, but all eyes will look at us coldly askance. Washington cannot be taken and the nation live.

And as I do not believe the death-bell of the nation has struck as yet, I do not believe that Washington is to be taken. Trusting to that, I give myself no thought of this town, but look to see what our army will do in their work of defeating and destroying this audacious detachment of rebels who have crossed so boldly into Maryland. It is an eternal blight and shame to every General and every private in the National army, if those half-starved rogues ever get back to Virginia alive. Our men are fresh, vigorous, healthy, well fed, well armed, perfectly equipped. Their rations are more than any man can eat, their marches have been short and easy, their clothing is comfortable, neat and soldierly. They are fighting in the best cause that ever blessed a banner. They have the proudest memories to cheer them; they have the best blood of the world running in their Saxon veins. They are opposed by a half-starved rabble, disorderly and miserable, perishing with disease and famine, gaunt, ragged and filthy, fired with whisky and fanatic hate, and led by perjured rebels and traitors. They subsist on what they can steal, and prepare in the intervals of their long and ruinous marches, wherein men drop dead by the wayside, the sharp stones are crimsoned with the blood of bare-footed wretches, the moanings of disease and misery resound through the army, and still the column marches to its aim, inflexible as death. These starving wretches, these feculent and malodorous scarecrows, defeated our fat and natty soldiers last week.

It was not cowardice that beat our troops. There was no panic in all those days. Men fought gloriously and continuously, as long as there was an officer to command them, or an object to fight for. And when they had done their share of the fighting they would file to the rear in perfect order, no man breaking step. It is the crowning shame and horror of the war, that we lost causelessly and wantonly those decisive battles. We were superior in numbers, in arms, in discipline, in everything but energy and morale.

It tempts one to go with those bilious and earnest radicals who say, "The rebels are fighting for an idea, and we are not." They say, "We will be independent," and we say, "You shall not." The negative of a question is always the weakest, and always will be while force is greater than weakness. Perhaps the time is coming when the President, so long forbearing, so long suffering with the South and the border, will give the word long waited for, which will breathe the life that is needed, the fire that seems extinguished, in the breasts of our men at arms.

If we are not gloriously victorious before the frosts of October redden the leaves, with their falling will fall our hopes and the hopes of liberty in the world.[42]

WASHINGTON CORRESPONDENCE, 22 SEPTEMBER 1862

There has probably never been a ruler who in times of such deep public excitement, has so long and successfully maintained an attitude of dignified reticence as has Abraham Lincoln, in the two years that have elapsed since his election. Especially for the last six months, he has been alternately the target of extremists from the North and the border, each charging him with faithlessness to principles and a weak subservience to the influence of the other. He has been equally unmoved by the eloquent fury of the inspired maniac, Wendell Phillips, and the impotent malignity that oozed from the withered lips of Gov. Wickliffe. Thaddeus Stevens might speak bitterness and disappointment, in his place in the House of Representatives, and the President would never allude to it. Ben Wood might print the seditious utterances that he lacked wit to write, and the President never thought of it. The border States might form in solemn procession, and invade the Executive mansion; he gave them no assurances of any safety, save that they could find in the sure leeway of emancipation. The Progressive Friends might attack him in force, blazing upon him in the gorgeous costume of the shadbellied dandies, but he only told them that he had thought of that subject more than they, and they must wait his time and the Lord's.

He had the best possible reasons for his reticence. He was not undecided, apathetic or stubborn in the matter. He knew that, in the first place, the contest in which we are engaged is the one unique of its kind, without precedents or analogies in history. Its character shifts with the shifting seasons; its complexion changes with the staining leaves. He knew that any declaration of opinion which he might publicly make would be rendered obsolete by the progress of events before it had reached the newer States. Secondly, his utterances would instantly form an issue upon which would divide and fiercely fight those who were now most strongly united in the defense of the Union. While the contest could be better carried on without an executive pronunciamento, the President thought best to keep silent.

Yet, even at that time, he spoke freely and frankly in regard to the great questions that agitated the minds of all good people, in conversation with those who had a right to his confidence, either from official position or known discretion. Once or twice he clearly and strongly defined his position in set remarks to the Cabinet, once to the men of the Border States, several times to Senatorial and Representative delegations. His confidence was generally, but not always, worthily bestowed. On one occasion, talking with Harlan, of Iowa, and Pomeroy, of Kansas, he discussed the question of slavery with great freedom. Soon after, an utterly false report of the conversation appeared in the *Cincinnati Gazette,* which stated that one of the Senators had said, "I wish to God you would resign, Mr. President, and let Mr. Hamlin try it."

Absurd as this lie was, it was generally copied and some people believed it. The bad taste of the insolent remark is no proof that it was not uttered, but its unparalleled impudence is too much for even the brazen cheek of the Senator, who is supposed to have invented it while thinking over the incidents of the conversation, under the mild inspiration of the reporter's whisky. The other day, Wilkinson, of Minnesota, went—sober—to the executive mansion, and talked with the President soberly about the Indian massacres. In the afternoon he met the bilious and ill-conditioned arrangement that does the correspondence of the *Evening Post,* and in that day's letter of this latter worthy, appeared the statement that a "distinguished Northwestern Senator had gone to the President and told him the people of the Northwest had lost all confidence in him." Now, Wilkinson was known to be sober *in the morning,* and so, of course, said nothing of the kind.

The programme of the President, as shown by several of the best-considered utterances mentioned above, seemed to be as follows:

1. To carry on the war, in such a way as to make it to the interest of the people of the rebellious States to forsake their ambitious and wicked leaders and to return to their allegiance. Judicious severity was to be employed with this view, so that life should be more comfortable under national rule than in a state of rebellion. Where distinctions of treatment were to be made, they were to be made most decidedly in favor of Unionists, and against rebels.

2. Not to return to slavery those slaves who fall necessarily into our hands in the course of the war—not to entice them in, nor to incite them to rise, but not to use the National arms in any case to return them to their masters, at the same time to compensate loyal owners for losses thus sustained.

3. A liberal system of colonization to be adopted—not in any sense compulsory, but in the interest of both blacks and their former owners, this being a sort of corollary to the preceding point.

4. To use all possible means to induce the border States to adopt the eminently just and liberal policy of gradual emancipation. This is the object nearest the President's heart. He considers it the only way of dignity and safety for the Border States. Slavery has received its death-blow in the house of its friends. He wishes the loyal States of the Border to free themselves from the contagion while they may with both honor and profit. The nation will not be so able and willing to assist them, after several more years of debilitating war, as now.

5. The President has always favored a reasonable confiscation act, by which the property of rebels should be made to pay a large portion of the expense of their rebellion. He favored also the granting of a pretty wide executive discretion of amnesty and exemption.

6. He still holds to that provision of the Chicago platform prohibiting slavery in the territories and willingly signed the bill for that purpose.

7. He was in favor, finally, at the close of the war when it should be closed by the suppression of the rebellion, of restoring the Union as it was and maintaining the Constitution as it is. The radical measures proposed by many, of utterly abolishing existing forms of government and trying out of that chaos to evolve a form which might possibly be better, never met with any countenance of favor from him. His highest hope has been the restoration of the Old Union, as founded by men who understood the theory of government perhaps as well as we, which made us proud and happy and prosperous for eighty-five years, and would have maintained us always so, but for one disturbing element in our political system.

Such, I have good reason to believe, was the attitude of the President up to a recent period. How earnestly and sincerely he has labored to do his whole duty in this regard, and with what wonderful success he has met, in forming and guiding the public opinion which he seemed all the while to follow and obey, the world has recognized and history will record. Especially is due to him the love and gratitude of the loyal Border Slave States. He has been their champion in the court where he himself presided. He has stood up, at times, almost alone in the Government and acted with promptness and energy in preserving from what he deemed unconstitutional and illegal attack, the institution to which every impulse of his heart, every thought of his mind, was abhorrent. Frémont was his trusted General. He annulled his acts, which were done in the interest of freedom. Hunter was his intimate and life-long friend. He repudiated his proclamation against the clamors of nearly his whole party. He has stood between slavery and those who would destroy it, as a strong and steadfast bulwark, waiting, hoping, praying to God that the Border States would read the signs of the times that the National arms would prevail, that the maniacy of treason would give way to the truth and the light of returning loyalty.

Yet the contest continues. The costliest blood of the nation is poured out like water in wasteful devotion on every battle-plain. The national finances tremble with the terrible strain of our unnumbered outlays. The shock of our lingering conflict convulses the world; and the world looks on amazed and wonders why the keenest and brightest and deadliest weapon in the whole arsenal of justice still hangs suspended over the weakest joint in the armor of red-handed and defiant treason.

The President determines the stroke shall be delayed no longer. He has withheld it as long as seemed to him just or expedient. We do not seem to advance as rapidly as we should. Some new step must be taken. This seems the best one possible. To-night, as I write, the Proclamation of the President, Commander-in-Chief of the Army and the Navy, by virtue of that authority that lies without question in him, the exercise of which by subordinates he has so jealously forbidden, flashes over the wires to every quarter of our waiting land, declaring that the Government has done with leniency or paltering with murderous traitors, and has given them but one more opportunity for repentance and safety.

If they reject this, let their ruin rest upon their own heads.[43]

Washington correspondence, 25 September 1862

Last night a demonstration took place which, considering the time and the latitude, was perfectly marvelous. The first loud and emphatic token of approval which the President's most recent and most momentous proclamation has received, has taken place in the City of Washington, among a population always opposed to radical measures, always, until within a limited period, devoted to the interests of slavery. If this may be taken as an earnest of the feeling of the average masses in the loyal States, the safety of the Union becomes at once a fixed fact, and the hands of the Government are strengthened to do and to dare all things. For a people who are so devoted to the best interests of the Government as to look on with approval, while that Government, to save its own life, strikes at their most cherished prejudices, and convictions are capable of any and everything which a righteous cause may demand. For such sacrifices there must be co-equal triumphs. The spirit of utter loyalty and self-abnegation which inspired the crowd of last night, moulds into forms of enduring valor and unceasing effort the mind and heart of a people determined to be free, and to preserve their liberties from all assaults of foreign attack or domestic treason. The nation will be stronger than ever before, if it stands unmoved the shock of the President's proclamation. With what breathless anxiety will the eye of the patriot watch for the earliest responses from Missouri and Kentucky. Maryland is entirely safe in all contingencies. The *Baltimore American,* a most earnest, intelligent and enterprising journal, takes the irrefragable position that this issue has been forced upon the nation by the traitors, and they have only themselves to blame. The *Clipper* says little for and nothing against the proclamation. The *Sun,* which has ceased to shine save as a luminary of news, says of course nothing. I should very much like to write the leading editorial for that able contemporary. If the leading editor gets a good salary, he certainly has all day to spend it in. Yet people wait in great anxiety to hear from the Western border. Little anxiety is felt for Missouri; her loyalty is considered above stain. Not so Kentucky. Though the Union men of that State have in great part outgrown that loyalty which makes conditions for its existence, the factious and uneasy spirit of rebellion is far from being yet thoroughly extinguished. Some of the best men of Kentucky have within a very short time assured the President that while they consider the emancipation policy for the present inexpedient, they were confident that whatever might be done with the negro, the loyalty of Kentucky was secure. Yet we cannot forget that Mr. Wickliffe lives in Kentucky and has been elected to Congress, and that, therefore, there must be men of his way of thinking in his district at least. So the country waits with some anxiety for the response of that powerful State.

There was no doubt about the feeling that animated the floating population of Washington last night. They collected in large numbers at Brown's Hotel and moved up the Avenue, keeping time to the music of the Marine Band, and halted before the white columns of the portico of the Executive Mansion, standing lucid and diaphanous in the clear obscure like the architecture of a dream. The crowd flowed in and filled every nook and corner of the grand entrance as instantly and quietly as molten metal fills a mould. The portico was filled, the pedestals of the outer columns were crowded; eager hands clung to the spikes of the iron railings, and an adventurous crowd clambered over the gates and dropped into the basement area. The band burst into a strain of stirring and triumphant harmony, and as it closed, the tall President appeared at the window. He said only half a dozen words, but his voice was full of an earnest solemnity, and there was something of unusual dignity in his manner. He seemed to think he had placed himself sufficiently clearly on the record, and his acts should be justified by results and not by argument. He bade the crowd good night, and while they were clamoring for more speech, he entered a carriage in waiting at a side door, accompanied by Mr. Hay, his Secretary, and drove through the shouting throng unnoticed to the Soldier's Home.

At Governor Chase's, however, we had more talking. The Secretary himself said little, but said it with singular felicity. He is a very statuesque sort of man. He is never ungraceful—never out of place. He has a habit of always appearing well, and at ease. His sentences in his most careless utterances, come out in chrystallized forms—bright, polished and cold. Thoroughly honest, and devoted to his principles, with an earnestness which borders on enthusiasm, he is never passionate in his utterances, never fervid in his manner. His very coldness is the coldness of the iceberg, not of the avalanche. His convictions, though powerful, never enslave his reason; they only add weight and force to his processes of thought, and stamp his deductions with the seal of purpose. Last night he, like the President, seemed to think that a great work had been done, whose best commentary would be the progress of events. He believed in it thoroughly, but preferred to let his reasons for belief be developed by the logic of the immediate future.

General [*Cassius M.*] Clay, who followed him, had no scruples against freeing his mind to the fullest extent on this particular act and the general issue. He launched into a lively and energetic harangue, which pleased the crowd immensely, who were delighted at finding at last, after an evening's search, a man who would talk. One enthusiastic auditor, of a financial turn, who evidently preferred the General's style of talk to the Secretary's, said "he liked Cash better than old Treasury notes," which, striking a sympathetic chord in his neighborhood, was received with applause which would have disconcerted any orator but the unabashed Cassius.

He made a good speech. He was particularly happy in the manner and style in which he paid his respects to the hypocrisy and greed which has characterized England in this war. This is a matter which has sunk deeper into the hearts of Abolitionists than any other. The treachery and meanness which was discovered in the British character when the world saw plainly that their century's abuse of slavery meant simply hatred and jealousy of the Union, was a surprise such as one rarely sees in the *denouement* of the most improbable farce. General Clay thought that even the mouth of England would be closed in very shame by the President's Proclamation, but General Clay is sanguine England will become honest and decent when Parson Brownlow turns Locofoco.

If the spirit of the people of this mixed population can be taken as an earnest of that of the country at large, the augury is most cheering. What most particularly pleased the vast audience last night, was not the fiery apostrophe to the Genius of Universal Freedom, but the calculation of probable profit in which Clay indulged. The emancipation of the non-slaveholding white population of the South, upon which he most specially dwelt as the result of the President's action, seemed to be received with more cordial and intelligent assent than any other proposition advanced. If this people have been educated by the fiery discipline of the last two years into capacity for making this enormous and momentous change in their social system, without wrack or ruin, the Great Republic has passed from the realm of experiment, and has taken an assured and everlasting place in history.[44]

WASHINGTON CORRESPONDENCE, 30 SEPTEMBER 1862

It seems to-day from the long lines of soldiers that go filing through the streets that we may soon expect some news. We have to a great extent overcome those early habits of sending divisions on railroad excursions and back without object or result. Now when we see a movement of troops we infer that it means something. Whatever the fighting qualities of General Halleck may be, there is no question that he understands theoretically the science of strategy better than any man in America. His combinations are always wise and sagacious, and if his instruments were always well chosen he would never be unsuccessful.

The troops are now going to General McClellan. The Commander of the army of the Potomac has a monomania for massing troops. If you were to give him a million, he would find a place where just another regiment was absolutely essential, and say he could not fight till he got it. Even in his last campaign, where under the spur of recent occurrences, he acted with more energy and vigor than ever before, I am informed there was not a day in which he did not appeal to General Halleck for more men, alleging that the enemy was largely superior to him in his front.

Yet the official reports of the rebels assert that they had in all but 60,000 men, (exactly the number, by the way, that Gen. Sigel always contended they had), while our force was nearly twice that. It is true, they had greatly the advantage of position, but even with that, we whipped them out of every field, and they only escaped into Virginia by our kind permission. The rout and demoralization which was alleged to exist in their ranks has unhappily not yet made its appearance. When it comes the enemy will have suffered by the Maryland campaign, and we will have gained something. Until then, honors are easy.

General McClellan unquestionably shows very great and very useful qualities on occasion, and when we begin to hope that the cloud has passed from him, and that we have found at last a chief whom we can trust, some act of singular meaning, which may be carelessness, indolence or indecision, dashes the brimming chalice of hope from our lips, and we resume our weary search for a leader.

After the sacrifice of Pope, the soldiers, their hearts heavy with defeat and disappointment, clamored for McClellan. The Government knew that he, better than any man living, could bring that beaten army into order again. He did more in two days than most men could have done in as many months. His success was instant and marvelous. It vindicated the action of the President, which had been taken in the face of strong remonstrances. And when the reorganized army was to be led against the enemy, who, maddened by unexpected success, and tempting fate, had crossed into Maryland, there seemed no better man at hand to lead them than McClellan. He marched against the enemy, and, for the first time in his history, attacked him. He beat him, of course, and pursued him to Antietam. There he again attacked and again defeated him. Then, while all the world looked on and cried, "Bravo! God bless you, General," he sat absolutely motionless on the field of battle, not sending out a picket nor firing a gun till the beaten and routed enemy had safely crossed the Potomac, and the work of the year was to be begun at the beginning again.

People are bewildered, and do not know how to look at these things. Conjecture runs riot and flowers into ridiculous and outrageous slanders of treachery, cowardice, K[*nights of the*] G[*olden*] C[*ircle*], and other wretched offshoots of ignorance and prejudice. A man who calls General McClellan a coward or a traitor—and there are many who do—is either a fool or a knave. He is thoroughly brave and thoroughly patriotic. In every fibre of his being and every impulse of his soul he desires nothing but victory and honorable peace for his country. Even the wretched squabbles which his partisans indulge in over his reputation and those of his brother officers find no support or countenance in him.

I know no better patriot or truer gentleman than George B. McClellan. But there are acts of his which I cannot understand, except upon the supposition of an inherent vice of mind, often the accompaniment of great organizing power, which makes him *never ready to act*. The whole power and energy of his nature seems to be devoted to *making* armies, not *using* them. He has too clear and distinct ideas of the wants of an army, too accurate a conception of its deficiencies. He works and toils unceasingly to bring an army to a pitch of perfection which can never be reached, and in the meanwhile, a ragged, half-starved, miserable mob of filthy and disorderly wretches, who know how to move, and having nothing but their legs, move fast, outmarches and outgenerals him.

Who compares, for instance, Stonewall Jackson with McClellan—the shaggy, unkempt fanatic with the chivalrous and accomplished soldier? At West Point, Jackson was a blundering, awkward, stupid booby, the butt of his class; McClellan was the admiration and pride of his. In the army, Jackson was a failure, and resigned because he felt himself incapable. McClellan stood higher than any man of his age, and left the army to better his position. They entered this war, the one obscure, indigent, awkward, unconscious of great merit, and for a great while unsuccessful, the other with a great name, the idol of the country, the trusted chief commander of our armies. Stonewall Jackson has done nothing well; he has always blundered and floundered around, killing his horses and wearing out his men, making bold dashes without aim or object, gaining successes which were worthless, and positions which he instantly gave up, and acting constantly in defiant ignorance of the rules of military science. McClellan, on the contrary, has done everything well that he has done; he has never made a positive blunder, he has never once offended against the masters who have written of war. But out of Jackson's audacious follies and aimless blundering energy, has grown success and honor to the rebel arms, while our careful and scientific strategy has landed us, after a year's hard fighting, at the place where we began.

With all this the spirit in Washington at this time is hopeful. I mention this to show how elastic is human nature. We hope that from the movements of this week will come great store of victory and honor, that General Mc-

Clellan and the brave men who go with him, and whose trust is in him, may succeed in every undertaking. If industry, courage, and undaunted patriotism can accomplish good results, we are sure of these in McClellan. For all things else, let us follow him with our hopes and prayers.[45]

Washington correspondence, 1 October 1862

As a recent act of the President dismissing from the service of the United States an officer, for words spoken in conversation, is exciting a good deal of remark, the true version of the matter may as well be given, although a comparatively unimportant affair, it is not destitute of a certain significance.

Major John J. Key, Additional Aid de Camp to General Halleck, and brother of Col. T. M. Key, Judge Advocate upon the Staff of Gen. McClellan, said, in answer to the question propounded to him by another officer, "Why were not the rebels bagged by McClellan after the battle of Antietam?"—"That is not the game. The object is for the two armies to keep the field as long as possible, neither gaining any decisive advantage, until both are tired out, and a compromise may be made by which we can save slavery."

This shameful utterance was reported to the President. He sent a message to Major Key, through Mr. Hay, his secretary, requesting that he would, within twenty-four hours, disprove the charges of having made the above remark.

Major Key answered the summons by bringing to the Executive office the officer to whom he had made this exposition of his principles. But instead of disproving the utterance of the statement, he proceeded to justify it. He said he thought that slavery was a divine institution, and any issue in this conflict that did not save it would be disastrous.

The President told him that any discussion of the question of slavery was irrelevant to the matter in hand. "You may think about that as you please," he continued, "but no man shall bear a commission of mine, who is not in favor of gaining victories over the rebels, at any and all times. You can go, sir." He immediately ordered him dismissed from the service.

This has been the first public utterance of a spirit that has long been known to exist in the ranks of the army in regard to the war—a spirit though not disloyal, still lacking utterly that spirit of uncompromising energy without which no war can be successful. In this case, especially, such expressions called for immediate and exemplary punishment.

The Major spoken of was a member of General Halleck's staff. His brother is the most intimate confidential adviser of General McClellan. It would be thought by every one that he reflected the sentiments of his brother, to whom he owes his appointment. This, of course, could not be permitted. It would be a daily disgrace to the Government to permit an officer to wear its uniform, eat its bread, and avow himself opposed to the army winning decisive victories. Politics are very well in their way, but when they carry a man so far as this, they had better carry him a little farther, and carry him out of the army.

Of course nobody accuses General McClellan of this sort of thing; nobody at least but a set of radical and impracticable men who are determined to see no good in him. General McClellan unquestionably wants to whip the rebels decisively and finally. But the fact is becoming irresistibly ascertained that a large number of his most bitter partisans hold opinions identical with those whose indiscreet utterance brought Major Key to grief. They use the great and popular name of the General as an all embracing mantle to cover their own multitude of sins. They try to hide and obscure the question really at issue by blowing clouds of sophistry around it, and raising a great dust of "Abolition," "Horace Greeley," "Damn John Brown." All this—as Pelissier said at Balaklava—may be very magnificent, but it is not war. A soldier whose devotion to a played-out political principle leads him to disloyalty or even luke-warmness towards his own Government, and who, in his eager anxiety for the safety of his hobby, takes no thought of the honor of his country's arms, has evidently mistaken his sphere, and should be at once remanded to the position in the political machinery of his ward or county, for which Providence designed him, and from which a boyish fancy for shoulder straps has for the time beguiled him.

It is to be hoped that the example of the luckless Major, who was only more indiscreet than others, will result in good to those ardent young persons who garrison Willard's, and evade the liquor ordinance in quiet places of the Capital. Striking him down may silence others like him, as a stone dropped into the noisiest frog pond will reduce to instant reticence the whole batrachian orchestra.

People are gloomy here over the death of General Nelson. He was well known in Washington as a brave, hearty, proud, honorable man, not without a certain offensive vanity and arrogance of manner, and with a style of address contracted by years of rough sea service. The President was his especial friend. His bluff heartiness and geniality of manner, which to his superiors was tempered by deference and respect, was very engaging. He was a wonderful talker. His experience had been very varied, and his fund of anecdote and reminiscence was inexhaustible. He was a man of a warm and generous nature, and of a lively and versatile mind. He was one of the best officers of his rank in the navy, and he stepped at once from ship-board into camp, as if his life had been spent in the army.

He did a work in Kentucky which few man could have done as well. He went there in the days when the State was trembling in the delusive balance of avowed neutrality, and with little assistance from the Government, further than the mere furnishing of arms, he organized the Union men into a defensive guard, and gave the crushed and cowed spirit of loyalty something to live by. He organized the first camp in the State, as the spirit of resistance to rebel arrogance grew stronger, and succeeded admirably in those fighting counties of Garrard and Rockcastle. He was a Kentuckian, and hated an Abolitionist. He had many feelings in common with the men he influenced. He was the right man in the right place.

His subsequent history in the war has been full of the alternate lights and shades of his character. He has acted with undaunted and desperate bravery in every action, and his avenging sword has hung like a baleful meteor over the head of the coward and the skulker from his own ranks. An officer who has been reprimanded coarsely by this General for misconduct will not feel kindly towards him for a while, and a dastardly scoundrel whose scalp is bleeding from his General's saber, will not bless the hand that smote him. In this and other ways, many stories have arisen which have sullied the fair fame which Nelson took to the West. But no man can stand by his grave and deny that there lies a true patriot, a gallant soldier, and a generous man.[46]

Washington correspondence, 20 October 1862

In spite of the slow sinking of currency and the collapse of credit, in spite of the faineant army that still hangs as if fixed by a spell of glamour on the Virginian hills, in spite of the low and ominous murmurs that come up from the stay-at-home populations of the Northern States, in spite of the general flavor of bad meaning that pervades the air, and unhealthily permeates the thoughts and serious speeches of men, Washington is now jollier than ever before. The elastic good humor of this city is something very surprising. From abroad, this town is looked upon as the centre of a world's excitement, and people think how powerful must be the turmoil and trouble of the fountain, when streams of so sanguine a color have their origin there. Our cousins in the country imagine that all our talk is of affairs of state; that we take a course of political economy with our morning muffins; that at dinner we discuss soup and strategy together, and that we drink no tea but gunpowder.

I believe there is no people in the North that apparently cares so little for the result of this fight, as the heterogeneous multitude that inhabits this vast caravanserai. I have seen nowhere since the miserable war began, a people so volatile, so pleasure-loving, so nonchalant, as that which forms the population of Washington to-day. The vast influx of busy life that has followed the new wants and exigencies of these novel times, brings with it a demand for means of enjoyment and recreation that never before existed here. The result is seen in several strange and daring innovations. A thrill of horror ran through the staid and prim circles of the resident population, when the course of abolition lectures was announced to be given in the Smithsonian Institution. The echoes of the lecture hall which had been dozing for years, never more than half aroused by the drowsy utterances of the white headed fogies of science, started madly from their crypts when Cheever thundered his hot anathemas against the powers that be, and the eloquent tongue of Phillips launched its bolts of splendid maniacy. The pristine peace will never come back to that lecture room. The charm of silence is broken there forever.

And concerts came and went away with postage stamps galore. And the mob of "Professors" with a cosmopolitan assortment of names and brogues came swarming in upon the scene. One enthusiastic Gaul advertised very extensively a course of lectures upon French literature. He delivered the beginning of the first to a select audience of two, consisting of himself and the doorkeeper. He went away in a blasphemous frame of mind. Professor Phineas Taylor Barnum has run away from the draft in New York, and brought with him his abridged editions of the "Essay on Man," whom he calls Thumb and Nutt—General and Commodore. One would think there were dwarfs enough in Washington already. The Concert Halls which have been driven from New York have also found rest in the Metropolis for the soles of their feet, and swarms of young heroes air their virgin uniforms nightly in these "Halls of Mirth and Melody," as I believe the gushing young person who does their posters calls them. They make the night hideous and the sidewalks a nuisance with the brass-banditti, whose doleful strains drag on as by some horrible fascination a motlier crowd of "Canterbury Pilgrims" than those that Chaucer wrote of.

Yet this scum and froth that floats upon the surface of this wave of pleasure-seeking life developed by the novel conditions of society in Washington, is not the only result we find. The intellectual activity and appreciation awakened by the stirring times, and the impulse thus given to the dramatic art in this city, is something upon which we residents can most heartily congratulate ourselves. It has always been the most difficult thing in the world to keep a theatre alive here. The dead apathy that seemed to becloud the minds of the people as with a fall of Beotian density, prevented any successful efforts in this direction. The art which has been in all ages the test of popular culture, languished and sickened here. Its vital flame came near going quietly out in the early days of the reign of Abraham I, when the "star-spangled banner" was hissed, and the sleepy dozens would only applaud Dixie or the Marseillaise.

But all this is bravely changed. An enterprising manager named Grover, bought a circus, turned out the horses and turned in Setchell, who makes people laugh, and, therefore, deserves well of the Republic. Mr. Ford, seeing the path to usefulness lay in the same direction, entered a Baptist Church, kicked out the Deacons, and made private boxes of their stalls, and with commendable despatch cushioned the mortified pews into comfort, and consecrated the temple anew to Thalia.

Ford's Theatre has been, during the last month, the scene of a most brilliant dramatic triumph, one which does as much honor to the audience as to the artist. Miss Maggie Mitchell, whose name has been for a few years well known to theatre goers, as that of a bright, vivacious, and dashing young girl, with fine eyes and a pretty mouth, great *aplomb,* and a perfect knowledge of stage business, who could sustain with ease an indefinite number of impossible characters in the course of an evening, and whose performances, though perfect in their kind, were without use or purpose, appeared early in September, in the character of "Fanchon, the Cricket." She was unheralded except by a reported success in New York; no arts of puffing were resorted to; the Theatre was in an out-of-the-way street, and the town was deeply interested in other things.

Yet never was there a success more instant and decided. Her wonderful personation of the elfish witch-child of the mountains, with a beautiful nature, turned momentarily awry by the world's unkindness, brought by a true love out of the shadows of early neglect and abandonment to the light and beauty of perfect womanliness, touched the hearts and compelled the admiration of all who saw it—The wild and startling grace of the Moonlight Dance with her shadow—the simple pathos and modest dignity of her dialogue with her peasant lover in the gathering twilight—the winning and most lovable charm that surrounds her at the close of the triumphant struggle with her little world's hard opinion—were delineated with that exquisite naturalness which we thought had vanished from the American stage. It is a picture which combines ideal grace with pre-Raphaelite finish and realism.

It indicates no ordinary moral courage for so young an artist as Miss Mitchell to enter at once upon a path before almost untrodden, to turn from Protean farces to a five-act drama of domestic life, to throw her past behind her, and venture alone upon a higher future. Her success is a voice of cheer to American art. It proves that there is nothing so foolish as for actors to think of playing *down* to their audiences. The people will recognize merit and reward it. In this town, which seemed to me last year hopelessly apathetic on the subject of the drama, a theatre is nightly filled to excess with an intelligent crowd, who come to listen to a simple uneventful story of a humble life, as proper as a sermon and as pure as a prayer.

To Miss Mitchell, who, by a happy inspiration of genius, has discovered in the morning of her career, the path of true success and unfading honor, let us offer our sincere congratulations. It is not too much to hope that in the warm welcome of this beautiful Idyl of the Actual we see the promise of a better day for American comedy.[47]

WASHINGTON CORRESPONDENCE, 6 DECEMBER 1862

The interest of the Capital now centres in the court-martial of Fitz John Porter and the court of inquiry requested by General McDowell to investigate the truth of the reckless charges so constantly made against him for the last year. The intense interest with which people read the reports of these solemn tribunals day after day, proves that however flippantly newspapers may attack and blacken the character of officers, the public appreciates the vast stake in the keeping of their Generals, and the incalculable importance of having it entrusted into proper hands.

In McDowell's case nothing has been as yet proved. He has easily and without special effort shown the falsity and absurdity of the statements so freely made of correspondence and cordial feeling between himself and the enemy. He has shown that in his conduct, which has been characterized as protecting rebel property and crushing Union feeling—charges so easily made and so readily believed by the prejudiced and unthinking—he has been actuated only by the principles of common humanity and a regard for the discipline of his troops.

If he had granted furloughs by the thousand, like some generals, or suffered his men to plunder and outrage with impunity, like others, he would have been more popular with his soldiers. Had he devoted his time to writing Napoleonic speeches to his troops; had he surrounded himself with a staff of ready writers, to cover up his defects and magnify his achievements before the people, he would have been a great General in the newspapers and an available man for a needy caucus. But McDowell has utterly neglected the arts of popularity. His manner is cold and haughty. His address to his inferiors is brusque and imperious, to his equals distant and reserved. He has no enthusiasms, no political aims or ambitions. He was a martinet in the peace establishment; he is a most rigid disciplinarian in war. He is the most accomplished man in the army in general erudition, save, perhaps, Gen. Hitchcock, yet a man of little versatility or sprightliness of mind. His culture has been most catholic and liberal, embracing the finest educational resources of Europe and America; yet he is as cold as an Englishman, as exclusive as a Hidalgo. He is certainly not the ideal of a Republican soldier, but he is an honest, honorable and energetic officer, a pure and disinterested patriot, and the worst abused man in America.

The most amusing incident of McDowell's court has been the evidence given by a little wretch named Goodwin, a creature who is all fool except a small portion, which is knave. He testifies, upon oath, to having seen McDowell repeatedly drunk on Pennsylvania Avenue and in camp. The fact is, that McDowell is fanatical on the subject of temperance, and drinks nothing but water. He has not for years tasted any spirituous liquors in any form.

And yet this contemptible little shrimp, who hardly comprehends the difference between truth and falsehood, is allowed to give, under oath, this statement of a lie, which excels the wildest romance, and the telegraph spreads the absurd slander over the world. The fame of McDowell carries the infamous libel not only to the shores of the Pacific, but to every capital in Europe. And by the incomprehensible usages of the Court, General McDowell was not allowed to prove that this reckless little liar was a forger, a thief, and a jail-bird, facts of wide notoriety.

The Court-Martial of Major General Fitz John Porter is developing more than any one expected. The report of General Halleck, so convincing, so clear in its statements, so unimpassioned and so calm in tone, came with great force and effect upon the public mind, just previous to the opening of the court and naturally created a great anxiety to hear the further disclosures which this most important trial would bring to light. It is perhaps unfair to form a judgment upon the evidence already adduced, as it is all upon one side, and throws the darkest shadow upon the characters of officers previously of good repute.[48]

WASHINGTON CORRESPONDENCE, 21 DECEMBER 1862

There seems to be one General, at least, in the army, who has not laid off his sense of honor with his citizen's weeds, and who holds himself bound by the same principles of integrity in his intercourse with the Government as in that with his friends and equals. I mean General Burnside. If the unfortunate occurrences at Fredericksburg have no other ray of light to relieve them, we may still congratulate ourselves that they have shown us a General who prefers justice to unfounded praise, and refuses to allow blame to rest upon the undeserving through his reticence.

General Burnside is this morning in Washington. He says to every one with whom he converses, that the clamors against General Halleck and the Secretary of War, on account of the affair at Fredericksburg, are utterly unjust and unfounded; that the march upon Fredericksburg was his own original idea; that it was opposed both by General Halleck and the Secretary, as well as by the President, who all afterwards yielded to the representations of General Burnside; that he received no orders from Washington in regard to his movements; that he crossed the river because he expected to beat the enemy; that he came back because he thought a further advance had become impracticable; that he asked for nothing from the Government which he had not received, and had no cause of complaint, but rather of sincere gratitude for the cordial and unwavering support he had received from the President, Secretary of War, and General Halleck.

He says, further, that he has observed with pain the efforts that have been made, by newspapers of a certain class, to praise him at the expense of the Administration; to give to him all the credit, and to them all the blame, for recent movements. He thinks it would be cowardly and unmanly for him, by silence, to give a seeming assent to these atrocious insinuations, and it is understood that he has prepared a dispatch for the Associated Press giving an abstract of what I have stated.

It is also understood that he has freely and frankly assured the President, that he hopes the Government will not have the least hesitation in removing him from the command of the army, if they can place there a man in whom they or the people have more confidence; that he will serve with cheerfulness under any commander they may choose to designate; and that he will not for an instant allow his personal feelings to weigh in the balance against what is, or seems to be, the public interest.

It is further understood that he has been met in the same spirit of honest frankness by the President. He has been told that no blame was attached to him by the Administration; that General Halleck, after a full survey of the army and the field, had reported that his dispositions were excellent, and that nothing but a chain of untoward circumstances prevented the realization of his most sanguine hopes.

What those circumstances were will soon be given to the public. It will then be seen how unjust were the clamors, how malicious were the insinuations which have been made against the Government for this truly distressing occurrence. It is to be hoped that the recollections of it may soon be effaced by the light of new victories. Until then it is useless to cry "patience." No administration can expect to receive the applause of the country for well-intentioned failures. No man has monuments built to him in grateful recognition of his energy in macadamizing hell. By their fruits we judge our rulers, and they must stand or fall by success or failure. But the people should not take a cloud for an eclipse. Least of all should we allow the mists of partisan malice to obscure the white light of truth, through which we should look at current events. The man who distorts the sad history of this bloody war to the base uses of politics is unfit for other company than that of hyenas and ghouls.

There are, however, such men, and we blush to say there are such in the army. There are Democratic Generals who poultice the shame of defeat by the hope of consequent opposition victories in elections, and there are Abolition Generals who, conscious that the prolongation of the war will assuredly destroy slavery, care not how long it continues.

By the side of reptiles like these, how sublime is the attitude of Burnside. He is prouder in this moral victory of his, over his own ambition and his own partisan feelings, than he would be crowned with the purple wreath of blood-bought victory. He is the first General who has not tried to ascribe his failure to the government. He is the first Democrat who has not tried to cripple the Abolition ascendancy by imputing to them the blame of disaster. He is the first adherent of General McClellan who has not preferred the fame of his chief to the good repute of the administration.

His conduct is the more admirable that it was not called for. He had only to keep silent, as other Generals have done in failure, and let his friends abuse the government and the people would have sided with him, and all would have praised his "heroic reticence." (I believe that is the stock phrase which is used when a man finds concealment and evasion more prudent than speech.) But to a man like Burnside, insincerity is a crime. His want of ambition verges upon a fault. He went into this war with the sole thought and intention of doing his duty. He has remained in it, to the daily sacrifice of his inclinations and detriment of his business. He is a life-long Democrat, but a better patriot. So that he will not allow his friends to attack his superiors to shield him. He will not countenance his party in charging the Administration with that for which, right or wrong, he is responsible. He has conquered, in this act of splendid manliness, the promptings of personal ambition and the instigations of party pressure. And in so doing, he has done what no leading General has done before since the war began.

We cannot afford to lose such a man. The examples of this manly honor and magnanimity are not so frequent that they should pass by unnoticed. We have enough fight, and enough genius, and enough science in our army. But we have not enough of that self-denying patriotism which subordinates not only ambition, but even partisanship, to the common good. The first brilliant instance of this quality is that which I have to-day recorded, and for that let the people always hold Burnside in grateful remembrance.

When the truthful record of these days is made up you will see that Burnside, more than any General in the field, properly appreciated the strength of the enemy, and the requirements of the situation; that he moved to his object firmly and swiftly; that he fought bravely and well; that when he found the opportunity he had hoped to catch had slipped from his grasp, he saved his army with consummate skill and efficiency, and then crowned the works of those brilliant but unlucky days, by turning his back on his flatterers and sycophants, and bravely told the truth to the world.

To believe that such a man has not a future bright with unknown splendors, is to believe that truth itself is a blunder, and that justice is dethroned on the earth.[49]

EDITORIAL, 30 DECEMBER 1862

The veil has at last been removed from the best-kept secret of the age, and the first announcement of the destination of General Banks is the news of the arrival of his expedition at New Orleans. If there be those who have thought it unwise to detach from our main army so large a force at this time, and others who could see no adequate reason for sending this expeditionary corps to the Gulf of Mexico, both questions have doubtless been solved before this. General Burnside has frankly stated that he had all the men at Fredericksburg who could be handled to advantage there, and military men have universally rejected the idea, which was so fondly cherished for a while by the public at large, of causing a diversion of the enemy by a movement on Richmond from the peninsula—a movement which would inevitably have ended in the destruction of the detachment attempting it, without in the least facilitating the operations for the main army.

The duty to which the Government has assigned so fine an army, and a general of such pre-eminent military and executive ability, is clearly foreshadowed in the admirable address of General Banks, which we published yesterday. The opening of the Mississippi to the commerce of the world, the reclamation of the rich and populous States that lie along its winding borders, the pacification of their citizens, and the reconstruction of their political systems, is the work for which the Administration, with distinguished judgment and discretion, has selected a general of such tried ability, such calm patriotism, and such varied experience as Nathaniel P. Banks. There is no greater work to be done in this tremendous struggle, and there is no better man to do it.

The vast importance of this movement can best be seen by considering the earnestness with which the rebel leaders have endeavored to prevent and forestall it. They have ever considered the valley of the Mississippi their choicest possession, and the vast regions watered by its westward tributaries the sure refuge of their failure or the splendid arena of their future development. There has not been a rebel general from Buckner to Bragg who has not advanced to the Kentucky border, sending before him a snow-shower of proclamations declaring the fated unity of the Northwest, and calling upon the dwellers by the shore of the Mississippi to combine for mutual safety and common glory. The great truth of the evident purpose of Heaven to make of that opulent basin a home for one united community was so manifest that even the mists of treason could not obscure it, and they strove to turn this powerful weapon against its own possessors. The true logic of these gigantic facts will be seen before long, and the vagaries of rebellion will seem on the shores of that mighty and peaceful river like the shadows of an ugly dream.

The momentous questions of social and political philosophy which to-day agitate the minds of all true men, and variously tinge our possible future with the lights of liberty and peace or the shadows of blood and tumult, must in this Western tribunal have their fullest test and trial. We congratulate the nation on the felicitous choice which has been made of the clear and acute judicial minds which are to conduct affairs in the Department of the Gulf.[50]

EDITORIAL, 31 DECEMBER 1862

We stand to-day in the broadening twilight of great events. There is a solemn hush of expectation in the air, and the hearts of true men are stirred with a vague forewarning of good to come. In the morning skies the forerunning shadows that herald the day are flushed with a tinge of a light, before unseen. We hope that in its roseate folds lurks the welcome promise of a purer day, and not the angrier redness of tumult and slaughter. As in the morning twilight we know that the day is surely coming, but cannot foretell whether its hours shall be serene or stormy, so as we approach the solemn threshold of a new political dispensation, we cannot say whether the great Disposer of national destinies will permit us to pluck peace from amid the flowering blooms of accomplished justice, or whether we are to suffer, unto farther purification, the penalty of violated law and tardy retribution. Conscious at last of right, we are sure of ultimate victory, but of what lies before us in the immediate future, God only is cognizant.

A most encouraging symptom is the desperation and madness which all the foul creatures which hate the day exhibit, as the light grows less uncertain. Like the ghosts which must vanish with the sunrise, they shudder at the first grey beams that mottle the east. Before the coming revelations the false lights which have been misleading the people begin to pale their ineffectual fires. The evil spirits rage sorely, for their time is short.

The rebel chieftain sitting sad and desolate at Richmond, in the midst of a deluded people who are indulging in futile rejoicings over a barren success, can find no better way of relieving the fearful forebodings of his sinking heart, than by issuing a frantic threat of vengeance against that power which seems the most dreadful to him. He launches his fulmination against General Butler and his officers, but none knew better than the wily rebel that Gen. Butler had been for more than a week relieved from command in the South. He feared the execution of his own slaughterous threat, and based his proclamation upon a state of things which he knew had no existence. General Butler's was a convenient name to use. But the culprit against whom these furious threats were directed, was a greater [one] than any General. It was the spirit of avenging justice and triumphant liberty.

Not in the South alone is there trouble in the camp of disloyalty. The pensioned apologists of treason in the North, fearful of the fiat which will be the beginning of their end, catch eagerly at this late sword-of-lath which their master brandishes, and speak of its power and keenness admiringly. The New York *World* talks of the "great cause for complaint which President Davis had," and of the powerful effect which this mass of raving will "produce in Europe."

If the bloody-minded rebel who penned this document and the wretched hirelings who defend it, suppose that they can thus delay for an instant the lightnings which they fear from the clouds of their own preparing, they mistake the temper of the North and the requirements of the situation. And, if their madness runs into bloody deeds, upon their own heads be the forfeit of the crime. The administration of the War Department has never been accused by its worst enemies of hesitation or cowardice, and we are sure it only waits a proper occasion to vindicate the claims of violated law and outraged humanity.

If the blade of enfranchised justice when but half unsheathed causes such consternation among the hosts of rebellion, how can they stand the fierce light of its naked brilliancy, unveiled in the face of day?[51]

4

1863–1864

EDITORIAL, 1 JANUARY 1863

ALTHOUGH OUR MILITARY POSITION IS NOT ALL WE COULD WISH ON this first day of the New Year, we have much to congratulate ourselves upon, if we compare our situation to-day with that of a year ago. In the impatient fretfulness with which we are too apt to criticise the progress of events, we say that nothing is done, when our full expectations are not realized. The careless observer who stands by the seaside sees the ceaseless backward and forward play of the ripples and can mark no permanent change in the line of sea and sand. But let him be absent for an hour, and he will find the tide swelling irresistibly up the shelving shore, and filling with its persistent flow every inlet, creek, and bay. We have talked so much of check, and so little of success, that we shall need a moment of retrospection, to convince us that we have really done a great work during the year of grace 1862.

One year ago, the unbroken armies of rebellion boldly confronted Washington. The spell of inactivity was lying heavily on all our forces. Even the slight success at Drainsville had failed to excite them to farther effort. They were waiting for the enemy to attack them. The President's War Order No. 1 had not yet issued from the Executive Mansion. Stanton had not yet infused his fiery energy into the administration of the War Department. Norfolk was still the busy workshop of the rebellion, and an army lay virtually besieged in Fortress Monroe. North Carolina and her outlying islands flaunted undisturbed the banners of treason. Not a fortress from Virginia to Mexico bore the flag of the Union in the face of heaven, except Fort Pickens, which sternly frowned defiance on the rebel forts of the mainland. The commercial metropolis of the South [*New Orleans*] revelled in haughty security at the mouth of the Mississippi, guarded by the twin Cerberi, St. Philip and Jackson, and the redoubtable navy of the C.S.A. In the West, the death of Zolli-

coffer had not yet indicated the turning of the tide, and the triumphs of Forts
Henry and Donelson, and the long line of successes that followed, brilliant as
the trail of a meteor, were as yet unaccomplished, and generally unexpected.
From Cairo to the Balize, our central river was entirely in rebel hands, and its
wasted waters never rippled to the passage of a loyal keel. Arkansas was a *terra
incognita* to our armies, and the soil of Missouri was daily watered by the
blood of peaceful citizens brutally murdered by roving guerrillas.

In spite of all the most grumbling patriot or malignant malcontent can
say of our slowness and unsuccess, it cannot be denied that our progress in
the year that has passed has been substantial and decided. Not only has peace
been restored to the State of Missouri, but the enemy that had so harried her
has been driven headlong over the border, and the irresistible divisions of
Blunt and Herron have pursued them with rout and slaughter to the
Arkansas river. Andrew Johnson sits in the Executive Office at Nashville, and
the great-hearted patriots of East Tennessee catch at last a glimpse of the long
expected light of deliverance gilding the summits of their mountains. A murmur of preparation is heard on the winding shores of the gigantic river of
the West, and the men of the prairies, that never were beaten, are marshalling
to follow their leaders to the South. Before long, their vanguard will meet, in
the embrace of victory, the magnificent army of the Gulf, under the Iron
Man of Waltham [*Nathaniel P. Banks*].

We do not like to be too sanguine, or to indulge in the vagaries of opti-
mism. But there is no good reason why we may not expect the greatest results from our Western armies very soon. The country which they are to tra-
verse and to liberate is the opulent storehouse of the nation. The conquest
of the States of the Gulf is the liberation and new life of Illinois and Iowa,
and their powerful sisters of the Northwest. The electric influence of victory
will remove the benumbing paralysis which has fallen on their trade and
prosperity, and with success, wealth and ease will again come to them. This
is a consummation so necessary in this moment of our struggle, that we
are sure the Government, to effect it, will cast from them no instrument,
however humble, which God has placed in their way, and spare no efforts
however great, which may be required at their hands.

With the tramp of these tremendous armies sounding upon the air as
they march from the North and from the South on their mission of liberation; with our new created Navy preparing to fasten its teeth of iron upon

those spots of the coast where treason is yet obdurate and defiant; with generals who know what they are fighting for; with an Administration working harmoniously together for the good of the Commonwealth; with a President combining the zeal of a crusader with the common sense of an American; with a cause in which at last the feet of Liberty and Union, wedded forever, keep time to the measured tread of our soldiers, can we doubt that the smile of the God of Hosts will rest upon our banners, and conduct us through the dark and troublous days that are remaining, into the unfading sunshine of a righteous peace?[1]

EDITORIAL, JULY 1863

In a communication which we publish in our outside columns to-day, from Gen. Robert E. Lee, addressed to the rebel Adjutant General, the former officer contradicts the report of Gen. Meade, announcing a skirmish at Falling Waters and the capture of two pieces of artillery and numerous prisoners. It is of course no manner of consequence what Gen. Lee says to his confreres in treason to break the force of his own terrible disaster, but, in justice to Gen. Meade, it should be stated that his dispatch to the Government of the affair at Falling Waters is correct, despite the contradiction of the baffled and retreating rebel.

We would ask Gen. Lee if he has ever heard of a rebel general named Pettigrew, who was mortally wounded in the skirmish at Falling Waters, *that did not take place,* and died a few days thereafter?

Men are not generally killed and wounded without cause. If there was no fight at Falling Waters what is the meaning of the hospital full of the wounded near there?

While we have the two captured guns in our own batteries; the wounded in our own hospitals; the prisoners in our own jails; and read the obituaries of the rebels slain in that affair, in the Richmond papers, we must be permitted to credit the concurring statement of General Meade, rather than the spiteful contradiction of the baffled traitor who audaciously makes this [*an*] issue of veracity.

Robert E. Lee, of the American army, was once considered a gentleman and a christian. But bad company and bad luck have spoiled his morals and his temper.[2]

Editorial, 7 August 1863

Nothing shows more clearly that the rebellion is nearing its close than the utter disorganization of its votaries in the North and South. As long as it had the least apparent chance of success, a power of cohesion and a concert of action were everywhere evident among its supporters that have now entirely vanished. Its organs utter falsehoods as profusely as ever, but without homogeneousness. They vituperate as malignantly as ever, but their vituperation has lost congruity. They attack in feeble spasms. They fall back in disordered masses. They have been stunned by the heavy blows of Gettysburg, Vicksburg, and Port Hudson, and they fight wildly.

This is clearly seen in the way they receive the news from Kentucky. It is of course a terrible defeat. Instead of receiving it with resignation, they recalcitrate against it with a fury which comes of despair, but with an obstinacy borrowed from rebellion. But they cannot agree upon a plan of falsehood. The *New York World,* the organ of the Mackerelville Democracy, says that it is an abolition triumph, carried by military despotism, and represents the successful candidates in all the negritude of misguided Republicanism, as forced down the throats of reluctant "Kentucky chaps," on the point of very bright and exceedingly long bayonets. Mr. Lincoln is a judicious combination of Nero and Mumbo Jumbo, and General Burnside is a satrap and a butcher and an abolition horde.

This is bold, original, and racy. It indicates anger, defeat, assured disgrace, but still is instinct with pluck undying. It is infinitely better than the elaborate air of dignified satisfaction which an antique journal of this city [*the National Intelligencer*] brings to *its* misrepresentations. It comes to the rescue of a falling cause with unusual haste, in contravention of its rule of not mentioning events till people have forgotten them; an admirable rule, by the way, insuring impunity to mendacity, as nobody cares to correct a misstatement a month old. Instead of admitting a defeat, and being angry over it like the fiery young rebel of the *World,* the ancient newspaper aforesaid prefers to break its fall by the soft, convenient and accustomed cushion of a falsehood. It claims, with a breezy impudence that is overwhelming, that the election is a victory for its own side of the house. It says:

> The returns from the election in Kentucky on Monday last, so far as received, indicate the success of the "Union Democratic" ticket for State officers by a large majority. The candidates of the same party for Congress

are supposed to be elected in nearly all the districts. The "Union Democrats" of Kentucky do not indorse the President's Proclamation of Emancipation, and are opposed to arming negroes, and to other measures that make up what is called the "radical party."

Now the facts of the case are these. The Governor-elect, Colonel Bramlette, United States District Attorney of the State, formerly commandant of the Third Kentucky regiment, one of the earliest war men of the border States, and always a firm and outspoken unconditional Unionist, made a careful speech at the opening of the canvass at Carlisle, Kentucky, which was published and extensively used during the campaign. An extract or two will convince any candid person of the falsehood of the above quoted assertion. Colonel Bramlette said:

> You say the Emancipation Proclamation is all wrong, and Kentucky should not sanction it. You are a Kentuckian, and let us see where you stand. The President carefully excluded from his Emancipation Proclamation all the border States; even Tennessee was excepted from its operation; and between its first enunciation and the time it was authoritatively promulgated, portions of Louisiana and North Carolina have been recovered from the rebels; those portions were embraced in the territory excepted. All territories were excepted where it could not be used to effect some useful purpose in suppressing the rebellion. . . . But yet you Kentuckians who are not to be affected by it, turn around and want to help Jeff. Davis. You sympathize with him in regard to his slaves; and to that extent, at least, you are for the rebellion and against the Union. For my part, I would say, if emancipation will effect anything down there, go ahead. I am for the Government, and for Kentucky; but you turn against the border States, and wish to assist the cotton States, to plunder us of our slaves, rather than Lincoln should dispossess them of their property. You would rather bring waste and ruin upon your own country than stand by your Government.

Does this read very denunciatorily against the proclamation? The fossil journal already quoted from says the successful candidates are opposed to arming negroes, but Colonel Bramlette's address showed that this plea, too, is false. He said:

> You object to negro soldiers. Who began this business? Who raised the first negro regiment? Did Lincoln? Don't you know that in the beginning of this strife, in New Orleans, they heralded it abroad that they had already organized two negro regiments to fight the Yankees with? Don't you know

that the first act in the Tennessee rebel legislature was the organization of free negro regiments? Don't you know it to be a fact, furthermore, that they have regiments of Indians in their service, to tomahawk and scalp our women and children? And yet not one of you here assembled, I will venture to say, have heard these constitutional Union gentlemen object to their using negro regiments to fight us with. You never heard one of them object to enlisting the Indians against us. Why is it that you have grown so terribly repugnant to negro aid? You are willing it should be employed against us, but now that it is being employed to help us you are terribly disturbed. The reason seems irresistible, that they were fighting on the side you were anxious should win; but as soon as they are employed against that side you object. [Applause]

Suppose one of you were assaulted by robbers, who threatened to burn your house and murder your family if you didn't give up your money; that your neighbor came rushing to your assistance, and with him one or two stout negroes, with clubs and axes and guns; that while you are engaged in a close hand to hand conflict with one of them you should see that brawny negro having one of them down, would you say, "Hold on! I don't want any negro to help me. Here, Mr. Robber, I am not going to succeed in driving you off by any such aid as that; you may burn my house and take my property." Is this what any sane man would do? But it is just in this way that Southern sympathizers—Constitutional Union men—talk. They would have us, because the President does not use just such weapons as they think proper, say: "Here, Jeff Davis, take all we have, and slay us as soon as you please; not another man or another dollar can we give until Lincoln quits fighting with these things."

I am for the Constitution framed by Washington and his compeers— those good and great men who were touched with more than human wisdom—at all hazards and at all expense. Are you for it? Alas, I fear you are for the constitution and the union of the Southern confederacy, for every means and measure that you object to being used by the Federal Government, you are perfectly willing that the rebel government should use. You are opposed to the Union being maintained by unconstitutional measures, but you are willing Jeff Davis should fight unconstitutionally to destroy the Union and the Constitution. This shows where your heart is better than your formal professions of Unionism.

If the opponents of the Government are satisfied with this style of talk so are we. Indeed we only wish we had the space to print the whole of Colonel Bramlette's most admirable and patriotic address, but the above extracts will show how much cause for congratulation the organs of mutiny and anarchy have in the result of the Kentucky elections.

Nor can this class of journalists take refuge in the Congressional elections, for in these they will find still less comfort, if possible. Brutus Clay will not listen with a very good grace to such twaddle, and General Green Clay Smith, fresh from his triumph over the conservative Menzies, would be disgusted with a veiled treason more odious than the open rebellion with which he has so gloriously contended in camp and forum.

It seems impossible for these journals "suckled in a creed worn out" to form any conception of the course of events and the changing exigencies of the times. They are too old and too infirm to keep abreast of the advancing truth. The representative in this city of mutiny and treason especially had better confine its disquisitions to Greek and Roman politics and its narratives to the incidents of the Deluge, and it will still be capital reading to those who look at the world through double-convex lenses. It simply makes itself absurd when it claims to stand in relation with any party of the present day. Especially when it arrogates to itself any connexion with the powerful and aggressive young Union party regenerated in Kentucky, it will be met with the stern rebuke with which the reformed Henry of England replied to the ribald congratulations of Falstaff, the foolish old representative of riot and debauchery:

> I know thee not, old man. Fall to thy prayers;
> How ill white hairs become a fool and jester!
> I have long dreamed of such a kind of man,
> So surfeit-swelled, so old, and so profane;
> But being awake I do despise my dream.
> Presume not that I am the thing I was;
> For Heaven doeth know, so shall the world perceive,
> That I have turned away my former self;
> So will I those that kept me company.[3]

NEWSPAPER ARTICLE, 26 MAY 1864

The following telegram appeared in the *New York Tribune* of yesterday, under the date of "May 24":

> The subject of arbitrary arrests was incidentally discussed in Cabinet council to-day. Mr. Chase manfully denounced them. The suppression

of the New York papers and extradition of Arguelles were both condemned by him as devoid of policy and wanting law. The defence of these
measures was more irritable than logical and assured.

1. The Cabinet councils of the President being private and confidential,
the correspondent could have learned this incident from no one but Mr.
Chase.

2. It is impossible that an official so sagacious and discreet as Mr. Chase
should have made to any newspaper correspondent such a statement in
regard to himself and his colleagues in the Government.

3. We have, therefore, no hesitation in pronouncing this statement unauthorized and unfounded.

4. The subject named was not discussed in the Cabinet on Tuesday.

5. *Mr. Chase was not in Cabinet council on that day.*[4]

EDITORIAL, CA. 28 MAY 1864

The Washington correspondent of the *New York Tribune,* in his dispatches
published in the *Tribune* of the 27th, states that a caucus of radical Republican Representatives has been held, which has decided that Mr. Fishback,
recently elected Senator from Arkansas, shall not be admitted to his seat; and
adds with shameless effrontery as a reason for excluding Senator Fishback,
that "his rejection will have some influence on the vote of the Baltimore
Convention."

We do not see how the Senate can pass over so gross and glaring an im-
putation on its honor and integrity without an investigation. This terrible
charge is made in a prominent Republican journal. It demands the attention
of the Senate and the country. Are those Senators who call themselves radical Republicans willing to admit that the power of faction so masters them
as to render them incapable of deciding an election case upon the law and
the fact? Are they so blinded and infatuated as to openly declare that the
defeat of the will of the people, as unanimously expressed in every convention so far held, in favor of Mr. Lincoln, is an object so desirable as to justify all means however dishonorable to compass it?

We express no opinion in relation to Mr. Fishback's case. But we demand,
in the name of justice and decency, that it be decided without any reference
to its bearing on any political convention. And how the members of the
House of Representatives have anything at all to say in the matter passes our
comprehension.[5]

NOTES

INDEX

NOTES

The following abbreviations for frequently cited sources are used in the notes:

AL MSS Robert Todd Lincoln Collection of Abraham Lincoln Papers

Basler, *CWL* Roy P. Basler et al., eds., *The Collected Works of Abraham Lincoln,* 8 vols. plus index (New Brunswick, N.J.: Rutgers University Press, 1953–55)

DLC Library of Congress

IHi Illinois State Historical Library, Springfield

JH MSS John Hay Papers

MD *The Missouri Democrat* (St. Louis)

MR *The Missouri Republican* (St. Louis)

RPB Brown University, Providence, Rhode Island

INTRODUCTION

1. On the publishing history of Hay's diaries, which are permanently housed in the Brown University Library, see the editors' introduction, Michael Burlingame and John R. Turner Ettlinger, eds., *Inside Lincoln's White House: The Complete Civil War Diary of John Hay* (Carbondale: Southern Illinois University Press, 1997). All excerpts from Hay's diary are taken from that edition, hereafter referred to as *Diary of John Hay.*

2. Henry B. Van Hoesen, "Lincoln and Hay," *Books at Brown* 18 (1960): 155–56.

3. Walter B. Stevens, *Centennial History of Missouri, the Center State* (St. Louis: S. J. Clarke, 1921), 2:137–38. See also Jim Allee Hart, *A History of the St. Louis Globe Democrat* (Columbia: University of Missouri Press, 1961), 70. Hart incorrectly said that Hay covered the Lincoln-Douglas debates for the *Democrat.* Hay spent the summer and fall of 1858 in Warsaw, Illinois.

4. Arthur Hill's summary of conversations with Angell, *Detroit Journal,* 13 July 1890; *The Reminiscences of James Burrill Angell* (New York: Longmans, Green, 1912), 117–18.

5. On Hay's authorship of the Bixby letter, see Michael Burlingame, "New Light on the Bixby Letter," *Journal of the Abraham Lincoln Association* 16 (1995): 59–71.

6. Cincinnati correspondence, 12 Feb. 1861, "from our special correspondent," *New York World,* 15 Feb. 1861, p. 4, cc. 3–5; Nelson Thomasson to Dr. C. H. Leonard, Providence, R.I., 16 Feb. 1927, JH MSS, RPB.

7. Long Branch, N.J., correspondence, 16 August 1861, "from our own correspondent," *New York World,* 17 Aug. 1861, p. 4, c. 6.

8. Hay to James A. Hamilton, Washington, 19 Aug. 1861, JH MSS, RPB.

9. Barlow to Edwin M. Stanton, New York, 11 Dec. 1861, Barlow Letters, vol. 7, Huntington Library, San Marino, California.

10. Nicolay to Simon Cameron, Washington, 23 Dec. 1864, Cameron MSS, DLC.

11. On Hay's fondness for the word *beguile,* see Burlingame, "New Light on the Bixby Letter," 65–66.

12. "Talking from the Teeth Outwards," *New York Tribune,* 17 Aug. 1872.

13. "Confidence Men," *New York Tribune,* 29 May 1874, clipping in Hay's scrapbook, vol. 56, JH MSS, DLC.

14. "Colonel Baker," *Harper's New Monthly Magazine* 24 (Dec. 1861): 106.

15. Hay to Andrew Johnson, Washington, 20 Jan. 1862, Leroy P. Graf et al., eds., *The Papers of Andrew Johnson* (Knoxville: University of Tennessee Press, 1967–), 5:109. Hay probably delivered this note in person at Lincoln's request in order to relieve the anxious Johnson, the only senator from a seceding state who remained loyal to the Union.

16. Forney to Hay, Washington, 8 Dec. 1862, JH MSS, RPB.

17. Hay to Nicolay, Washington, 7 Aug. 1863, JH MSS, RPB.

18. "Literary Gossip at Washington," clipping identified as "Correspondence of the *Cincinnati Gazette,* Washington, August 10," by "Agate," scrapbook, vol. 54, JH MSS, DLC.

19. John Hay, *Castilian Days,* rev. ed. (Boston: Houghton Mifflin, 1890), iv.

20. John Hay to Milton Hay, Springfield, 30 Sept. 1866, JH MSS, RPB.

21. Hay to John Russell Young, Paris, 9 Oct. 1866, letterpress copy; Hay to "My Dear Colonel [*Halpine?*]," Paris, 16 Sept. 1865, letterpress copy; Hay to "My Dear Old Boy," Madrid, 31 Jan. 1870, letterpress copy, JH MSS, RPB. Hay wrote all the editorial matter while working for the *Journal.*

22. See, for example, his editorial dated 12 Dec. 1860, in Basler, *CWL,* 4:150. See also Glenn H. Seymour, "'Conservative'—Another Lincoln Pseudonym?" *Journal of the Illinois State Historical Society* 29 (July 1936): 135–50; "Lincoln—Author of Letters by a Conservative," *Bulletin of the Abraham Lincoln Association,* no. 50 (Dec. 1937): 8–9. J. G. Randall thought that Seymour's thesis "is ingeniously presented, and the reasoning seems pretty sound. . . . The main arguments for Lincoln's authorship seem to be his connection with the *Journal* and the test of literary style. The letters do seem to have a kind of Lincoln tang." Randall to Arthur C. Cole, 20 March 1936, copy, J. G. Randall MSS, DLC. See also James H. Matheny, interview with William Herndon, November 1866, in *Herndon's Informants: Letters, Interviews, and Statements about Abraham Lincoln,* ed. Douglas L. Wilson and Rodney O. Davis (Urbana: University of Illinois Press, 1998), 431; Simeon Francis to Anson G. Henry, 14 July 1855, Henry MSS, IHi; Andy Van Meter, *Always My Friend: A History of the State Journal-Register* (Springfield, Ill.: Copley Press, 1981), 48–49, 67–68; Audus Waton Shipton, "Lincoln's Association with the *Journal:* An Address Delivered by A. W. Shipton, Publisher of the *Illinois State Journal,* Springfield, Illinois, at a conference of newspaper publishers and executives, at Coronado, California, September 27, 1939" (pamphlet; 1939); Paul M. Angle, ed., *Herndon's Lincoln* (Cleveland: World, 1942), 184, 197, 296–97;

Robert S. Harper, *Lincoln and the Press* (New York: McGraw-Hill, 1951), 2, 14–15; memo by William Henry Bailhache, San Diego, 14 Jan. 1898, Ida M. Tarbell MSS, Allegheny College; statement of Col. J. D. Roper, 22 Oct. 1897, enclosed in J. McCan Davis to Ida M. Tarbell, ibid.; Albert J. Beveridge, *Abraham Lincoln, 1809–1858*, 2 vols. (Boston: Houghton Mifflin, 1928), 1:171n, 183, 205n; William E. Barton, "Abraham Lincoln, Newspaper Man," typescript, and "Lincoln Editorials," handwritten memo, Springfield, 28 Dec. 1928, Barton MSS, University of Chicago.

23. Dated 3 June 1857, in Basler, *CWL*, 2:410.

24. McKee and Fishback to Ozias M. Hatch, St. Louis, 6 Dec. 1858, Hatch MSS, IHi.

25. Basler, *CWL*, 3:383.

26. Harper, *Lincoln and the Press*, 76; Harry J. Carman and Reinhold H. Luthin, *Lincoln and the Patronage* (New York: Columbia University Press, 1943), 121–29.

27. Brooks's San Francisco dispatch of 15 July 1865, *Sacramento Daily Union*, 2 Aug. 1865.

28. Draft of an introduction to Nicolay and Hay, *Abraham Lincoln: A History*, in the hand of Nicolay, Nicolay-Hay MSS, IHi.

29. John W. Bunn to Jesse W. Weik, Springfield, 20 July 1916, in Jesse W. Weik, *The Real Lincoln: A Portrait* (Boston: Houghton Mifflin, 1922), 282–88. During the Civil War, other White House secretaries and clerks, including Gustave Matile and Nathaniel S. Howe, were similarly employed in the Interior Department. Hay was commissioned a major on 12 January 1864, and was promoted on 31 May 1865 to brevet colonel of volunteers for faithful and meritorious service in the war. On 8 April 1867, he was honorably mustered out of the service.

30. Charles G. Halpine's headnote to Hay's poem, "God's Vengeance," undated clipping from the *New York Citizen*, scrapbook, JH MSS, RPB. According to Hay's biographer Tyler Dennett, "The personal relations of Lincoln and Hay came closely to resemble those of father and son" (*John Hay: From Poetry to Politics* [New York: Dodd, Mead, 1934], 39). Two more recent scholars have maintained that "John Hay's relationship with Abraham Lincoln was a paramount influence over his life. For Hay, Lincoln proved to be a father figure who combined the values and personalities of both John's father and uncle" (Howard I. Kushner and Anne Hummel Sherrill, *John Milton Hay: The Union of Poetry and Politics* [Boston: Twayne, 1977], 27). A new biography of Hay is needed. On Lincoln's tendency to act as a surrogate father to young men, see Michael Burlingame, *The Inner World of Abraham Lincoln* (Urbana: University of Illinois Press, 1994), 73–91.

31. Galusha Grow, quoted in James T. DuBois and Gertrude S. Mathews, *Galusha A. Grow: Father of the Homestead Law* (Boston: Houghton Mifflin, 1917), 266–67.

32. Nicolay and Hay, *Abraham Lincoln: A History*, 10 vols. (New York: Century, 1890), 1:xii; draft of an introduction to Nicolay and Hay, *Abraham Lincoln: A History*, in the hand of Nicolay, Nicolay-Hay MSS, IHi.

33. John Russell Young, "John Hay, Secretary of State," *Munsey's Magazine*, 8 Jan. 1899, 247; Young in the *Philadelphia Evening Star*, 22 Aug. 1891, p. 4, cc. 3–6, p. 4, c. 1; Young, writing in 1898, quoted in T. C. Evans, "Personal Reminiscences of John Hay," *Chattanooga Sunday Times*, 30 July 1905.

34. Hay to Young, Newbury, N.H., 27 Aug. 1891, Young MSS, DLC.

35. Clark E. Carr, *The Illini: A Story of the Prairies* (Chicago: McClurg, 1904), 139.

36. Logan Hay, "Notes on the History of the Logan and Hay Families," 30 May 1939, Stuart-Hay MSS, IHi.

37. *St. Louis Dispatch,* 30 May [no year indicated], clipping in a scrapbook, JH MSS, RPB.

38. F. A. Mitchel to Hay, East Orange, N.J., 12 Feb. 1905, JH MSS, RPB.

39. William Leete Stone, "John Hay, 1858," in *Memories of Brown: Traditions and Recollections Gathered from Many Sources,* ed. Robert Perkins Brown et al. (Providence, R.I.: Brown Alumni Magazine, 1909), 153–54.

40. Ibid., 152.

41. Manuscript diary of Anna Ridgely Hudson, entry for 22 Jan. 1860, IHi; Anna Ridgely Hudson, "Springfield, Illinois, in 1860, by a Native Springfielder," typescript dated December 1912, JH MSS, RPB.

42. Amy Duer to Elizabeth Meads Duer, Washington, 6 May 1862, JH MSS, RPB.

43. Helen Nicolay in an interview with William R. Thayer, Washington, D.C., 18 Jan. 1914, JH MSS, RPB.

44. Hannah Angell in an interview with William R. Thayer, Providence, 6 Dec. 1913, JH MSS, RPB. Cf. *A College Friendship: A Series of Letters from John Hay to Hannah Angell* (Boston: privately printed, 1938).

45. Octavia Roberts Corneau, "A Girl in the Sixties: Excerpts from the Journal of Anna Ridgely (Mrs. James L. Hudson)," entry for 26 June 1864, *Journal of the Illinois State Historical Society* 22 (1929): 437.

46. T. C. Evans, "Personal Reminiscences of John Hay," *Chattanooga Sunday Times,* 30 July 1905. Evans, who represented the *New York World,* befriended Hay on the train trip to Washington in February 1861.

47. *Sedalia (Mo.) Times,* 11 May 1871.

48. Stoddard, "White House Sketches," *New York Citizen,* 25 Aug. 1866; William O. Stoddard Jr., ed., *Lincoln's Third Secretary: The Memoirs of William O. Stoddard* (New York: Exposition Press, 1955), 166. Stoddard was at first the "Secretary to the President to Sign Land Patents." After the war began, as Nicolay recalled, "business became very slack so that he had scarcely any official work to do. He was therefore assigned to duty as one of my clerks at the White House, being able just as well to sign there the few Land Patents which were issued from time to time. Also on one or two occasions when Hay and I were both absent, he carried a message to Congress. So that you see he . . . was not in any proper sense either a real or acting President[']s Private Secretary" (Nicolay to Paul Selby, Washington, 11 March 1895, draft, Nicolay MSS, DLC).

49. Charles H. Philbrick to Ozias M. Hatch, Washington, 30 Dec. 1864, Hatch MSS, IHi. The three others were Nicolay, Edward D. Neill, and Philbrick.

50. Higginson to his mother, 25 May 1863, in Mary Thatcher Higginson, ed., *Letters and Journals of Thomas Wentworth Higginson, 1846–1906* (Boston: Houghton Mifflin, 1921), 201–2.

51. King, chief editorial writer for the *St. Louis Globe-Democrat,* quoted in "Col. John Hay—A Sketch of His Life," unidentified clipping, scrapbook, JH MSS, RPB.

52. Weed to Bigelow, n.p., n.d., quoted in William Roscoe Thayer, *Life and Letters of John Hay*, 2 vols. (Boston: Houghton Mifflin, 1929), 1:222.

53. Henry M. Smith to Charles Henry Ray and Joseph Medill, [Washington], 4 Nov. 1861, Charles H. Ray MSS, Huntington Library, San Marino, California.

54. "Hay's Florida Expedition," unidentified clipping, Hay scrapbook, vol. 56, JH MSS, DLC.

55. "Mr. Major Hay," unidentified clipping, [3 Aug. 1864], scrapbook, vol. 56, JH MSS, DLC.

56. David Rankin Barbee to Stephen I. Gilchrist, Washington, 2 April 1933, quoted in William H. Townsend to Edward C. Stone, Lexington, Ky., 6 March 1945, copy, F. Lauriston Bullard MSS, Boston University.

57. Hay to Nicolay, Warsaw, Ill., 22 Nov. 1872, JH MSS, DLC.

58. Hay to Charles Hay, Paris, 9 Sept. 1866, letterpress copy, JH MSS, RPB.

1. 1860

1. "Ecarte," *Providence Journal*, 26 May 1860, p. 2, c. 3, scrapbook, vol. 54, JH MSS, DLC. Friedrich Hassaurek (1831–85) immigrated from Austria to the United States after the failure of the Revolution of 1848; he settled in Cincinnati, where he won renown as a journalist, lawyer, and fiery antislavery orator. He was an Ohio delegate at the Chicago convention. Upon being named to represent the United States in Quito, Ecuador, a city 9,500 feet above sea level, he thanked Lincoln for appointing him "to the highest place in his gift." Amos Tuck (1811–79) had helped found the Republican Party in New Hampshire, and played a prominent role at the Republican National Conventions of 1856 and 1860. In Congress he had befriended Lincoln, who in 1861 named him naval officer for Boston and Charleston. George S. Boutwell (1818–1905) was a prominent lawyer and antislavery leader who helped found the Republican Party in Massachusetts. Attorney David K. Cartter (1812–87) represented an Ohio district in Congress (1849–53). In 1861 Lincoln named him minister to Bolivia; two years later he became chief justice of the Supreme Court of Washington, D.C. A prominent lawyer and judge in Philadelphia, William D. Kelley (1814–90) helped found the Republican Party in Pennsylvania. In 1860 he was elected to the first of fourteen consecutive terms in the House of Representatives, where he was identified with the Radical wing of the party. Born near Bonn, Germany, Carl Schurz (1829–1906) fled to the United States after the Revolution of 1848 failed. In Wisconsin he became a leading member of the Republican party and served as a delegate at the 1860 Chicago convention. Lincoln rewarded his efforts in the 1860 campaign by naming him minister to Spain, then later a major general in the Union army. Congressman George Ashmun (1804–70) came from Springfield, Mass. Lincoln's remarks, the address by Ashmun, and Lincoln's acceptance letter are in Basler, *CWL*, 4:50–52.

2. "Ecarte," *MD*, 11 Aug. 1860, p. 1, c. 8, scrapbook, vol. 54, JH MSS, DLC. Attorney and politician Joseph Gillespie (1809–85) was a judge of the Illinois state circuit court (1861–73). Rufus Choate (1799–1859) of Massachusetts was an orator, lawyer,

and politician. Lyman Trumbull (1813–96) had beaten Lincoln for a Senate seat in 1855. He served in that body until 1873. James Rood Doolittle (1815–97) represented Wisconsin in the Senate (1857–69). Attorney Orville Hickman Browning (1806–81) from Quincy, Ill., served in the Senate (1861–63). John M. Palmer (1817–1900) broke with the Democratic Party in 1854 and helped Lyman Trumbull win the Senate seat in 1855. During the Civil War, he served as a general in the western theater. Wilson was perhaps John Wilson of Chicago, a native of Washington, D.C., who moved to Illinois in 1855. He had served as commissioner of the General Land Office during the presidency of Millard Fillmore. He became third auditor of the Treasury late in the Civil War. John Wilson to ?, Chicago, 28 Nov. 1860, AL MSS, DLC. Cowan was perhaps Edgar Cowan (1815–85), a Republican leader from Pennsylvania who served in the Senate (1861–67). Attorney Richard J. Oglesby (1824–99) was born in Kentucky and moved to Illinois, where he practiced law and dabbled in politics. At the 1860 Illinois Republican convention, he helped establish Lincoln's reputation as "the rail splitter." Lincoln called him "an intimate personal friend" and made him a general. Lincoln's remarks are in Basler, *CWL*, 4:91–92. Wide-Awakes were young Republicans who, while marching in quasi-military fashion at political rallies, wore glazed hats and oilcloth capes to protect them from sparks generated by their torches.

3. "Ecarte," *Providence Journal*, 29 Aug. 1860, p. 2, c. 3, scrapbook, vol. 54, JH MSS, DLC. Forrest was perhaps Edwin Forrest (1806–72), a celebrated American actor. A lawyer from Jacksonville, Richard Yates (1815–73) served as governor of Illinois (1861–65). Leonard Swett (1825–89) of Bloomington played a key role in winning the presidential nomination for his close friend at the Chicago convention. In Cairo, opponents of the Rev. Mr. Ferree of Lebanon pelted him with eggs. In the 1830s, Jesse K. Dubois (1811–76) served with Lincoln in the Illinois state legislature, where he became his devoted friend and ally. He won election as state auditor in 1856 and 1860; in the latter year he helped David Davis and Leonard Swett secure the nomination for Lincoln at the Chicago convention. The gentleman with the Swabian accent was a Mr. Aratzen. The "Irish cooper" was Hugh Maher. A resident of Springfield, William Butler (1797–1876) had provided board for Lincoln in his early years in the city and was a close friend. "Ex pede Herculem" is a quotation from *The Histories of Herodotus,* book 4, line 82, meaning "From the foot, Hercules." Pythagoras inferred the height of Hercules from the size of his foot.

4. "Ecarte," *Providence Journal*, 19 Sept. 1860, p. 1, cc. 7–8. In 1833 Lincoln was a bondsman for Thomas S. Edwards, a farmer in Clary's Grove, when he was indicted for rape and for incitement to riot. Three years later Edwards sold Lincoln two lots in Springfield. John Todd Stuart described Edwards to Caroline Owsley Brown thus: "As the years passed and education advanced, Edwards ceased to be a leader of men and made a scant living as a bee hunter and a basket maker. About every three months he would get a neighbor to bring him to town [*Springfield*], where he would remain till he sold out his stock. Lincoln, Logan and Stuart being among his most liberal customers, he made their respective offices his headquarters." During the Civil War, Edwards persuaded Lincoln to discharge his grandson from the army (Brown, "A Girl in Lincoln's Town," *Continent,* 8 Feb. 1917, 156). Clary's

Grove was a settlement about three miles from New Salem, known for its roughneck young men. Denton Offutt (1803/1807?–1861?) employed Lincoln in 1831 to help take cargo to New Orleans. After his return from the Crescent City, Lincoln was hired by Offutt to clerk in his New Salem store. The store "winked out" after a short while, prompting Offutt to leave New Salem. The most prominent of the Clary's Grove boys, Jack Armstrong (?–1857?), wrestled Lincoln in 1831 and became his fast friend. A famous circuit-riding minister in central Illinois, Peter Cartwright (1785–1872) was born in Virginia and settled in Sangamon County, Ill., in 1824. He served in the state legislature and in 1846 unsuccessfully opposed Lincoln for a seat in Congress. Arrested for the murder of a man during a drunken brawl, William "Duff" Armstrong (1833–99) was successfully defended by Lincoln in May 1858. Hannah was Duff Armstrong's mother. Edward D. Baker (1811–61) was Lincoln's close friend and political ally. In 1852 he left Illinois for California, and finally settled in Oregon seven years later. There he was elected senator.

5. *MD*, 15 Oct. 1860, scrapbook, vol. 54, JH MSS, DLC. Unlike Indiana and Pennsylvania, Ohio had gone for the Republican candidate in the 1856 presidential election.

6. "Ecarte," *Providence Journal,* 15 Nov. 1860, p. 1, cc. 7–8. Ozias M. Hatch (1814–93) was Illinois secretary of state. The corpulent David Davis (1815–86) was Lincoln's friend and ally in law and politics. Born in Maryland, Davis settled in Bloomington, Ill., where he became a successful attorney and judge. At the Chicago convention in 1860, Davis served as Lincoln's campaign manager and adviser. Lincoln named him to the Supreme Court in 1862. The Chenery House was an important hotel in Springfield and a favorite gathering place for Republicans. John G. Nicolay (1832–1905) was Lincoln's personal secretary. Norman B. Judd (1815–78) was a prominent Illinois Republican who helped Lincoln win the presidential nomination at Chicago in 1860. In 1861 Lincoln rewarded him with the job of minister to Prussia.

2. 1861

1. *MD*, 8 Jan. 1861, p. 3, c. 6, scrapbook, vol. 54, JH MSS, DLC. In late December 1860, Nicolay told his fiancée, "Mr. Lincoln and I moved out of our room at the State House yesterday. He went down to his own house where he will stay most of the time to receive visitors, and I have come to a room in what is called Johnson's Building, just across the street from the Chenery House. It is quite a good room, about twenty feet square, newly painted papered and carpeted, and pretty well furnished. This I shall occupy both as a bedroom and office. I shall be here all the time at work, and Mr. Lincoln will come here occasionally, when I need his advice or he my immediate assistance. It is a very comfortable place if I can keep the crowd out during the session [*of the state legislature*]" (Nicolay to Therena Bates, Springfield, 30 Dec. 1860, Nicolay MSS, DLC).

2. *MD*, 11 Jan. 1861, p. 3, c. 6, scrapbook, vol. 54, JH MSS, DLC. Lt. Gov. Francis Arnold Hoffmann (1822–1903), a German-born banker in Chicago, had been the first editor of the *Illinois Staats-Zeitung.* Gustav P. Koerner (1809–96), a German-born Republican leader from Belleville, had served as lieutenant governor (1852–56). In

the Capitol, Lincoln had suffered defeat in his bids to become a senator in 1855 and 1859. Shelby M. Cullom (1829–1914) of Springfield was speaker of the Illinois House of Representatives.

3. *MD*, 12 Jan. 1861, p. 3, c. 5, scrapbook, vol. 54, JH MSS, DLC.

4. *MD*, 14 Jan. 1861, p. 3, c. 5, scrapbook, vol. 54, JH MSS, DLC. Churchman was probably James Churchman of the town of Nevada, Calif.

5. *MD*, 15 Jan. 1861, p. 3, c. 6. John P. Sanderson of Philadelphia, a leader of the Pennsylvania Republican Party, was an attorney, editor, and author who became chief clerk of the War Department in 1861. Simon Cameron was a crafty Pennsylvania politician noted for his ethical insensitivity. When urged to appoint him to a cabinet post, Lincoln expressed reluctance, declaring that Cameron's "very name stinks in the nostrils of the people for his corruption" (Michael Burlingame, ed., *An Oral History of Abraham Lincoln: John G. Nicolay's Interviews and Essays* [Carbondale: Southern Illinois University Press, 1996], 28).

6. *MD*, 16 Jan. 1861, p. 2, c. 5.

7. *MD*, 21 Jan. 1861, p. 2, c. 5, scrapbook, vol. 54, JH MSS, DLC. Senator John Jay Crittenden (1786–1863) of Kentucky introduced a compromise package whose central feature was the extension of the Missouri Compromise line across the territories of New Mexico and Utah. On 12 January Seward had made a speech in the Senate endorsing a constitutional amendment guaranteeing slavery in the states where it already existed and calling for a national convention to consider other amendments that might defuse the secession crisis. Lincoln's support for Seward's proposal was lukewarm (Basler, *CWL*, 4:175–76).

8. *MD*, 23 Jan. 1861, p. 2, c. 4, scrapbook, vol. 54, JH MSS, DLC. Romero was at that time chargé d'affaires; he became Mexico's minister to the United States in 1863. Mexican president Benito P. Juarez has instructed Romero to visit Lincoln and express his country's desire for cordial relations with the United States. Romero spoke with Lincoln on 19 and 21 January.

9. *MD*, 24 Jan. 1861, p. 2, c. 4. The *Springfield Register* was a Democratic newspaper. The *Daily State Journal* editorial Hay refers to, and which he may have written, is as follows:

> Mr. Buchanan in his annual message, while denying the right of secession, and asserting the necessity of enforcing the laws, sought excuse for evading the performance of his duty in such a case by showing that it could not be done without "Coercion" and "Making War on a State." This he argued he had no constitutional power to do. Mr. Black, his Attorney General, also furnished an elaborate official opinion, in which he argued very justly that, as the war making power was vested in the General Government for the protection and defense of the people of the United States, against their enemies, that power could not be used against one of themselves. He contended that the Government could not constitutionally use its powers for such a purpose—that a State could not be placed in such an attitude as to be the object of war, and that, therefore, the powers of the Executive did not extend to coercion of a Sovereign State. Both President and Attorney General arrived at the unfortunate and illogical conclusion that in the absence of this power of "Coercing a State," or "Making War on a State," the evils existing in South

Carolina were without remedy, save by concession and compromise satisfactory to the resisting State. And in all subsequent discussions of the subject, the right to coerce a State to remain in the Union or to return to its allegiance—the right to levy war on a State to enforce the performance of her duties and to execute the laws, seem to have been accepted by all parties as the *real* issue. In Congressional speeches and reports—in the Messages of Governors and the proceedings of Legislatures—in public meetings—in the late State Democratic Convention—and in the columns of the newspapers, the same leading idea has been allowed to predominate; and the friends of the Union have been placed in the wrong, *not* by the force of the argument, but by the false premises. Read the speeches of Toombs, Jefferson Davis, Garnett, Pryor and the other disunionists of both Houses—read the protests and appeals of all the moderate men who are striving to stay the tide of evil—read the discussions in our own Legislature, and the same false impression colors everything—the horrid thought that relief from disunion and national rottenness can only be found in making war upon a sister State.

Now, we do not choose to accept either of these alternatives—both the invention of the enemies of the Union and of Constitutional Liberty. We begin setting ourselves right by announcing our hearty and unreserved acceptance of the doctrine that—

1. *Congress has no Constitutional right of Coercion over a State of this Union!*

2. *The Constitution has not created, nor do its provisions render possible any relation between the Government and the States of the Union out of which a state of war can arise.*

This doctrine is of course inconsistent with the theory of secession; repels the presumption and denies the right. For, if a State may secede and put herself outside the pale of constitutional duty, she also goes beyond the reach of constitutional protection. The tie broken, she becomes a *foreign* State, the object of coercion and war, as if never one of us. We may conquer and "acquire" her territory, as we did New Mexico and California, or treat with her as we did with Mexico.

A State *cannot secede* from the others and become independent of them, at its own will. The idea of an indivisible Union goes back beyond the Constitution, beyond the articles of Confederation, beyond the declaration of independence. We were "united colonies"—we rebelled as "a people"—we became the "United States of America." The "articles of confederation" declared the supremacy of the Government and that the Union should "be perpetual." The Constitution came "to form a *more perfect* Union." The Constitution is the bond between the people; and the States have assented to it in that sense that it takes the subject of avoiding its operation or of setting it aside, out of their reach. That instrument makes the terms of its own amendment. When amended according to those terms so as to discharge a State, and restore those attributes of sovereignty with which she had parted. She may then "go out of the Union." Now, it is idle talk and waste paper, and a thousand ordinances are nothing because void—and South Carolina is as truly a State of this Union to-day as Illinois. South Carolina then being still in the Union, still subject to the operation of the Constitution and laws, and the duties and rights of her people remaining unchanged by her void laws and ordinances, the duty of Mr. Buchanan becomes very plain. It is simply to *execute the laws*. Mr. Douglas gave up this point in despair and acknowledged that South Carolina was out of the

Union and the Government nevertheless, because the officers had resigned. Why not supply their places with men who will *not* resign? and if they are resisted then bring the *posse,* and if the *posse* is not strong enough or faithful enough to sustain the officers, then bring the militia, then the army, an hundred thousand strong if need be. This is the way Washington quelled the whisky insurrection in Pennsylvania—the very way that President Pierce took Anthony Burns out of Boston. If the existing laws do not provide for the exigencies of the present case let them be made stronger. What we mean to say is: let the laws of the United States be executed, with as little force as possible; but with enough to make sure work of it. We are met, however, with the objection that this is *coercion,* this is *making war on a State.* Not at all, and we will give the reason. The laws of Congress, passed in pursuance of the Constitution, are in full force in the State of South Carolina. They operate without reference to what the Legislature or Convention of that State may do, and cannot be contravened nor interfered with by State laws. Abolish the State Government and repeal all its laws, and the laws of Congress still operate. If the State pass laws contravening those of Congress, forbidding their execution, and releasing their people from obeying them, still the laws of Congress stand and the people are bound. Why?

"This Constitution, and the laws of the United States which shall be made in pursuance thereof, and all treaties made, or which shall be made under the authority of the United States, shall be the *supreme law of the land;* and the Judges in every State shall be bound thereby; *anything in the Constitution or laws of any State to the contrary notwithstanding*" [*Constitution, Art. 6, Sec. 2*].

Here is the unfailing test. All laws of Congress passed in pursuance of this Constitution must prevail. All the States, South Carolina included, have solemnly covenanted that it shall be so. And each has parted with the right to say it shall *not* be so. South Carolina has parted with so much of her sovereignty, and renounced the right to make laws within the scope of Congressional action. This is forbidden ground upon which she cannot enter. Over all the field of legislation reserved to the State, her own laws prevail. The laws of Congress operate upon all her people as citizens of the United States, on all subjects covered by the Constitution. The laws of the State operate as fully on all subjects of *State* legislation. There is no clashing. Two sets of Courts, juries, witnesses and other appliances of justice, may operate at the same time in the same vicinage, and even upon the same parties, and all move in harmony. It is only when a State law contravenes a law of Congress that it must give way; for the latter is "the supreme law." So well instructed on this point are all parties, that from Governor Pickens down to a constable in the streets of Charleston, they have sworn on taking office "to support the Constitution of the United States." The members of the Legislature who passed the laws of nullification and secession took (and violated) the same oath.

There being no power then in the Legislature of South Carolina to secede from the Union—no power to nullify the laws of the United States—no power to absolve their citizens from their allegiance or their fealty to the laws—it remains only for the execution of the laws to go right on. If resisted, the resistance must be overcome. If the civil arm cannot do it, the military must aid. If organized insurrection follows, it is the duty of the President to "see that the laws be faithfully executed." And if ten thousand armed men are necessary to execute the laws of

Congress within a State, it does not follow that a single law of that State need be disturbed in its operation, or a single State right infringed. These things involve legal "coercion," not of the *State*, but of the offender who resists. And no amount of force necessary to be used in enforcing a law of Congress constitutes "*making war on a State.*" The proceeding has nothing to do with the State. Nor has the State any concern with the proceeding. That matter is not within the reach of State interference. On ratifying the Constitution the State renounced that power. Suppose the United States offices in South Carolina to be again filled, and the incumbents protected and aided by the President in the performance of their duties. The traitors now making war on the United States and violating in various ways the laws, are arrested and put upon trial. They plead in bar the laws and ordinances of South Carolina. The court decides that the law of Congress, charged to have been violated, is "the supreme law of the land," and the State law opposing it void, and the offender is without defense. A State has no more right to oppose its legislation to an act of Congress than a county or city has to oppose *its* resolves or ordinances to the law of a State.

We end where we began, deprecating and denouncing the weak and delusive argument of Mr. Buchanan and his Attorney-General, that to execute the laws within a State is to "coerce a State," and that to protect the property of the United States from plunder and preserve the national flag from dishonor, is to "make war on a sovereign State." We would restore words to their honest use, and have the truth shine out that a State cannot secede, nor by any act of its Legislature or Convention, oust the Government of its jurisdiction; nor change its own relation or the relation of its citizens to the Government one jot or tittle; but if aggrieved must seek the remedy in the manner prescribed by the Constitution for its own amendment. (*Illinois Daily State Journal,* 22 Jan. 1861, p. 2, cc. 1–2, scrapbook, vol. 54, JH MSS, DLC)

Attorney General Jeremiah S. Black (1810–83) of Pennsylvania advised the president that while he could not coerce a state that seceded, he must enforce federal laws and protect federal property. Robert Toombs (1810–85) of Georgia was a senator (1852–61). Muscoe Russell Hunter Garnett (1821–64) and Roger A. Pryor (1828–1919) represented Virginia districts in the House. In 1794, President Washington called up several state militias to crush the Whiskey Rebellion waged by farmers in western Pennsylvania. In 1854 President Pierce dispatched troops to Boston to thwart attempts to free runaway slave Anthony Burns from federal custody. Francis W. Pickens (1807–69) was governor of South Carolina (1860–62).

10. *MD,* 29 Jan. 1861, p. 2, c. 4, scrapbook, vol. 55, JH MSS, DLC. Caleb Blood Smith (1808–64) was an Indiana politician who was Lincoln's secretary of the interior (1861–63). An Indiana attorney and politician, Schyler Colfax (1823–85) served in the House (1855–69). David Hunter (1802–86) was a West Point graduate who became a controversial Union general during the Civil War. Edwin V. "Bull Head" Sumner (1797–1863) of Massachusetts became the oldest corps commander in the Union army during the Civil War. The newspaper piece Hay alludes to was "The Position of the Republican Party," *Illinois Daily State Journal,* 28 Jan. 1861, p. 2, c. 1. This editorial, perhaps written by Hay, emphatically declared that the Republicans were far more moderate than their opponents would have the public believe: "The Re-

publican Party *does not* favor the equality of the black and white races—*does not* oppose the admission of more Slave States—*does not* propose to interfere with slavery in the States where it lawfully exists—*does not* propose to deny to the South the benefit of a Fugitive Slave Law—*is not* in favor of inciting slaves to escape, nor in aiding them in doing so—*did not* approve of John Brown's invasion of Virginia, but severely condemned it—and, finally, *does not* cherish hatred toward the people of the South, nor seek to deprive them of any Constitutional right."

11. *MD*, 30 Jan. 1861, p. 2, c. 4. Rodgers was perhaps attorney John B. Rodgers (1799–1873), a Whig politician who attended the 1860 Chicago convention and stumped Tennessee for Lincoln. See Rodgers to Edward Bates, South Rock Island, 14 May 1861, AL MSS, DLC.

12. *MD*, 31 Jan. 1861, p. 2, c. 3. Lincoln was visiting his stepmother, Sarah Bush Johnston Lincoln. John G. Nicolay took verbatim notes on Lincoln's conversation with Bates. Nicolay MSS, DLC.

13. *MD*, 1 Feb. 1861, p. 2, c. 4. Joseph A. Nunes, president of the California Republican conventions in 1856 and 1860, served in the Civil War as a paymaster. While in Springfield he urged Lincoln to name to his cabinet someone from the Pacific Coast (Nunes to Lincoln, Springfield, 2 Feb. 1861, AL MSS, DLC).

14. "From our special correspondent," *New York World*, 15 Feb. 1861, p. 4, cc. 3–5, Hay's scrapbook, privately owned by Robert Hoffman of Rochester, N.Y. I am grateful to Mr. Hoffman for allowing me to consult this scrapbook. As the Prince of Wales, the future king Edward VII (1841–1910) of England had toured the United States in 1860. Oliver P. Morton (1823–77) was governor of Indiana (1861–67). Newton Bateman (1822–97) supervised public instruction in Illinois. Joseph Jackson Grimshaw (1820–75), an Illinois lawyer and Republican politician, had practiced law in Pittsfield, then moved to Quincy, where he ran unsuccessfully for Congress in 1856 and 1858. Morrison was perhaps Democrat William R. Morrison (1824–1909), a representative from Illinois (1863–65, 1873–87). Underwood was William S. Underwood. James M. Burgess of Janesville, Wisc., had journeyed to Springfield to offer his help on the train trip to Washington; Lincoln accepted the offer gladly. Burgess "had been charged by his state with guarding Lincoln's person on the journey and until inaugurated. It was a thoughtful move on the part of Wisconsin Governor Alex W. Randall and state officials" (Victor Searcher, *Lincoln's Journey to Greatness: A Factual Account of the Twelve-Day Inaugural Trip* [Philadelphia: Winston, 1960], 8). The others included Capt. John Pope (1822–92) of the Topographical Engineers, who would command the Army of Virginia in the summer of 1862; Capt. George W. Hazard (West Point, class of 1847) of the Fourth Artillery; William Butler, Lincoln's close friend in Springfield; Ward Hill Lamon (1828–93) of Danville, Ill., another close friend, who became marshal of the District of Columbia (1861–65); Norman B. Judd; the young militia leader, Elmer Ephraim Ellsworth (1837–61), a kind of surrogate son to Lincoln who had worked in Lincoln's law office in 1860 and campaigned for him; William S. Wood, who was in charge of the arrangements for the train journey; Wood's assistant, Burnett Forbes; David Davis; Dr. William S. Wallace, the husband of Mary Todd Lincoln's sister Ann; Capt. Lockwood M. Todd, Mary Todd Lincoln's cousin; George C. Latham, a Springfield friend of Robert Todd Lincoln; Robert

Irwin, the cashier of the Springfield Marine and Fire Insurance Company and Lincoln's financial agent; John James Speed Wilson, superintendent of the Union Telegraph Company and bureau chief of the Caton Line in Springfield; J. A. Hough; Martin H. Cassell; Hall Wilson; D. H. Gilder; Edward F. Leonard (1837–1915) worked in the office of the state auditor, Lincoln's friend Jesse K. Dubois; W. Jameson; William H. Carlin, a Democratic state senator from Adams County; L. W. Ross; attorney Ebenezer Peck of Chicago, a leading Republican political strategist and organizer whom Lincoln later appointed a judge of the U.S. Court of Claims; Orville H. Browning; Jesse K. Dubois; and William H. Johnson (d. 1864?), a black man from Springfield. Springfield correspondence, 11 Feb. 1861, *Cincinnati Commercial*, undated clipping in Hay's scrapbook owned by Robert Hoffman. Johnson later worked in the White House and in the Treasury Department. As Lincoln's body servant, Johnson shaved him, attended his wardrobe, and performed similar services. To earn extra money, Johnson also was a messenger for the Treasury Department. Roy P. Basler, "Did President Lincoln Give the Smallpox to William H. Johnson?" *Huntington Library Quarterly* 34 (May 1972), 279–84; John E. Washington, *They Knew Lincoln* (New York: E. P. Dutton, 1942), 127–34. Dubois, Browning, and Hatch traveled only as far as Indianapolis before returning to Illinois. Among the journalists on board were T. C. Evans (*New York World*), Henry Villard (*New York Herald*), Joseph Howard Jr. (*New York Times*), O. H. Dutton (*New York Tribune*), Henri Lovie (*Leslie's Weekly*), Uriah Hunt Painter (*Philadelphia Inquirer*), W. G. Terrell (*Cincinnati Gazette*), Henry M. Smith (*Chicago Tribune*), S. D. Page, J. H. A. Bone, A. W. Griswold, J. R. Drake (Associated Press), and Theodore Stager. Lincoln's speeches are in Basler, *CWL*, 4:190–91, 194–96.

15. "From our special correspondent," *New York World*, 15 Feb. 1861, p. 4, cc. 5–6. A clipping of this item is pasted into Hay's scrapbook, privately owned by Robert Hoffman. William Dennison (1815–82) was governor of Ohio (1859–61) and U.S. postmaster general (1864–66). John Reeve (1799–1838) was a popular English farceur. Henry Liston (1771–1846) was an English comic actor. Lincoln's speeches are in Basler, *CWL*, 4:196–99.

16. "From our own correspondent," *New York World*, 19 Feb. 1861, p. 5, cc. 1–2. Grace Bedell (1848–1936) of Westfield, N.Y., suggested in a letter dated 15 October that Lincoln grow a beard. Lincoln's response is in Basler, *CWL*, 4:129–30. Lincoln's remarks at Painesville, Ashtabula, Conneaut, Erie, Dunkirk, and Westfield are ibid., 4:218–19. Joshua R. Giddings (1795–1864) was not a senator but rather a representative (1839–59); in 1861 Lincoln appointed him U.S. consul general to Canada. Horace Greeley (1811–72) founded and edited the *New York Tribune*.

17. *New York World*, 19 Feb. 1861, p. 5, c. 2. Millard Fillmore (1800–1874) became president upon the death of Zachary Taylor in 1850. Asaph S. Bemis was the president of the common council, not the mayor. Edwin D. Morgan (1811–83) was governor of New York from 1858 to 1862.

18. "From our special correspondent," *New York World*, 21 Feb. 1861, p. 3, cc. 1–3. A clipping of this item is pasted into Hay's scrapbook, owned by Robert Hoffman. Johann Kaspar Lavater (1741–1801) was a German poet and physiognomist. William S. Wood of New York supervised the train trip. Lincoln, under pressure from his wife,

reluctantly appointed him commissioner of public buildings. Wood was revealed to be corrupt and dismissed. See Michael Burlingame, *Honest Abe, Dishonest Mary* (Racine: Lincoln Fellowship of Wisconsin, 1994), 11–15.

19. "From Our Special Correspondent," *New York World*, 25 Feb. 1861, p. 3, cc. 4–5. Lincoln's remarks are in Basler, *CWL*, 4:235–37.

20. "Special Dispatch," *New York World*, 23 Feb. 1861, p. 4, c. 6. R. B. Coleman was proprietor of the Eutaw House. Ellsworth recruited a regiment in New York and dressed them in the uniforms of Algerian soldiers serving in the French army.

21. "From our own correspondent," *New York World*, 27 Feb. 1861, p. 3, cc. 2–3. Allen Pinkerton (1819–84), head of a Chicago detective agency, had been hired by the Philadelphia, Wilmington, and Baltimore Railroad to investigate rumors of sabotage against the line's property. He alleged that the plot against Lincoln's life was a genuine threat. Detectives working for Col. Charles P. Stone, U.S.A., supported Pinkerton's claim. François-Eugéne Vidocq (1775–1857) was a police chief and fabled sleuth. The barber who purportedly led a plot was one Fernandina, who headed a secret military organization in Baltimore. Democrat Erastus Corning of Albany, N.Y., was a rich iron manufacturer. Frederick W. Seward (1830–1915) was the son of William Henry Seward. Norman B. Judd and railroad president Samuel M. Felton urged Lincoln to take the warnings seriously.

22. "From our own correspondent," *New York World*, 28 Feb. 1861, p. 3, c. 1. "Straight-outs" were militant opponents of slavery. They disliked Cameron because they thought him insufficiently ardent in his antislavery views and because his integrity was suspect. John Bell (1797–1869) had run for president in 1860 on the Constitutional Union ticket, which carried Tennessee, Kentucky, and Virginia. David E. Twiggs (1790–1862), commander of the Department of Texas when the war broke out, surrendered to Ben McCulloch of the Confederate army on 18 February. Lewis Cass (1782–1866) of Michigan, the unsuccessful Democratic candidate for president in 1848, was Buchanan's secretary of state (1857–60).

23. "From Our Special Correspondent," *New York World*, 4 March 1861, p. 3, c. 2. The *World* published a prosaic, reportorial Washington dispatch of the same date by "our own correspondent." Sculptor Thomas Crawford (ca. 1813–57) executed a statue of "Armed Liberty," which was placed atop the Capitol dome when it was finally completed.

24. "From Our Special Correspondent," *New York World*, 5 March 1861, p. 3, c. 2. A prosaic, reportorial dispatch by "our own correspondent," dated 2 March, appeared on the same page. The most powerful champion of the Counter-Reformation, Philip II (1527–98), ruled the Holy Roman Empire from Spain. Buchanan's home was in Lancaster, Pennsylvania. Actaeon was a mythological Greek hunter who was killed by his own dogs after he glimpsed Artemis in her bath and she transformed him into a stag. John Tyler (1790–1862) was tenth president of the United States (1841–45).

25. "Correspondence of the World," *New York World*, 6 March 1861, p. 3, c. 1. The preliminary and final versions of Lincoln's first inaugural are in Basler, *CWL*, 4:249–71.

26. "Our own correspondent," *New York World*, 8 March 1861, p. 4, c. 6, p. 5, c. 1. John J. Crittenden (1787–1863), a leading Kentucky Unionist, was not appointed to

the Supreme Court. The commissioners dispatched by the Confederacy to negotiate about the forts were Martin J. Crawford, John Forsyth, and A. B. Roman.

27. "Ecarte," *Illinois Daily State Journal,* 23 April 1861, p. 2, c. 4. A clipping of this article is pasted into one of Hay's scrapbooks, vol. 56, Hay MSS, DLC. The editor of the paper thanked Hay for this contribution (Edward L. Baker to Hay, Springfield, 29 April 1861, JH MSS, RPB). On 12 December 1860, Lewis Cass resigned from James Buchanan's cabinet because the president failed to reinforce U.S. forts in Charleston. On 26 December, Maj. Robert Anderson (1805–71) had transferred his troops from Charleston's Fort Moultrie, on the mainland, to Fort Sumter, an island in the middle of the harbor. William Sprague (1830–1915) was elected governor of Rhode Island as a Democrat in 1859 and again in 1861. A Republican Congressman from Pennsylvania, John Covode (1808–71) had made a fortune in business. On 15 April, patriotic mobs in Philadelphia threatened the printing offices of newspapers that supported the South. The mayor raised a U.S. flag over the *Palmetto Flag* building and gave a pro-Union speech, while urging his listeners to respect the rights of private property (*New York Tribune,* 16 April 1861). On 15 April, when the *New York Herald,* which militantly opposed abolition and had expressed sympathy for the South, made no comment about the firing on Fort Sumter, a crowd converged on the newspaper's office and insisted that owner James Gordon Bennett raise the U.S. flag over it. Fearing violence, Bennett complied and bowed to the mob after one flag was hoisted on a staff and another was draped from a window. The next day Bennett announced in the *Herald* that "the actual presence of war cuts short all debate. . . . There will now be but one party, one question, one issue, one purpose in the Northern States—that of sustaining the government."

28. "From our own correspondent," *New York World,* 10 May 1861, p. 4, cc. 5–6. Hay's diary entry for 7 May 1861 indicates that he observed the events described in this dispatch. Irvin McDowell (1818–85) would lead the Union army to defeat at Bull Run in July. Mrs. John Jacob Astor was the doyenne of New York society.

29. "Ecarte," *Illinois Daily State Journal,* 20 May 1861, p. 2, c. 4. When a tailor's shop adjacent to Willard's hotel caught fire, the general commanding Washington ordered Ellsworth's regiment to the scene because the local firemen were notoriously incompetent. The shop burned to the ground, but the soldiers saved the hotel.

30. *Illinois Daily State Journal,* 3 June 1861, p. 1, cc. 2–3. Cf. Hay, "A Young Hero," *New York World,* 16 Feb. 1890, p. 26, cc. 4–5, and *Atlantic,* July 1865, 119–25. Ellsworth was killed as his troops seized Alexandria, Va., on 24 May. Ned Buntline was the pen name for Edward Zane Carroll Judson (1821–86), who wrote more than four hundred dime novels. He served in the First New York Mounted Rifles (1862–64). Henry W. Halleck (1815–72), who was to become commander in chief of the Union armies (1862–64), had written *Elements of Military Art and Science,* among other books. Ellsworth's death crushed Lincoln, who "mourned him as a son." Upon receipt of the news, he burst into tears, telling his official callers, "Excuse me, but I cannot talk." After he had collected himself, he explained: "I will make no apology, gentlemen, for my weakness; but I knew poor Ellsworth well, and held him in great regard" (Washington correspondence, 24 May 1861, *New York Herald,* 25 May 1861, p. 1, c. 5). When a congressman expressed satisfaction that the Stars and Stripes now

flew in Alexandria, Lincoln replied: "'Yes, but it was at a terrible cost!' and the tears rushed into his eyes as he said it" (John A. Kasson in Allen Thorndike Rice, ed., *Reminiscences of Abraham Lincoln by Distinguished Men of His Time* [New York: North American Review, 1888], 36). At the funeral conducted in the White House, the president cried out as he viewed the corpse, "My boy! my boy! was it necessary this sacrifice should be made!" See Walter B. Stevens, "The Avenger's Story," unidentified clipping, Lincoln Museum, Fort Wayne, Ind.

31. "From our own correspondent," *New York World*, 11 July 1861, p. 4, c. 5. Senator Stephen A. Douglas of Illinois had died on June 3. James A. McDougall (1817–67) was a senator from California (1861–67). Jacob Collamer (1792–1865) was a senator from Vermont (1855–65). Robert John Walker (1801–69) had represented Mississippi in the Senate (1835–45) and was secretary of the treasury (1845–49).

32. "From our own correspondent," *New York World*, 12 July 1861, p. 4, cc. 5–6. The *St. Nicholas* was a double-decked barge. Clement L. Vallandigham (1820–71), a representative from Ohio (1858–63), was a leading Democratic critic of the Lincoln administration. Journalist James E. Harvey wrote for the *New York Tribune* and edited the *Philadelphia North American*. In 1861 Lincoln appointed him U.S. minister to Portugal. His loyalty to the Union was questioned because, during the secession crisis, he corresponded with some friends in his native South Carolina.

33. "From our own correspondent," *New York World*, 24 July 1861, p. 3, cc. 4–5. William R. Montgomery (1801–71) was the colonel of the First New Jersey Volunteers. Israel R. Richardson (1815–62) commanded the Fourth Brigade of the First Division, Army of Northeastern Virginia.

34. "From our own correspondent," *New York World*, 30 July 1861, p. 4, c. 5. James Cameron, brother of Secretary of War Simon Cameron, served in William T. Sherman's brigade. Henry W. Slocum (1826–94) commanded the 27th New York Volunteers. Col. Noah L. Farnham served with the 11th New York Volunteers.

35. "From our own correspondent," *New York World*, 1 Aug. 1861, p. 3, c. 3. George B. McClellan (1826–85) took command of Union forces around Washington after the battle of Bull Run.

36. *Illinois Daily State Journal*, 3 Aug. 1861, p. 2, cc. 1–2. Joel Roberts Poinsett (1779–1851) of South Carolina was secretary of war (1837–41). Capt. William G. Williams of the U.S. Topographical Corps, an 1824 graduate of West Point, had supervised the Great Lakes surveys. Joseph Nicolas Nicolett (1786–1843) took Frémont with him in 1838 to survey the upper Missouri River. Frémont's wife was Jessie Benton Frémont (1824–1902). Thomas Hart Benton (1782–1858) of Missouri been a colonel in the War of 1812 and a senator (1821–51). The United States declared war on Mexico in May 1846. In the fall of 1846 Stephen Watts Kearny (1794–1848) had set out from New Mexico with three hundred dragoons. In 1847 Kearny charged Frémont with mutiny. In a trial ending in January 1848, Frémont was found guilty, but the court recommended clemency. Accordingly, President Polk pardoned Frémont and restored him to his post in the army. Frémont represented California in the Senate (1850–51).

37. "From our own correspondent," *New York World*, 8 Aug. 1861, p. 3, cc. 1–2, scrap-

book, vol. 54, JH MSS, DLC. Prince Napoleon Joseph (1822–91), cousin of the French emperor Napoleon III, was known as "Plon-Plon" because he had been a fat baby. He was a "man of the Bonaparte type and indomitable character, half Jacobin, half autocrat." A French wit thought him "a good copy of the first Emperor dipped in German grease" (Georges Joyaux, trans., *Prince Napoleon in America, 1861: Letters from His Aide-de-Camp, Lieutenant-Colonel Camille Ferri Pisani* [Bloomington: Indiana University Press, 1959], 5). Edouard Henri Mercier (1816–86) was French minister to the United States (1861–63). Jules Baroche (1802–70) was a French politician. Ragon was a Crimean War hero. Lt. Col. Camille Ferri Pisani was aide-de-camp to Prince Napoleon. A captain in the French navy, Bonfils had been governor of Guadeloupe and was a personal friend of Prince Napoleon. Maurice Sand was the son of the novelist George Sand. In 1861 Elizabeth Todd Grimsley (1825–95) of Springfield spent six months at the White House helping her cousin, Mary Todd Lincoln, adjust to life in Washington. Charles Sumner (1811–74) of Massachusetts was the chairman of the Senate Committee on Foreign Relations.

38. "Our Own Correspondent," *New York World,* 14 Aug. 1861, p. 3, cc. 2–3, scrapbook, vol. 54, JH MSS, DLC. Commander John Dahlgren (1809–70), inventor of the Dahlgren gun, was in charge of the Washington Navy Yard. Aimable-Jean-Jacques Pélissier (1794–1864), marshal of France, commanded French forces in the Crimea in 1855. The British Light Brigade rode to its death at Balaklava in the Crimean War. The "rebel general" was Joseph E. Johnston (1807–91). "Stewart" was perhaps J. E. B. Stuart (1833–64), later to achieve fame as Robert E. Lee's chief of cavalry. He was promoted from colonel to general on 24 September 1861.

39. "From our own correspondent," *New York World,* 17 Aug. 1861, p. 4, c. 6. Long Branch was a fashionable beach resort. Hay had accompanied Mrs. Lincoln's party from Washington to New York on 14 August and continued on to Long Branch, where she vacationed briefly (*New York Tribune,* 16 Aug. 1861). Lester Wallack (1820–88) was a popular comic actor (*New York Herald,* 19 Aug. 1861).

40. "From our own correspondent," *New York World,* 19 Aug. 1861, p. 4, cc. 5–6. In 1792 army captain Claude-Joseph Rouget de Lisle wrote "La Marseillaise," the French national anthem. The Empress Eugenie of France regularly vacationed at Biarritz. The Empress Elizabeth of Austria vacationed at Madeira.

41. "From our own correspondent," *New York World,* 19 Aug. 1861, p. 3, c. 3. Meeker was perhaps Samuel Meeker, president of the State Bank. Mrs. John Henry Shearer (née Hannah Miner) was the sister of the Lincolns' friend Noyes W. Miner, a Baptist minister in Springfield.

42. "From our own correspondent," *New York World,* 20 Aug. 1861, p. 4, c. 5.

43. *New York World,* 24 Sept. 1861, p. 4, cc. 5–6, scrapbook, vol. 54, JH MSS, DLC. New Madrid, Mo., was taken by the Confederates on July 28. They seized Columbus, Ky., in September.

44. *MR,* 13 Oct. 1861, p. 2, c. 4. Frémont was accused of corruption and inefficiency. He ordered one of his critics, Frank Blair (1821–75), brother of Postmaster General Montgomery Blair, arrested. Union general John E. Wool (1784–1869) commanded the Department of Virginia. Union general J. K. F. Mansfield (1803–62) com-

manded the Department of Washington. Joseph Rodman Drake de Kay (1836–86) was provost of Washington. A New York merchant and prominent War Democrat, W. K. Strong (1805–67) was appointed a general for political reasons. Henry C. De Ahna was found guilty of conduct unbecoming an officer after he forced his way past General Frémont's sentinel, whom he denounced as a "damned body guard" and "a Hungarian humbug" (Washington correspondence, 11 Sept. 1861, *Chicago Tribune*, 12 Sept. 1861, p. 1, c. 5). Lochiel was Cameron's home in Pennsylvania. Thomas A. Scott (1823–81) was assistant secretary of war. In late July in the New Mexico Territory, a Confederate band of 250 men under Capt. John R. Baylor captured a Union force of 500 under Maj. Isaac Lynde without firing a shot. Lynde was cashiered in November.

45. *MR*, 15 Oct. 1861, p. 2, c. 4, scrapbook, vol. 54, JH MSS, DLC. The "Anaconda plan" was General Scott's original strategy for defeating the Confederacy, squeezing it to death by controlling the Mississippi River and tightly blockading Southern ports. A prominent Massachusetts politician before the war, Gen. Nathaniel P. Banks (1816–94) was at this time in charge of the Department of Annapolis. On 6 October, the president consulted with Banks at Rockville, Md. Smith was probably William F. Smith (1824–1903), known as "Baldy," who later became a corps commander. He is best known for his timidity during the first attacks on Petersburg, which he might have captured had he been bolder. Gen. George Archibald McCall (1802–68) commanded the Pennsylvania Reserves Division. A division commander at this time, Fitz John Porter (1822–1901) took charge of a corps in 1862. In 1863 he was cashiered for disobeying orders at Second Bull Run. The commander of the Union forces at First Bull Run, Irvin McDowell (1818–85) was at this time in charge of a division. The *Vanderbilt* was a 1,700-ton side-wheel steamer given to the U.S. government by Commodore Vanderbilt. Gideon Welles (1802–78), Lincoln's secretary of the navy, was criticized in the press for remoteness, for not using his distribution of patronage and contracts to help the Republican party, and for his grandfatherly appearance. In 1861 John F. Potter (1817–99), a representative from Wisconsin (1857–63), chaired a House committee to investigate the loyalty of government employees. In 1861 New York congressman Charles Henry Van Wyck (1824–95) chaired a House committee to investigate government contractors.

46. *MR*, 19 Oct. 1861, p. 2, c. 4, scrapbook, vol. 54, JH MSS, DLC. Charles Francis Adams (1807–86) of Massachusetts was U.S. minister to Great Britain. Hay wrote in his diary on 12 October: "Seward spoke also of [*John Lothrop*] Motley's despatch which seems to contain a most cheering account of the real sentiment of honest sympathy existing in the best class of English Society towards us. Motley's letter embraced free and cordial conversations with Earl Russell, Earl Grey, Cobden, Mr. Layard, Prince Albert and the Queen." George Charles Grantley Fitzhardinge Berkeley (1800–1861) was a notorious bully, duelist, pugilist, and huntsman. John Mitchel (1815–75) of Ireland, a fugitive in the United States from British justice, championed the cause of the Confederacy. William Howard Russell recorded that "Sir James Ferguson and Mr. R. Bourke, who have been traveling in the South and have seen something of the Confederate government and armies, visited us this evening after

dinner. They do not seem at all desirous of testing by comparison the relative efficiency of the two armies, which Sir James, at all events, is competent to do. They are impressed by the energy and animosity of the South" (*My Diary North and South* [Boston: T. O. H. P. Burnham, 1863], 555 [entry for 15 October]).

47. *MR*, 21 Oct. 1861, p. 3, c. 1. On 7 October, Lincoln dispatched Cameron to Missouri to inspect allegations of incompetence and corruption in Frémont's command. In August 1861, the former mayor of Washington, James Berret, was jailed for disloyalty when he refused to take the oath of allegiance. In mid-September, Mrs. Lincoln denounced Wood as "a very bad man," "a most unprincipled man," who "does not know, what *truth* means" (Mary Todd Lincoln to John F. Potter, 13 Sept. 1861, in Justin G. Turner and Linda Levitt Turner, eds., *Mary Todd Lincoln: Her Life and Letters* [New York: Knopf, 1972], 104). When a congressional investigating committee informed Lincoln that Wood was corrupt, the president removed him from his post. Burlingame, *Honest Abe, Dishonest Mary*, 11–15. John P. Hale (1806–73) was a Radical Republican senator from New Hampshire who was noted for abolishing the grog ration and flogging in the Navy. During the war he was chairman of the Senate Committee on Naval Affairs.

48. *MR*, 22 Oct. 1861, p. 2, c. 5, scrapbook, vol. 54, JH MSS, DLC. Parrotts were rifled, muzzle-loading cannon designed by Robert Parker Parrott (1840–77). Gideon J. Pillow (1806–78) was a Confederate general. John W. Geary (1819–73) was wounded at Harper's Ferry on 16 October. The son of Henry Clay, Thomas Hart Clay (1803–71) of Kentucky, was a vigorous Unionist whom Lincoln named minister to Honduras in 1862. Lincoln's closest friend during his early adulthood, Joshua Fry Speed (1814–82), and his attorney general (appointed in December 1864), James Speed (1812–87), were members of this Louisville family. For a different assessment of Robert Anderson, see *Diary of John Hay*, 21 (entry for 9 May). William T. Sherman (1820–91) was Anderson's second-in-command in Kentucky at this time. Abigail Kelley Foster (1810–87) was a "dogmatic, fanatical, virtually humorless" abolitionist and feminist (*Notable American Women*, 1:649). John B. Floyd (1806–63), Buchanan's secretary of war (1857–60), was at this time leading a Confederate brigade in western Virginia. Confederate general Henry Alexander Wise (1806–76), former governor of Virginia, served as a brigadier general in western Virginia. Wise and Floyd squabbled fiercely, especially after the 10 September battle at Carnifex Ferry, where Floyd managed to repulse Union assaults even though Wise failed to reinforce him. James Murray Mason (1798–1871) of Virginia was Confederate diplomatic commissioner to Great Britain. John Slidell (1793–1871) of Louisiana was appointed the Confederacy's diplomatic commissioner to France.

49. *MR*, 25 Oct. 1861, p. 3, c. 1, scrapbook, vol. 54, JH MSS, DLC. On 14 October, Seward sent a circular to all governors of Northern states on the seacoast or on lakes urging them to improve their shore defenses. William L. Dayton (1807–64) was U.S. minister to France. Richard Bickerton Pemell Lyons (1817–87), British minister to the United States, had written a sharp protest against the arrest by U.S. authorities of two British subjects in violation of the habeas corpus provision of the Constitution. Seward tartly replied that the U.S. government would interpret the Con-

stitution for itself. Don Gabriel Garcia y Tassara was Spain's minister to the United States. Frémont was removed from the command of the Western Department on 2 November. Lincoln was disappointed by Frémont's ineptitude and by his unauthorized order, dated 30 August, freeing the slaves of rebel slaveholders and declaring martial law in Missouri. Cameron's report to Lincoln on 14 October is in the AL MSS, DLC.

50. *MR,* 27 Oct. 1861, p. 2, c. 5. Charles P. Stone (1824–87) commanded a "corps of observation" in the Army of the Potomac. Randolph B. Marcy (1812–87) was McClellan's father-in-law and chief of staff. According to Noah Brooks, the news of Baker's death "smote" Lincoln "like a whirlwind from a desert." The president deemed it the "keenest blow" he suffered in "all the war." Upon learning Baker's fate, Lincoln emerged from the telegraph office "with bowed head, and tears rolling down his furrowed cheeks, his face pale and wan, his heart heaving with emotion" and "almost fell as he stepped into the street. . . . With both hands pressed upon his heart he walked down the street, not returning the salute of the sentinel pacing his beat before the door" (Michael Burlingame, ed., *Lincoln Observed: Civil War Dispatches of Noah Brooks* [Baltimore: Johns Hopkins University Press, 1998], 215). On 22 October, Hay recorded in his diary: "This has been a heavy day. Last night Col. Baker was killed at Leesburg at the head of his Brigade. McClellan & the President talked sadly over it. McClellan said, [']There is many a good fellow that wears the shoulder-straps going under the sod before this thing is over'" (*Diary of John Hay,* 27).

51. *MR,* 31 Oct. 1861, p. 2, c. 3. Sterling Price (1809–67) was the Confederate general in charge of Missouri. On 20 October, Union forces attacked Confederate guerrillas at Pilot Knob in Missouri. Camp Wild Cat was the site of a minor battle in Kentucky on 21 October. McClellan held Gen. Winfield Scott in contempt and was maneuvering to have him ousted. On 10 October, Hay noted in his diary: "As we left, McClellan said, 'I think we shall have our arrangements made for a strong reconnaissance about Monday to feel the strength of the enemy. I intend to be careful, and do as well as possible. Don't let them hurry me, is all I ask.' 'You shall have your own way in the matter I assure you,' said the Tycoon, and went home" (*Diary of John Hay,* 25). Thomas Tinsey Craven (1808–87) was in command of the Potomac River flotilla. The CSS *George Page,* a side-wheel river steamer with two guns, had been blockaded in Acquia Creek. In March 1862, the Confederates burned it lest it fall into Union hands. Stephen W. Stryker was colonel of the 44th New York Infantry.

52. *MR,* 8 Nov. 1861, p. 2, c. 6, scrapbook, vol. 54, JH MSS, DLC. The "howling dervishes" were Senators Benjamin F. Wade (1800–1878) of Ohio, Zachariah Chandler (1813–79) of Michigan, and Lyman Trumbull of Illinois. John Addison Gurley (1813–63) was a Universalist minister and an Ohio congressman (1859–63). From August to October 1861, he had served as a colonel on General Frémont's staff. Lorenzo Thomas (1804–75), adjutant general of the U.S. army, had been sent to St. Louis with Cameron to investigate Frémont. His report concluded, "The opinion entertained by gentlemen who have approached and observed him is that he is more fond of the pomp than of the stern realities of war; that his mind is incapable of fixed attention or strong concentration; that by his mismanagement of affairs since his arrival in Missouri the State has almost been lost, and that if he is continued in command, the worst results may be anticipated" (*Official Records of the War of the Re-*

bellion, ser. 1, 3:547). Sam Wilkeson, head of the Washington bureau of the *New York Tribune*, ran a story about Thomas's report on 30 October.

53. *MR*, 8 Nov. 1861, p. 2, c. 5, scrapbook, vol. 54, JH MSS, DLC. Charles Stewart was assistant adjutant general to Charles P. Stone. Havelock was presumably the namesake son of Henry Havelock (1795–1857), hero of British arms in Asia, especially during the Indian Mutiny of 1857. Militia colonel Arthur Rankin (1816–93) tried to recruit Canadians to serve in the Union army under his command. In October, Canadian authorities arrested him for violating the Foreign Enlistment Act. Giuseppe Garibaldi (1807–82) was the leading Italian revolutionary general. The Garde di Garibaldi (39th New York Regiment) consisted of Hungarians, Germans, Italians, Algerians, French Foreign Legionnaires, Cossacks, Sepoys, English, Swiss, Turks, Croats, Bavarians, Spaniards, Portuguese, and Platt Deutsch. Col. Philippe Regis Denis de Keredern Trobriand (1816–97) commanded the Garde Lafayette of New York, a Franco-American unit. François-Ferdinand-Philippe-Louis-Marie d'Orleans, Prince de Joinville (1818–1900), drew on his experiences with McClellan's staff to write *The Army of the Potomac: Its Organization, Its Commander, and Its Campaign* (New York: Randolph, 1862). The exiled Orleans prince and pretender to the throne, Louis Phillipe Albert d'Orleans, Comte de Paris (1838–94), was an officer on McClellan's staff, as was his brother, Robert Philippe Louis Eugene Ferdinand d' Orleans, Duc de Chartres (1840–1910). The Union troops called them Captain Perry and Captain Chatters. On 3 August, Mrs. Lincoln gave a state dinner for Prince Napoleon, for which she overbilled the government drastically (Burlingame, *Honest Abe, Dishonest Mary*, 16–20). John G. Nicolay described Georgiana Fane thus: "Daughter of the Earl of Westminster, I believe, a very rich, reasonably intelligent, horribly ugly, English old maid, who is traveling in the United States" (Nicolay to Therena Bates, Washington, 30 June 1861, Nicolay MSS, DLC).

54. *MR*, 12 Nov. 1861, p. 2, c. 4, scrapbook, vol. 54, JH MSS, DLC. When Maj. Charles Zagonyi defeated a small Confederate force in Springfield, Missouri, on 25 October, Frémont's supporters exaggerated the importance of the event. Union general Samuel R. Curtis (1817–66) had represented Iowa in the U.S. House of Representatives.

55. *MR*, 16 Nov. 1861, p. 2, c. 4. On 7 November, Union forces captured Beaufort, Port Royal, and Hilton Head. Confederate general Braxton Bragg (1817–76) was in charge of the coast between Pensacola and Mobile. Gen. Samuel Peter Heintzelman (1805–80) commanded the Third Division of the Army of the Potomac.

56. *MR*, 17 Nov. 1861, p. 2, c. 3, scrapbook, vol. 54, JH MSS, DLC. Bill Pennington, secretary of the legation in Paris, was the son of William Pennington (1796–1862), former governor of New Jersey (1837–43) and Republican Speaker of the House (1859–61). Antoine Edouard Thouvenel (1818–66) was foreign minister of France (1860–62). Carl Schurz (1829–1906) of Wisconsin was U.S. minister to Spain. George P. Marsh (1801–82) of Massachusetts was U.S. minister to Italy. The historian John Lothrop Motley (1814–77) was U.S. minister to Austria. Cassius M. Clay (1810–1903), an antislavery leader from Kentucky, was U.S. minister to Russia. Henry Shelton Sanford (1823–91) of Derby, Conn., had been chargé d'affaires in Paris under President Taylor; Lincoln named him U.S. minister to Belgium. At the request of Secretary of

State Seward, Sanford visited the Italian revolutionary general Giuseppe Garibaldi to offer him a commission as a major general in the Union army. Hoping to win recognition for the Confederacy, William Lowndes Yancey (1814–63) of Alabama led a three-man diplomatic team to Europe. His colleagues were Pierre A. Rost of Louisiana (1797–1868) and A. Dudley Mann of Georgia (1801–89). In the winter of 1861–62, at Lincoln's request, Thurlow Weed and John Joseph Hughes (1797–1864), archbishop of New York, visited Europe as informal Union diplomats. Edward Everett (1794–1865) of Boston, a renowned orator, had served as governor of Massachusetts and as secretary of state under Millard Fillmore. John Pendleton Kennedy (1795–1870) of Baltimore was an author who suffered ostracism for his devotion to the Union. Charles P. McIlvaine (1799–1873), Episcopal bishop of Ohio, visited England at Lincoln's urging and helped promote sympathy for the Union. Gen. William Nelson (1824–62) successfully recruited for the Union army in his native Kentucky.

57. *MR*, 22 Nov. 1861, p. 2, c. 3, scrapbook, vol. 54, JH MSS, DLC. Confederate general John B. Floyd (1806–63), while serving as secretary of war in Buchanan's administration (1857–60), had misappropriated funds. Union general William S. Rosecrans (1819–98) had participated in the West Virginia campaign early in the war and had nearly captured Floyd at the battle of Carnifex Ferry on 10 September. Union general Henry W. Benham (1813–84) led troops West Virginia in 1861. Alexander H. Stephens (1812–83) was vice president of the Confederacy. Robert A. Toombs (1810–85) was the Confederacy's secretary of state and later a general in the army. Roger A. Pryor (1828–1919), a member of the Confederate Congress, later became a general in the Confederate army. The CSS *Theodora* left Charleston on 12 October with Confederate diplomats James M. Mason and John Slidell aboard. It sailed to Nassau and then to Cuba, where Mason and Slidell bought tickets on a British mail steamship, the *Trent*. Charles Wilkes (1798–1877) commanded the USS *San Jacinto*, which had stopped the *Trent* on the high seas. Fox was perhaps the British Whig leader Charles James Fox (1749–1806). Irish-born Michael Corcoran (1827–63), a colonel in the New York militia, had been captured at Bull Run. The Confederates were threatening to hang him if the Union executed Confederate privateers.

58. *MR*, 29 Nov. 1861, p. 1, c. 8, scrapbook, vol. 54, JH MSS, DLC. "The American Flag" by Joseph Rodman Drake (1795–1820) was a paean to the United States in 640 lines. Josephine Chesney, daughter of James Chesney, married a nephew of Benjamin Butler. Anna Cora Mowatt (1819–70) had a brief but highly successful career as an actress (1845–54). William Ritchie, editor of the *Richmond Enquirer*, married Anna Mowatt on 6 June 1854, three days after her final stage appearance. Jean Margaret Davenport Lander (1829–1903), a celebrated English-born actress, took over the direction of Union hospitals in Port Royal, S.C., shortly after the death of her husband, Gen. Frederick West Lander, on 2 March 1862. After the war she returned to the stage, where she won acclaim. The British poet Horatio Smith (1779–1849) was also known as Horace Smith.

59. *MR*, 4 Dec. 1861, p. 3, c. 1. In 1861 Britain, France, and Spain sent a joint mili-

tary expedition to Mexico, ostensibly to collect debts. On 24 April 1862, the Senate passed a bill calling for the appointment of diplomatic representatives to Haiti and Liberia. After the House approved the same measure on 3 June, Lincoln signed it. In 1846 Congress ceded one-third of the city of Washington, including the area known as Alexandria, back to Virginia. In 1863 Congress established a national banking system at the urging of the president and the secretary of the treasury. The Pembina country was in North Dakota. John McLean (1785–1865) was an associate justice of the Supreme Court (1829–61). He presided over the seventh circuit (Ohio, Indiana, Illinois, and Michigan). In 1862 Lincoln filled the three vacant seats on Supreme Court with David Davis of Illinois, Noah H. Swayne of Ohio, and Samuel F. Miller of Iowa.

60. *MR*, 5 Dec. 1861, p. 2, c. 4, scrapbook, vol. 54, JH MSS, DLC. Col. William Wilson's 6th New York Infantry, known as "Wilson's Zouaves," was sent to Santa Rosa Island, Fla., where Confederates under Gen. Richard Heron Anderson routed them on the night of 8–9 October 1861. Confederate Capt. Josiah Tattnall (1795–1871) was in charge of the naval defense of Georgia and South Carolina. Doubtless he is the "hero of Greytown." Federal troops occupied Tybee Island, Ga., in late November, posing a threat to the mouth of the Savannah River. Gen. Braxton Bragg (1817–76) commanded Confederate forces at Pensacola, Fla., where Fort McRee was located. Union general Harvey Brown (1796–1874) commanded Fort Pickens. Union forces bombarded Fort McRee on 22 November.

61. *MR*, n.d., scrapbook, vol. 54, JH MSS, DLC. This may have appeared in either the 7 or 9 December issue, neither of which is included on the microfilm version of the *Missouri Republican*. John C. Breckinridge (1821–75) of Kentucky had been Buchanan's vice president. Beriah Magoffin (1815–85) was governor of Kentucky. Lazarus W. Powell (1812–67) represented Kentucky in the Senate (1859–65). Charles Anderson Wickliffe (1788–1869) of Kentucky served in the House (1861–63). Henry Cornelius Burnett (1825–66) of Kentucky also served in the House (1855–61). He was expelled on 3 December 1861, and joined the Confederate army. "Prog" was a slang term for food, usually acquired by begging. Lincoln's message is in Basler, *CWL*, 5:35–53. Lincoln's friend and a vigorous opponent of slavery, Owen Lovejoy (1811–64) of Illinois served in the House (1857–64). James Henry Lane (1814–66) was a Radical senator from Kansas.

62. *MR*, 10 Dec. 1861, p. 3, c. 2, scrapbook, vol. 54, JH MSS, DLC. On 30 November, Secretary of War Simon Cameron submitted to the president his annual report, which among other things called for the liberation and arming of slaves to put down the rebellion. On 1 December, Lincoln read the document and asked Cameron to strike the passage dealing with slaves. Reluctantly the secretary complied. But Cameron had already dispatched copies of his report to the press, which published it. Radicals applauded Cameron and denounced Lincoln for forcing him to modify the report. On 11 January, Lincoln dismissed Cameron from the cabinet and named him minister to Russia. Former congressman John Cochrane (1813–98) was a New York politician who served in the army (1861–63). On 14 March 1861, Cochrane

had told an audience in Richmond that New York would sustain Virginia if she seceded. When, however, she did secede, Cochrane became a Unionist and in 1864 was nominated by the Radical Republicans for vice president. On 13 November 1861, he delivered a rousing emancipation speech to his troops. Gen. Benjamin F. Butler (1818–93) of Massachusetts, who had been a Jefferson Davis Democrat in 1860, became a radical foe of slavery in 1861. Daniel S. Dickinson (1800–1866) of New York was a Democrat who had hoped to win the presidential nomination in 1860. When Fort Sumter was fired upon, he became a vigorous Republican. On 13 November, after John Cochrane had told his regiment (the U.S. Chasseurs in Joseph Hooker's division) that he favored emancipation of the slaves as a military measure, Cameron reportedly said: "I approve every sentiment uttered by your noble commander. All the doctrines he has laid down I approve of, as if they were uttered in my own words. These are my sentiments and the sentiments which will eventually lead to victory. 'Tis no time to talk to these people, but meet them on their own terms and treat them as enemies, and punish them as our enemies, until they learn to behave themselves. Every means which God has placed in our hands we must use, until they are subdued" (Washington correspondence, 13 Nov. 1861, *Chicago Tribune*, 14 Nov. 1861, p. 1, c. 7). Pennsylvanian John W. Forney (1817–81) edited the *Philadelphia Press* and the *Washington Chronicle*. On 19 November, at Forney's dinner honoring George D. Prentiss of the *Louisville Journal*, Cameron "reiterated his opinion that as a last resort *we ought to arm every man who desires to strike for human liberty*" (Washington correspondence, 20 Nov. 1861, *Chicago Tribune*, 21 Nov. 1861, p. 1, c. 4).

63. *MR*, 17 Dec. 1861, p. 2, c. 5, scrapbook, vol. 54, JH MSS, DLC. Radical congressman Thaddeus Stevens (1792–1868) of Pennsylvania chaired the House Ways and Means Committee. On 26 November, Gen. Henry W. Halleck, from his St. Louis headquarters, issued an order denouncing the Union troops' seizure of Confederate private property. On 18 November 1861, a convention of Unionist delegates from forty-five counties gathered at Hatteras and chose Marble Nash Taylor provisional governor of North Carolina. A lawyer from Maine, Charles Henry Foster had settled in Murfreesboro and edited a newspaper, the *Citizen*. Because of their unpopular Unionism, both he and Taylor were forced to flee to the North.

64. *MR*, 18 Dec. 1861, p. 2, c. 3, scrapbook, vol. 54, JH MSS, DLC. Republican Kinsley Scott Bingham (1808–61) represented Michigan in the Senate (1859–61). Democrat James W. Nesmith (1820–85) represented Oregon in the Senate (1861–67). Democrat James A. McDougall (1817–67) represented California in the Senate (1861–67). Democrat Milton S. Latham (1827–1882) also represented California in the Senate (1860–63). George Bancroft (1800–1891) was a historian and diplomat.

65. *MR*, 20 Dec. 1861, p. 2, cc. 3–4.

66. *MR*, 21 Dec. 1861, p. 2, c. 7, scrapbook, vol. 54, JH MSS, DLC. On 3 December, a Union force captured Ship Island, Miss., which served as a base for operations against New Orleans. Gen. Albin F. Schoepf (1822–86) was leading Union forces in eastern Kentucky. Henry John Temple, Third Viscount Palmerston (1784–1865), was prime minister of Great Britain. During the War of 1812, British and American

soldiers had clashed repeatedly along the Niagara frontier. The battle of Lundy's Lane, between British and American forces in Canada, took place on 25 July 1814. "Cotton bales" refers to the battle of New Orleans (8 Jan. 1815).

67. *MR,* 24 Dec. 1861, p. 2, c. 6, scrapbook, vol. 54, JH MSS, DLC. On 18 December, Lane was appointed a brigadier general; on 21 March 1862, that appointment was canceled. Charles Robinson (1818–94), governor of the state of Kansas, was Lane's chief rival for political dominance there. Frederick Perry Stanton (1801–64) was governor of Kansas (1858–60). Trusten Polk (1811–76) of Missouri entered the Senate in 1857; on 10 January 1862, he was expelled for disloyalty (Polk to P. S. Wilkes, n.p., n.d., *Congressional Globe,* 37th Congress, 2d sess., pt. 1, p. 126, c. 1 [18 Dec. 1861]). Wilkes edited a secessionist paper in Springfield. Democrat Willard Saulsbury (1820–92) was a senator from Delaware (1859–71). Democrat James A. Bayard Jr. (1799–1880) also represented Delaware in the Senate (1851–64). Charles Ellet (1810–62) wrote *Military Incapacity and What It Costs the Country* (Philadelphia: Ross and Tousey, 1862), a fifteen-page document criticizing McClellan.

68. *MR,* 28 Dec. 1861, p. 2, c. 2.

69. *MR,* 30 Dec. 1861, p. 2, c. 5, scrapbook, vol. 54, JH MSS, DLC. O'Neil was perhaps Hugh O'Neill (1550–1616), who led Irish resistance to British rule and became known as the Prince of Ireland. O'Brien was perhaps William Smith O'Brien (1803–64), an Irish nationalist. Irish-born James Shields (1810–79) was living in Mazatlan, Mexico, when Fort Sumter was bombarded. On the heels of that event, he offered his services to Lincoln, who appointed him a brigadier general of volunteers on 19 August 1861. He had been made a brevet major general after the battle of Cerro Gordo in the Mexican War. He served as a senator from Illinois, Minnesota, and Missouri. In 1852 Francis Meagher (1823–67) escaped a British prison and came to the United States, where he organized and led the Irish Brigade during the Civil War. He tried to get James Shields to head the brigade. The Irish nationalist poet James Clarence Mangan (1803–49) published translations of "Dark Rosaleen" from the Gaelic.

70. *MR,* 1 Jan. 1862, p. 2, c. 2, scrapbook, vol. 54, JH MSS, DLC. In 1860, Congressman John Covode of Pennsylvania had chaired a House investigation into President Buchanan's actions during the congressional debate over the Lecompton bill in 1858. On 12 December, Trumbull introduced a resolution demanding that Seward forward information about all arrests he had made and under what statutes. During the debate four days later, Trumbull was attacked by Dixon of Connecticut, and former allies like Henry Wilson of Massachusetts and Browning of Illinois opposed his resolution. On the motion of Senator James R. Doolittle of Wisconsin, the matter was postponed for six months. On 3 March 1863, he secured passage of a law regulating arrests made under the suspension of the privilege of the writ of habeas corpus (Horace White, *The Life of Lyman Trumbull* [Boston: Houghton Mifflin, 1913], 190–96). Hale was a bitter, dyspeptic, combative man in his later years (Richard H. Sewell, *John P. Hale and the Politics of Abolition* [Cambridge: Harvard University Press, 1965], 230–31).

3. 1862

1. *MR,* 10 Jan. 1862, p. 2, c. 3, scrapbook, vol. 54, JH MSS, DLC. In late December, McClellan contracted typhoid fever, which afflicted him until 10 January. Lawrence A. Gobright (1816–81) was the Washington agent for the Associated Press. Andrew Gregg Curtin (1817–94), a leader of the anti-Cameron faction in the Pennsylvania Republican Party, served as governor (1861–67). On 2 November 1861, Curtin told Seward that it was up to Congress, not the states, to provide for proper coastal defenses. In December, Secretary of War Simon Cameron and Thaddeus Stevens, who had refused to speak to each other for years, ended their feud. On the night of 9 December, Stevens, referring to Cameron's annual report, "spoke of him in the highest terms." Four days later the secretary visited the Capitol and shook Stevens's hand. During the previous fall, Lincoln had expressed to John G. Nicolay serious dissatisfaction with Cameron. In his notes of a conversation with the president, Nicolay recorded: "Cameron utterly ignorant and regardless of the course of things. . . . Selfish and openly discourteous to the President. Obnoxious to the country. Incapable of either organizing details or conceiving and advising general plans" ("Conversation with the President," 2 Oct. 1861, Nicolay MSS, DLC).

2. *MR,* 14 Jan. 1862, p. 2, c. 3. A prominent Kentucky Unionist, Garrett Davis (1801–72) was a senator (1861–72). The Louisiana-born Benjamin Stark (1820–98) represented Oregon in the Senate from October 1861 to September 1862. John Whiteaker (1820–1902), a pro-slavery Democrat, was governor of Oregon from July 1858 to September 1862. Senator Jacob M. Howard (1805–71) represented Michigan from 1862 to 1871. Democrat Waldo Porter Johnson (1817–85) represented Missouri in the Senate from March 1861 until 10 January 1862, when he was expelled for joining the Confederate army.

3. *MR,* 18 Jan. 1862, p. 2, c. 4. Isaac Sturgeon was president of the Northern Missouri Railroad Company. Adolphus Meier was an importer and jobber of foreign and domestic hardware and cutlery. Democrat James Craig (1818–88) was a representative from Missouri (1857–61).

4. *MR,* 19 Jan. 1862, p. 2, c. 5. A lawyer from Pennsylvania, Edwin M. Stanton (1814–69) served as secretary of war (1862–68). Kentucky abolitionist Cassius Marcellus Clay (1810–1903) had been appointed U.S. minister to Russia in 1861. He returned the following year to serve in the army. As Buchanan's secretary of war, Joseph Holt (1807–94) had labored hard in 1861 to keep his native state of Kentucky loyal to the Union; the following year he became judge advocate general of the army. John A. Dix (1798–1879) had served in Buchanan's cabinet as secretary of the treasury (1861) and was at this time commander of the Department of the East.

5. *MR,* 25 Jan. 1862, p. 2, c. 4. Pierce Egan (1772–1849) wrote *Life in London* (1821), which introduced many slang phrases. James W. Grimes (1816–72) was a senator from Iowa (1859–69).

6. *MR,* 28 Jan. 1862, p. 2, c. 2, scrapbook, vol. 54, JH MSS, DLC. Jesse D. Bright (1812–75) of Indiana was a senator from 1845 until his expulsion (5 Feb. 1862).

7. *MR,* 31 Jan. 1862, p. 2, c. 2, scrapbook, vol. 54, JH MSS, DLC. At Dranesville,

Va., Gen. Edward O. C. Ord (1818–83) commanded forces which on 20 December 1861 secured one of the Union's first victories in the eastern theater.

8. *MR*, 8 Feb. 1862, p. 2, c. 2. From December 1861 to April 1862, Ambrose E. Burnside (1824–81) of Rhode Island commanded the North Carolina Expedition Corps, which captured Roanoke Island and New Bern. He later became commander of the Army of the Potomac (November 1862–January 1863). Louis M. Goldsborough (1805–77), commander of the North Atlantic Blockading Squadron, was in charge of the naval units supporting Burnside's campaign.

9. *MR*, 11 Feb. 1862, p. 2, c. 3, scrapbook, vol. 54, JH MSS, DLC. On 1 March 1861, Bright had written to Jefferson Davis, whom he addressed as "His Excellency," introducing a friend from Texas who had devised "a great improvement in firearms." Bright failed to regain his seat in 1863.

10. *MR*, 14 Feb. 1862, p. 1, c. 6. Fort Pulaski was located on Cockspur Island close to the entrance to the port of Savannah, Ga. Capt. Josiah Tattnall (1795–1871) commanded the Confederacy's fleet, which in November 1861 attacked the Union ships in the Port Royal expedition. Confederate captain William F. Lynch (1801–65) commanded the fleet opposing Burnside's assault on Roanoke Island and Elizabeth City, N.C.; in 1848 he had explored the Jordan River and the Dead Sea. On 7 February, Lander had reoccupied the town of Romney in western Virginia. In the winter of 1861–62, Thomas J. "Stonewall" Jackson (1824–63) enjoyed little success campaigning in western Virginia. In 1830 Joseph Smith (1805–44) founded the Church of Jesus Christ of the Latter-Day Saints. When Lincoln ordered a column of Union troops under David Hunter to march on Texas, James Lane tried to supplant Hunter. Although the president rebuked Lane and upheld Hunter, the whole project was scrapped in March 1862.

11. *MR*, 17 Feb. 1862, p. 2, c. 4, scrapbook, vol. 54, JH MSS, DLC. Charles P. Stone commanded a "corps of observation" in the Army of the Potomac. As a scapegoat for the Union defeat at Ball's Bluff on 21 October 1861, he was imprisoned without charges for 189 days. John A. Andrew (1818–67) was governor of Massachusetts (1861–66). Malcolm Ives was a Washington correspondent for the *New York Herald* whose highhanded manner led to his arrest by Stanton.

12. *MR*, 18 Feb. 1862, p. 2, c. 4, scrapbook, vol. 54, JH MSS, DLC. The battle for Roanoke Island took place on 7 February. The *Evening Day Book* was published in New York. At Roanoke, 37 Federals were killed, 214 wounded, and 13 reported missing; 23 Confederates were killed and 2,500 were captured. Gen. Henry A. Wise (1806–76) commanded Confederate forces on Roanoke Island. His eldest son, Obadiah Jennings Wise, was killed in the battle. Sherrard Clemens (1820–81) was a U.S. representative from Virginia (1857–61). Hamilton Fish (1808–93), a prominent New York politician, was appointed by Lincoln to serve on a board of commissioners to expedite prisoner exchanges. Later he served as President Grant's secretary of state (1869–77). Edward Raymond Ames (1806–79) was bishop of the Methodist Episcopal Church.

13. *MR*, 26 Feb. 1862, p. 2, c. 4, scrapbook, vol. 54, JH MSS, DLC. Confederate general Thomas C. Hindman (1828–68) commanded the First Brigade in Hardee's

Division of the Central Army of Kentucky. The *Benton* was a 1,000-ton ironclad gunboat delivered to the U.S. government on 5 December 1861. Engineer James Buchanan Eads (1820–87) built fourteen armor-plated gunboats for use on the western rivers. Union forces occupied Nashville on 25 February. Gen. Francis Marion (c. 1732–95), a hero of the American Revolutionary War, led militia units in the South. Gimry Shamil (1796?–1871), the third imam of Dagestan, led Chechen and Dagestan forces in a holy war against the Russian occupiers of the Caucasus (1834–59).

14. *MR,* 26 Feb. 1862, p. 2, cc. 3–4, scrapbook, vol. 54, JH MSS, DLC. James Lane remained in the Senate until his death in 1866. The editor of the *Chicago Tribune* was Joseph Medill (1823–99).

15. *MR,* 4 March 1862, p. 2, c. 5, scrapbook, vol. 54, JH MSS, DLC. Stanton had grown so disenchanted with McClellan by March that he offered command of the Army of the Potomac to other generals, without consulting Lincoln. McClellan called Stanton "the vilest man I ever knew or heard of." Charles A. Dana (1819–97) was managing editor of the *New York Tribune.* Dana's dispatch giving Halleck and Stanton credit for the Union victory at Fort Donelson, dated 18 Feb. 1862, appeared in the *New York Tribune,* 19 Feb. 1862, p. 5, c. 2. Stanton disclaimed credit for "organizing the victory" at Donelson in a letter to Dana, who published it in the *New York Tribune,* 20 Feb. 1862, p. 4, c. 2. Commodore Andrew H. Foote (1806–63) commanded the Union naval forces on the upper Mississippi River. Sam Wilkeson headed the Washington bureau of the *New York Tribune.*

16. *MR,* 4 March 1862, p. 2, c. 6, scrapbook, vol. 54, JH MSS, DLC. On 25 February, the War Department took control of all telegraph lines and Stanton imposed rigid censorship on them. Daniel E. Sickles (1825–1914) murdered his wife's lover in 1859 and was acquitted on the ground of temporary insanity. New York congressman Benjamin Wood (1820–1900) edited the *New York Daily News.* Thomas T. Eckert (1825–1910) was superintendent of the military telegraph in the Department of the Potomac. On 26 February, Col. Anson Stager (1825–85) was named to head the U.S. military telegraph. Ship Island is in the Gulf of Mexico, off the southeast coast of Mississippi. Col. E. R. S. Canby (1817–73) commanded the Department of New Mexico (1861–62). Capt. Samuel Francis Du Pont (1803–65) commanded the South Atlantic Blockading Squadron. Union troops occupied Bowling Green on 14 February as part of their Nashville campaign. Isham G. Harris (1818–97) was governor of Tennessee (1857–62). When Union forces took Nashville, Harris fled to Memphis, which became the new state capital in the eyes of the Confederacy. Samuel R. Curtis (1805–66) commanded the Army of Southwest Missouri (1861–62). Union forces captured Roanoke Island in early February. William L. Maury was an officer in the Confederate navy.

17. *MR,* 15 March 1862, p. 2, c. 3, scrapbook, vol. 54, JH MSS, DLC. Gen. Simon B. Buckner (1823–1914) surrendered Fort Donelson to Grant. The *Merrimack* was a Union ship scuttled in 1861, raised by the Confederates, and converted into an ironclad ram, which they christened the CSS *Virginia.* The USS *Cumberland* was a 30-gun ship sunk by the *Merrimack.* The USS *Congress* was a 50-gun ship that sur-

rendered to the *Merrimack*. The USS *Minnesota* was a steam frigate that had run aground during the battle with the *Merrimack* on 8 March; she was saved the next day by the arrival of the USS *Monitor,* commanded by John L. Worden (1818–97). Swedish-born John Ericsson (1803–89) designed the ironclad monitors.

18. *MR,* 27 March 1862, p. 1, c. 7. On 8 March, Lincoln invited the abolitionist champion Wendell Phillips (1811–84) to the White House. Phillips recalled telling the president "that if he started the experiment of emancipation, and honestly devoted his energies to making it a fact, he would deserve to hold the helm until the experiment was finished—that the people would not allow him to quit while it was trying." He went on to urge that Seward be dismissed from the cabinet. According to Phillips, at the close of their meeting Lincoln said, "It's a big job; the country little knows how big." Phillips also recalled Lincoln saying, "The Negro who has once touched the hem of the Government's garment shall never again be a slave." (It is not clear whether that statement was made during their interview.) Phillips's speech in Chicago, 28 March 1862, *Chicago Tribune,* 29 March 1862, p. 4, cc. 2–3; Washington correspondence, 8 March 1862, ibid., 20 March 1862, p. 2, c. 4; Carlos Martyn, *Wendell Phillips, the Agitator* (New York: Funk and Wagnalls, 1890), 325; Irving H. Bartlett, *Wendell Phillips: Brahmin Radical* (Boston: Beacon Press, 1961), 249. Believing that his native state of Maryland would secede, Franklin Buchanan (1800–1874) resigned from the U.S. navy on 22 April 1861 and joined the Confederate navy. He commanded the *Merrimack* in its epic battle with the *Monitor* in March 1862.

19. *MR,* 4 April 1862, p. 2, c. 3. The two *Tribunes* were the *New York Tribune* and the *Chicago Tribune.* The "outburst" was contained in the editorials on McClellan, *New York Tribune,* 22 Feb. 1862, p. 4, c. 2, and 12 March 1862, p. 4, c. 4. Frémont was appointed to head the Mountain Division on 29 March 1862. Republican John Peter Cleaver Shanks (1826–1901) of Indiana served in the House (1861–63). The Rev. Mr. George B. Cheever (1807–90), pastor of the Church of the Puritans in New York, championed Frémont's cause. The president's emancipation message of 6 March to Congress is in Basler, *CWL,* 5:144–46. McClellan was removed as commander in chief of all Union armies on 11 March and entrusted solely with command of the Army of the Potomac.

20. *MR,* 2 April 1862, p. 2, c. 2. Abolitionist general John W. Phelps (1813–85) attempted to recruit black troops in the Department of the Gulf. Gen. James Shields commanded troops in western Virginia. William A. Richardson (1811–75), who represented an Illinois district in the U.S. House (1847–56, 1861–63), was appointed a brigadier general of volunteers on 2 Sept. 1861. The Baden Revolution was part of the German Revolution of 1848–49. A veteran of that struggle, Gen. Franz Sigel (1824–1902) commanded a brigade in the Army of Southwest Missouri. A refugee from Germany, Gen. Louis Blenker (1812–63) commanded a division in the Army of the Potomac.

21. *MR,* 10 April 1862, p. 2, c. 2, scrapbook, vol. 54, JH MSS, DLC. In the skirmish at Big Bethel on 10 June 1861, Union forces under the inexperienced Gen. Ebenezer W. Pierce of the Massachusetts Militia were defeated by the Confederates under Col.

D. H. Hill. Theodore Winthrop (1828–61), military secretary to Gen. Benjamin F. Butler, was a poet and novelist. The "Rip Raps" was a term used to describe an artificial island in Chesapeake Bay near Fortress Monroe.

22. *MR*, 25 April 1862, p. 1, c. 7. John Letcher (1813–84) was governor of Virginia (1861–63). Democrat Charles John Biddle (1819–73) of Pennsylvania was a representative (1861–63). Democrat Samuel Sullivan "Sunset" Cox (1824–89) of Ohio was a representative (1857–65). On 7 March 1862, McClellan launched his long-delayed offensive against Manassas; to his surprise, the Confederates had abandoned their position before he arrived. When it was discovered that the enemy had intimidated the Army of the Potomac for months with "cannons" that proved to be painted logs, McClellan was widely criticized in the North.

23. *MR*, 26 April 1862, p. 2, c. 3. Zachariah Chandler (1813–1879), who had represented Michigan in the Senate since 1857, served on the Joint Congressional Committee on the Conduct of the War, which was established on 10 December 1861. When Pierce Butler of Philadelphia, a native of South Carolina, was arrested on 15 August 1861 for allegedly accepting a commission in the Confederate army, he sued Secretary of War Cameron for false imprisonment.

24. *MR*, 26 April 1862, p. 1, c. 7. Commodore Andrew H. Foote (1806–63) commanded naval forces on the upper Mississippi River.

25. *MR*, 27 April 1862, p. 2, c. 3, scrapbook, vol. 54, JH MSS, DLC. John B. Henderson (1826–1913) was a senator from Missouri (1862–69). Lincoln's approval of the statute emancipating slaves in Washington is in Basler, *CWL*, 5:192.

26. *MR*, 2 May 1862, p. 1, c. 7, scrapbook, vol. 54, JH MSS, DLC. At the battle of Somerset (or Mill Springs) in Kentucky on 19 January, Union forces defeated Gen. George B. Crittenden's Confederates and killed Gen. Felix Zollicoffer. Federal troops occupied Winchester on 12 March 1862. The battle of Pittsburg Landing, Tenn. (or Shiloh), was fought on 6–7 April. On 25 April Farragut entered New Orleans, which surrendered officially two days later. Gen. Mansfield Lovell (1822–84) commanded Confederate forces at New Orleans. Pierre Soulé (1801–70) was provost marshal of New Orleans. He had been a senator from Louisiana (1849–53) and U.S. minister to Spain (1853–55).

27. *MR*, 15 May 1862, p. 2, c. 3, scrapbook, vol. 54, JH MSS, DLC. At Williamsburg on 4 and 5 May, sharp fighting took place between the retreating Confederates and the pursing Union troops. On 5 May, McClellan told Stanton, "I find Joe Johnston in front of me in strong force, probably greater a good deal than my own & very strongly entrenched. . . . My entire force is undoubtedly considerably inferior to that of the Rebels, who still fight well, but I will do all I can with the force at my disposal." Henman was perhaps Washington M. Henman, an interpreter of American Indian languages.

28. *MR*, 23 May 1862, p. 2, c. 4, scrapbook, vol. 54, JH MSS, DLC. When Gen. David Hunter emancipated the slaves of rebellious owners in the Department of the South on 9 May, Lincoln overruled him (Basler, *CWL*, 5:222–23).

29. *MR*, 25 June 1862, p. 2, c. 4, scrapbook, vol. 54, JH MSS, DLC. Norfolk was taken

by Union forces under Gen. John E. Wool on 10 May. The Gosport Navy Yard had been burned by Union forces when they felt compelled to abandon it on 20 April 1861. In May 1862, the retreating Confederates once again burned that facility.

30. *MR*, 26 June 1862, p. 1, c. 5, scrapbook, vol. 54, JH MSS, DLC. John Franklin Farnsworth (1837–63) was colonel of the 8th Illinois Cavalry. On 13 June at Tunstall's Station, Confederate cavalry under J. E. B. Stuart attacked a Union train, which managed to escape. Horace Maynard (1814–82), a devout Tennessee Unionist, served in Congress (1857–63) and as the state's attorney general (1863–65).

31. *MR*, 27 June 1862, p. 2, cc. 2–3. In 1821 Reginald Heber (1783–1826), Bishop of Calcutta, wrote the hymn "From Greenland's Icy Mountains," which contains these lines: "Though every prospect pleases / and only man is vile." Hay's paternal great-grandfather migrated from Pennsylvania to Virginia, and his grandfather migrated from Virginia to Kentucky. The Blackstone River flows through western Massachusetts and Rhode Island, passing Providence, where Hay attended college. Below Pawtucket, R.I., the river is called the Seekonk. Exeter Hall was a meeting place in London where antislavery forces often convened. Hinton Rowan Helper (1829–1909) of North Carolina condemned slavery in his book, *The Impending Crisis of the South* (1857). Gen. Benjamin F. Butler referred to slaves who reached Union lines as "contraband of war." Thomas Fuller (1608–61), an English preacher and historian, wrote in *The Holy State and the Profane State* (1642): "But our captain counts the Image of God nevertheless his image, cut in ebony as if done in ivory." Hiram Berdan (1823?–93) commanded the First U.S. Sharpshooters, who performed especially well at Yorktown as they disabled Confederate artillery. Gen. John B. Magruder (1807–71) commanded the Confederate forces at Yorktown, which held up McClellan's advance for a month.

32. *MR*, 1 July 1862, p. 2, c. 3, scrapbook, vol. 54, JH MSS, DLC. West Hughes Humphreys (1806–83) had been appointed U.S. district judge in 1853; after his impeachment and removal from the federal bench, the Confederate government made him a district judge. Solomon Foot (1802–66) of Vermont was a senator (1851–66). John A. Bingham (1815–1900) of Ohio was a representative (1855–63, 1865–73). Charles R. Train (1817–85) of Massachusetts was a representative (1859–63). George W. Dunlap (1813–80) of Kentucky was a representative (1861–63). Willard Saulsbury (1820–92) was a senator from Delaware (1859–71). William Pitt Fessenden (1806–69) of Maine was a senator (1854–64). Anthony Kennedy (1810–92), a member of the American Party, was a senator from Maryland (1857–63). Garrett Davis (1801–72) of Kentucky was a senator (1861–72). James F. Simmons (1795–1864) of Rhode Island was a senator (1857–62). Lot M. Morrill (1813–83) of Maine was a senator (1861–76). Henry B. Anthony (1815–84) of Rhode Island was a senator (1859–84). Milton S. Latham (1827–82) of California was a senator (1860–63). Preston King (1806–65) of New York was a senator (1857–63). William G. "Parson" Brownlow (1805–77) was a leading Tennessee Unionist.

33. *MR*, 18 July 1862, p. 3, c. 2, scrapbook, vol. 54, JH MSS, DLC. Thomas Corwin (1794–1865) of Ohio was U.S. minister to Mexico (1861–64).

34. *MR*, 21 July 1862, p. 2, c. 5. On 11 May, the Confederates scuttled the *Merrimack* to keep it from falling into Union hands. The "obelisk" was the Washington Monument.

35. *MR*, n.d., scrapbook, vol. 54, JH MSS, DLC. The microfilm edition of the *Missouri Republican* lacks all issues between 30 July and 8 August 1862. Gen. Ormsby M. Mitchel (1809–62) was a prominent astronomer. Col. Jesse Norton, whom Mitchel had charged with being absent from his command, spread rumors about Mitchel's alleged theft of cotton and his pillaging.

36. *MR*, 17 Aug. 1862, p. 1, c. 4. Confederate general Richard S. Ewell (1817–72) commanded the Second Corps of the Army of Northern Virginia. Union general James B. Ricketts (1817–87) commanded the Second Division of the Third Corps of the Army of Virginia. Union general George D. Bayard (1835–62) commanded the cavalry of the Third Corps, Army of Virginia. Union general Samuel W. Crawford (1829–92) commanded a division in the Second Corps of the Army of Virginia. Union general Alpheus S. Williams (1810–78) commanded the First Division of Crawford's Corps. The battle of Cedar Mountain took place on 9 August. Union general Rufus King (1814–76) commanded the Third Corps of the Army of Virginia.

37. *MR*, 22 Aug. 1862, p. 1, c. 5. The battle of Malvern Hill, in which the Union forces, fighting on the defensive, inflicted severe losses on the attacking Confederates, took place on 1 July, bringing to an end the Seven Days' Campaign. James Ryder Randall, a native of Baltimore and a professor of English at Poydras College in Louisiana, wrote the poem "Maryland, My Maryland" on 23–24 April 1861. Gen. Silas Casey (1807–82) was in charge of a provisional brigade in the forces defending Washington. His division of the Fourth Corps had been struck by the Confederates' initial assault at the battle of Fair Oaks on 31 May.

38. *MR*, 25 Aug. 1862, p. 2, c. 3, scrapbook, vol. 54, JH MSS, DLC. On 14 August, McClellan evacuated Harrison's Landing, his base on the Virginia Peninsula. Pope's "pyrotechnic order" was the notorious address issued on 14 July in which he criticized eastern troops for being too defensive-minded.

39. *MR*, 30 Aug. 1862, p. 1, c. 4. Gen. Fitz John Porter (1822–1901) was court-martialed for misconduct at the second battle of Bull Run. Found guilty on 10 January 1863, he was dismissed from the service. In 1878 an inquiry found him innocent and he was eventually reinstated. Samuel P. Heintzelman (1805–80) commanded the Third Corps of the Army of the Potomac. Philip Kearney (1814–62) commanded the First Division of the Third Corps of the Army of the Potomac.

40. *MR*, 5 Sept. 1862, p. 1, c. 6, scrapbook, vol. 54, JH MSS, DLC. Gen. William B. Franklin (1823–1903) commanded the Sixth Corps of the Army of the Potomac.

41. *MR*, 7 Sept. 1862, p. 2, c. 4. Gen. Jesse L. Reno (1823–62), who commanded that Second Division of the Ninth Corps, was killed at South Mountain. Isaac I. Stevens (1818–62), commander of the First Division of the Ninth Corps of the Army of the Potomac, was killed on 1 September at Chantilly. On 16 June 1862, Gen. Henry W. Benham had suffered a crushing defeat when, against orders, he attacked Secessionville, S.C. (James Island).

42. *MR*, 11 Sept. 1862, p. 2, c. 3. Wendell Phillips denounced Lincoln often. In May

1862, he said, "The President and the Cabinet are treasonable. The President . . . should be impeached."

43. *MR*, 26 Sept. 1862, p. 2, c. 3, scrapbook, vol. 54, JH MSS, DLC. Charles A. Wickliffe (1788–1869) of Bowling Green, Ky., was a representative (1823–33, 1861–63). James Harlan (1820–99) of Iowa was a senator (1857–65). Samuel C. Pomeroy (1816–91) of Kansas was a senator (1861–73). The sharp remark to Lincoln was reported in the Washington correspondence, 4 and 5 Aug. 1862, *Cincinnati Gazette*, 5 Aug. 1862, p. 3, c. 3, and 6 Aug. 1862, p. 3, c. 3; Washington correspondence, 5 Aug. 1862, *Chicago Tribune*, 6 Aug. 1862, p. 1, c. 5; *Chicago Morning Post*, 7 Aug. 1862, copy, Allan Nevins MSS, Columbia University. According to a letter by the *Gazette* correspondent to the *Washington Republican* of 11 Aug., ibid., 14 Aug., p. 3, c. 3, the source was the senator who retorted so boldly. That was doubtless Pomeroy, for Harlan did not include the insolent words in his reminiscences. See undated reminiscences of James Harlan, and Harlan to Ida Tarbell, Mount Pleasant, Iowa, 15 Dec. 1898, Tarbell MSS, Allegheny College. Cf. Basler, *CWL*, 5:356–57. Morton S. Wilkinson (1819–94) was a senator from Minnesota (1859–65). The Washington correspondents for the *Evening Post* were Harry Norman Hudson, Richard Cunningham McCormick, Augustus Maverick, and Philip Ripley.

44. *MR*, 29 Sept. 1862, p. 2, c. 3, scrapbook, vol. 54, JH MSS, DLC. Cassius M. Clay (1810–1903) was an antislavery leader from Kentucky. *Locofoco* was a slang term for a Democrat.

45. *MR*, 5 Oct. 1862, p. 1, c. 4. The Knights of the Golden Circle was a secret pro-Southern order in the North.

46. *MR*, 6 Oct. 1862, p. 2, c. 2. Major Key had allegedly declared that the Army of the Potomac did not intend to crush Lee: "The object is that neither army shall get much advantage of the other; that both shall be kept in the field till they are exhausted, when we will make a compromise and save slavery." See Lincoln to Key, Washington, 26 Sept. 1862, Basler, *CWL*, 5:442; "Record of Dismissal of John J. Key," 26–27 September 1862, ibid., 442–43. Cf. Lincoln to Key, Washington, 24 Nov. 1862, ibid., 5:508; Howard K. Beale, ed., *The Diary of Gideon Welles*, 3 vols. (New York: Norton, 1960), 1:146 (entry for 24 Sept. 1862); *Diary of John Hay*, 41 (entry for 26 Sept. 1862); Key's brother, Col. Thomas Key of Cincinnati, reported that many of McClellan's staff officers wanted Lincoln to treat slavery conservatively. According to one journalist, some of those officers in mid-September planned to march on Washington to intimidate the administration. See Nathaniel Paige, interviewed in the *New York Tribune*, n.d., in the *Washington Capital*, 21 March 1880, copy, Allan Nevins MSS, Columbia University. The officers, according to the author of the *Capital* article, "had a contempt of Lincoln and a hatred of Stanton, with a fixed belief that the war was a folly and bound to be a failure." They referred to the president and his advisers as "old women." William Nelson (1824–62) had served twenty years in the U.S. navy before becoming an army general in 1861. He was shot to death by Union general Jefferson C. Davis on 19 September.

47. *MR*, n.d., scrapbook, vol. 54, JH MSS, DLC. The microfilmed edition of the *Missouri Republican* contains no issues from 24 October through 2 November 1862.

48. *MR*, 10 Dec. 1862, p. 2, c. 2. Gen. Ethan Allen Hitchcock (1798–1870) was commissioner for the exchange of prisoners of war (1862–65). Gen. Irvin McDowell (1818–85) demanded a court of inquiry when he was blamed for the Union failure at Second Bull Run; the court cleared him.

49. *MR*, 25 Dec. 1862, p. 1, c. 3, scrapbook, vol. 54, JH MSS, DLC. At the battle of Fredericksburg on 13 December, the Army of the Potomac suffered a crushing defeat. Burnside's letter to Halleck, dated Falmouth, Va., 19 Dec. 1862, appeared in the *New York Times*, 23 Dec. 1861, p. 1, c. 1.

50. *Washington Daily Morning Chronicle*, 30 Dec. 1862, p. 2, cc. 1–2, scrapbook, vol. 54, JH MSS, DLC. Banks assumed command of the Department of the Gulf on 16 December.

51. *Washington Chronicle*, 31 Dec. 1862, p. 2, c. 2, scrapbook, vol. 54, JH MSS, DLC. On 23 December, Davis issued a proclamation denouncing Butler as "a felon deserving of capital punishment" and "an outlaw and common enemy of mankind" who was to be hanged if captured. On 9 November, Lincoln issued an order replacing Butler with Gen. N. P. Banks in command of the Department of the Gulf. Butler first heard of this order when Banks handed it to him on 12 December.

4. 1863–1864

1. *Washington Chronicle*, 1 Jan. 1863, p. 2, c. 2, scrapbook, vol. 54, JH MSS, DLC. At Dranesville, Va., brisk fighting had taken place on 20 December 1861. On 27 January 1862, the president issued a war order commanding the Army of the Potomac to occupy a point on the Confederate railroad south of Manassas. The movement was to begin no later than 22 February. A balize is a beacon erected at sea; Hay evidently uses it figuratively to refer to the mouth of the Mississippi River. Forts Jackson and St. Philip were located on the banks of the Mississippi, ninety miles below New Orleans. Gen. Francis Jay Herron (1837–1902) and Gen. James G. Blunt (1826–81) commanded divisions of the Army of the Frontier, Department of the Missouri.

2. Scrapbook, vol. 54, JH MSS, DLC. Hay wrote "July 1863 Republican" beside this clipping. During the minor skirmishing that took place at Falling Waters, W. Va., on 14 July, Gen. James J. Pettigrew (1828–63) C.S.A., who commanded a division in the Second Corps of the Army of Northern Virginia, was killed.

3. *Washington Chronicle*, 7 Aug. 1863, p. 2, cc. 1–2, scrapbook, vol. 54, JH MSS, DLC. Thomas E. Bramlette (1817–75) was elected governor of Kentucky on 3 August as a Union Democrat; he held the post until 1867. Brutus Junius Clay (1808–78) of Kentucky was a representative (1863–65). Gen. Green Clay Smith (1826–95), who had defeated John Hunt Morgan at Lebanon, Tenn., in May 1862, won election to Congress in Kentucky in 1863. John W. Menzies (1819–97) of Kentucky was a U.S. representative (1861–63).

4. *Washington National Republican*, n.d., clipping in scrapbook, vol. 54, JH MSS, DLC. On 18 May, the president ordered the *World* and the *Journal of Commerce* suppressed. Jose A. Arguelles, a Spanish officer who had come to New York from

Cuba, was turned over to Spanish authorities, even though Spain and the United States had no extradition treaty.

5. Unidentified clipping, scrapbook, vol. 54, JH MSS, DLC. William Meade Fishback (1831–1903) was a leading Arkansas Unionist who won election to the Senate in 1864, but because the Arkansas constitution limited suffrage to whites, Congress refused to seat him.

INDEX

abolitionists, 194, 235, 253, 254, 263–65
Accomac (Va.), 197
Acquia Creek (Va.), 127
Adams, Charles Francis, 109, 141, 358n. 46
Adams, John, 141
Adams, John Quincy, 141
Alabama, 361n. 55
Albany (N.Y.), 38
Albemarle Sound (N.C.), 218
Albert, Prince, xx, 109, 358n. 46
Alexandria (Va.), 66, 356n. 30, 363n. 59;
    blockade of, 145; hospital, 79; retroces-
    sion of, 151; secessionists in, 77
Allen, Capt., 83
Ames, Edward Raymond, 219, 367n. 12
Anaconda Plan, 122, 194, 211, 358n. 45
Anderson, Richard Heron, 363n. 60
Anderson, Robert, 56, 117, 355n. 27, 359n.
    48
Andrew, John A., 215, 367n. 11
Angell, James B., xi
Anthony, Henry B., 277, 371n. 32
Antietam, battle of, 315, 317
Arago, 179
Aratzen, 8, 346n. 3
Arguelles, Jose A., 374–75n. 4
Arizona, 105
Arkansas, 332, 338
Arlington (Va.), 66
Armstrong, Duff, 11–12, 347n. 4
Armstrong, Hannah, 11, 347n. 4
Armstrong, Jack, 10, 347n. 4
Army of Northern Virginia, 307, 316
Army of the Frontier, 374n. 1
Army of the Gulf, 332
Army of the Potomac, 301, 369n. 19,
    374nn. 1, 49; inaction of, 240; and G. B.
    McClellan, 242, 262, 275, 291–97, 314–15;

preparedness of, 242, 244, 306–7; re-
    views, 148
Army of Virginia, 292, 295, 296, 352n. 14,
    372n. 36
Ashmun, George, 3, 345n. 1
Ashtabula (Ohio), 32, 353n. 16
assassination rumors: in Baltimore,
    43–45, 354n. 21; in Richmond, 47
Associated Press, 104, 150, 187, 300, 325,
    366n. 1
Astor, Mrs. John Jacob, 62, 355n. 28

Baden Revolution, 241, 369n. 20
Baker, Edward D., xvii–xviii, 347n. 4;
    character of, 164, 191; death of, 122–23,
    164, 190, 215; oratory of, 123
Baker, Ned, 12
Ball's Bluff (Va.), 122, 125, 190, 215
Baltimore (Md.), 43–45, 100, 197, 254; and
    J. C. Breckinridge, 156; secessionists in,
    77, 82
Baltimore American, 256–57, 312
Baltimore Sun, xvi
Bancroft, George, 166, 364n. 64
banking legislation, 195; proposal, 151
Banks, Nathaniel P., 82, 122, 206, 241, 245,
    296, 301, 305, 332, 358n. 45, 374nn. 50, 51;
    and cabinet appointments, 197; com-
    mand of, 244; expeditions of, 288–93,
    327–28; at Frederick, 212; preparedness
    of, 105; report of, 116; and rumors, 228
Barbee, David Rankin, xxvii
Bardolf, Orlando, 83
Barlow, S. L. M., xvi
Barnum, Phineas Taylor, 320
Baroche, Jules, 88, 357n. 37
Barrett's Hill, 106
Bateman, Newton, 24, 352n. 14

Michael Burlingame is a professor of history at Connecticut College in New London. His previous books include *The Inner World of Abraham Lincoln, Inside Lincoln's White House: The Complete Civil War Diary of John Hay, Lincoln Observed: Civil War Dispatches of Noah Brooks*, and *An Oral History of Abraham Lincoln*, which won the 1995 Abraham Lincoln Association Prize.